SPORT FACILITY OPERATIONS MANAGEMENT

Now in a fully revised and updated third edition, *Sport Facility Operations Management* goes beyond the basic theories of sport facility management to include relevant practical professional experiences connecting facilities, people, and technology.

This is a comprehensive and engaging textbook introducing cutting-edge concepts and best practice in sport facility operations management. Each chapter contains real-world case studies and discussion questions, innovative 'Technology Now' and new 'Facility Focus' features, and 'In the Field' segments about what is going on in the industry. This new edition also provides new content in the areas of project management, social and digital media, revenue generation and diversification, performance analytics, and impacts and legacies.

This is a vital resource for sport management educators and students, especially those studying facility management. It is also an interesting read for industry professionals working in sport facility management, from grassroots and community complexes to global mega stadiums and arenas.

Dedicated online materials include PowerPoint presentations for each chapter; multiple-choice and essay questions; online appendices with diagrams, schematics, manuals, and forms; a glossary; and a sample master syllabus.

Eric C. Schwarz is Chair of the Postgraduate Courses in Sport Business and Integrity at Victoria University in Melbourne, Australia.

Stacey A. Hall is Senior Associate Dean of the College of Business and Economic Development and Professor of Sport Management at The University of Southern Mississippi, United States.

Simon Shibli is Professor of Sport Management and Director of the Sport Industry Research Centre at Sheffield Hallam University, UK.

SPORT FACILITY OPERATIONS MANAGEMENT

A GLOBAL PERSPECTIVE

THIRD EDITION

ERIC C. SCHWARZ, STACEY A. HALL, AND SIMON SHIBLI

Routledge
Taylor & Francis Group

LONDON AND NEW YORK

Third edition published 2020
by Routledge

2 Park Square, Milton Park, Abingdon, Oxon, OX14 4RN
and by Routledge

52 Vanderbilt Avenue, New York, NY 10017

Routledge is an imprint of the Taylor & Francis Group, an informa business

First edition published by Elsevier 2009

Second edition published by Routledge 2015

British Library Cataloguing-in-Publication Data
A catalogue record for this book is available from the British Library

Library of Congress Cataloging-in-Publication Data
A catalog record for this book has been requested

ISBN: 978-0-367-34555-6 (hbk)
ISBN: 978-0-367-13364-1 (pbk)
ISBN: 978-0-429-02610-2 (ebk)

Typeset in Melior
by Apex CoVantage, LLC

Visit the eResources: www.routledge.com/9780367133641

ERIC C. SCHWARZ

I would like to dedicate this book to my wife, Loan. I am very fortunate to have found a person to be my partner in life who shows unconditional love and unwavering support for my work, my writing, and me. I love you with all of my heart and soul!!!

In addition, I would like to recognize my coauthors on this project, Stacey A. Hall and Simon Shibli. Cannot believe we are now writing our third edition . . . and it was as much a pleasure working with both of you on this edition as it was on the first two. I look forward to future collaborations with both of you.

And finally, to Max . . .

STACEY A. HALL

I would like to thank my family in Northern Ireland for their unconditional love and support in both my professional and personal endeavors. I would also like to thank my friends and colleagues at Southern Miss for their support and guidance. Lastly, I thank Eric C. Schwarz for the opportunity to contribute to this book. Eric's leadership skills and professionalism made this project an enjoyable experience.

SIMON SHIBLI

Never in my wildest dreams did I imagine that my modest career in academia would involve a third edition of anything. That Routledge saw fit to commission this third edition speaks volumes for the vision of Eric C. Schwarz for conceiving the idea of *Sport Facility Operations Management: A Global Perspective*. Eric and our coauthor, Stacey A. Hall, have been the driving forces for this enterprise, and I have been lucky enough to hang on to their coattails.

My colleagues in the Sport Industry Research Centre (SIRC) are a pillar of support and create the time for me to step off the remorseless treadmill of contract research every now and again to pursue projects like this. There is a culture and work ethic within the SIRC team that make it a privilege to belong to such a group. It has been an honor to lead you.

I would like to place on record my thanks to the Brand Protection Team at Manchester United. They gave me permission to use the image in Chapter 10 of the layout of Old Trafford and the season ticket details. Not only was I pleased to get a response to my request, but I was also delighted that the response was positive. It is said that one good picture is worth a thousand words and in this regard, I am inclined to agree.

To my wife Tracey, and to our children Alice, James (Jim), and Mary, thank you for your continued tolerance of my work sometimes being my way of life. As the children get closer to flying the nest, I am looking forward to seeing them all flourish and reach their considerable potential.

Finally, it would be remiss of me not to mention my friend and colleague Dan Porter, who passed away in February 2018 after a courageous ten-year battle against cancer. Dan was Head of Sport Services at Sheffield Hallam University, and his passing is a sad loss to our community.

CONTENTS

List of figures ix
List of tables x
Case studies xii
List of facility focus xiii
List of technology now! xiv
List of in the field xv
Preface xvi

1 Introduction to sport facility operations management 1

SECTION I
Pre-management and pre-operational issues 11

2 Ownership structures 13
3 Financing sport facilities 36
4 Capital investment appraisal 59
5 Project management: planning, design, and construction 83

SECTION II
Application of management and operations principles for sport facilities 107

6 Organizational leadership and human resource management 109
7 Financial management, operational decision making, and budgeting 136
8 Operations management 161

SECTION III
Implementing sport facility operations management 187

9   Multichannel marketing and communications   189
10 Revenue generation and diversification   213
11 Customer experiences – from event planning to activation   233
12 Legal issues and risk assessment   254
13 Security planning for facility management   279

SECTION IV
Effectiveness of management and operations 303

14 Performance analytics for sport facilities   305
15 Impacts and legacies through sustainability   334

    Index   340

FIGURES

2.1	Three elements of a trust	25
4.1	Compounding and discounting	70
4.2	Internal rate of return (IRR) represented graphically	73
5.1	Example of a Gantt chart	88
5.2	Sport facility space allocation and management process	95
7.1	Cost, revenue, and break-even chart	143
7.2	Budgets as steps in a logically sequenced planning process	151
10.1	Season ticket prices and segments at Old Trafford 2018/2019	218
11.1	SESA Assessment Cycle	249
12.1	Risk probability and consequence severity	259
12.2	Sport Event Security Assessment Model (SESAM)	260
12.3	Risk logic matrix	272
13.1	Sport event security stakeholders	280
13.2	Situational crime prevention (SCP) model	294
13.3	Principles and components of sport event emergency management	295
14.1	Business Excellence Model: EFQM	309
14.2	Why measure performance?	311
14.3	Balanced Scorecard structure	323
14.4	Cost recovery rates in UK sport and leisure centers in 2018	324

TABLES

2.1	Models of organizational effectiveness	30
3.1	Considerations for life cycle costing	39
3.2	Delivering positive economic benefits for sport facilities	42
3.3	Examples of hard and soft taxes	45
3.4	Types of municipal bonds	46
3.5	Spillover benefits justifying public subsidies	47
3.6	Private sources of revenue	48
3.7	Public–private partnership models	50
4.1	Capital investment appraisal (CIA) data for gym example	63
4.2	The payback method	65
4.3	Alternative project competing for a $250,000 investment	65
4.4	Accounting rate of return (ARR) data	67
4.5	Net present value (NPV) calculation assuming interest rates of 10%	71
4.6	Iterative method to deriving the internal rate of return (IRR)	72
4.7	Internal rate of return (IRR) = Point at which net present value (NPV) = $0	74
4.8	Discounted payback period	74
4.9	Summary of capital investment appraisal (CIA) analysis $250,000 investment in a gym	76
4.10	Sensitivity analysis	77
4.11	CIA of three competing projects	79
5.1	Feasibility study components	89
6.1	Cross-cultural values	115
7.1	Costing matrix to show contribution	140
7.2	Complete costing matrix	141
7.3	What-if scenario	145

7.4	Sensitivity analysis	146
7.5	Swimming pool annual running costs	148
8.1	Prioritization chart for the main gymnasium – university sports complex	164
9.1	Global sport facility naming rights deals	203
10.1	Manchester United matchday revenues and games, 2014–2018	216
10.2	Sample naming rights deals in the United States	222
12.1	Sport venue assets	261
12.2	Global sport event incidents	264
12.3	Risk control and response matrix	276
13.1	Game day security operations checklist	282
13.2	Continuity capability checklist	296
14.1	Criteria for good performance indicators	315
14.2	Criteria for suitable performance indicators' data	316
14.3	Performance ratios for commercial organizations	317
14.4	Performance indicators for Sport England's National Benchmarking Service	320

CASE STUDIES

2	Private management of public facilities	22
3	Sport facility financing investment: a look ahead	52
4	The United States' most expensive sport stadia	60
5	Natural grass or synthetic turf – which option is better?	96
6	Global volunteerism	118
7	Highmark Stadium and the Pittsburgh Riverhounds	137
8	Panorama Stadium	181
9	eSports and the new sport arena for Millennials and Gen Z	208
10	Seating manifests: how much to charge for entry?	217
11	'Dis'agreements between facility naming rights versus hallmark event sponsors	238
12	Panorama Stadium threat assessment	269
13	2013 Boston Marathon bombing	297
14	Sport England's National Benchmarking Service (NBS)	325

FACILITY FOCUS

2   Transnational venue management: Mercedes-Benz Arena,
    Shanghai, China   29
3   Investing for the future: Melbourne Park Redevelopment,
    Melbourne, Australia   40
4   Investing for competitive advantage: Hallamshire Tennis and
    Squash Club, Sheffield, United Kingdom   75
5   Recycled stadium construction: Ras Abu Aboud Stadium,
    Doha, Qatar   99
6   Hiring, training, and retention: Mercedes-Benz Stadium,
    Atlanta, Georgia, United States   117
7   Increasing income via facility hire: Hathersage Swimming
    Pool, United Kingdom   153
8   Customized corporates boxes: Santiago Bernabéu Stadium,
    Madrid, Spain   169
9   Marketing Singapore as a sporting destination: Singapore
    Sports Hub, Singapore   205
10 Stadium design for diverse revenue generation: Tottenham
    Hotspur Stadium, London, United Kingdom   229
11 Facility and event sponsorship conflicts: Pepsi Center, Denver,
    Colorado, United States   252
12 Managing security for 100k guests: Darrell K Royal (DKR)–Texas
    Memorial Stadium, Austin, Texas, United States   267
13 Security in the outfield: Citi Field Ballpark, New York City,
    United States   289
14 Efficiency analysis of an anonymous facility using the National
    Benchmarking Service: United Kingdom   328

TECHNOLOGY NOW!

2   Financial Analysis Made Easy – FAME (United Kingdom)   20
3   eventIMPACTS (United Kingdom)   43
4   Capital works and environmental impact (United Kingdom)   79
5   AutoCAD (United States)   93
6   TeamWork Online (United States)   124
7   SIVTickets.com (United Kingdom)   143
8   AwareManager (United States)   174
9   1HUDDLE (United States)   199
10 Hallam Active (United Kingdom)   226
11 CERM PI (Australia)   250
12 Sport security and technology (generic/global)   273
13 Unmanned aircraft systems (generic/global)   288
14 A new and improved National Benchmarking Service
    (United Kingdom)   330

IN THE FIELD

2   Mike Tatoian, executive vice president and chief operating officer, Dover Motorsports Inc., Dover, Delaware, United States   33

3   Dev Pathik, founder and chief executive officer, The Sports Facilities Advisory and The Sports Facilities Management, St. Petersburg, Florida, United States   57

4   Matt Whitaker, director, We Do Tennis Ltd, Welton, United Kingdom   82

5   Ronnie Hurst, project director of Optus Stadium, Perth, Western Australia   104

6   Kristin Houston, director of human resources, Tampa Bay Buccaneers, Tampa, Florida, United States   134

7   Steve Brailey MBE, former chief executive officer, Sheffield International Venues Ltd (SIV), Sheffield, United Kingdom   158

8   Charlotte Jensen-Murphy, senior vice president, sports and entertainment, ABM Industries, New York City, United States   183

9   Naming rights at Marvel Stadium, Melbourne, Australia   210

10   Iain Mckinney, head of sport services, Sheffield Hallam University, Sheffield, United Kingdom   231

11   Customer experiences at Marvel Stadium, Melbourne, Australia   246

12   David Born, senior director of security, STAPLES Center, Los Angeles, California, United States   277

13   Various sport security leaders from the United States and Puerto Rico   300

14   Mike Hill, joint director of Leisure-net Solutions Limited, Norfolk, United Kingdom   332

PREFACE

Sport facilities, from grassroots and community multipurpose spaces to mega stadiums, are an integral part of the global sport business management landscape. As such, those who enter the field of sport management will inevitably interact with the management and operations of a sport facility at some point during their careers. This book is being published with the sport management educator and student in mind, specifically aimed at those sport management programs that require a facility management unit as a part of their curriculum.

The third edition of *Sport Facility Operations Management: A Global Perspective* goes beyond the basic theoretical framework of sport facility management to include the concepts inherent to the traditional operations management units taught in business management. In addition, this book connects relevant practical professional experience through facilities, people, and technology. This comprehensive sport facility management textbook is a leader in the marketplace today, addressing this important area of sport management from a global perspective.

This book brings together three authors with significant experience teaching sport business management and working with the facility and event management industry in the United States, Europe, and Australia. This includes having conducted significant research related to sport facility management and operations around the globe and having practical experience in sport facility operations management. With this background, the purpose of the textbook is to provide a theoretical and applied foundation for sport facility operations management and is supplemented with practical applications via case study scenarios, real-world excerpts, and functional documentation that can be utilized by the sport facility operations manager. In addition, each author has infused research and experiences from sport facilities around the world (North America, Europe, Middle East/Asia, Australia and New Zealand) to ensure that a global perspective for the textbook is achieved.

The initial chapter of the book serves to provide an overview of sport facility operations management, including a basic review of those topics commonly covered in an introductory sport facility operations management course. The remainder of this text will provide the reader with a framework understanding of sport facility operations management from a global perspective. In pre-management and pre-operational issues, readers will learn about ownership structures, financing, capital investment appraisal, and project management. This will lead to an explanation of the application of management and operations principles for sport facilities including organizational leadership, human resource management, financial management, budgeting, operational decision making, and operations management. From there, the implementation of sport facilities operations management across multichannel marketing and communications, revenue generation and diversification, and customer experiences from event planning to activation will be covered. This will include an investigation into legal issues, risk assessment, and security planning and management. Bringing this all together to evaluate the effectiveness of the sport facility operations management processes will be an investigation into performance analytics used to measure success. The book will conclude with a look at the short-term impacts and the long-term legacies inherent to sustainable sport facility operations management.

PEDAGOGICAL FEATURES

The third edition of *Sport Facility Operations Management: A Global Perspective* enhances learning with the following pedagogical devices:

- Each chapter opens with a chapter outline and a list of chapter objectives.
- Key terms are defined in the text when it first appears. They are also defined alphabetically on flashcards found on the website for the book.
- Each chapter has an updated case study embedded within the text to enhance critical thinking related to real-world concepts associated with the chapter material. Questions associated with each case study allow the learner to apply theoretical knowledge to the scenarios.
- Each chapter has an 'In the field' piece written by a professional currently employed in the field of sport facility operation management.
- Each chapter has a 'Facility focus' piece describing a global sport facility in terms of the concepts in the specific chapter.
- Each chapter has a 'Technology now!' excerpt spotlighting relevant technology to enhance the awareness of readers.
- A comprehensive chapter review at the end of each chapter reviews the chapter objectives and pertinent information from the chapter.

SUPPLEMENTS

The third edition of *Sport Facility Operations Management: A Global Perspective*, is available in paperback, traditional hardcopy, and online e-book formats. Instructors are provided with the following teaching aids:

- Updated case studies within each chapter with suggested discussion topics
- 'In the field,' 'Facility focus,' and 'Technology now!' excerpts to be used to further discussion about current real-world concepts
- A website dedicated to this book, including:
  - PowerPoint presentations for each chapter
  - An electronic test bank with both multiple-choice and essay questions
  - Online appendices with diagrams, schematics, manuals, and forms
  - Flashcards for students to test their knowledge of terms and definitions
  - Sample master course syllabus with suggested class activities connected to chapters in the book

CHAPTER 1

INTRODUCTION TO SPORT FACILITY OPERATIONS MANAGEMENT

CHAPTER OUTLINE

- What is sport facility operations management?
- Why sport facility operations management is important
- The discipline of sport facility operations management
- Chapter review

CHAPTER OBJECTIVES

The purpose of this prologue is to provide the reader with some initial background on the concept of sport facility operations management. First is an explanation of the concepts of facility management and operations management in general terms, followed by how these concepts interact with one another in terms of sport facilities. This is followed by a presentation of global scenarios where poor management and/or operations of a sport facility have led to significant problems. This prologue concludes an explanation of how this book will help the reader learn to deal with the scenarios presented – and much more. This is accomplished through a description of the discipline of sport facility operations management in terms of the various concepts covered in this textbook.

WHAT IS SPORT FACILITY OPERATIONS MANAGEMENT?

In order to effectively understand sport facility operations management, it is important to consider each of the two main concepts – facility management and operations management. *Facility management* is an all-encompassing term referring to the maintenance and care of commercial and nonprofit buildings, including but not limited to sport facilities, including heating, ventilation, and air-conditioning (HVAC); electrical; plumbing; sound and lighting systems; cleaning, grounds keeping, and housekeeping; security; and general operations. The goal of facility management is to organize and supervise the safe and secure maintenance and operation of the facility in a financially and environmentally sound manner.

Numerous associations oversee the profession of facility management worldwide. These associations have further clarified the definition of facility management and also provide guidance and education for those who are employed in the field. The world's largest and most widely recognized international association for professional facility managers is the International Facility Management Association (IFMA). According to their website (www.ifma.org), they support more than 24,000 members in over 100 countries across 136 regions, 16 councils, and six community areas of interest, comprised of 78 billion square feet of property that purchase more than $526 billion in products and services. They define facility management as 'a profession that encompasses multiple disciplines to ensure the functionality of the built environment by integrating people, place, process, and technology,' and they further clarify this definition as 'the practice of coordinating the physical workplace with the people and work of the organization; integrat[ing] the principles of business administration, architecture, and the behavioral and engineering sciences.' Other organizations include the British Institute of Facilities Management (BIFM – www. bifm.org.uk), the Facility Management Association of Australia (FMA Australia – www.fma.com.au), the Venue Managers Association Asia and Pacific (www.vma. org.au), the International Association for Sports and Leisure Facilities (www.iaks. org), and the International Association of Venue Managers (IAAM – www.iavm.org).

While facility management focuses on the overall maintenance and care of a building, *operations management* focuses on administrating the processes to produce and distribute the products and services offered through a facility. This would include the processes of production (tangible and intangible), inventory control, supply chain management, purchasing, logistics, scheduling, staffing, and general services – with the goal of maintaining, controlling, and improving organizational activities. The operations management field also has numerous associations that support the profession. The largest is the Association for Operations Management (APICS – www.apics.org). While on the surface they are the association for supply chain management, their mission is to build knowledge and skills among operations management professionals in order to enhance and validate abilities and accelerate careers. Their body and knowledge framework and principles for operations management are industry leading and globally recognized. Beyond APICS, other global organizations that support the profession of operations management include the European Operations Management Association (EurOMA – www.euroma-online. org), the Production and Operations Management Society (POMS – www.poms. org), and the Chartered Institute of Logistics and Transport (www.ciltuk.org.uk).

WHY SPORT FACILITY OPERATIONS MANAGEMENT IS IMPORTANT

Every day, thousands of facilities around the globe host sport, recreation, and leisure activities with minimal or no problems. But when a problem occurs or when there is a lack of planning ahead for activities, the results can be harmful and damaging. This can range from damage to the facility or equipment to injuries to personnel, participants, and visitors – with the injuries ranging in severity from minor (cuts, bruises, sprains) to major (broken bones, torn ligaments, back and eye injuries) to catastrophic (loss of limb, paralysis, death). Sport facility operations management seeks to maintain and care for public, private, and nonprofit facilities used for sport, recreation, and leisure in order to ensure the safe and secure production and distribution of products and services to users.

The discipline of sport facilities operations management has many different components that need to be understood. However, before an explanation of these various subdisciplines is provided, let us take a look at a number of historical scenarios where poor facility operations and management have led to significant problems.

- In 1972, 11 Israeli athletes (along with one German police officer and five terrorists) were killed by the Palestinian terrorist group Black September due to inadequate security at the Munich Olympic Games. Eight Palestinians, with bags of weapons, were able to scale the fence that surrounded the Olympic village and then proceeded to enter the Israeli accommodation to take the athletes hostage.
- In 1985 at Valley Parade football stadium, the home of Bradford City in the United Kingdom, a flash fire broke out during a match with Lincoln City. The fire consumed one side of the stadium, killing 56 people and injuring over 250. The fire was believed to have been caused by either a match or cigarette that fell through a hole in the stands and into rubbish below. Even though the fire brigade was called, there was no way to keep the fire at bay as fire extinguishers had been removed from passageways to prevent vandalism.
- Also in 1985, Liverpool and Juventus were facing each other in the European Cup final at Heysel Stadium in Belgium. Before the match started, Liverpool supporters reacted to taunts from the Italian fans by charging through the lines of the Belgian police. The Juventus fans could do nothing but retreat as far as a wall, which collapsed under the pressure onto their own fans below. In the ensuing panic, 39 supporters died and over 600 were injured. Based on further inquiries, as well as an evaluation of concerns voiced prior to the event, it was determined that 58,000 people being allowed into a stadium to watch the game at a stadium that was crumbling from disrepair and that could hold only 50,000 contributed significantly to the disaster.
- In 1988 in Katmandu, Nepal, 80 soccer fans seeking cover during a violent hailstorm at the national stadium were trampled to death in a stampede. The reason: The stadium doors were locked.

- In 1989 at Hillsborough Stadium in the United Kingdom (the home of the Shef-field Wednesday Football Club), a human crush occurred during an FA semifi-nal match with Liverpool that resulted in the deaths of 96 people. This deadliest stadium-related disaster in British history (and one of the worst in international football history) could have been prevented, as the inquiry into the disaster (the Taylor Report) named the cause as a failure of police and security control.
- On 1992, 18 were killed and 2,300 were injured as one of the terraces of the Armand Cesari Stadium in Bastia on the island of Corsica in France collapsed prior to a semifinal French Cup match between SC Bastia and Olympique de Marseille. Structural problems and instability were noticeable before the match, and improper construction of the temporary terrace was the main issue respon-sible for the disaster. Further investigation also disclosed violations in the man-agement of ticketing and the attitudes of the management executives as also contributing to the disaster.
- In 1993, during a quarterfinal tennis match in Hamburg, Germany, a fan ran from the middle of the crowd to the edge of the court between games and stabbed Monica Seles between the shoulder blades. The individual (who was deemed to be 'psychologically abnormal' by the courts) was a fan of Seles's rival, Steffi Graf (who was not Seles's opponent in this match). While her injuries were not life-threatening, she did not return to professional tennis for over two years.
- In 1996 at the Mateo Flores National Stadium in Guatemala City (seating capacity 45,800), Costa Rica and Guatemala were playing a World Cup qualifier. According to FIFA (Fédération Internationale de Football Association, the world soccer asso-ciation), forgers apparently had sold fake tickets to the match, bringing far more people to the stadium than it could fit (estimated at over 60,000). This crowd, combined with gate-crashers (people without tickets), pushed into the bleachers through a concrete causeway, overwhelmed other fans below, and caused a mass of people to tumble down on top of one another. Ticket takers were seen to also continue admitting fans even after bleachers were clearly filled to capacity.
- In the so-called Accra Sports Stadium disaster in 2001, a match between two teams from the West African nation of Ghana was expected to create unrest, and extra security was provided. The losing team's fans started throwing plastic seats and bottles onto the soccer pitch expressing their displeasure with the result. Police responded by shooting tear gas and plastic bullets into the crowd, creating a stampede of people that resulted in the deaths of 127 spectators. This was the worst stadium disaster in Africa to date.
- In 2007 at the Australian Open tennis tournament, a brawl between Serbian and Croatian spectators erupted outside a merchandise tent when the two groups began trading insults. Punches, bottles, and beer cups were thrown as about 150 members of the two groups rivals clashed. No injuries were reported, but 150 people were ejected from the event, and Tennis Australia announced the need to revise plans for handling these types of situations in the future.

4

- Multiple reports published between 2006 and 2009 have examined significant risks to players and spectators due to air poisoning from exhaust systems from ice resurfacing machines because of a lack of ventilation in ice rinks. Medical studies have shown the results can cause a significant increase in asthma and chronic coughs in hockey players who play in poorly ventilated rinks due to carbon monoxide and nitrogen dioxide poisoning. In a related concept, ventilation problems have also been related to so-called sick pool syndrome in aquatic centers/natatoriums due to the high humidity and the contaminants caused by chemicals and biologics.
- In 2009 at the Dallas Cowboys practice facility, a thunderstorm ripped the roof off the inflatable bubble and collapsed the infrastructure, injuring 12 people, including the paralysis of one coach. Questions of negligence on behalf of the Cowboys have arisen due to a number of factors: (1) Was this an adequate and safe facility to be holding practice in during tornadic weather conditions? (2) Was the maintenance on the facility to withstand the winds from the storm substandard and a cause? (3) Should the Cowboys have used Summit Structures LLC to build the facility when they had prior knowledge that a similar type of facility built for the Philadelphia Regional Port Authority collapsed under similar weather conditions (which are more regular in Texas)?
- In the lead-up to the 2010 FIFA World Cup in South Africa, a 64-year-old person was crushed to death while in line to buy tickets in central Cape Town, There were riots across the country at other selling points – to the point that police in Pretoria needed to use pepper spray on the people fighting to get into a FIFA ticket outlet. The cause of so many irate fans: The computer system serving many of those outlets crashed minutes after opening, and people were not able to buy the discounted tickets for matches.
- Also in 2010 in Minneapolis, Minnesota, the roof to the Metrodome, home to the Minnesota Vikings, collapsed under the weight of the snow that had collected on it over the weekend. Fortunately, nobody was in the stadium at the time, and it forced the game versus the New York Giants to be moved to Detroit.
- In 2012 in Port Said, Egypt, at least 74 people were killed and many dozens injured in a fight between the fans of two rival soccer clubs. Security measures at the stadium come into question as many fans used knives and other weapons in the fight. Fans were also easily able to storm the field after the match and attack players and fans alike, in addition to setting part of the stadium on fire.
- In 2013, two bombs exploded near the finish line of the Boston Marathon in the United States as runners were finishing the race. Three people were killed and more than 175 injured. Three other devices were found at other locations nearby.
- According to a report published by the International Trade Union Confederation (ITUC), 1,200 deaths have been attributed to stadium constructions since Qatar was awarded the 2022 FIFA World Cup in 2010.

5

So – how would you deal with each of these scenarios? Could they have been prevented? What would you have done differently? You probably cannot answer those questions right now, but the goal of this book is to provide you with a body of knowledge in sport facility operations management that can be transferred to any type of facility around the globe. As with any textbook, the theoretical foundations presented here offer the reader the opportunity to conceptualize the practices within a subject, then take that knowledge and apply it in practical settings. This book does not and cannot cover every individual, unique aspect of sport facility operations management with respect to every type of facility – this would be impossible. It does, however, provide the framework for an understanding that will allow individuals to enter a sport facility operations management situation, have a base understanding of what is happening, and conceptually understand how to start the process of managing the situation.

THE DISCIPLINE OF SPORT FACILITY OPERATIONS MANAGEMENT

The first section of the book seeks to provide the reader with an understanding of behind-the-scenes concepts that must be understood before even entering into the management and operations of sport facilities. First is an explanation of the various business, ownership, and governance structures for sport facilities across the globe. It is equally important to understand the legal authority under which the sport facility can operate as a business, as well as the business, governance, and organizational effectiveness structures. Second is an analysis of the intricacies of financing sport facilities, including the costs of conducting business, life cycle costing, cost-effectiveness/efficiency, and the importance of economic impact analyses. By understanding these financing concepts, sport facility operations managers can connect financing options to ownership and governance structures and understand how the facility came into being. Furthermore, this information serves as a foundation for looking at the current and future trends that will affect the management and operation of sport facilities. The third concept involves capital investment appraisal, which focuses on how the decisions to build new facilities, upgrade existing facilities, or invest in new equipment have a significant effect on the future financial well-being of a sport organization. To help make these decisions on an informed basis, a variety of techniques known as capital investment appraisal are available. Such decisions will be examined through an analysis of traditional methods, such as the payback method and the accounting return on investment, as well as contemporary approaches based on the time value of money, such as discounted cash flows and the internal rate of return. The final area to be covered in this section is project management and the planning, design, and construction processes for sport facilities. While not all individuals are involved in these processes from the initial conceptualization of a facility, it is inevitable that facility management professionals will be involved with the modification, refurbishment, and/or expansion of a facility sometime in their careers. The goal is to provide background about preliminary planning, developing designs, construction processes, and preparation planning for training and management of the facility

The second section of the book will focus on the implementation of management and operations in sport facilities, including organizational and human resource management; financial management, budgeting, and operational decision making; and operations management. Organizational management involves the planning, organizing, leading, and coordinating functions within a business to create an environment that supports the continuous improvement of personnel, the organization, and the customers. Human resource management is the logical and strategic supervision and managing of the most important asset within an organization: the employees. Without a quality group of individuals working for the facility, goals and objectives cannot be met, tasks cannot be completed, and customers are not served. Understanding the various types of human resources and the generally accepted practices of human resource management is crucial to the success of sport facility operations management. Equally important is financial management, as concepts such as financial reporting, budgeting, and break-even analysis are vital to the fiscal health of the sport facility and hence to the ability to continue business operations. In addition, operational decision making is crucial to success. To manage facilities efficiently and effectively, managers need to understand the concept of cost and how to apply it in real-world situations, as well as understanding the nature of cost and using this knowledge to improve a sport facility's financial performance. All of these concepts lead to actual operations management, which is the maintenance, control, and improvement of the organizational activities required to produce products and services for consumers of the sport facility. In order to effectively manage operations, a sport facility manager must understand how the operational structure integrates with the operation of the sport facility in terms of total quality management and generating operating procedures to be utilized in various facility operations and services.

The third section of the text will focus on ancillary issues in sport facility operations management, including multichannel marketing and communications, revenue generation and diversification, customer experiences from event planning to activation, legal issues and risk assessment, and security planning. In the multichannel marketing and communications chapter, basic theories and principles of global sport marketing and communications will be covered to provide the reader with broad knowledge and skill in the marketing process related to understanding the sport consumer, logistics, promotions, and public relations activities ranging from traditional methods to the use of social, digital, and mobile media. In terms of revenue generation and diversification, the various ways revenue can be generated by facilities through advertising, sponsorship, and sales including the role of managing a box office, and the diversification of facility offerings including nontraditional events, corporate and conference usage, hospitality and VIP events, stadium tours, and museums. Without the customer experience across the event planning-to-activation spectrum – without events – a facility would have no purpose. Hence it is important to understand that the goals and operational procedures of facilities are often not the same as that of an event manager. Thus the intent is to articulate the role that facility management plays in supporting event management through the sport facility event planning process; the sport facility's role in pre-event, during the event, and post-event operations, including the activation of a facility event marketing plan; actual event implementation; the level of involvement in managing events; preparing for unexpected circumstances; and the evaluation of events after they have taken place. As with almost any activity related to sport, recreation, or leisure, there is some element of risk. The next chapter articulates the need to plan for all types of emergencies that may disrupt normal operations through knowledge about risk management practices and be able to identify potential facility threats, vulnerabilities, and security countermeasures. In addition, general legal concerns for sport facility owners and managers will be covered, including the effects of the legal environment on sport facilities; general legal principles and standards inherent to sport facility operations management; and an explanation of the level of legal expertise an owner or manager needs. In the final part of this section, security planning and management are expanded upon by introducing security best practices, systems, and planning options to equip the 21st century sport manager with an all-hazards approach to facility security planning through the development of plans, policies, and protective measures.

The final section of the text focuses on performance analytics for sport facilities and on the impacts and legacies leading to sustainability. The performance analytics chapter brings together the various strands of performance management to provide clarity that anything a facility manager completes must be measured and hence the need to understand both the priorities and the measures required to monitor and demonstrate personal, team, facility, and corporate effectiveness. The chapter will specifically discuss the concepts of benchmarking and performance analytics, how measuring performance helps sport facility managers achieve better results, and techniques that can be utilized to integrate performance analytics data within the organizational culture to provide a clear focus on business essentials and that offer courses of action for continuous improvement. The chapter on impacts and legacies looks at the short-term (first ten years) and the longer-term influences of sport facilities on society. Impacts and legacies have often been linked to the concept of sustainable sport and leisure development and are becoming vital components for measuring the effectiveness of sport facility management operations in terms of managing and operating sport facilities for sport, recreation, leisure, and entertainment events. This is examined across a range of perspectives from sustainable infrastructure development to the evaluation of the long-term performance of sport facilities in terms of the triple bottom line of economic, social, and environmental impacts.

CHAPTER REVIEW

Facility management is an all-encompassing term referring to the maintenance and care of commercial and nonprofit buildings, with the goal of organizing and supervising the safe and secure maintenance and operation of a facility in a financially and environmentally sound manner. Operations management focuses on administrating the processes required to produce and distribute the products and services offered through a facility, with the goal of maintaining, controlling, and improving organizational activities. Therefore, sport facility operations management seeks to maintain and care for public, private, and nonprofit facilities used for sport, recreation, and leisure to ensure the safe and secure production and distribution of products and services to users. To be successful, a sport facility owner or manager must understand the various components of sport facility operations management including (1) pre-management and pre-operations issues (ownership structures, financing, capital investment appraisal, and planning/design/construction); (2) the implementation of management and operations (organizational and human resource management; financial management, budgeting, and operational decision making; and operations management); (3) ancillary issues in management and operations (multichannel marketing and communications, revenue generation and diversification, customer experiences from event planning to activation, legal issues and risk assessment, and security planning); (4) measuring the effectiveness of management and operations (performance analytics and impacts and legacies via sustainability).

BIBLIOGRAPHY

APICS. (2018). *About APICS*. Retrieved July 17, 2018, from www.apics.org/About

Big D Disaster. (2009, May). *Sports Illustrated*, *110*(19), 30. Retrieved June 21, 2014, from Research Library Core database, https://www.si.com/vault/2009/05/11/105810886/big-d-disaster

Bodden, V. (2014). *The Boston Marathon bombings*. North Mankato, MN: ABDO Publishing.

Cocking, C., & Drury, J. (2014). Talking about Hillsborough: "Panic" as discourse in survivors' accounts of the 1989 football stadium disaster. *Journal of Community and Applied Social Psychology*, *24*(2), 86–99. https://doi.org/10.1002/casp.2153

Darby, P. (2012). Accra Sports Stadium disaster. In J. Nauright & C. Parrish (Eds.), *Sports around the world: History, culture, and practice* (pp. 80–81). Santa Barbara: ABC-Clio Inc.

Dickie, J. F. (1995). Major crowd catastrophes. *Safety Science*, *18*(4), 309–320. https://doi.org/10.1016/0925-7535(94)00048-8

Evans, R. (1996). Bogus tickets blamed for overflow crowd. *Amusement Business*, *108*(44), 15.

Gangi, S. (2016). Leveraging the World Cup: Mega sporting events, human rights risk, and worker welfare reform in Qatar. *Journal on Migration and Human Security*, *4*(4), 221–259.

International Facility Management Association. (2018). *About us*. Retrieved July 15, 2018, from www.ifma.org/about/about-ifma

International Trade Union Confederation. (2014). *The case against Qatar: Host of the FIFA 2022 World Cup*. ITUC Special Report. Brussels: ITUC. Retrieved July 15, 2018, from https://eldis.org/document/A68054

Taylor, I. (1987). Putting the boot into a working-class sport: British soccer after Bradford and Brussels. *Sociology of Sport Journal*, *4*(2), 171–191. https://doi.org/10.1123/ssj.4.2.171

Webster, M. (2007, January 16). Ethnic rivalry mars first day of Aussie Open [Echosport Edition]. *Northern Echo*, p. 19. Retrieved June 12, 2014, from ABI/INFORM Trade & Industry database.

Wolff, A., Cazeneuve, B., & Yaeger, D. (2002, August). When the terror began. *Sports Illustrated*, *97*(8), 58–72. Retrieved June 12, 2014, from Research Library Core database.

World Wrestling Entertainment, Inc., & WWE vs. NBA. (2009, June). *Entertainment Business Newsweekly*, 45. Retrieved May 17, 2014, from ABI/INFORM Trade & Industry database.

SECTION I

PRE-MANAGEMENT AND PRE-OPERATIONAL ISSUES

CHAPTER 2

OWNERSHIP STRUCTURES

CHAPTER OUTLINE

- General business structures for sport facilities
  - Sole proprietorships
  - Partnerships
    - General partnerships
    - Limited partnerships
  - Corporations
    - Types of corporations
- Sport facility ownership and governance structures
  - Public
  - Private
  - Nonprofit/voluntary governance
  - Trusts
- Models of organizational effectiveness
- Chapter review

CHAPTER OBJECTIVES

This chapter will cover the various business, ownership, and governance structures for sport facilities across the globe. Sport facility owners must first understand the legal authority under which the sport facility can operate as a business, including as a sole proprietorship, as a partnership, or under a number of forms of corporations. At the same time, the sport facility owners must determine how they want to structure their sport business. Sport business organizations are generally structured in three ways: public, nonprofit, or commercial. While these categories are general and independent in definition, many sport business organizations can operate under multiple structures. As a result, the owner must also make choices regarding the governance of the structure, which may be as a public entity, a private entity, a public–private partnership, or under a voluntary structure. Each of these structures is examined to provide the reader with a holistic understanding of the various configurations of sport facility ownership. In addition, models of organizational effectiveness will be presented to assist the sport facility manager in efficiently managing the ownership structure. Models to be covered include the goals model, the system resource model, the process model, and the multiple constituency model. The chapter will conclude with an explanation that ownership and sport facilities managers, in order to be most effective and efficient, must use a contingency approach in all they do because there is no best model – only an optimum solution for a specific set of circumstances.

GENERAL BUSINESS STRUCTURES FOR SPORT FACILITIES

As with any type of business, a sport facility must operate under a specific legal business structure to be a viable business. Understanding these various business structures and the operational framework that each allows is crucial to the operations and management of a sport facility from the legal and functional standpoints. The three main categories of business structures are sole proprietorships, partnerships, and corporations. While these main structures are generic in nature, partnerships and corporations have numerous substructures that need to be considered for the maximum effectiveness and efficiency in managing the sport facility business.

Sole proprietorships

The most basic form of business ownership is the *sole proprietorship*. In a sport facility under this form of ownership, only one individual owns the facility, and hence that individual is responsible for the overall administration of the sport facility. In addition, the sole proprietor is accountable for all business operations, including the management of all assets, and has personal responsibility for all debt and liabilities incurred by the sport facility. This includes the tax liability, which is incurred by the owner as a part of his or her personal income tax. Sole proprietors will often pass their business down to their heirs, as in the case of most family-owned sport facilities.

In addition to having complete control over the decision-making and management processes of the sport facility, a sole proprietorship has a number of additional advantages. There are relatively minimal legal costs and few formal business requirements to creating a sole proprietorship, and the owner who chooses to sell the facility can do so without consultation with others. Sole proprietorship businesses can usually open their doors easily; however, it is important to recognize the unique licensing, legal, and zoning regulations of different jurisdictions. A further advantage of sole proprietorships and arguably a disadvantage for other ownership types is the degree of scrutiny that outside bodies can have on the financial performance of a sole proprietorship. In practice, the financial affairs of sole proprietors are confidential between them and the tax authorities. As you will discover later in the chapter, one of the prices to be paid for the more complex types of business entity is the requirement for a higher level of scrutiny over an entity's financial affairs.

There are some disadvantages to sole proprietorship for sport facilities over and above the personal liability of the sport facility from business operations. First, the owner is personally liable for the actions of employees; hence any acts of negligence or other illegal conduct related to the sport facility become the legal responsibility of the sole proprietor. Second, since investors and venture capitalists usually do not invest in sole proprietorships, it is difficult for businesses of this type to raise additional funding (or capital) for expansion and development. Most sole proprietors rely on profits, bank loans, and personal assets to finance their sport facility initially, which has the effect of limiting the funding that can be sourced to support the business. In the future, if the business grows, the sole proprietor may choose to take on partners or incorporate to secure additional funding, but obviously that changes the entire structure of the business.

Sole proprietorships come in all sizes. Many sole proprietorships are small 'mom-and-pop'–type businesses such as a hot dog vendor, golf course owners, fitness and recreation clubs, or local retail shop owners. However, a sole proprietorship can be a large business with thousands of employees. From a sport team perspective, one example is Paul Allen, who co-founded Microsoft with Bill Gates. Ranked the 43rd richest person in the world in 2018, he is the sole owner of two sport franchises – the Seattle Seahawks of the National Football League (NFL) and the Portland Trailblazers of the National Basketball Association (NBA) – as well as of the Virginia Mason Athletic Center outside Seattle (the training facility for the Seahawks) and the Moda Center in Portland (home of the Trailblazers).

Partnerships

A *partnership* is an ownership structure where more than one individual shares the overall administration and business operations of the sport facility. A number of partnership structures are utilized for sport facilities, including general partnerships and limited partnerships.

General partnerships

The most basic form of partnership is a *general partnership*, where two or more partners are responsible for all business operations and management responsibilities for a sport facility. The structure is similar to that of a sole proprietorship in that there is a personal responsibility for all debt and liabilities incurred by the sport facility include the tax liability, but it differs in that the partners share the liabilities based on the percentage of ownership each partner has in the sport facility. In addition to the shared financial commitment and the relative ease of creation, a partnership allows for a stronger top management structure, as multiple owners bring multiple strengths to the business, and often one partner's strength is another's weakness. This allows for more effective and efficient management of the sport facility, a stronger business plan, and the potential for acquiring additional resources and investors.

However, if the partners have different personalities, especially as it comes to how each views the management and administration of the sport facility, problems can occur. This is especially true if the goals and vision of the partners differ and consensus cannot be reached. This can become even more contentious if a majority partner tries to drive the business because of his majority ownership in the sport facility. Another disadvantage of a partnership, which is the same as in a sole proprietorship, is that the partners are personally liable for the negligence or illegal conduct of their employees when acting as an agent of the sport facility. This disadvantage is amplified in a partnership because each partner is liable for all the decisions made and all the actions taken by the other partner(s), including any debt they incur in the name of the partnership. As a result of these disadvantages, general partnerships should have agreements that are drawn up by lawyers, that are mutually agreed upon and signed, and that include provisions for the dissolution of the partnership. Reasons for dissolution may include the death or disability of one or more of the partners or if a partner wishes to sell her share of the sport facility or chooses to cease involvement in the business.

Limited partnerships

Limited partnerships are different from general partnerships specifically in the way the roles and responsibilities are undertaken by the partners. Also known as a limited liability partnership (LLP), the limited partnership provides financial backing but does not take an active role in the day-to-day operation and management of the sport facility (this responsibility reverts solely to the general partner[s] in the limited partnership). This is an attractive financial investment for an individual who does not have the expertise or time to run the sport facility. Limited partners still have a say in major decisions that affect the sport facility and take on the financial risk of the sport facility, although they do not take on the liability risk because they are not involved with the management or day-to-day operations. However, this

Pre-management and pre-operational issues

does not include protection from personal negligence related to a limited partner's actions in the sport facility or that of an employee acting under the direct supervision of a limited partner.

Corporations

A *corporation* is a business structure created under the laws and regulations of a governmental authority, which is made up of a group of individuals who obtain a charter authorizing them as a legal body and whose powers, rights, authority, and liabilities are distinct from the individuals making up the group. The individuals in charge of the corporation are normally referred to as shareholders, and the corporation acts as a legally recognized entity in its own right – eligible to enter into contracts, obtain assets, be responsible for liabilities, and conduct day-to-day management and business operations.

The process of incorporation, or company, formation is a very complex process that may vary from jurisdiction to jurisdiction and that is based on the type of corporation chosen for the business – such as a C-Corporation, a close corporation, an S-corporation, a limited liability corporation, a publicly traded corporation, or a nonprofit corporation. Generally, there is a three-step process to incorporate. First is to determine a name for the corporation and verify with the appropriate jurisdiction that the company name is available for incorporation. The name must be unique and cannot create deception in its similarity to another incorporate business. The second step is to file all the necessary documentation as required by the specific incorporation. This documentation is usually referred to as the Articles of Incorporation but can also be called a Certificate of Incorporation, a Corporate Charter, or Articles of Association. These articles of incorporation include the name of the corporation, names and contact information of the directors of the corporation, information about membership (if applicable), where the registered office and/or principal location are, the purpose of the corporation, the limitations of the corporation, the activities of the corporation, and how the corporation would be dissolved. The final step is to pay any fees charged by your jurisdiction. This may include governmental fees, franchise taxes, and business initiation fees. In addition, if you have any legal representation assisting in the incorporation of the business, fees incurred would also need to be paid.

Setting up a sport facility as a corporation has numerous advantages. The major reason is that the limited liability provided to owners protects the personal assets of the owners and hence are not at risk for the debts or liabilities of the corporation. This is extended to tax liabilities since the corporation is a separate legal entity – the corporation pays the taxes, not the owners. Corporations are also generally considered attractive investments; therefore, it is often easier to attract investors for funding to improve the corporation. From an employee standpoint, there are a few interesting advantages. General employees may enjoy opportunities for profit sharing and stock ownership – a benefit that often attracts higher-quality employees. For owner-employees, many of the general expenses incurred by the individual, including insurance, can often be reimbursed through the corporation or used as a tax deduction at the end of the year. From a structural standpoint, the management structure is usually very clear and ordered, and the organization has perpetual existence until all of the shareholders either dissolve the corporation or merge with another company.

There are also disadvantages to incorporating a sport facility, not the least of which is the cost to file the articles of incorporation, prepay taxes, file governmental documentation, and pay for legal fees. Paperwork is very extensive, including corporate reports, tax filings, banking and accounting records, minutes of corporate actions and shareholder meetings, and documents related to any licenses and certifications. In addition, the formalities required to run a corporation are significant. This is why many corporate meetings use Robert's Rules of Order or the Democratic Rules of Order and why there is a need for such a strict organizational structure. In addition, the dissolution of a corporation is very time-consuming and complex, as a result of the processes related to liquidating assets, organizing payments to creditors, and distributing remaining cash value to shareholders.

Types of corporations

A corporation can take on a variety of legal structures for sport facilities, including C-Corporations, close corporations, S-Corporations, limited liability corporations (LLC), publicly traded corporations, or nonprofit corporations. The general structure discussed in the previous section on corporations is indicative of the most common structure – a C-Corporation. A *C-Corporation* is the form taken by for-profit, incorporated sport facilities and provides a structure that allows for an unlimited number of owners, shareholders, and shares of stock. Another type of corporation – a close corporation – has a structure similar to that of a C- Corporation; however, it is designed for sport facilities that have a corporate structure with as few as one owner (a sole proprietor that chooses to use a corporate structure) to a maximum of usually no more than 50 owners/shareholders.

The other types of corporations have some unique characteristics that may be beneficial to various sport facility owners. For example, while the *S-Corporation* is formed in a similar manner to C-Corporations and close corporations, its tax structure is very different because taxes are paid similarly to a sole proprietorship or partnership – where the income from the S-Corporation is passed on to the shareholders, rather than the corporation, and they pay the taxes on the profit (or take the deduction in case of a loss). The advantage of this type of corporation for the owners of the sport facility is that they can act as a sole proprietor of a partnership with all the tax and liability benefits of a corporation. Also by operating under a corporate structure, investors are more likely to invest funds into a corporation, as it is seen as a more attractive investment option as compared to sole proprietorships and partnerships. On the negative side, there are significant regulations on S-Corporations, including limits on the number of shareholders, and scrutiny by governmental agencies regarding the compensation of shareholders who are also employees of the sport facility. S-Corporations are relatively expensive to set up in comparison to sole proprietorships and partnerships and have unique governmental regulations that vary from jurisdiction to jurisdiction. In addition, to avoid any legal problems, the owners need to be diligent to keep personal financial records and corporate financial records separate. Many private sporting facilities will utilize these types of structures.

Similar to a limited liability partnership (LLP), a *limited liability corporation* (LLC) has the characteristics of both a partnership and a corporation. Over the past decade, this has become the single most popular form of ownership for sport-related business entities not only because of its hybrid structure but also because of the status of the individuals who act as the owners. An LLC is formed by members of the organization, not shareholders. In the case of a sport facility, they create an operating agreement to run the facility without the strict guidelines and organizational structures of a corporation. This includes not having to write annual reports, run structured meetings, and deal with shareholder issues. By not having to operate under these strict formalities, the ownership can focus on the operation of the facility, have more flexibility in the management of the facility (including developing and implementing contracts, assigning human and physical resources, and allocating income), and meeting the needs of clients. In addition, the LLC provides the same personal liability protection as any other corporation. Examples are the Boston Red Sox of Major League Baseball (MLB) and Liverpool Football Club in the English Premier League (EPL), both owned by the Fenway Sports Group. They also own the stadiums for both teams (Fenway Park and Anfield, respectively).

Publicly traded (or *publicly owned*) *corporations* have a number of meanings based on the part of the world. In general, the concept of a public corporation refers to a business entity that has registered securities such as stocks and/or bonds that can be sold to the general population through stock offerings. Public corporations have also been referred to as government-owned corporations because of the public ownership of the assets and because the benefits provided by the business entity are for the interest of the public. This latter reference is most commonly used globally in terms of sport facilities. The benefits of being a publicly owned/government-owned corporation center on the ability to have better access to capital through the sales of stocks and/or bonds and a higher level of support as a result of governmental backing. However, this type of corporation requires total public disclosure of all financial and operational actions. An example of this is the Manchester United Football Club, who own their stadium Old Trafford and is a publicly traded corporation.

A final corporation that is prevalent in community and charity sport facilities (as well as in many of the events and companies that use sport facilities) is the nonprofit corporation. A *non-profit corporation* is a business whose purpose is not to make a profit but rather to offer services that are beneficial to the general public. Most nonprofit corporations are tax exempt due to their nature as a public benefit business. Examples of sport facilities that may be categorized under nonprofit status include those related to religious, charitable, and educational purposes. Many facilities that have the purpose of fostering international sporting events are often categorized as nonprofit, such as those hosting the Olympics. In addition, facilities that are owned and operated by civic leagues and recreational clubs are often classified as nonprofit. These types of corporations are kept under scrutiny by the government as a result of the benefits they receive.

TECHNOLOGY NOW! FINANCIAL ANALYSIS MADE EASY – FAME (UNITED KINGDOM)

One of the challenges facing owners and investors who want partial ownership of a company is finding detailed information about a business that is accurate, in-depth, and functional. One such resource used by owners and investors alike across the United Kingdom and Ireland is FAME, which stands for Financial Analysis Made Easy. FAME is a comprehensive business intelligence tool used by owners and investors alike when considering mergers, acquisitions, and investments in companies throughout the UK and Ireland. The tool, which includes information on millions of active and dissolved companies, allows for the researching general company information, investigating specific profiles of companies, and analyzing the business intelligence.

FAME provides an abundance of information for owners and investors, including:

- Financial information on companies – with up to a decade of financial history in many cases;
- Financial strength indicators;
- Organizational structure information, including key executive personnel and their contact info;
- Ownership, shareholders, and subsidiary information;
- Original tax filings information;
- Any filings against the company;
- Stock data for companies that are publically traded; and
- Industry research, company news, and any merger/acquisition reports

As a day-to-day practical tool, FAME can be very useful in providing insight into the people and the businesses you might deal with. If the person who rings you up to hire your stadium seems too good to be true, use FAME to check things out.

- What is the financial track record of their company?
- What's their liquidity rating like, and can they pay their bills?
- Have any of the directors ever been disqualified?
- Is your contact really a mouse with a lion's roar?

FAME is an excellent tool for owners and investors alike to gather significant business intelligence and to learn more about leads, prospects, and potential investors, and it can enhance the information available with a company's customer relationship management (CRM) system.

Source: Bureau Van Duk. (2019). Retrieved May 30, 2019, from www.bvdinfo.com/en-gb/our-products/data/national/fame

SPORT FACILITY OWNERSHIP AND GOVERNANCE STRUCTURES

In looking at the general business structures for sport facilities as discussed previously, we can generalize the types of sport business facility ownership into three basic categories. Public sport facilities are usually operated under governmental or quasi-governmental ownership either through federal, regional, or local jurisdictions. Nonprofit sport facilities are those managed by volunteer executives and hire paid staff to carry out day-to-day operations, with the ultimate goal based not on profit but on public benefit. The main goal of commercial sport facilities is to make a profit.

While the three sport facility ownerships structures are generic in nature, the methods employed to govern these structures can vary. For sport facilities, four main governance structures are prevalent globally: public governance, private governance, nonprofit/voluntary governance, and governance via trusts. It is important to remember that these governance structures can be applied individually or can also be applied in combination with one another, such as in a public–private governance.

Public

Public governance of sport facilities is usually conducted as a responsibility of an elected public body for a governmental jurisdiction and is usually assigned as the main responsibility of a specifically appointed governmental official. The main reason for a publicly owned facility is often related to the importance of offering high-quality facilities for the use of the population based on their needs. When it comes to larger facilities for the purpose of holding large events and/or having a professional team, municipalities believe that these sport facilities are important engines of economic development – especially in urban areas. These officials believe that the sport facilities contribute new spending and jobs to the municipality, hence providing justification for public subsidies for the construction and maintenance of these sport facilities.

In this type of governance, the facility manager usually reports directly to these government officials and must work within the operational efficiency constraints, regulations, and procedures evident in bureaucratic management. This often has a direct effect on many of the operational functions of a sport facility manager, including purchasing processes (which often must go through a tedious bidding and approval process), contract approvals (which must go through the various levels of legislative bureaucracy), and human resource management (hiring, promotion, and firing – which all must go through government approval and clearance procedures). There are also challenges when the governmental officials/bodies who are overseeing the public facilities are politicians who truly do not understand the managerial processes of a sport facility. As a result, many publicly governed sport facilities have commissioned independent boards to oversee the facilities – made up of individuals who understand facility management but who still report to the governmental agencies. Another viable option is noted in the case, 'Private Management of Public Facilities.'

PRIVATE MANAGEMENT OF PUBLIC FACILITIES

In many cases, public bodies have chosen to outsource the management of municipal sport stadiums, arenas, and recreational facilities by hiring private management groups to manage the day-to-day operations of the sport facility and provide reports to the governmental agency. Three of the major companies in the world who offer this type of service to sport facilities are SMG, Global Spectrum, and AEG.

SMG (www.smgworld.com) is one of the largest companies in the world focused on venue management, marketing, and development. It manages convention centers, exhibition halls and trade centers, arenas, stadiums, performing arts centers, theaters, and specialized-use venues and has partnerships and relationships with both municipal and private clients. SMG has a global reach in sport arena and stadium management – just a few examples of prominent sport facilities are in the United States (NRG Stadium in Houston, the Mercedes-Benz Superdome in New Orleans, and Soldier Field in Chicago) and in Europe (König Pilsener Arena in Germany, the Odyssey Arena in Northern Ireland, and Wroclaw Stadium in Poland). SMG is also in the process of expanding its operations into Latin America through their offices in Puerto Rico with the management of the Coliseo de Puerto Rico.

Global Spectrum (www.global-spectrum.com), a subsidiary of Comcast Spectacor, provides management, marketing, operations, and event booking services for public assembly facilities, including arenas, convention and exhibition centers, stadiums, theaters and performing arts centers, ice facilities, fairgrounds, amphitheaters, and entertainment and retail districts. In addition to providing full scope-of-services for existing facilities that decide to privatize, Global Spectrum also provides preopening design and construction consulting services for the development phase of facilities under construction. The global reach of this company is growing – some examples of current facilities around the world managed by Global Spectrum are in the United States (Wells Fargo Center in Philadelphia and the University of Phoenix Stadium in Arizona), in Canada (Budweiser Gardens in London, Ontario, and Abbotsford Centre in British Columbia), and in Asia (Singapore Sports Hub [Arena, National Stadium, and Indoor Stadium] and Du Forum in Abu Dhabi, UAE).

AEG (www.aegworldwide.com) has been one of the world's leading sport and live entertainment businesses for 20 years. Through its global network of venues and associated sport and entertainment products, it strives to deliver an innovative experience to its customers. They also offer significant philanthropy, sustainability, and diversity initiatives through subsidiaries, including AEG 1COMMUNITY, AEG 1EARTH, and AEG 1FORCE. A sample of their global reach in the area of sport facility operations management includes facilities in the United States (Staples Center in Los Angeles, T-Mobile Arena in Las Vegas, Barclays Center in Brooklyn, New York), in Canada (Videotron Centre in Quebec City), in Europe (Ericsson Globe Arena in Stockholm, O2 Arena in London), in South America (Buenos Aires Arena, Argentina and Antel Arena, Montevideo, Uruguay), in Australia (Qudos Bank Arena, Sydney, Perth Arena, Perth, Suncorp Stadium, Brisbane), in China (Cadillac Arena, Beijing, and Mercedes-Benz Arena, Shanghai), and in the UAE (Dubai Arena, Dubai).

Sources

AEG. (2018). *We Are AEG*. Retrieved July 18, 2018, from www.aegworldwide.com/about

Global Spectrum. (2014). *Company Background*. Retrieved March 28, 2014, from www. spectraexperiences.com/venue/

SMG. (2014). *About SMG*. Retrieved March 28, 2014, from http://smgworld.com/company-history

Suggested discussion topics

1   What are the advantages and disadvantages of outsourcing the management of public sport facilities?
2   Other than SMG, Global Spectrum, and AEG, identify two other private management companies for sport facilities. Compare and contrast the mission and service offerings – how are each of those companies similar to and different from the three just described?

Private

The fastest growing structure for governing sport facilities of all types is *private governance*. As public funding dries up because of changes in the economy, the determination that other municipal projects are more needed, and the lack of human resources to appropriately manage and oversee sport facilities, private enterprises have evolved to meet the needs of communities. These privately managed sport facilities run as independent businesses under any number of ownership structures, including sole proprietorships, partnerships, or corporations – and can be either commercial or nonprofit. The owners have the ability to exercise their own power and authority over the entire governance structure of the sport facility, including the development of the mission and vision and determining who the users of the facility are, and they are the regulatory power for anything that happens within the sport facility.

Nonprofit/voluntary governance

Nonprofit and *voluntary governance* organizations are an integral part of the sport business landscape, especially as related to sport facilities that are part of educational, charitable, and religious sport entities. Involvement of individuals in the day-to-day operation of these sport facilities is usually voluntary in nature, although there may be some compensated employees within the organization. However, the governance of the sport facility is usually voluntary. The main responsibilities as related to voluntary governance involve the ability to work within the external environments to secure resources from market operations, from governmental subsidies, or from reciprocity (volunteering, donations), while pursuing the goals and objectives set forth for the sport facility. Organizations under a voluntary governance structure usually work under a constitution and a set of bylaws. The constitution is a document that outlines the purpose, structure, and limits of the organization. The bylaws are the rules adopted to define and direct the internal structure, policies, and procedures of the sport facility.

Trusts

The importance of managers being aware of the jurisdiction in which they are working is well illustrated by the case of the United Kingdom where the use of sport and leisure 'trusts' is an increasingly common trend. The term 'trust' does not really have a legal definition and tends to be used as a catch-all description for organizations that are specifically set up to run local authority leisure services independently, for the public good rather than financial gain. The essence of what a trust is can be appreciated from the three-stage diagram presented in Figure 2.1.

Local authorities can consider using three types of trust: (1) a company limited by guarantee with or without charitable status, (2) an industrial and provident society (IPS) with or without charitable status, and (3) a public interest company (PIC).

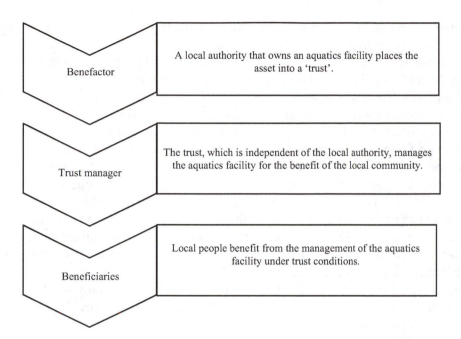

Figure 2.1 Three elements of a trust

A *company limited by guarantee* is a legally recognized business entity in its own right – the same as any other limited company. However, unlike conventional limited companies where owners' liability is limited to the extent of their investment in the business, in a company limited by guarantee, there is no individual investment, and the liability of the owners is limited to a guarantee of a fixed amount in the event of the company failing. In practice, the amount that directors of companies limited by guarantee are asked to contribute in the event of failure is a nominal amount should it be called for. In order to achieve limited by guarantee status, a company needs to have objectives that are for the public good, such as the provision of recreational or cultural opportunities for the community. A further distinguishing feature of a company limited by guarantee is that surpluses or profits are not allowed to be distributed to the directors or trustees. This does not mean that it is not permitted for companies of this type to make profits; rather, those who control the company are not permitted to benefit financially from its trading performance. Indeed, it may be essential for companies limited by guarantee to make profits in order to maintain their facilities and to reinvest in the business. For many facility providers in the UK, achieving the status of a company limited by guarantee is but a stepping-stone to achieving charitable status. Charitable status provides desirable tax advantages for organizations whose objectives include the relief of poverty, the advancement of education, the advancement of religion, or other purposes deemed beneficial to the community. The provision of sport facilities and sporting opportunities falls into the 'other purposes' category, and there are plenty of precedents whereby charitable status has been awarded to sport organizations. The major financial benefits of charitable status are an exemption from corporation tax on the profits plus mandatory relief of 80% of local authority business rates (a form of local taxation) with the potential to increase this to 100% at the discretion of the local authority. Thus, simply from rate relief alone, registered charities have a significant financial competitive advantage over suppliers that are not registered charities. Some companies that are limited by guarantee do not pursue charitable status and are content with the protection that their status provides the directors of the company, that is, a nominal limit on their liability in the event of failure. Regardless of charitable status, one of the key benefits of being a company limited by guarantee is the ability to attract competent directors from the community who are happy to offer their expertise for free because they are safe in the knowledge that their liability for debts is limited by the value of their (usually nominal) guarantee.

Industrial and provident societies (IPS) are recognized as being legal entities in their own right and have broadly the same benefits as companies limited by guarantee. To achieve IPS status in the context of sports, applicants are required to demonstrate that they are providing benefits for the community and not just the membership. The key features of an industrial and provident society are that it will have:

- A written set of rules that govern its activities;
- A recognized separate legal identity;
- The right to own property;
- The right to enter into contracts;
- Additional legal requirements made of it such as company law;
- Limited liability (i.e., the liability of the management committee is usually limited to a nominal amount); and
- The ability to make a profit, which is put back into the organization.

Greenwich Leisure Limited (GLL) is an innovative example of a staff-led 'Leisure Trust,' which uses the industrial and provident society format. GLL manages more than 65 public leisure centers in Greater London. Not only is the legal format of the business an ideal way to run the trust, but it also benefits from economies of scale in terms of procurement whereby it can negotiate bulk discounts on energy costs and other supplies. Like companies limited by guarantee, industrial and provident societies may also qualify for charitable status and hence benefit from mandatory rate relief.

A *public interest company* (PIC) is a relatively new legal format for delivering public services and exists to deliver a specific public benefit such as providing equitable sporting opportunities for the community. This benefit cannot be changed without direct agreement from the appropriate publicly accountable body, protecting the public's interest in the services provided and distinguishing PICs from commercial companies and the not-for-profit sector. PICs are independent bodies. The government cannot manage them directly or interfere with management processes and day-to-day decisions. PICs can be held accountable by the government only for their results and the standards of delivery. This makes PICs different from public sector organizations and allows them to be entrepreneurial and responsive to the needs of users.

The intricacies of what type of business format to adopt are best left to those with current legal skills and experience who can provide expert advice to managers. However, as a manager, you should have a working knowledge of the available options and should be conversant with the advice that lawyers give you. It is therefore worthwhile knowing the strengths and weaknesses of various formats so that decisions are made using the best available information.

In sum, the strengths of 'trust' status are as follows:

- Trusts operate as 'social enterprises,' which provides them with the ability to run as businesses while working toward the community's needs and a local authority's strategic direction.
- There is a proven record of trusts improving the performance of their partners through the achievement of social targets and the setting of clear strategic goals.
- Evidence gathered over a long period suggests that trusts reduce the cost of services to the local authority, in turn reducing an authority's financial risk. Trusts do not pay tax on profits; they qualify for rate relief and tend to find it easier than local authorities to fund-raise for both revenue and capital projects.
- Local authorities retain some control over trusts by agreeing on shared targets to ensure that sport facilities are managed to optimize the achievement of an authority's objectives. In practice, this is achieved through partnerships in the form of working and service-level agreements.
- Local authorities can retain influence on the board of a trust via the nomination of trustees who will protect the authority's interests.
- Sport facilities can be operated with greater financial and management autonomy, enabling them to respond to market changes dynamically and hence remain competitive.
- Trustees have the ability to develop business and financial plans over sustainable periods of time, creating the ability to plan for the future.
- Previous evidence suggests that trusts improve the opportunity for community involvement in service delivery.
- Trusts have the ability to deliver a wide spectrum of varying leisure facilities, as long as the activities can be considered 'charitable.' Examples include running sport facilities ('other purposes beneficial to the community') and arts facilities ('advancing education').

- The trust option creates a perceived 'middle ground' toward outsourcing public services and does not necessarily involve such a fundamental shift in political ideology as contracting facilities and services out to the private sector.
- The board of trustees, if appointed successfully, should add expert financial, business, and marketing experience with no additional cost to the service as these are voluntary posts.

In contrast, the weaknesses of trust status are:

- There is a widely held view that establishing a trust is resource intensive both in terms of financial outlay and the time required to see the process through from inception to completion.
- By placing a facility or service into trust, there is an inevitable loss of integration with other local authority services. For example, in the case of an emergency, the authority would not be able to convert a trust-managed sports hall into a temporary shelter for homeless people as easily as it could if the facility were managed in-house.
- The success or failure of a trust hinges crucially on the ability to recruit a suitable board of trustees, with the requisite skills, experience, and knowledge to provide strategic direction and leadership. There is the danger that, in deprived areas particularly, appropriate community leadership will not emerge, and under these conditions, trust status can be more of a hindrance than a help.
- In the early stages of running a trust, it may be difficult to attract financing owing to the company's unproven trading record. Potential trading partners prefer to vet the accounts of companies they do business with. If a trust does not have a financial track record and is unable to provide copies of its last three years' worth of audited accounts, some firms may be reluctant to trade or will set punitive trading conditions, such as payment in advance.
- Facilities often receive hidden subsidies from local authorities such as help with central administration and maintenance costs. These should be planned for so that there is no duplication of effort or that the trust becomes more expensive to run than under an in-house model.
- If a trust fails financially, a potentially large financial risk may need to be borne by the Authority. This type of situation can be seen as local authorities bearing much of the risk but not benefiting from the rewards. However, evidence to date indicates that in the last 20 years, very few trusts have failed.

The essential points emerging from the information presented on the types of ownership structure presented in this chapter are twofold. First, numerous types of legal format are available to the sport facility manager. The reality is that in the early part of your career, this type of activity will have been taken care of, and you will work in a predetermined ownership structure over which you have no strategic control. As your career develops and you take on a more strategic role, which could involve deciding the ownership model and legal identity of a facility, you will be required to explore and advise on various options accordingly. Second, the issues around ownership structures and legal identity are complex. While you should be conversant with the issues, it is also important to realize the limitations of your knowledge. Some things are best left to specialists, and the sign of a good manager is one who knows when to ask for help.

FACILITY FOCUS: TRANSNATIONAL VENUE MANAGEMENT: MERCEDES-BENZ ARENA, SHANGHAI, CHINA

The management and operation of sport venues involve the safe and secure maintenance and upkeep of the mechanical functions of commercial and non-profit venues in an environmentally and fiscally sound fashion. Sport facility owners need to decide at some point whether they are going to directly manage the venue or outsource it to an external manager. The outsourcing of these management and operational functions takes place at all levels of sport – from local community facilities to large stadiums and arena. Numerous companies operate in this transnational space including the Anschutz Entertainment Group (AEG), who manages the Mercedes-Benz Arena in Shanghai.

Traditionally, sport venues in China are considered state-owned assets because their major investor is government, and hence they are usually managed by either government-affiliated institutions or state-owned enterprises. However, the convergence of outsourcing venue management and traditional Chinese venue operations management came together in 2008 when AEG, the National Basketball Association (NBA), and the owner of PAC-Shanghai Oriental Pearl (Group) Co. Ltd. (OPG) entered into a partnership to co-fund AEG-OPG Culture and Sports (Shanghai) Co., Ltd. Its main purpose was to manage and operate the Shanghai World Expo Cultural Center, which after Expo 2010 became the Mercedes-Benz Arena as part of a 10-year facility sponsorship deal.

The role of AEG in this unique multistakeholder management and operations partnership is to provide their expertise as a transnational venue management corporation. The structure provided by AEG helps to ensure that the Mercedes-Benz Arena became a vibrant cultural and lifestyle destination in Shanghai for residents, as well as to attract global brand awareness for sporting events, entertainment tours, and other leisure and recreational events.

Source: Excerpts from Yao, Q. & Schwarz, E. C. (2017). Transnational venue management corporations and local embeddedness: A case study on the Mercedes-Benz Arena in Shanghai, China. *International Journal of Sports Marketing and Sponsorship*, *18*(1), 70–80. http://dx.doi.org/10.1108/IJSMS-05-2016-0008

MODELS OF ORGANIZATIONAL EFFECTIVENESS

To be able to appropriately govern a sport facility, a manager must have a clear understanding of the concept of organizational effectiveness. Organizational effectiveness is the concept of how successful a business is in achieving the outcomes set forth in the planning processes. Measuring organizational effectiveness is central to the evaluation of what a sport facility delivers from programmatic, operational, and managerial perspectives. It is an integral process to proving to investors and donors that the money being provided is being used to accomplish the goals of the organization, to evaluate the communication processes and ethical actions of the business, and to serve as a foundational process for determining strategic growth.

For a sport facility to be effective and achieve its goals and objectives, the ownership and the governance structures must be able to successfully respond to changes in its environment. Changes in the environment may be internal to the sport facility organization/management/ operation or external (examples include customers' needs, the economy, politics, legal issues, and the media). At the same time, an organization needs to understand the attributes of flexibility in correlation to control. Flexibility allows faster change, whereas control allows a firmer grasp on current operations. How these two concerns work in congruency in both the internal and external environments is a significant measure of organizational effectiveness.

Numerous models have been developed to help sport facilities measure organizational effectiveness based on the varying levels of environmental and organizational attributes. Table 2.1 articulates the major models of organizational effectiveness that are utilized in sport facilities globally.

Table 2.1 Models of organizational effectiveness

Model/approach	Description
Goal (or rational goal)	▪ The achievement of specific organizational goals determines effectiveness. ▪ Establishes a general goal. ▪ Discovers the objectives for accomplishment. ▪ Defines activities for each objective. ▪ Measures the level of success. ▪ Designed to enhance strategic planning by linking program goals and resource allocation levels. ▪ Is output based on measurable terms? Not always good because not all effectiveness is output based.
Process (or internal process)	▪ Focuses on the effectiveness of the internal transformation process. ▪ Emphasis is on control and the internal focus and stresses the roles of information management, communication, stability, and control.

Pre-management and pre-operational issues

Model/approach	Description
Systems resources	Effectiveness is determined in terms of the ability to attract and secure valuable resources, such as operating capital, physical resources, and quality human resources.
Multiple constituency	Effectiveness is not internally judged but is based on the judgment of its constituents. In the case of a sport facility, it may include spectators, promoters, resident teams, and vendors Often is used as a viable alternative to the goal and systems approaches.
Strategic constituency	Effectiveness is determined by the extent to which the organization satisfies all of its strategic constituencies. For a sport facility, it would include spectators, vendors, home teams, the media, sponsors, etc.
Open system	Effectiveness is measured as a result of the degree that an organization acquires inputs from its environment and has outputs accepted by its environment.
Competing values	Effectiveness is measured based on the interaction among four sets of competing values: – Internal focus and integration – External focus and differentiation – Flexibility and discretion – Control and stability
High-performing system	Effectiveness is a measurement that compares itself to other similar organizations (to be covered in more detail in Chapter 14 on performance analytics).
Human relations	Effectiveness is measured based on the development of the organization's personnel. Places emphasis on flexibility and internal focus. Stresses cohesion, morale, and human resources as criteria for developing effectiveness.
Legitimacy	Effectiveness is measured by acting lawfully and ethically in the eyes of the internal and external environments.
Fault-driven	Effectiveness seeks to eliminate traces of ineffectiveness in its internal functioning through the design of backup plans to be reliable even if some components fail.

On a final note, sport facility managers and owners need to acknowledge a contingency approach to organizational effectiveness, as there is no best model. Numerous variables influence organizational effectiveness, including changes in the organizational structure, the implementation of new technologies, opportunities and threats in the environment that affect the sport facility, and the people using the sport facility (both customers and human resources) – to name a few. As a result, owners and managers of sport facilities must take a situational approach to organizational effectiveness in order to attain an optimum solution for a specific set of circumstances that may arise.

CHAPTER REVIEW

A sport facility must operate under a specific legal business structure to be viable. Understanding these various business structures and the operational framework each allows is crucial to the operations and management of a sport facility from a legal and functional standpoint. The three main categories of business structures are sole proprietorships, partnerships, and corporations. The most basic form of business ownership is a sole proprietorship, where only one individual owns the facility and is responsible for the overall administration and liabilities of the sport facility. In a partnership, more than one individual shares the overall administration and business operations of the sport facility. A number of partnership structures are utilized for sport facilities, including general partnerships and limited partnerships. General partners are directly involved with the day-to-day operations of the facility and have full liability, whereas limited partners have financial liability but not operational liability or responsibility. The corporation is a business structure created under the laws and regulations of governmental authority and is made up of a group of individuals who obtain a charter authorizing them as a legal body where the powers, rights, authority, and liabilities of the entity are distinct from the individuals making up the group. There are various corporate structures for sport facilities, including C-Corporation, a close corporation, an S-Corporation, a limited liability corporation, a publicly traded corporation, and a nonprofit corporation.

Sport facility ownership usually falls under one of three governance structures. Public sport facilities are usually operated under governmental or quasi-governmental ownership through either federal, regional, or local jurisdiction. Nonprofit sport facilities are managed by volunteer executives who hire paid staff to carry out day-to-day operations, with the ultimate goal based not on profit but for public benefit. Commercial sport facilities' main goal is to make a profit. A unique governance structure is a governance by trust, where a benefactor places an asset (such as a sport facility) into a trust that is managed by an assigned party (trust manager) to ensure that the customers (beneficiaries) benefit from the services of the sport facility. These trusts can be either a charitable organization, a nonprofit without charitable status, or a public interest company.

To appropriately govern a sport facility, a manager must have a clear understanding of the concept of organizational effectiveness, which is the concept of how successful a business is in achieving the outcomes set forth in the planning processes. While there are multiple models of organizational effectiveness, it is important to recognize and acknowledge the need for a contingency approach to governing a sport facility, as there is no best model – only an optimum solution for a specific set of circumstances.

IN THE FIELD . . .

With Mike Tatoian, executive vice president and chief operating officer, Dover Motorsports Inc., Dover, Delaware, United States

Mike has been the executive vice president and chief operating officer of Dover Motorsports, Inc. (NYSE: DVD) since 2007. The organization includes Dover International Speedway (capacity 113,000) and Nashville Super Speedway (capacity 35,000). He is responsible for all facets of the organization, which are primarily focused around NASCAR race weekends, Firefly Music Festival, and other special events held at the facility.

Dover, Delaware, takes on a carnival-like atmosphere as the most popular names in NASCAR's premier series come to Dover International Speedway, affectionately known as the Monster Mile. The venue plays host to the largest sporting events in the Mid-Atlantic region and is known as the fastest one-mile oval in the world. Also held on the speedway's property since 2012, Firefly Music Festival is a four-day music festival attracting 80,000 fans per day and in three years has become the fastest growing, most successful music festival of all time according to *Rolling Stone* magazine.

Mike has over 25 years of experience as a senior level sport and entertainment executive successfully managing over $750 million in sport teams, facilities, and properties in his career. The first opportunity he had to get into sport management was back in the mid-1980s working for the Tulsa Drillers AA minor league baseball team as a telemarketing sales representative. In a brief three-year period, he became an administrative assistant, followed by becoming director of stadium operations (aka groundskeeper) and shortly after director of media relations for the team. Mike then was afforded the opportunity to move to his hometown of Bettendorf, Iowa, to become the assistant general manager of the Quad City Angels (class A affiliate of the then California Angels) and quickly moved into the GM position of that team shortly thereafter. After a few years there, he launched a brand new team in Fort Wayne, Indiana (Fort Wayne Wizards, class A affiliate of the Minnesota Twins).

At this point, Mike decided to enter into a more corporate/ownership position when he became the chief operating officer of United Sports Ventures. Over the next seven years as COO, he was involved with building, owning, managing, or operating minor league baseball and hockey teams all over the country. For him, it was a terrific experience learning the fundamentals of municipal financing, politics, building teams from the ground up, learning new sports, assembling business plans, meeting new people, testing time management skills, and balancing priorities. He then decided to launch another sport management and ownership company, Victory Sports Group (VSG). After success in that venture, he then moved to his current position at Dover Motorsports.

Mike believes that a successful career in the field of sport facility ownership and management requires a diverse understanding of the various components that all equally contribute to the success. The focus of various departments such as sales, operations, safety, security, food and beverage, and communications, which are inextricably linked to fans, sponsors, and members of the media, combined with the pressure of meeting budget goals and objectives, all need to be balanced, prioritized, and understood to have a long and successful career.

BIBLIOGRAPHY

Ackerman, A. M. (1994). Privatization of public-assembly-facility management. *Cornell Hotel and Restaurant Administration Quarterly*, *35*(2), 72–83. https://doi.org/10.1016/0010-8804(94)90022-1

Anand, A., Milne, F., & Purda, L. (2006). *Voluntary adoption of corporate governance mechanisms*. Retrieved March 28, 2014, from http://law.bepress.com/expresso/eps/1277

Bushardt, S. C., Debnath, S. C., & Fowler, A. F. (1990). A contingency approach to organizational effectiveness through structural adaptation. *American Business Review*, *8*(1), 16–24.

Coates, D., & Humphreys, B. R. (2003). Professional sport facilities, franchises and urban economic development. *Public Finance and Management*, *3*(3), 335–357.

Ferkins, L., Shilbury, D., & McDonald, G. (2009). Board involvement in strategy: Advancing the governance of sport organizations. *Journal of Sport Management*, *23*(3), 245–277. https://doi.org/ 10.1123/jsm.23.3.245

Mahoney, K., Esckilsen, L. A., & Jeralds, A. (2015). *Public assembly venue management: Sports, entertainment, meeting, and convention venues*. Dallas: Brook Books Publishing Group.

Martinez-Tur, V., Piero, J. M., & Ramos, J. (2001). Linking service structural complexity to customer satisfaction: The moderating role of type of ownership. *International Journal of Service Industry Management*, *12*(3/4), 295–306. https://doi.org/10.1108/eum0000000005522

McNamee, M. J., & Fleming, S. (2007). Ethics audits and corporate governance: The case of public sector sports organizations. *Journal of Business Ethics*, *73*(4), 425–437. https://doi.org/10.1007/s10551-006-9216-0

Misener, K., & Doherty, A. (2009). A case study of organizational capacity in nonprofit community sport. *Journal of Sport Management*, *23*(4), 457–482. https://doi.org/10.1123/jsm.23.4.457

O'Boyle, I. (2012). Corporate governance applicability and theories within not-for-profit sport management. *Corporate Ownership and Control*, *9*(2–3), 335–342. https://doi.org/10.22495/cocv9i2c3art3

Rosentraub, M. S. (2009). *City shaping: The summary report of the leadership committee for a new sports/entertainment facility for Edmonton*. Retrieved July 18, 2018, from www.edmonton.ca/attractions_events/documents/PDF/City_Shaping_PDF.pdf

Rosentraub, M. S., & Swindell, D. (2009). Of devils and details: Bargaining for successful public/private partnerships between cities and sports teams. *Public Administration Quarterly, 33*(1), 118–148.

Torkildsen, G., & Taylor, P. (Eds.). (2010). *Leisure and recreation management* (6th ed.). London: Routledge.

Trenberth, L., & Hassan, D. (Eds.). (2011). *Managing sport business*. London: Routledge.

Unison. (2006). *Leisure trusts briefing 148 December 2006: Charitable trusts delivering public leisure and cultural services*. Retrieved June 8, 2011, from www.unison-scotland.org.uk/briefings/leisuretrusts.html

CHAPTER 3

FINANCING SPORT FACILITIES

CHAPTER OUTLINE

- Financing concepts
    - Business issues
    - The costs of ownership and life cycle costing
    - The principles of economic impact analysis
- Sources of financing for sport facilities
    - Public sector funding
    - Private sources of revenue
    - Public–private partnerships
- History of sport facility financing
- Future trends in sport facility financing
- Chapter review

CHAPTER OBJECTIVES

This chapter will delve into the intricacies of financing sport facilities. Recurring themes in financing will be discussed, including business issues, the costs of ownership, life cycle costing, cost-effectiveness/efficiency, and the principles of economic impact analysis. The recurring issues have a direct effect on the source of financing to be used for sport facilities, such as public sector funding, private sources of revenue, public–private partnerships, and the influence of the voluntary sector. Sport facility investment has been significantly affected by the economic changes that have taken place early in the 21st century; hence the chapter will conclude with a look at the current and future trends that will affect the management and operation of sport facilities.

Pre-management and pre-operational issues

FINANCING CONCEPTS

Financing is defined as the act of obtaining or providing money or capital for the purchase of a business enterprise. For a sport facility, many of these financing issues are related to the types of financing available and the significant changes that have occurred in sport facility investment in the 21st century. However, prior to delving into those topics, it is important to understand recurring themes that are central to the understanding of basis financing themes. In addition to basic business issues related to financing sport facilities, other concepts to be understood include the costs of ownership/life cycle costing; and the principles of economic impact analysis.

Business issues

Developing new sport facilities is a risky process that invariably requires complex financial arrangements. These two points are interrelated. First, it is unlikely that any organization from any sector will have the spare cash available to develop and build a sport facility from the outset of a project. It is, therefore, a current practice that the financing of sport facilities tends to be made with financial contributions from a variety of sources. For example, Wembley Stadium in England opened in 2007 with an estimated cost of £757 million ($1.157 billion). The stadium was funded by the Football Association (FA), distributions from the National Lottery, the London Development Agency, and a series of commercial banks. It is essential for businesses to make a profit and to be able to service their debts. In 2017, Wembley National Stadium Ltd. had long-term debts of £285.70 million ($373.14 million) and paid £42.85 million ($55.96 million) in interest to service those debts. Second, because of the risks involved and the scale of developing sport facilities, developers seek to share the risk involved in a project with partners. These are drawn from those who wish to risk their money on taking a stake in a business by buying the right to share in future profits (equity financing) and from those who are prepared to loan money for development in return for a fixed rate of interest and the knowledge that in the event of business failure they will get their money back (debt financing). The bigger the project, the more complex the web of relationships underpinning it is. When public sector money is involved, there is also the scope for controversy as perhaps best demonstrated by the adverse publicity surrounding the $450 million public sector subsidies provided by the New York authorities for Yankee Stadium and the £120 million ($194.9 million) provided by the National Lottery for Wembley Stadium.

When borrowed money (or debt) is used to finance a development, the stance of those borrowing the money is the belief that they can make sufficient profit to be able to service interest costs and still make a profit. For the providers of loans, the stance taken is that the interest being paid on the loans justifies the risk of lending to the developer. In practice, the two parties' fates are inextricably linked: For everyone to get a fair return on their investment, the development has to succeed.

The complex nature of sport facility development helps to provide further insight into the role and responsibilities of the sport facility manager. At the most basic level, it is important that day-to-day operations are profitable and sustainable. There is little point in using public subsidies and other people's money to develop a facility for sport only for further money to be required to underwrite operating losses. One of the first rules of business is that you need to make a profit if your business is to have a long-term future. In the case of public sector facilities, for which there may be legitimate grounds to subsidize operating costs, managers must operate within the subsidy levels that have been allocated to them. The importance of appropriate financial performance can also be appreciated by looking at the bigger picture. If as a manager you do not deliver, then you place at risk the livelihoods of your staff, your suppliers, and other stakeholders. Equally, by performing well, you create the conditions for growth, reinvestment, higher salaries, more staff, and so on. While this is a weighty responsibility in its own right, things do not stop at sound financial performance. Sport facilities are investments that have the potential to grow in value. Most property tends to increase in value over time, and sport facilities are no different. One method by which investors can profit from their initial investment in a sport facility is by selling it for a higher price than the facility cost to develop in the first place. Some of the key factors that determine how much a business is worth include how well the business is performing financially; the condition of the land, buildings, fixtures, and local infrastructure; and the opportunity for future development in the locality.

Thus a further set of responsibilities for the sport facility manager is the importance of ensuring that the asset is well maintained and kept in a suitable condition such that it is attractive to potential purchasers or indeed new investors. Finally, the managers of sport facilities should be aware of the wider context in which they operate. When a facility is built, it supports jobs in the construction industry, and when the facility is operational, numerous other people may be directly or indirectly dependent on the facility for some or all of their income. With this responsibility comes the importance of being a good corporate citizen, looking after not only your own interests but also those of the wider community. A good facility manager will operate at all three levels and look after the interests of the business, the facility, and the wider community. You should now realize that effective sport facility management is much more than taking care of day-to-day operations.

The costs of ownership and life cycle costing

Considerations around financing sport facilities are not confined to how much a building costs to construct in the first instance. In our own lives, we know that buying a car is simply the start of an expensive relationship with an asset, which will require further expense in terms of tax, insurance, fuel servicing, parking, and valeting. A second-hand luxury car might cost the same as a new small car, but we all know that the costs of owning the former will be much greater than the latter. The same type of commonsense thinking is applicable to sport facilities. For both buildings and equipment, due consideration must be given to what are known as 'life cycle costs,' which are defined by the Chartered Institute of Management Accountants (CIMA) as 'the maintenance of physical asset cost records over the entire asset lives, so that decisions concerning the acquisition, use, or disposal of the assets can be made in a way that achieves the optimum asset usage at the lowest cost to the entity' (CIMA, 2005).

The importance of being aware of life cycle costing can be appreciated by the finding that as much as 90% of the lifetime costs attributable to an asset are determined by decisions made in the early part of the asset's life. For example, in the case of a swimming pool, the purchase costs of an ozone treatment plant for water cleansing compared with a chlorine-based plant might make the ozone option seem prohibitive in price. However, when the full lifetime costs of each option are evaluated to account for costs such as energy usage, chemical costs, and plant maintenance, it may well be the case that the more expensive option to buy actually works out to less expensive to own and operate in the longer term than the cheaper option. It is important to avoid buy-now-pay-later situations as cheaper items may have higher running costs and a lower disposal value. Managers of sport facilities are routinely required to make long-term judgments about the optimal solution for a given set of circumstances. For example, is it more cost-effective to purchase fitness center equipment such as selectorized and cardiovascular machinery outright and to take responsibility for maintaining and replacing it, or is a better option to lease the equipment whereby maintenance is part of the service level agreement? By using the principles of lifetime costing, these decisions can be made on the evidence of the best information available and in the best interests of the business.

The evidence that life cycle costing for an asset is based on can be complicated, as indicated in the range of considerations listed in Table 3.1

Table 3.1 Considerations for life cycle costing

Purchase costs	How much does an asset cost to purchase?
Running costs	What are the operational costs of using an asset, such as the hourly costs of running air-conditioning in a sport stadium?
Maintenance costs	How much does it cost to retain an asset in a fit-for-purpose condition?
Training costs	How much will it cost to train staff in the use of a new box office system?
Decommissioning and disposal costs	How much will it cost to wind down an asset and to dispose of it bearing in mind operational and environmental issues?

In reality, it is difficult to forecast what might happen in the future, and life cycle costing decisions are based on the attitudes of individuals toward risk and financial issues such as how quickly they want their money back. Nonetheless, the importance of making good decisions can be appreciated by examining the case of health and fitness clubs that are part of a chain. If proper life cycle costing is carried out to inform an organization's business model, then when the model is rolled out to multiple sites, the benefits will be reaped at every site. Conversely, if you get it wrong at one site and roll out a flawed business model, then the error will be compounded in every site affected. An alternative way of looking at life cycle costing is to call it cost-effectiveness, which is defined as an assessment before a decision is made based on the available options that are assumed to deliver the same outcomes in terms of their relative costs. Thus, whether we are talking about the construction materials for a multipurpose gymnasium, the type of plant to use to cleanse the water in a swimming pool, or the purchase or leasing of fitness equipment, sport facility managers should always be mindful of the importance of cost effectiveness and the impact of decisions on costs in the future.

FACILITY FOCUS: INVESTING FOR THE FUTURE: MELBOURNE PARK REDEVELOPMENT, MELBOURNE, AUSTRALIA

Part of the forecasting for sport facilities is the need for redevelopment to stay ahead of the competition and either secure or retain valuable event properties. This is especially true in Melbourne, Australia, where there is a desire to retaining their title as one of the world's leading sport cities with competition less than 1,000 kilometers down the road in Sydney.

One such project is the Melbourne Part redevelopment, a commitment of nearly AU$1 billion and $700 million across three phases to ensure that the facility caters to maintaining the hosting of the Australian Open through 2036, while also creating a world-class sport and event precinct. In the first phase already completed, the numerous improvements and upgrades include:

- Adding 1,500 seats and a retractable roof to Margaret Court Arena (making it the third retractable roof facility in the complex);
- Upgrades to Rod Laver Arena including the concourse and food and beverage services; and
- The addition of eight indoor and 13 outdoor tennis courts at the National Tennis Center.

Phase 2, which is set to be completed by the end of 2020, features:

- Further renovation to Rod Laver Arena;
- A new bridge to create better walking and cycling access from downtown to Melbourne Park; and
- A new administrative headquarters for Tennis Australia.

Phase 3 is currently underway and features:

- A new 5,000-seat sunken show court and arena;
- New elevated outdoor public spaces;
- A new function and media center including broadcast studios;
- A new logistics hub;
- New and improved pathways for visitors; and
- New scoreboards and signage throughout the complex.

The principles of economic impact analysis

The justification for financing many sport facilities is often based on arguments made about the economic benefits that the development will have on the local community. Indeed, it is precisely this argument that developers present to public bodies in order to lever funding or other financially advantageous concessions for proposed projects. In recent years, there has been no higher-profile example of economic impact arguments being used to justify investment in sport facilities than the London 2012 Olympic and Paralympic Games. London 2012 was staged during a time of global recession with a degree of severity that had previously been unseen since the Great Depression of the 1930s. There is a proven logic for governments to spend their way out of financial trouble during recessions, and the expenditure of around £9.2 billion ($14.9 billion) on sport facilities and supporting infrastructure can be looked upon as a financial lifeline contributing to bringing the economy out of recession rather than an expensive luxury.

Given the claimed benefits of investing in sport facilities, what is meant by economic impact, and what are the benefits that it brings? A simple definition of economic impact is the net economic change in a host community that is directly attributable to a facility or an event. Two points of note arise from this definition. First, the word 'net' means that it is important to take into account both positive and negative aspects of economic impact. Thus, the opening of a new health club might create 50 new jobs, but it also might lead to the closure of a rival facility with the loss of say 30 existing jobs. The 'net' economic impact, in this case, would be

20 new jobs. Second, the words 'directly attributable' mean that the facility or event must cause the economic impact to occur. If people attending a convention in a city decide to attend a game of basketball as part of their visit, the economic impact is actually attributable to the conference and not the game of basketball. That is to say, the visitors were in the area for a primary reason (the conference), and the basketball game just happened to be at the same time and was secondary to the main purpose of the visit. There is something of a culture in the sport industry for people to exaggerate the economic impact of facilities and events in order to make them look more attractive for public funding.

As noted in Table 3.2, positive economic benefits can be delivered for sport facilities in five key areas.

Table 3.2 Delivering positive economic benefits for sport facilities

Construction	▪ During the construction phase of a facility, jobs will be supported or created in the building industry. ▪ In the UK, it is widely accepted by economists that every £100,000 ($153,000) of construction costs will support or create one job in the industry. ▪ Therefore, it is no surprise that in 2009 some 4,500 construction workers were employed on the Olympic Park site in London. ▪ There can also be positive economic benefits in the construction supply chain with increased demand for building materials and for the fixtures and fittings needed to equip a new building.
Employment	▪ When a facility opens, it will need staff to operate it, and this leads to increased employment opportunities for the local community. ▪ Working in sport is a customer-focused occupation, and people can acquire useful customer care and operations management experiences that are transferable to many other occupations.

Supply chain	▪ Sport facilities need:
	  – Supplies such as merchandise to be sold to customers;
	  – Equipment such as treadmills and weights to be used by customers; and
	  – Services such as utilities to keep the facility running.
	▪ Those businesses that provide services to new sport facilities will see an increase in the demand for their products as the ripples of economic impact spread wider.

Local income	▪ The presence of more money in the local community from the spending of employees, the increased demand in the supply chain, and increased tax revenues mean that the community as a whole will enjoy the increased prosperity that can be linked to the opening of a new sport facility.

Events	▪ Some new sport facilities change the local infrastructure and enable activities that were previously not possible to occur. For example:
	  – If a new stadium is built to host an NFL franchise, there will be a guaranteed eight regular-season home matches per year.
	  – Therefore, the stadium will have to be put to other uses such as staging concerts, conferences, and exhibitions.
	  – Without the stadium, these would not have been possible, and the spending from out-of-town visitors at these events can provide a welcome additional revenue stream to the local community.

The manner in which potential economic impacts are quantified is by the use of specially commissioned *economic impact studies*. These studies attempt to model the future economic impacts of a sport facility or to measure the actual economic impact of a facility or an event. They are as much art as science, and radically different figures can be derived for the same development by consultants depending on who they are working for and the assumptions they use to drive their models. It is therefore important that economic impact studies are carried out independently and make full use of all of the data available. Furthermore, there should be a transparent audit trail of how the economic impact has been derived and what the key drivers of it are. As a manager, you should have an awareness of the economic impact of your facility on the local community. Where appropriate, you should also develop the skills necessary to exploit this knowledge for the benefit of your organization.

TECHNOLOGY NOW! eventIMPACTS (UNITED KINGDOM)

Without sport facilities, sport events would not have a location to operate. Moreover, without sport events, there would be no reason to have a sport facility. Hence, facilities and events are closely linked when looking at a multitude of factors – one of which is impact. As such, sport facility managers must not only work closely with event managers but also understand how to measure the impact of events on their community. While economic impact is a widely used tool for this evaluation, additional impacts such as attendance, social, environmental, and media impacts are of equal importance to sport facilities.

The eventIMPACTS tool kit is a collaboration between UK Sport and multiple public sector partners, including the Department for Culture, Media and Sport and EventScotland, to provide a free-to-use event evaluation framework. Built into eventIMPACTS is an economic impact calculator that allows event managers to input the details about their event and then receive an estimate of the event's likely economic impact. It also provides guidance on how to choose the most appropriate measurement to use for a specific event.

From an attendance standpoint, the tool kit assists with calculating attendance numbers and measuring the profile of spectators and attendees. Social impact looks at providing guidance on how to measure the sense of place, identity, and image of a target market, which in turn plays a crucial role in funding decisions for sport facilities and events. Environmental impact focuses on providing guidance related to the sustainability, planning, viability, and sponsorship of events. Media impact measures how the venues and events are viewed across print, broadcast, and digital media platforms.

43

eventIMPACTS has been a highly regarded and trusted tool that delivers credible, 'at least' estimates that can be supported by an audit trail of evidence and reasonable assumptions. This is demonstrated through their various case studies of successful implementation, as well as the vast resources available, including published research and survey tools.

Source: eventIMPACTS. (2019). Retrieved May 30, 2019, from www.eventimpacts.com

SOURCES OF FINANCING FOR SPORT FACILITIES

Financing of sport facilities comes in three basic forms – public financing, private funding, and public–private partnerships. All three have had a significant effect on financing sport facilities throughout modern history. *Public financing* involves the collection of taxes from those who receive benefits from the provision of public goods by the government and then uses those tax revenues to produce and distribute them to the beneficiaries. *Private financing* is providing funding for capital investments by nongovernmental individuals and/or businesses to provide products and services to the public under the management and operation of the private entity, with the public usually paying a fee to utilize the products and services. *Public–private partnerships* are agreements between the government and the private sector regarding the provision of public services or infrastructure. The public municipality transfers the burden of capital expenditures and risks of cost overruns to the private entity but maintains a partnership in the offering of products and services to the public.

Public sector funding

As with any type of governmental funding, the appropriations have to come from some type of taxation. Public funding of sport facilities comes from both hard taxes and soft taxes. Hard taxes are assessments that are applied to the entire population, whereas soft taxes are assessments applied to specific product users or to nonresidents of a municipality. Examples of hard and soft taxes can be found in Table 3.3.

Bonds are interest-bearing certificates that are issued by either a jurisdiction or a business that is a binding promise to repay the initial investment of money (called the principal) and an agreed-upon level of interest at a specified date in the future. Quality bonds are usually issued by businesses and/or jurisdictions with a good repayment history and are bought by investors seeking the most favorable interest rates or tax benefits. Bonds have similar characteristics to long-term loans, as they are effectively contracts where a borrower makes payments on certain dates over a

44

Table 3.3 Examples of hard and soft taxes

Hard taxes	Soft taxes
Real estate tax	Tourist development tax
Property tax	Lodging or hotel/motel tax
Income tax	Restaurant or food service tax
General sales tax	Automobile rental service tax
Road tax	Taxi/limousine/livery service tax
Utility tax	Sin tax (liquor, tobacco)
	Players tax
	Team tax
	Business license/permit tax
	Lottery and gaming tax

defined period of time in exchange for receiving repayment of the principal with interest at a date in the future. The advantages of investing in bonds include that they are relatively inexpensive – especially for those organizations that have a long history and a good credit rating – the bond market is fairly strong and established, and interest on bonds is tax deductible. The disadvantages of bonds include interest (a fixed amount that must always be paid periodically regardless of earning revenue/making a profit) and the principal (the amount loaned, which must be paid on the maturity date, again regardless of earning revenue/making a profit). In addition, if a bond is secured with collateral, a jurisdiction or company cannot sell the collateral asset without bondholder approval, and bondholders have the upper hand in collecting their principal and interest if a jurisdiction or corporation goes into bankruptcy.

There are various types of bonds but most fall under two categories – taxable bonds and municipal bonds. *Taxable bonds* are usually issued by corporations and do not offer the same tax-exempt benefits of a municipal bond. While these types of bonds are used less often in the financing of sport facilities, the two types that have been used are private placement bonds and asset-backed securitizations. *Private-placement bonds* are long-term, fixed-interest certificates issued by a nonmunicipal organization developing a sport facility to venture capitalists and other private lenders of funds. The total revenues generated by the sport facility secure these bonds. *Asset-backed securitizations* are similar to private-placement bonds, however, only the most financially viable revenues streams are bundled into the bond offering (example: naming the right sponsorships, luxury suite, and PSLs (permanent/personal seat licenses) that might be part of the asset-backed security, whereas concessions and parking revenues revert directly to the facility).

On the other hand, municipal bonds are widely used to finance sport facilities. Municipal bonds are issued by a governmental agency, and the interest is tax exempt. A variety of bond options are available under this category, either guaranteed or nonguaranteed. The most often used guaranteed bonds (also known as full-faith or credit obligations) utilized in financing sport facilities are general obligation bonds and certificate of obligation. A variety of nonguaranteed bonds are utilized for the financing of sport facilities, including revenue bonds, certificates of participation, tax increment financing, special authority bonds, straight governmental appropriations, and public grants. An explanation of these various types of bonds is described in more detail in Table 3.4.

Table 3.4 Types of municipal bonds

Guaranteed bonds	
General obligation bonds	Bonds that are repaid with a portion of the general property tax – also known as an ad valorem tax – and that are backed by the full faith and credit of the issuing body (in most cases the jurisdiction).
Certificates of obligation	Bonds that are secured by unlimited claims on tax revenues usually have a low-interest rate and are easily obtained through governmental sources because the issuance does not require approval by a vote of the population.
Nonguaranteed bonds	
Revenue bonds	Bonds are backed exclusively from the revenue that accrues from the sport facility or associated revenue sources.
Certificates of participation (COP)	Bonds involve a jurisdiction purchasing the sport facility and leasing parts of the facility back to the general public or associated agencies, with the revenue from those lease payments being utilized to pay off the capital expenses for the facility.
Tax-increment financing (TIF)	Bonds are utilized when there is an area identified as needing some type of renewal or redevelopment, and the jurisdiction freezes the tax base in that area until the development or renewal takes place so that taxes can be raised to pay off the TIF.
Special authority bonds	Bonds are financed through public organizations that have jurisdictional power outside the normal constraints of the government; most often used when the general public is against financing sport facilities but the local government wants the sport facility built. Hence the jurisdiction uses these agencies, including power authorities, turnpike/roadway authorities, waterworks authorities, and other public works departments, to fund sport facilities through raised fees.
Straight government appropriations	Public funding from a municipality's budget is set aside for a specific purpose, such as financing a sport facility.
Public grants	Awards of financial assistance from a municipality to carry out a project of support or stimulation for the good of the public where the financing does not have to be repaid since it is technically not categorized as government assistance or individual loans.

In addition to these public finding options, other types of public sector contributions include the purchase of donated land; the funding of site improvements, parking garages, or surrounding infrastructure; direct equity investments; and the construction of related facilities. Regardless of the source of funding, there are always questions as to whether public financing is appropriate for the use of sport facilities. These questions center on uncertainty among the public about whether available alternative sources of private financing should supersede the use of public financing and the contention that the economic returns accruing from public investments do not necessarily equate to the initial investment in the sport facility. However, there are alternate sources of spillover benefits that justify these public subsidies, as documented in Table 3.5.

Table 3.5 Spillover benefits justifying public subsidies

Increased community visibility	▪ A professional sport facility often results in a significant increase in the amount of media coverage for the municipality in which it is located. ▪ It also keeps the community's name in front of regional, national, and sometimes even international/global audiences.
Enhanced community image	▪ Many municipalities engage in place marketing, which strives to sell the image of a place so as to make it more attractive to businesses, tourists, and inhabitants. ▪ The omnipresent popularity of sport in the media has persuaded many municipalities to realize that sport facilities may be useful vehicles to enhance their image.
Making a 'major league city'	▪ There is a lot of public interest in the belief that a municipality cannot be considered a 'major league city' or 'first-tier city' without a 'major league' sports team. ▪ As such, it is nearly impossible to have a 'major league' sports team without a quality sport facility. In many municipalities, the facility is seen as being indicative of their character and as defining the external perceptions of the city.
Loss of a major sports team	▪ If a municipality loses a sports franchise, it may create the impression that local businesses and government officials are not supportive of the community, that the community is declining, and that its residents lack civic pride. ▪ Hence, if a municipality does not provide quality sport facilities, they may create a worse image for themselves than if they never had the teams or facilities at all.
Stimulation of other development	▪ Municipalities believe that investment in sport facilities will stimulate additional development and hence contribute to the expansion of a city's tax base. ▪ There are three types of development to be addressed when financing a sport facility: – *Proximate development* is utilized to stimulate economic development as part of an integrated redevelopment plan around the sport facility

(*Continued*)

Table 3.5 (Continued)

	– *Complementary development* comes from the need to support the proximate development around the sport facility, either because of the municipality's desire to host a hallmark or mega event or to upgrade the level of service near the sport facility (restaurants, bars, retail stores, etc.)
	– *General development* goes beyond proximate and complementary development into the increased availability of public services including roadways and public transportation.
Psychic income	▨ Psychic income is the emotional and psychological benefit that residents of a municipality perceive they receive, even though they do not physically attend events at the facility and are not involved in organizing them.
	▨ Sport facilities are a medium through which cities and their residents express their personality, enhance their status, and promote their quality of life to a regional, national, and even international/global audience.
	▨ This is often measured using the contingent valuation method (CVM), which places currency values on goods/services not exchanged in the marketplace.

Private sources of revenue

A sport facility cannot be financed solely from public sources. Sport businesses need to create sources of revenue to enhance its financing efforts for a facility. When we look at the traditional forms of obtaining revenue in business, we typically look at donations of cash, gifts, in-kind contributions, bequests, endowments, trusts, and revenues from fund-raising efforts. In sport facilities, numerous additional sources of revenue play a crucial role as economic generators for a sport facility. Table 3.6 depicts these various revenue sources.

Table 3.6 Private sources of revenue

Naming rights and sponsorships	The entitlement to name a sport facility (or a part thereof) in exchange for financial considerations
Lease agreements/ building rentals	The amount of money earned by the facility for its use, either by tenants (usually sport teams but may include outside vendors who can fill spaces not used by the sport facility for sports), outside traveling events (examples include concerts, WWE [World Wrestling Entertainment], and monster truck shows), and local events (municipal gatherings, graduations, corporate gathering, etc.)
Advertising rights	The percentage of revenue earned by the facility for signage and other advertisements within the sport facility
Luxury suites and corporate/private boxes	Yearly leases of specialized seating typically located near the middle section of the sport facility that allows the best view of events, usually including glass paneling that can open to the playing area, as well as amenities such as a bar, TVs, wi-fi, private seats, and a bathroom; catered food service; and private parking and entrances to the facility.

Preferred/ premium/club seating	A level below luxury boxes that offers special amenities above and beyond general admission seating, including private restaurants, lounge areas, and merchandise stands, and whose main difference is that the seating is not enclosed as with the luxury box – it is open-air similar to general admissions –hence providing the elements of both
Permanent/ personal seat licenses (PSLs)	Known as debentures in Europe, a fee paid to buy tickets for a specific seat within a specific sport facility, usually limited to those buying season tickets
Ticket sales	The percentage a sport facility gets back for every ticket sold for events within the facility, with a higher percentage coming back for tickets sold through the box office
Concessionaire exclusivity/ restaurant rights	Organizations' purchases of the sole rights for all concessions within a sport facility
Concessions revenue	The percentage of revenue that comes back to the sport facility for all food service and merchandising sold within the facility
Parking fees	The amount a sport facility makes for allowing parking at the facility, whether it is the full parking price minus expenses when management is kept in-house or the percentage of the fee when parking management is outsourced
Ancillary entertainment revenue	Revenue earned from extras within the stadium such as amusement parks, halls of fame, museums, and facility tours

Public–private partnerships

Many times, to effectively finance sport facilities, there is a need for a relationship between municipalities and private entrepreneurs. The public sector has the authority to implement project funding through the governing process, while the private sector has the ability to contribute financing and management expertise in the area of sport facilities. While there are advantages to combining the funding and revenue resources as discussed in the previous two sections, there are two major challenges to facilitating a successful public–private partnership.

The first challenge is for public and private entities to understand, respect, and acknowledge the differences between each other, especially as related to value systems and customer expectations. Public sector organizations exist to meet the needs and wants of their target population as related to social benefits and outcomes. Private business looks to maximize financial return and/or return on investments (i.e., be able to pay off their investors), and hence they target their efforts to those who can provide the greatest opportunity to earn revenue and make a profit. There is a need within these types of partnerships to ensure that social and financial considerations are included in the decision-making process related to financing for a sport facility.

The second challenge is the concern that each element of the partnership only looks out for itself – hence unfairly competing against each other through the partnership. Usually, the public agency must address this issue, as many private entities serve to help the public sector satisfy the needs of their constituents in areas they cannot provide service for.

Numerous models have been created to articulate the various public–private partnerships evident in sport facility financing. The models used most often utilized are documented in Table 3.7.

Table 3.7 Public–private partnership models

Public sector leasing	This is the most common form of public–private sport facility partnership, where private entities pay a lease fee in order to use the publically funded and managed sport facility
Leaseback agreements (private sector leasing)	Where a municipal agency uses a sport facility that it has leased from a private owner
Public sector takeovers	The seizing of a struggling or failing private sport facility in order to help in the effort to keep an existing sport asset within the municipality because, without it, the sport/entertainment opportunity would cease to exist in the area
Private sector takeovers	A private organization taking over responsibility for the operation of a sport facility owned by the public sector because the municipality either does not have the expertise or funding to appropriately manage/operate the facility
Private pump-priming	A private entity using its assets to force a public entity to invest in a sport facility project
Multiparty arrangements	Multiple financial partners initiating a complex agreement to finance the sport facility, usually seen in large-scale public–private sport partnerships and are most often organized by independent quasi-governmental bodies that facilitate collaborative exchange between the various public and private entities involved with the project

HISTORY OF SPORT FACILITY FINANCING

Prior to understanding the specific sources of financing, it is important to understand the history of financing for sport facilities. Generally, the period before 1960 can be referred to as the Period of Antiquity for sport facilities. During this period, the government was the primary source of funding for sport facilities – although there were still privately financed stadiums and arenas (but very few). Most of these sport facilities were funded through the government via general obligation bonds, where the repayment of the bonds came from the general property tax.

During the 1960s (1960–1969), there was the start of a transformation as to how sport facilities were funded. This Period of Growth was when municipalities started building sport facilities that focused on multipurpose use and unique architectural designs – some of which became cookie cutter in nature, that is, similar designs repeated in numerous cities. From a financing standpoint, the money was still flowing from public sector funding through the government; however, with the increase in the need for funding, the government started offering bonds secured through a multitude of hard taxes (on the entire population) and soft taxes (on targeted parts of the population).

The 1970s through 1983 saw significant public subsidy offer to sport facilities. This Period of Revitalization in sport facilities focused on building sport facilities in conjunction with improving the infrastructure of cities. As a result of the multipurpose function of financing, municipalities extended their public subsidies through more revenue bonds borne from taxes, continued the issuance of general obligation bonds from the general property tax, and enhanced both with annual appropriations from the government.

The Period of Discontinuance hit between 1984 and 1986. This was a significant time of change in the way in which sport facilities of the future were financed. There were significant questions regarding the logic of dumping significant amounts of money into sport facilities when bigger economic and financial issues needed to be addressed with governmental appropriations. In the United States, two laws were passed that had a direct effect on sport facility financing. The Deficit Reduction Act of 1984 mandated that because of the need to lower the national deficit, public funding of projects such as sport facilities were to be given a reduced priority. This was followed up two years later by the Tax Reform Act of 1986, which significantly reduced the availability of tax-exempt bonds for building sport facilities. Many other countries around the world followed this lead, exacting similar laws and regulations reducing the amount of public subsidy available for sport facility financing.

As a result, there was a need for change, and hence the period from 1986 to around 1995 is referred to as a Period of Change in sport facility financing. During this time, there was a transition from fully public financing to public–private partnerships, and some growth was taking place in privatized facilities. The public–private partnerships that were indicative of this period involved public entities providing land, investment capital through debt or equity financing, some operating knowledge, and the ability to reduce the risk associated with sport facilities. In turn, private entities paid taxes that resulted from facility operations and corporate guarantees, ushering in the introduction of alternative sources of revenue through luxury suites, premium seating, personal seat licenses, concessionaire rights, and naming rights.

Since 1995, sport facility financing has taken another shift into the Period of Partnerships, where the shift has been toward funding provided by both private and public entities and has extended into the running of sport facility operations. Since this era requires private owners to cover a percentage of the bill before governmental agencies will chip in, private entities are building new 'fully loaded' stadia and arenas with amenities including restaurants, fan experiences, and technology, as well as infrastructural designs such as retractable roofs and retractable fields of play. The price tags for these new facilities have increased exponentially, with new facilities that opened in Dallas (AT&T Stadium, 2009) and New York (MetLife Stadium, 2010) exceeding $1 billion and naming rights deals to help pay the private entities part of the bill around $20 million per year over average terms of 20–30 years. This has continued to date with Levi's Stadium in San Francisco (2014), U.S. Bank Stadium in Minneapolis (2016), and Mercedes-Benz Stadium in Atlanta (2017). Moreover, if communities refuse to contribute, the teams threatened may choose to relocate. One example of this was in St. Louis and San Diego, where both cities would not provide the desired facility, resulting in the National Football League's Rams and Chargers to relocate back to Los Angeles to move into a projected $5 billion stadium (with an associated entertainment district) in 2020. Another example is the Oakland Raiders, who will relocate to Las Vegas in 2020 and play in a new stadium currently projected to cost $1.8 billion.

FUTURE TRENDS IN SPORT FACILITY FINANCING

So now that multibillion-dollar stadiums have been and are being built in multiple cities, what is next? Will there be a return to multipurpose facilities that can be justified by public subsidy? Perhaps total privatization of stadia and arena, with municipalities showing their support as corporate sponsors? How about corporate ownership of facilities – taking it out of the hands of municipalities and team owners? Could changes in technology affect how we watch the sport experience in the stadium/arena, and how participants view spectators in the stadium? How about a reduction in the need of specialized seating, concessions, amenities, and the like (except for those deemed necessary for the participants to play), as a result of breakthroughs in technology such as virtual fans who dial in from home and sit in the virtual stadium?

SPORT FACILITY FINANCING INVESTMENT: A LOOK AHEAD

As the economy and public outcry results in reductions to public subsidies there are concerns as to where facility financing will come from. From a professional sport facility standpoint, if a municipality balked at providing funding for a new facility, the professional team would threaten to move, and the municipality would eventually come up with the money. One example in 2007 was when the owners of the NHL's Pittsburgh Penguins threatened to sell the team and secured a new facility agreement only a few hours before they were set to be sold and leave for Kansas City. However, there is a shift in this trend in recent times. In 2008, the NBA's Seattle Supersonics and the City of Seattle could not come up with a viable solution to replace the aging Key Arena – so the team picked up and moved to Oklahoma City. Another example is when the NHL's New York Islanders could not secure a partnership for a new facility to replace the aging Nassau Veterans Memorial Coliseum; in 2014, they opted to move from that facility and Nassau County on Long Island to the Borough of Brooklyn in New York City and the new Barclays Center. Ironically, three years later, this move ended up in an announcement that they would move back to Nassau Coliseum part-time in 2018 and then move to their new $1 billion 'arena village' at Belmont Park in 2021.

However, for smaller recreational and community sport facilities, the amount of public money available to construct these facilities has dropped significantly and has resulted in the private building of these types of complexes. With the increase in the privatization of sport facilities, the question is whether this will trickle up to the professional level – that is, fully privatized facilities with no governmental interaction. While the trends show less public involvement (and hence more private involvement), there does not seem to be a time in the near future that public subsidy totally disappears from sport facilities. Municipalities need to show support in their communities for sports since a large majority of the population has an interest in some aspect of sport, recreation, and/or leisure. Tax dollars need to support the interests of the public who pay those taxes; however, it is becoming abundantly clear that there is a cap to the spending recommended.

On the private side, it is possible that we are nearing an economic and financial cap. The money is not endless, and with shifts in the economic and financial climate globally, the amount corporations are willing to spend on naming rights may be reaching a crescendo. They are discovering other sponsorable products that offer the potential of a great return on investment and on objectives. Hence, facilities are trying to meet this shift by offering sponsorships and advertising on everything from turnstiles to steps in the arena so that they can get more money from more sponsors at a lower cost per sponsor.

Suggested discussion topics

1   How would you justify to a municipality (both the elected officials and the taxpayers) to enter into a public–private financial partnership to construct a new recreation or community sport facility?

2   Beyond naming and traditional signage rights, identify eight additional sponsorable inventories within a professional sport arena or stadium, and explain how you would utilize those areas for a greater return on the investment of the infrastructure without turning the facility into a mass of advertisements that distract from events?

We can make numerous projections here; however, only time will tell what will come down the road and how the changes will have a direct effect on the financing of sport facilities in the 21st century and beyond. However, three areas are projected to have a direct effect on the future of sport facility financing. The first is the influence of the voluntary sector as an additional niche having an increasingly important role in the provision of sport facilities for communities. The voluntary sector already owns and controls many facilities such as golf clubs, fields/pitches, and community halls. Rather than public authorities taking additional risk in trying to provide facilities themselves, there is some logic in the strategy of incentivizing the voluntary sector to open its facilities for the benefit of the wider community. An obvious example is the use of sport club facilities for after-school programs and as resources for young people to use during school holidays. It is widely accepted that sport and the voluntary sector can be used to help deliver wider government agendas such as health improvements, community cohesion, reductions in delinquency, and improvements in educational attainment. Therefore, it is more cost-effective to offer clubs financial contributions than it is to provide new facilities from scratch. Not only does this approach make sound commercial sense, but there are also strategic benefits as well. The voluntary sector is more dynamic than government and can react quickly to changes in the external environment, as it is not constrained by bureaucracy. The voluntary sector is also able to get closer to the customer than public authorities are. Furthermore, the voluntary sector is capable of operating at a lower cost than public authorities operate and is more able to attract funding from charities and lotteries. Thus for these reasons, it is a win-win situation for public and voluntary bodies to work together closely. In an era when public money for investment in sport facilities will be increasingly scarce, there will be a strong business and environmental case to make the best use of that which already exists before new facilities can be justified. Consequently, at the community level, the voluntary sector is likely to have an increasingly important role to play in helping to provide new sport facilities and wider community access to existing sport facilities.

The second is a shift of government investment toward community sports. The realization that community sports have more participants than any other type of sport, government at the local, state/province, and federal levels have been shifting their focus away from assisting professional sport teams and large-scale sporting facilities to community-focused facilities. An example of this is in the state of Victoria in Australia, where for the 2018–2019 budget the state government earmarked AUD$484.4 million ($356.2 million) for the future of sport across Victoria plus an additional AUD$100 million ($73.5 million) for a Community Sports Loan Scheme. This includes significant funding targeted to female sport facilities, including the creation of a Female Friendly Facilities Fund. In addition, a Change Our Game Sports Leadership Centre is to be created to focus on cultural change and female leadership in sport.

54

The third is the effects of currency values as related to international/global investments. The notion that sport is a global business is well illustrated by the fact that both domestic and international investors fund many high-profile sport facilities. Much of the debt that has been raised to support the development of the Wembley Stadium in London is owed to German banks. The United Kingdom uses sterling as its currency whereas Germany uses the Euro. The net effect of this situation is that if the two currencies fluctuate against each other, then one party will be better off than expected and the other worse off. For example, in 2009, sterling (UK currency) had fallen from £1 being worth around €1.40 to €1.10 (Euros) – a fall of just over 20%. As discussed earlier, the owners of Wembley Stadium paid £42.85m (€47.95) in interest in 2017. An adverse currency fluctuation of 20% potentially could have added around £8.5m (€9.5) per year to the company's interest charges and hence make the difference between the company being viable or being in financial trouble. Very few sport facilities could take a financial hit of £8.5m without its having an adverse effect on the business whether in the form of cutting costs or having to stage more events to recover the deficit. In real life, it is unlikely that such a stark situation would ever materialize. As part of Wembley Stadium's efforts to manage its financial risks, it would have negotiated sources of mitigation such as fixed exchange rates or exchange rates that float between two agreed fixed points but not beyond some point that would impact too unfavorably on one party. The existence of more advanced sources of mitigation, such as currency hedge funds and options, are beyond the scope of this text, but their existence and application in the financing of sport facilities serve to illustrate further the broad range of skills and knowledge that sport facility managers may be required to call upon throughout their careers.

CHAPTER REVIEW

Financing is defined as the act of obtaining or providing money or capital for the purchase of a business enterprise. Developing new sport facilities is a risky process that invariably requires complex financial arrangements, as it is unlikely that any organization from any sector will have the spare cash available to develop and build a sport facility from the outset of a project. It is, therefore, a current practice that the financing of sport facilities tends to be made with financial contributions from a variety of sources. When borrowed money (or debt) is used to finance a development, the stance of those borrowing the money is the belief that they can make sufficient profit to be able to service interest costs and still make a profit. For the providers of loans, the stance taken is that the interest being paid on the loans justifies the risk of lending to the developer. In practice, the two parties' fates are inextricably linked: For everyone to get a fair return on their investment, the development has to succeed.

Considerations around financing sport facilities are not confined to how much a building costs to construct in the first instance. For both buildings and equipment, due consideration must be given to what are known as 'life cycle costs,' which are defined as the maintenance of physical asset cost records over the entire asset lives, so that decisions concerning the acquisition, use, or disposal of the assets can be made in a way that achieves the optimum asset usage at the lowest cost to the entity. The importance of being aware of life cycle costing can be appreciated by the finding that as much as 90% of the lifetime costs attributable to an asset are determined by decisions made in the early part of the asset's life. The evidence is that life cycle costing for an asset can be complicated, as indicated in the range of considerations including purchase costs, running costs, maintenance costs, training costs, and decommissioning and disposal costs.

The justification for financing many sport facilities is often based on arguments made about the economic benefits that the development will have on the local community. For sport facilities, the positive economic benefits can be delivered in five key areas: construction, employment, supply chains, local income, and events. The manner in which potential economic impacts are quantified is by the use of specially commissioned economic impact studies, which attempt to model the future economic impacts of a sport facility or to measure the actual economic impact of a facility or an event.

Financing of sport facilities comes in three basic forms: public financing, private funding, and public–private partnerships. Public funding of sport facilities comes from hard taxes, soft taxes, and bonds. Private funding comes from revenue created by sport businesses to enhance the financing efforts for a sport facility. Many times, to effectively finance sport facilities, there is a need for there to be a relationship between municipalities and private entrepreneurs. The public sector has the authority to implement project funding through the governing process, while the private sector has the ability to contribute financing and management expertise in the area of sport facilities.

Until the mid-1980s, the financing for sport facilities evolved from a time where sport facilities were primarily funded through general obligation bonds funded by the government from general property taxes to bonds and public subsidies secured through a multitude of hard and soft taxes. In the mid-1980s, a significant change to how sport facilities would be financed occurred when there were questions regarding the logic of dumping significant amounts of money into sport facilities when bigger economic and financial issues needed to be addressed with government appropriations. This transition from full public financing to public–private partnerships across both financing and operations is the norm. So what does the future hold for sport facility financing? Only time will tell. However, we can safely project that economic issues affecting both public and private entities will be at the center of the discussion. In addition, the emergence of the voluntary sector as an additional niche in the financing of sport facilities, the increase of government investment in community sport, and the effects of currency values as related to international/global investments seem to be significant concerns related to the financing of sport facilities in the future.

IN THE FIELD . . .

With Dev Pathik, founder and chief executive officer, The Sports Facilities Advisory and The Sports Facilities Management, St. Petersburg, Florida, United States

Dev is the founder and CEO of The Sports Facilities Advisory (SFA) and The Sports Facilities Management (SFM). SFA is a sport center planning consultant. SFM is a sport center management company. Both companies assess feasibility, master-plan entire community programs, produce funding documents, structure public–private partnerships, oversee new facility openings, and manage and advise many of today's most notable community sport and recreation centers around the world. Since 2003, SFA I SFM have become the preeminent resource for public and private clients seeking to plan, fund, open, and optimize indoor and outdoor recreation venues. They have served over 2,000 communities with over $10 billion in projects planned by SFA and 20 million SFM guest visits each year.

One of SFA's specialties is financing and project funding. Obtaining funding is a challenge for many facility developers, especially in terms of time needed to secure the funding, the appropriate equity partners, and the land. With dedicated professionals in its Funding Support Services department, SFA stands ready to become a partner in the funding acquisition process. The team makes introductions to potential capital sources, assists in preparing funding presentations, helps develop financing strategies, and seeks to develop synergistic partnerships that range from private partners to public–private partnerships. They can also help structure tax referendums and bond issuances as needed.

According to Dev, it is important from a business perspective to understand the numbers. That means understanding every aspect of the budget and being able to read facility budgets and let them tell you the story of the operation. If you can read a budget and understand how it translates into the mission of the operation, you will be leaps and bounds ahead of others.

BIBLIOGRAPHY

Baade, R. A. (2003). Evaluating subsidies for professional sports in the United States and Europe: A public–sector primer. *Oxford Review of Economic Policy*, *19*(4), 585–597. https://doi.org/10.1093/oxrep/19.4.585

Baade, R. A., & Matheson, V. A. (2006). Have public finance principles been shut out in financing new stadiums for the NFL? *Public Finance and Management*, *6*(3), 284–305, 307–320.

Bovaird, T. (2007). Beyond engagement and participation: User and community coproduction of public services. *Public Administration Review*, *67*(5), 846–860. https://doi.org/10.1111/j.1540-6210.2007.00773.x

Bruning, J. K., & Chen, S. (2016). Trends in funding renovations and new facilities for National Football League team venues. *KAHPERD Journal*, *53*(2), 45–54.

Carey, M., & Mason, D. S. (2014). Building consent: Funding recreation, cultural, and sports amenities in a Canadian city. *Managing Leisure*, *19*(2), 105–120. https://doi.org/10.1080/13606719.2013.859458

Chartered Institute of Management Accountants. (2005). *CIMA's official terminology* (2nd ed.). London: CIMA.

Crompton, J. L. (2014). Proximate development: An alternate justification for public investment in major sport facilities? *Managing Leisure*, *19*(4), 263–282. https://doi.org/10.1080/13606719.2014.885712

Crompton, J. L., & Howard, D. R. (2013). Costs: The rest of the economic impact story. *Journal of Sport Management*, *27*(5), 379–392. https://doi.org/10.1123/jsm.27.5.379

The FA. (2017). *About the FA*. Retrieved July 19, 2018, from www.thefa.com/news/2018/mar/20/fa-financial-results-2016-17-210318

Feng, X., & Humphreys, B. (2018). Assessing the economic impact of sports facilities on residential property values: A spatial hedonic approach. *Journal of Sports Economics*, *19*(2), 188–210. https://doi.org/10.1177/1527002515622318

Harger, K., Humphreys, B. R., & Ross, A. (2016). Do new sports facilities attract new businesses? *Journal of Sports Economics*, *17*(5), 483–500. https://doi.org/10.1177/1527002516641168

Howard, D. R., & Crompton, J. L. (2018). *Financing sport* (4th ed.). Morgantown, WV: Fitness Information Technology.

McGehee, G. M., Marquez, A. A., Cianfrone, B. A., & Kellison, T. (2018). Understanding organizational and public perspectives on stadium redevelopment through social media: A case study of Georgia State University's 'new' stadium. *International Journal of Sport Communication*, *11*(2), 261–285. https://doi.org/10.1123/ijsc.2017-0108

Misener, K., & Doherty, A. (2009). A case study of organizational capacity in nonprofit community sport. *Journal of Sport Management*, *23*(4), 457–482. https://doi.org/10.1123/jsm.23.4.457

Propheter, G. (2012). Are basketball arenas catalysts of economic development? *Journal of Urban Affairs*, *34*(4), 441–459. https://doi.org/10.1111/j.1467-9906.2011.00597.x

Rosentraub, M., & Swindell, D. (2009). Of devils and details: Bargaining for successful public/private partnerships between cities and sports teams. *Public Administration Quarterly*, *33*(1), 118–148.

Santo, C. A., & Mildner, G. C. S. (2010). *Sport and public policy: Social, political, and economic perspectives*. Champaign, IL: Human Kinetics.

CHAPTER 4

CAPITAL INVESTMENT APPRAISAL

CHAPTER OUTLINE

- The purpose of capital investment appraisal
- Raw data
- Traditional methods of capital investment appraisal
- Modern methods of capital investment appraisal
- Using capital investment appraisal techniques in practice
- Chapter review

CHAPTER OBJECTIVES

Businesses face the twin challenges of making profits and being able to pay their bills as they fall due. Before a sport facility can generate any income and make profits, typically it will have to invest in fixed assets. If we take the case of a gym or fitness center, this will often be the cost of a building and the purchase of gym equipment. An expenditure of this type is called *capital investment*. There is a calculated risk attached to capital expenditure because there may be a considerable time lag between incurring the expenditure (often paid for through borrowed money), receiving a return on it from paying customers thereby making sufficient profit to meet their expenses, and having enough left over to make the decision worthwhile. The key phrase in the previous sentence is 'calculated risk,' and in this chapter, we will demonstrate the techniques that are routinely used to calculate risks and thus to evaluate whether to invest in a particular project. We will also examine the techniques that are used to frame capital investment choices and the techniques used to evaluate such choices.

Being responsible for capital investment decision making takes managerial responsibility to a new level and requires managers to have a new set of skills to support the decision-making process. More often than not, entrepreneurs do not have the cash required to fund capital expenditure themselves. To raise the money required means presenting a convincing business case to a supportive bank or supportive friends and family. Either way, the entrepreneur is taking a risk with other people's money, and there is pressure related to the responsibility of paying it back, often with interest.

THE UNITED STATES' MOST EXPENSIVE SPORT STADIA

MetLife Stadium, home to the New York Giants and the New York Jets
($1.6 billion)
Mercedes-Benz Stadium, home to the Atlanta Falcons and
Atlanta United FC ($1.6 billion)
Yankee Stadium, home to the New York Yankees and New York City FC
($1.5 billion)

With all three of these stadiums costing over $1.5 billion, there is clear evidence of the enormous financial scale and risk attached to the facility management side of professional team sports in the United States. Two forthcoming projects (at the time of writing) include new stadiums in Los Angeles and Las Vegas, both projected to exceed $2.4 billion. The new Los Angeles Stadium has an estimated development cost of $2.66 billion and will be home to both the Los Angeles Rams and the Los Angeles Chargers of the NFL, as well as being a venue for the 2028 Summer Olympic Games. The new Las Vegas Stadium has an estimated development cost of $2.4 billion and will become the home for University of Nevada–Las Vegas college football team, as well as the relocating Oakland Raiders of the NFL.

Where does the money come from to pay to for these stadia, and what kind of financial performance do they need to achieve in order to be viable propositions? Happily, these are not questions that have to be answered as you embark upon a career in sport facility management. However, the magnitude of the investment in these facilities gives an insight into the level of responsibility required by those who are involved in the decision-making process. Somewhere along the line, there will have been the involvement of people with Capital Investment Appraisal skills. These are the people who subject the business cases for these stadia to detailed financial scrutiny and who make the case to banks, investors, and local authorities for funding. In this chapter, we look at the principles involved in evaluating capital investment decisions – but on a much smaller scale. Use them consistently throughout your career and get them right . . . and in time it could be you working on the next multibillion-dollar stadium.

Suggested discussion questions

1   Think of a sport facility that you have used recently as a participant in an active sport activity such as a gym or a swimming pool and answer the following questions:
    a   Where did the money come from to pay for the construction of the facility?
    b   How long do you think it takes the investors to see a return on their funds?
    c   How would you feel about taking a risk on this type of investment?
    d   When you embark on your career, do you see yourself as an employee working for someone else or as an entrepreneur taking business risks and hiring employees?
2   During the regular season, NFL teams are guaranteed 8–13 home matches (including preseason and playoffs), yet there are 365 days in a year. What else do stadium owners do to ensure that sufficient activity takes place to justify the investment in their facilities?

THE PURPOSE OF CAPITAL INVESTMENT APPRAISAL

Because of the risks involved with capital expenditure, capital investment appraisal (CIA) techniques have evolved to inform the decision-making process. When we borrow money to fund a new project, we need to know that we can afford to pay back the loan (or principal), as well as any interest payable to service the loan. We also need to make sure that we do not run out of money and can pay our bills as they fall due. In this regard, CIA is concerned with the total investment needs of a project. When a gym is being constructed, it will need staff to sell memberships even though the facility is not yet open. Therefore, money will also be required to fund these day-to-day expenses as well as the purchase of fixed assets. Regardless of how good our business ideas might seem to us, there is no guarantee that funders will see things in the same way. The reality is that funding for capital investment will be limited in supply relative to the demand for it and therefore will be rationed. This means that in practice only the most advantageous loans for the banks will be made, where 'advantageous' means the likelihood of being paid and the amount of interest that can be charged. It is therefore vitally important that those people looking to make capital investment decisions do so on the basis of a sound business case. This point brings us to the purpose of capital investment appraisal, which can be described as comparing the cost of a project now with the expected benefits that will accrue in the future. The chances are that you are reading this book because you have made a decision to invest in your education now, with the expectation that your future lifetime earnings will compensate for the time you took out to go to university and the fees you incurred in so doing. In short, the purpose of CIA can be summarized as follows:

- To test the financial viability of a project
- To rank different projects so that limited funding is allocated to the best project

The techniques described in this chapter are decision support techniques and not decision-making techniques. An element of judgment is always required, and non-financial considerations also need to be factored in. For example, there are many instances in the United States where local authorities will invest in the construction of a new stadium to attract a professional sports franchise. The stadium might never recover the costs that were incurred. However, the prestige of having a franchise in their city, plus the economic impact a professional team might bring to the city may override the basic financial viability considerations. As you will see, there is a variety of capital investment appraisal techniques, and the answers derived from them may be conflicting. The proactive manager will gather as much information from different sources in order to make the best possible decision. However, there will always be a degree of subjectivity to the process because what we are trying to do is to model the future based on assumptions.

RAW DATA

Capital investment appraisal (CIA) involves creating a series of assumptions around an investment decision and then modeling the subsequent impacts of that decision. There is a recognized technique for laying out CIA data, and we will use the following data to conduct CIA on a project to illustrate the point. Imagine an entrepreneur decides to invest $250,000 in launching a new gym. We start by assuming that the building is leased and the majority of the investment is made on gym equipment. To populate our CIA tools, we need to know:

1 the amount of investment required ($250,000);
2 the duration of the project in years (let's assume five years);
3 the cash inflows arising from trading (in this case, gym memberships and other sales);
4 the cash outflows linked to the project such as interest to the bank and staff wages; and

5   any residual value left in the investment after the project's end (let us assume
    the gym equipment has a resale value of $25,000 after five years).

For items 3 and 4 in the preceding list, managers are required to produce detailed
business plans to model the cash inflows and outflows that will occur. As an example, in year one, the manager might assume that the facility will sell 1,000 memberships at $175 each, which will provide revenue in the first year of $175,000.
Similarly, the costs of running the gym might be $50,000 in year one. Taking all
of the assumptions into account, we can set the data up in a form suitable for CIA
analysis, as shown in Table 4.1

Table 4.1 Capital investment appraisal (CIA) data for gym example

	Inflows ($)	Outflows ($)	Net cash flow ($)
Year 0 (investment)		250,000	−250,000
Year 1	175,000	50,000	125,000
Year 2	175,000	50,000	125,000
Year 3	125,000	60,000	65,000
Year 4	200,000	70,000	130,000
Year 5	200,000	85,000	115,000
Residual value	25,000		25,000
Projected lifetime surplus			335,000

In essence, what Table 4.1 does is to structure the assumptions so that we can
offset the initial investment, with future net cash flows in order to derive a project's
lifetime surplus. Students often ask the question, 'Where does this data come from?'
In real life, the cost for the gym equipment will come from inviting suppliers of gym
equipment to tender for the right to supply you. You could choose the cheapest tender, or it could be the one that offers the greatest all-round value for money when
factoring in after-sales service and residual value. The project duration of five years
might be determined by the duration of the lease you have on the building or the
length of time the bank will loan you money. The inflows and outflows for each year
are the summary figures that fall out of the business planning processes in response
to questions such as:

▪   How many customers will we be able to attract?
▪   How much will they be willing to pay?
▪   How much revenue will this generate?
▪   How much will it cost to pay the interest on the loan?

- How much will it cost to rent the premises?
- How much will staff cost each week?
- How much are the total outgoings each year?How much will I get from the sale of the equipment in five years' time?

These are difficult questions because you are trying to predict an uncertain future. However, using research data, prior experience, and intuition, it is possible to model scenarios that provide a sense of what an investment might achieve. The important point of note is that techniques such as capital investment appraisal must be underpinned by high-quality data to power your assumptions; otherwise you face the age-old problem of 'garbage in equals garbage out.'

Simply by looking at the data in Table 4.1, we can see that in the most basic terms it delivers a project lifetime surplus after having paid off the initial loan. In principle, this is a positive finding, but how does CIA enable us to make an effective diagnosis of the data?

TRADITIONAL METHODS OF CAPITAL INVESTMENT APPRAISAL

'When will I get my money back?' That question demonstrates an intuitive grasp of the most basic CIA technique, the so-called payback method. Because of its simplicity, it is no surprise that the payback method is the most widely used technique in CIA. It is simply a measure of how quickly a project will repay its initial capital investment, in our case the $250,000 spent on gym equipment. Because the future is uncertain and there can be no guarantee that there will be any financial return, the speed with which a project repays its initial outlay is crucially important. Using our data in Table 4.1, we can add an extra column to compute the cumulative net cash flow.

What we can see in Table 4.2 is that after an initial investment of $250,000, there is a net cash inflow of $125,000 in years one and two. This is sufficient for the cumulative balance to be $0 at the end of year two, and at this point, the project has broken even. That is to say, we have paid off the loan after having also paid our operating costs (outflows) from the revenue generated by trading activities. Thus, our gym investment project has a two-year payback period. Is this good, bad, or average? Without having criteria against which to make a judgment, it is impossible to say. However, many entrepreneurs and businesses will have their own thresholds against which they judge projects. Therefore, for a business that works on a three-year pay-back period, a two-year payback would be a good outcome, whereas for a business that prefers a two-year payback period, it would be an average performance. Where the payback method is particularly helpful is in enabling managers to make informed decisions about two or more projects that are competing for the same investment. If you had two projects that both required $250,000 in initial investment and one paid back in two years and the other paid back in three years, then, all other things being

Table 4.2 The payback method

	Inflows ($)	Outflows ($)	Net cash flow ($)	Cumulative ($)
Year 0 (investment)		250,000	−250,000	**−250,000**
Year 1	175,000	50,000	125,000	**−125,000**
Year 2	175,000	50,000	125,000	**0**
Year 3	125,000	60,000	65,000	**65,000**
Year 4	200,000	70,000	130,000	**195,000**
Year 5	200,000	85,000	115,000	**310,000**
Residual value	25,000		25,000	**335,000**
Projected lifetime surplus			335,000	
Pays back by the end of Year 2				

equal, the two-year payback project would be the preferred option. This is because the investor would get the money back quicker, and therefore the level of risk is reduced relative to the three-year payback period. If you had $1,000 dollars to lend, would you lend it to the person who pays you back in two months or the person who pays back in three months? Relying on the payback method in isolation could, however, cause you to make some inappropriate decisions, which in turn could lead to expensive mistakes. Consider the case of a competing project that also required a $250,000 investment and had the data profile shown in Table 4.3.

Table 4.3 Alternative project competing for a $250,000 investment

	Inflows ($)	Outflows ($)	Net cash flow ($)	Cumulative ($)
Year 0 (investment)		250,000	−250,000	**−250,000**
Year 1	175,000	50,000	125,000	**−125,000**
Year 2	175,000	50,000	125,000	**0**
Year 3	0	0	0	**0**
Year 4	0	0	0	**0**
Year 5	0	0	0	**0**
Residual value	0		0	**0**
Projected lifetime surplus			0	
Pays back by the end of year 2				

Just like the data in Table 4.2, the project in Table 4.3 has a payback period of two years. Using the payback method in isolation would cause these two projects to be ranked equally. However, we can tell just by looking at the data that the project in Table 4.2 is far superior to the project in Table 4.3. This is because the project in Table 4.3 ends in year two and has no project lifetime surplus. The payback method has its strengths, but it also has its weaknesses and should not be used for CIA on its own.

▪ Strengths of the payback method:
  – It is simple to use and to understand, particularly for people in the decision-making process with little or no background in finance.
  – Many businesses suffer from cash flow problems, and to alleviate these they require a speedy return of investment. The payback method focuses people's attention on the time in which a project repays its investment.
  – Where an investment is risky, which is quite often the case in sport, the payback may be highly appropriate. This is because the forecasts of cash flows in the early years of a project are likely to be more accurate than those in later years. By concentrating on the short term, payback reduces the risks attached to forecasting. In our gym example, the equipment could become obsolete in three years, or a new competitor could open up that would completely undermine a five-year business plan. However, if we break even after two years, then these problems are not so severe.
▪ Weaknesses of the payback method:
  – Payback stops at the break-even point and does not recognize the overall return on the investment. It is clear that Table 4.2 presents a better investment than Table 4.3 does just by looking at the data, but payback would rank them evenly.
  – Payback ignores what is known as the time value of money. What would you rather have: $1,000 now or $1,000 in a year's time? If your answer is 'Now,' you intuitively understand the time value of money in that the certainty of money now is preferable to the risk of the same amount of money at some point in the future.

Despite its limitations, payback is the most widely used method of CIA, and most investors will have criteria about how quickly they would like to have their money back. Payback is often used as an initial filter for projects whereby those that do not meet an investor's basic repayment period will be rejected without further consideration because they are perceived to have too much risk attached to them. To overcome the limitations of payback, other methods have been devised to help provide a more rounded view of an investment, thereby enabling better decision making. The first of these that we consider is known as the *accounting rate of return* (ARR).

One of the most important measures is the return on capital employed percentage, which tells you how much a business is generating relative to the resources that are tied up in running the business. To put this into perspective, if we had $250,000 to invest, it would be fairly easy to go to a local bank, put the money on deposit, and in a year's time achieve a return of something like 3%; that is, we could withdraw our $250,000 plus a further $7,500 (3%) simply for keeping our money in the bank. Part of the thinking that entrepreneurs go through is to evaluate the return on their investment relative to what they could get from a safe investment such as putting money on deposit in a bank. If you put your money in a bank, you do not have to do anything else like fitting out a gym or hiring staff, and your investment is very safe. Therefore, if your return for taking a significant financial risk is no better than putting your money in a bank, then why bother running a business? Furthermore, the chances are that most businesspeople start by borrowing money because they do not have enough of their own. So now they are faced with having to pay the interest costs attached to a loan as well as the loan itself and still make a worthwhile return. As a result, certain questions are very important, such as, 'What kind of return will my business give me?' and 'How does this compare with putting my money in a safe investment like a bank?'

A weakness of payback is that it does not consider the full life of a project and stops at the point at which an investment breaks even. As a result, the accounting rate of return provides a different perspective by focusing on the overall profitability of a project, which is shown in Figures 4.2 and 4.3 as the project lifetime surplus. It follows that the higher the rate of ARR, the more profitable a project is, and the more attractive it is to an investor. There are different methods of calculating ARR, although they are variations on a basic theme. The basic point of note is that if you were using it to compare more than one project, you would use exactly the same formula for ARR on each of the different projects.

If we reuse our raw data from Table 4.1, it is possible to provide an illustration of how an ARR calculation is made in practice. (See Table 4.4.)

Table 4.4 Accounting rate of return (ARR) data

	Inflows ($)	Outflows ($)	Net cash flow ($)
Year 0 (investment)		250,000	−250,000
Year 1	175,000	50,000	125,000
Year 2	175,000	50,000	125,000
Year 3	125,000	60,000	65,000
Year 4	200,000	70,000	130,000
Year 5	200,000	85,000	115,000
Residual value	25,000		25,000
Projected lifetime surplus			335,000

Calculation of ARR involves a four-step process:

1 **Calculate the average yearly surplus of the project (the return).**
Project lifetime surplus/Duration of the project in years:
$335,000/5 years = $67,000 per year

2 **Calculate the net investment.**
Initial investment − Residual value:
$250,000 − $25,000 = $225,000

3 **Calculate the average investment.**
(Net investment/2) + Residual value:
This calculation is concerned with identifying the average amount of capital invested during the project's life. The initial capital of $250,000 is not tied up for the life of the project, as we already know from the payback method; it is actually paid back after two years. Thus a basic average of the investment tied up in the gym is the net investment divided by two. The residual value is added back to the basic average because it was a part of the investment that was genuinely tied up for the full five-year duration of the project.
($225,000/2) + $25,000 = $137,500

4 **Calculate the annual accounting rate of return (ARR).**
Average yearly surplus (step 1)/Average investment (step 3):
$67,000 per year/$137,500 average investment = 48.7%

With an annual accounting rate of return of 48.7%, the investment in the gym is much greater than could ever be achieved via a safe investment like a bank deposit account. The high return is the reward for taking a risk and being prepared to do the hard work to make a business idea a reality. Although the ARR looks at the full life of an investment, it does not address the issue of the time value of money. Clearly, a four-stage process to calculate ARR makes it mathematically more complex than the payback method and therefore less intuitive for untrained managers to grasp as a concept. Furthermore, it can be difficult to get your head around calculating the 'net investment' and the 'average investment.' Because the result of an ARR calculation is a percentage; it is not possible to distinguish between the scales of the projects. In looking at our gym example, the owner is achieving a return of 48.7% from profits of $67,000 per year. A sport stadium might deliver profits of $6.7 million per year, which is equivalent to, say, a 10% return on investment. Unless we took the scale of a project into account, there is a danger that we would favor a return of $67,000 per year over $6.7 million per year because the former has a higher ARR. Furthermore, because there are variations in the way the calculation of ARR can be made (e.g., the derivation of the average investment figure), it is a technique that is of limited usefulness. Payback and ARR are said to be traditional methods of capital investment appraisal because they do not account for the time value of money. This weakness in both methods is addressed in the next section when we look at modern methods of CIA that overcome some of the drawbacks of payback and ARR.

MODERN METHODS OF CAPITAL INVESTMENT APPRAISAL

Capital expenditure decisions involve committing resources to projects with no certain return (unlike bank deposits) for many years. The traditional CIA methods we have reviewed thus far, payback and accounting rate of return, use actual cash flows and do not take into account the time value of money. In our raw data, the investment in the gym generates a net cash flow of $125,000 in both year one and year two. To understand the relevance of the time value of money, ask yourself the question, 'What is better: $125,000 in a year's time or $125,000 in two years' time?' Most people will intuitively realize that $125,000 in a year's time is better than the same amount in two years' time because if we have the money sooner rather than later, we can put it to work either in a safe investment like a bank or in some other business project. Furthermore, there is greater uncertainty over two years than there is over one year; thus receiving your money back sooner rather than later reduces that risk. In reality, when we are making capital expenditure decisions that involve cash flows relating to years ahead, we need to take into account interest rates. Most adults will readily identify with the concept of interest rates because they affect how much we pay on our mortgages when buying a house or how much we pay in interest on credit cards. The methods involved in allowing for the time value of money are compounding and discounting. Discounting is used in CIA, but it helps to understand the principle by looking at compounding first. *Compounding*, or *compound interest*, is concerned with calculating the future value of a sum of money today at a given rate of interest. The technique is called compounding because the value of the investment increases over time as interest is earned on top of interest (i.e., interest is compounded). This point is best illustrated with an example. If our gym owner had $250,000 to invest and put it on deposit for a year at 3% interest at the end of the year, the initial investment would have grown to $257,500, that is, $250,000 + $7,500 (or 3%). If the investment was placed on deposit for a second year, the amount invested would now be $257,500 and 3% of this would be $7,725 giving a closing value at the end of year two of $265,225. The interest earned in year two is $225 more than in year one because the interest from year one has itself earned interest in year two. In contrast to compounding, discounting is concerned with converting the money earned in the future to today's value, or, as it is more commonly known, the *present value*. If compounding is concerned with calculating the future value of money invested today, discounting is concerned with calculating the present value of receiving money in the future. If we bought goods with a discount, we would be getting them for less than their face value. So too the promise

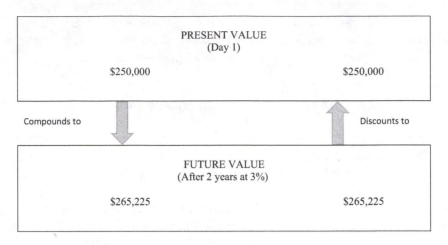

Figure 4.1 Compounding and discounting

of money in the future is worth less than money now, so we discount future cash flows to a present value. The relationship between discounting and compounding can be seen in Figure 4.1

After two years with interest rates of 3%, $250,000 is worth $265,225, and by the same logic, $265,225 in two years' time is worth the same as $250,000 today, which is demonstrated in longhand as follows:

- Compounding:

  $250,000 × 1.03 × 1.03 = $265,225
  or
  $250,000 × 1.0609 = $265,225 (note: 1.0609 is derived from 1.03 × 1.03, or 1.03^2)

- Discounting:

  $265,225 ÷1.03 = $257,500 and $257,500 ÷ 1.03 = $250,000
  or
  $265,225 × 0.9425 = $250,000 (note: 0.9425 is derived from 1 ÷ (1.03 × 1.03)

In practice, we source compounding and discounting factors from pre-prepared tables or from spreadsheets. An appendix to this chapter contains a list of discount factors for 0–25 years and from 0% to 25% interest. For a large-scale project such as a sport stadium, it is salutary to note that $1,000 in 20 years' time, assuming interest rates of 10%, would be worth just $149 now, that is, discount factor = 0.149. Take the time to look up this factor for yourself in the appendix. Find the row for 20 years, and run your finger along the columns of interest rates until you come to the intersection between 20 years and 10%; you will see the factor 0.149, which is

Pre-management and pre-operational issues

the value we used to multiply cash received in 20 years' time in order to convert it into today's value if interest rates were 10%.

The first method of CIA using discounting is called the *net present value* (NPV), where all future cash flows are discounted to today's value (the time at which we make the investment). The purpose of this exercise is to see whether the investment is viable when we allow for the fact that future cash flows are not worth as much as cash in the hand now. Using our $250,000 investment in a gym example and assuming interest rates of 10%, we can model the NPV of the project as shown in Table 4.5.

Table 4.5 Net present value (NPV) calculation assuming interest rates of 10%

	Inflows ($)	Outflows ($)	Net cash flow ($)	Discount factor (10%)	Present value
Year 0 (investment)		250,000	−250,000	1.000	−250,000
Year 1	175,000	50,000	125,000	0.909	113,636
Year 2	175,000	50,000	125,000	0.826	103,306
Year 3	125,000	60,000	65,000	0.751	48,835
Year 4	200,000	70,000	130,000	0.683	88,792
Year 5	200,000	85,000	115,000	0.621	71,406
Residual value	25,000		25,000	0.621	15,523
Projected lifetime surplus			335,000	**Net present value** = 191,498	

When we allow for the time value of money with interest rates of 10%, the gym investment has a net present value of $191,498, which, although positive, is considerably less than the project lifetime surplus of $335,000 calculated earlier (see Table 4.1), which does not take into account the time value of money. However, so long as a project returns a positive NPV, the investment is worthwhile at the level of interest specified. Thus in our case, if the gym owner could borrow $250,000 at an interest rate of 10%, he or she could be confident about servicing the bank loan. The net present value method is useful for appraising both single projects and multiple projects that are competing for the same capital funds. Where there is competition for funds, technically the best option is the project with the highest NPV, and this even includes investments that have different durations. The main problem with discounting, however, is that for some people it is too complex a skill to master, particularly for those with limited or no financial training. For those who do understand the basic principles, the mechanics of producing a discounted cash flow forecast as in Table 4.5 are quite straightforward. What is more difficult is being able to choose meaningful interest rates and discount factors for some time in the future. As an example of how hard it can be to model future interest rates, do you know what the interest rate will be on your credit card in three years' time? There is also the added problem of the reliability of the assumptions upon which the calculations are based. It is quite easy to assume that a gym can recruit 1,000 members at $175 per year and thereby generate revenue of $175,000, but if this does not happen or if running costs are higher than expected, then the apparent simplicity of CIA models is undermined by the quality of the data upon which they are based.

Uncertainty over interest rates and their discount rates gives rise to a second modern method of CIA, known as the *internal rate of return* (IRR). The IRR poses the simple question: At what rate of interest would the net present value of a particular project be equal to $0? If we cannot predict interest rates with any degree of accuracy, then the next best thing is to know the range of interest rates at which a project is still viable. In our gym example, we know that with interest rates at 10%, the investment is viable because there is a positive NPV, but at what rate of interest does the project in effect break even? This line of thinking is what is known as *sensitivity analysis*, which models how sensitive the viability of a project is to changes in the underlying assumptions. So in this case, how sensitive is the project to variations in interest rates? One straightforward method is simply to use trial and error, or what is also known as the iterative method. What this means is that you simply experiment with a range of interest rate values until you get as reasonably close to $0 as possible. Therefore, we know that at 10% the NPV is positive, so it follows that the IRR will be higher than this. We also know that the accounting rate of return is 48.7% (see the previous section of this chapter), and because this is based on the project lifetime surplus and is not discounted, then the IRR must be lower than the ARR. Therefore, in broad terms, we are working on a range of between more than 10% and less than 48.7%. We could narrow down this range by experimenting with, say, 30% as shown in Table 4.6.

Table 4.6 Iterative method to deriving the internal rate of return (IRR)

	Inflows ($)	Outflows ($)	Net cash flow ($)	Discount factor (30%)	Present value
Year 0 (investment)		250,000	−250,000	1.000	−250,000
Year 1	175,000	50,000	125,000	0.769	96,154
Year 2	175,000	50,000	125,000	0.592	73,964
Year 3	125,000	60,000	65,000	0.455	29,586
Year 4	200,000	70,000	130,000	0.350	45,517
Year 5	200,000	85,000	115,000	0.269	30,973
Residual value	25,000		25,000	0.269	6,733
Projected lifetime surplus			335,000	**Net present value** = 32,927	

At 30%, the NPV reduces to $32,927, which means that the project is still viable and therefore the IRR must be even higher than 30%. In practice, we can use a spreadsheet to experiment with different rates, and there is even an IRR function built into Excel, which will do the job automatically. If we went as high as 40%, we would get a negative NPV (–$13,380), which now tells us that we are looking for a figure somewhere between 30% and 40%. It is possible to plot the various iterations of NPV on a graph and to work out the IRR by finding the point at which the line for NPV crosses the interest rate axis as shown in Figure 4.2.

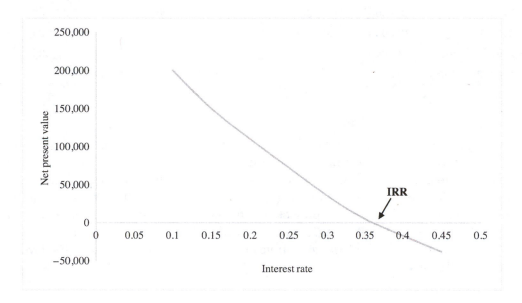

Figure 4.2 *Internal rate of return (IRR) represented graphically*

In Figure 4.2, we can see that NPV is positive for all interest rates up to 35% and negative at 40%. The NPV line crosses the x-axis at around 37% and we can confirm this using further iterations with the actual interest rate at which NPV = $0 being 36.8% as shown in Table 4.7.

Any project that has an IRR greater than the cost of the finance being borrowed to fund it is worth investing in because it means the investor can repay the loans, meet day-to-day expenses, and make a profit. In our case, the gym owner has borrowed $250,000 to invest in equipping a gym at 10%, and this rate of interest could increase to 36.8% before the NPV became negative. For the owner, this is comforting news and enables him or her to worry about selling the targeted number of memberships rather than fluctuations in interest rates.

Capital investment appraisal techniques are not cast in a tablet of stone and can be adapted to suit the needs of the users. Remember they are decision support

Table 4.7 Internal rate of return (IRR) = Point at which net present value (NPV) = $0

	Inflows ($)	Outflows ($)	Net cash flow ($)	Discount factor (36.8%)	Present value
Year 0 (investment)		250,000	−250,000	1.000	−250,000
Year 1	175,000	50,000	125,000	0.731	91,390
Year 2	175,000	50,000	125,000	0.535	66,817
Year 3	125,000	60,000	65,000	0.391	25,403
Year 4	200,000	70,000	130,000	0.286	37,145
Year 5	200,000	85,000	115,000	0.209	24,024
Residual value	25,000		25,000	0.209	5,223
Projected lifetime surplus			335,000	**Net present value = 0**	

techniques, not decision-making techniques. We have seen that the payback method is intuitive to use and easily understood, and we have seen that the net present value method is technically the most correct because it takes into account the time value of money. So why not combine the two? Combining payback with NPV gives us the *discounted payback* period of a project. Taking the relevant data from Table 4.5 and applying the payback method principles shown in Table 4.2 enables us to compute the discounted payback of the gym investment used throughout this chapter, as shown in Table 4.8.

Table 4.8 Discounted payback period

	Inflows ($)	Outflows ($)	Net cash flow ($)	Present value (10%)	Discounted payback period
Year 0 (investment)		250,000	−250,000	−250,000	−250,000
Year 1	175,000	50,000	125,000	113,625	−136,375
Year 2	175,000	50,000	125,000	103,250	−33,125
Year 3	125,000	60,000	65,000	48,815	**15,690**
Year 4	200,000	70,000	130,000	88,790	
Year 5	200,000	85,000	115,000	71,415	
Residual value	25,000		25,000	15,525	
Projected lifetime surplus			335,000	191,420	

Under the traditional payback method, the project repaid its investment after two years. However, using the discounted payback period approach, the project does not pay back the investment until sometime during year three. At the end of year two, the project still needs to recover $33,125 in order to repay the investment. In year three, the project makes a discounted surplus of $48,815, which is more than enough to repay the outstanding amount. If we assume that these cash flows occur evenly, then we can say that the number of months into year three that the project pays back under the discounted payback method is approximately 8 months, that is, (33,125/48,815) × 12 = 8 months. Being pragmatic and realizing that these things are not an exact science, we might conclude reasonably that traditional payback is two years and discounted payback is three years. This is yet more useful information from the decision support techniques to inform the investor about the attractiveness or otherwise of a capital investment opportunity.

FACILITY FOCUS: INVESTING FOR COMPETITIVE ADVANTAGE: HALLAMSHIRE TENNIS AND SQUASH CLUB, SHEFFIELD, UNITED KINGDOM

The Hallamshire Tennis and Squash Club has some 2,000 members who live mainly in the leafy suburbs of Sheffield and its surrounding areas. Racket sport players tend to be drawn from higher socioeconomic groups and are demanding in terms of what they expect from the use of their limited leisure time. In addition to this challenge is the fact that the vast majority of the club's costs are fixed and do not vary once opening hours have been agreed. Thus there is a need for managers to keep the club's offer as attractive as possible, while at the same time maximizing revenue to pay for the fixed costs. In practice, the club tackles these issues in two ways. First, there is a commitment to reinvest any surpluses back into the maintenance and upkeep of the club. This approach might involve resurfacing playing courts, upgrading social spaces, and improving communication with members via technology. By constantly improving the offer, it is more likely that members will be retained when it comes to renewing their subscriptions and more likely that there will be less resistance toward increasing prices. Second, by using technology such as access control, online booking, and linking bookings to the operation of court lights, it is possible to protect revenue and to prevent unauthorized use of the facilities by nonmembers or members who do not have access rights to particular areas. A random audit once found that 13% of people who were onsite did not have the appropriate access rights, which in turn was losing the club revenue. Subsequent investment has resulted in unauthorized use being eliminated, revenue increasing, and members having a better customer experience.

The five CIA methods we have looked at in this chapter have limitations when used in isolation, but when they are pulled together, our gym owner is provided with some powerful information with which to support the decision to invest or not, as shown in Table 4.9.

Table 4.9 Summary of capital investment appraisal (CIA) analysis $250,000 investment in a gym

Method	Score	Source of evidence
Payback	2 years	Table 4.2
Accounting rate of return	48.7%	Four-step process below Table 4.4
Net present value @ 10%	+$191,438	Table 4.5
Internal rate of return	36.8%	Figure 4.2 and Table 4.7
Discounted payback	c. 2 years, 8 months	Table 4.8

Assuming the forecasts of income generated and costs incurred are correct, then we are looking at an investment that has the following features:

■ It will be paid back in full at the end of two years according to the payback method.
■ It has an annual accounting rate of return (ARR) of 48.7%, which compares very favorably with return on capital employed calculations for money in safe deposits.
■ It has a positive net present value (NPV) of $191,498 when interest rates are at 10%.
■ It has an internal rate of return (IRR) of 36.8%.
■ It has a discounted payback period of around 2 years and 8 months.

These are precisely the sort of details that lenders of finance wish to see when entrepreneurs approach them. Investors can get their money back quickly; the gym generates returns that are way in excess of safe investments such as bank deposits; and with an IRR of 36.8%, the project is resilient to huge increases in interest rates. Anyone looking at a business proposal with this financial performance would be persuaded that it is a good business proposition, assuming the underlying assumptions were accurate. The argument is far more compelling than somebody walking in off the street and saying to a bank manager, 'I am a health and fitness enthusiast, and I think I can make some money running a gym, Please lend me $250,000.' What our case study demonstrates is that when making decisions about capital

76

expenditure, it pays to underpin the decision-making process with as much supporting information as possible. By conducting the full range of capital investment appraisal techniques at your disposal rather than relying solely on, say, payback, you enable decisions to be made from a far more rounded perspective. Having gone through this process, the gym owner can be in no doubt that the figures 'stack up' from an investment angle; the challenge is to deliver on the assumptions that underpin the business model.

At this point, the gym owner can impress the lenders even further by demonstrating that the business model has been tested for its sensitivity to changes in the key assumptions. The viability, or otherwise, of the proposed investment in the gym depends crucially on the ability to sell memberships at the level stated in the business plan. The income attributable to memberships is shown as 'inflows' in our various CIA calculations in previous figures and tables. Modeling the effects of changes in the assumptions is known as *sensitivity analysis* or *what-if analysis*. To illustrate the basic principles, let us consider the sensitivity of the base case model summarized in Table 4.9 to three different scenarios:

▧ Membership sales are 25% less than expected.
▧ Membership sales are 50% less than expected.
▧ The costs of running the gym (outflows) have been underestimated and are actually double those stated.

The process of establishing the impact of these scenarios can now be modeled easily by changing the data in the spreadsheet used to compile the base case, as shown in Table 4.10.

Table 4.10 Sensitivity analysis

Method	Base case	Membership sales −25%	Membership sales −50%	Operating costs +100%
Payback	2 years	3 years, 8 months	Never	5 years[1]
Accounting rate of return	48.7%	16.9%	−14.9%	2.9%
Net present value @ 10%	+$191,498	+$26,845	−$137,730	−$40,985
Internal rate of return	36.8%	14.1%	−15.2%	2.8%
Discounted payback	c. 2 years, 8 months	c. 4 years, 9 months	Never	Never

[1]Assumes the residual value of the equipment is realized in Year 5; otherwise the scenario does not pay back fully.

77

Relative to the base case assumptions, the proposed gym investment is shown to be highly sensitive to shortfalls in revenue and increases in costs. If membership sales were 25% less than anticipated, the project would still be viable in the sense that it has a positive net present value at 10% and all of the other CIA measures are positive. However, the comparison with the base case shows that the proposition is much less attractive than if the budgeted level of sales is achieved. This is because:

- the payback period increases from 2 years to 3 years and 8 months;
- the accounting rate of return (ARR) falls from 48.7% to 16.9%;
- the net present value (NPV) falls from $191,498 to $26,845;
- the internal rate of return (IRR) falls from 36.8% to 14.1%; and
- the discounted payback increases from 2 years and 8 months to 4 years and 9 months.

For the scenario in which there is a 50% reduction in sales, the project ceases to be viable as the net present value is negative at 10%; it never pays back the initial investment, and both the accounting rate of return and the internal rate of return are negative. In the case of a negative IRR, this means that the bank would be paying the borrower for the privilege of lending the money! This is not something that happens in the real world. By contrast, the scenario in which operating costs are double the base case shows that the project does pay back in five years and that the ARR and IRR at 2.9% and 2.8%, respectively, are positive. However, as we are working on the assumption that that cost of capital, or interest rate, is 10%; then at 10%, the net present value is negative (–$40,985), and therefore the project would be rejected. What the internal rate of return tells us is that in this scenario the maximum interest rate the project is capable of servicing is 2.8%, which is a very favorable rate for the borrower and provides little incentive for a lender to take a risk with $250,000. Having conducted this sort of analysis (as lenders invariably do), it focuses the mind of the gym owner on achieving the budgeted sales targets and on having contingency plans in place to take corrective action if these targets are not met, for example making savings on operating costs. In reality, borrowers should do their own sensitivity analyses to be able to preempt a lender's questions and concerns about project viability.

Where capital investment appraisal techniques become particularly powerful is in appraising different investments that are competing for the same money. If an investor has $250,000 to lend and three projects are competing for the money, then CIA really comes into its own. This point can be appreciated by looking at a situation whereby a lender has three proposals to borrow $250,000 for a tennis club, a sports retailer, and a swimming pool operator. The summary data for each project is shown in Table 4.10.

Table 4.11 CIA of three competing projects

	Tennis club	Sports retailer	Pool operator
Payback	2 years	3 years	4 years
Accounting rate of return	25%	20%	17%
Net present value @ 10%	+$69,730	+$62,190	+$58,400
Internal rate of return	22%	16%	13%
Discounted payback	3 years	3.5 years	5 years

Faced with the data in Table 4.11 and being able to fund only one project, which one represents the best option for an investor? The tennis club repays its investment in two years and has a positive NPV, which is also the highest NPV and the highest IRR. It is ranked highest on all of the CIA measures and would be the first to be funded. The sport retailer represents the second best option and the pool operator the third best option. There is always a surplus of demand for investment funds over the availability of the supply of such funds, and thus it is a competitive process. What CIA has done in this instance is produce directly comparable measures for three different projects that enable them to be compared on a like-for-like basis. The recommendation to support the investment in the tennis club is correct theoretically; it 'works' commercially, and it is the direct consequence of an objective process of evaluation. Used correctly, CIA is a powerful tool to help managers make decisions that involve taking calculated risks with large sums of money and that may have a significant impact on the future health of a business. Under these conditions, managers need all the help they can get, and being conversant in the principles of CIA is an important first step in getting that help.

TECHNOLOGY NOW! CAPITAL WORKS AND ENVIRONMENTAL IMPACT (UNITED KINGDOM)

The Hallamshire Tennis and Squash Club in Sheffield, England boasts former Wimbledon doubles tennis champion Jonny Marray and former World Squash Champion Nick Matthew among its members. It also serves some 2,000 people in the local community who make use of the 12 tennis courts, nine squash courts, gym, and social facilities. The club was awarded a National Lottery

79

grant of £177,000, as a contribution toward capital works designed to reduce the club's environmental impact as shown in the following table:

Improvement	Benefits
Installation of a more efficient boiler system and radiators	Lower energy consumption, lower costs, and fewer carbon emissions
Replacement of six squash floors	Enabled removal of old inefficient heaters
Air-conditioning to the gym	Better and more consistent customer experience
Replacement saunas for both the male and female changing rooms	Lower running costs and a source of competitive advantage
All lighting to tennis courts, squash courts, and viewing areas replaced with LED lights	Better lighting, lower energy costs, and reduced bulb replacement costs

The improvements and benefits have reduced the club's environmental impact by replacing old equipment with new, more energy-efficient alternatives. At the same time, there have been improvements in customer experience and a reduction in the club's future expenditure. This, in turn, will help the club to generate surpluses in the future and to keep costs down for the members. An intelligent approach to sport facility management such as this shows that capital investment is not solely confined to large-scale projects like stadia for professional sport franchises.

Source: Sport England. Retrieved May 30, 2019, from www.sportengland.org/media/4551/sheffield-hallamshire-tennis-and-squash-club.pdf

CHAPTER REVIEW

The key point of note in this chapter is that when we make capital expenditure on fixed assets such as a stadium or equipment, there will be a time delay between our making the investment and it is providing a return. A degree of risk is therefore attached to capital expenditure because, once your money has gone, it is gone, and whatever you have spent it on has to generate a return for you. Therefore, in practice there are two sets of risks: first, the delay between spending your money and getting a return and, second, whether the return received is sufficient to justify the investment in the first place. The purpose of capital investment appraisal can be summarized as being able to test the financial viability of a project and to rank different projects so that limited funding is allocated to the best project. What we are trying to do with CIA is to model the future, and this is not certain. There is the risk that an investment may cost more than planned, there is the risk that the forecasts on which future income generation is based are too optimistic, and there is the risk that interest rates might change and damage the viability of a project. What CIA does is to provide a set of tools that enable us to evaluate the anticipated outcomes of capital expenditure and to enable us to then make a decision as to whether the likely returns outweigh the risks.

The simplest and most commonly used method is payback, which simply poses the question, 'How long does it take for the investment to be repaid?' It is an intuitive, easily understood method that most people can relate to and understand. The key problem with the traditional measures of CIA such as payback and ARR is that they do not take into account the time value of money, notably that projected future cash flows are not worth the same as the same amount of money today. Given a choice, most people would take $1,000 today rather than the same amount in a year's time because they perceive (quite rightly) that $1,000 in a year's time is worth less than $1,000 now. The differential between money now and money in the future is called a discount and is determined by the prevailing rate of interest.

For long-term projects during periods of high interest rates, $1,000 now might be worth less than $150 in 20 years' time. To recognize this time value of money, we use discount factors to produce the net present value (NPV) and the internal rate of return (IRR). The net present value converts all future cash flows into their equivalent value today in order to test whether an investment is viable using this more demanding test relative to payback and ARR. Interest rates are rarely certain and will often fluctuate. Managers, therefore, need to know the range of interest rates within which an investment is viable. IRR identifies the interest rate at which the net present value (NPV) is $0, or in effect the break-even point. It is possible to combine the elements of CIA techniques to help inform the decision-making process even further. The discounted payback method combines the simplicity of payback with the technical correctness of net present value (NPV) to complement each method used in isolation.

CIA is at its most powerful when all of the techniques are used in combination to look at:

- a single investment from a variety of perspectives;
- the sensitivity of projects to changes in the business model's key assumptions; and
- ranking projects competing for the same funding.

Getting involved in capital investment decisions represents some of the greatest responsibility and excitement you will have in a career as a sport facility manager. The opportunity to work on capital projects is the domain of the few, and these select few inevitably have highly developed capital investment appraisal skills.

IN THE FIELD . . .

With Matt Whitaker, director, We Do Tennis Ltd, Welton, United Kingdom

After 16 years working in sport facility management for established UK brands such as Bannatyne Fitness Group, Nuffield, and David Lloyd plc, as well as private clubs such as the Hallamshire, Matt has recently become self-employed. His company, We Do Tennis Ltd, uses his experience of working in the sector to offer services to clubs that will help them improve their business operations. As a former club manager, he has been responsible for pretty much everything involved in the effective running of racket sport facilities. He has been responsible to boards and doing everything from organizing work rotations, staff training, health and safety, human resource management, dealing with new suppliers, managing club refurbishments, and preparing budgets. He now uses this broad base of experience to advise other clubs on how they might optimize their operations and their offerings to their customers.

The one piece of advice Matt would give anyone looking to work in this field would be to take on as many possible, diverse areas as possible. He has looked after physical training, beauty salons, hairdressers, spa treatments, cafe bars, and more . . . not all of which are his areas of expertise. Matt believes you will never know when the experience you have gained from years past will help you in the future.

BIBLIOGRAPHY

Beech, J., & Chadwick, S. (Eds.). (2004). *The business of sport management*. Essex, UK: Prentice Hall Financial Times.

Brown, M., Rascher, D., Nagel, M., & McEvoy, C. (2015). *Financial management in the sport industry*. New York: Routledge.

Emery, P. (2011). *The sports management toolkit*. Oxford, UK: Routledge.

Fried, G. (2015). *Managing sport facilities*. Champaign, IL: Human Kinetics.

Fried, G., DeSchriver, T., & Mondello, M. (2013). *Sport finance* (3rd ed.). Champaign, IL: Human Kinetics.

Russell, D., Patel, A., & Wilkinson-Riddle, G. J. (2002). *Cost accounting: An essential guide*. London: Pearson Educational.

Schwarz, E. C., Westerbeek, H., Liu, D., Emery, P., & Turner, P. (2017). *Managing sport facilities and major events* (2nd ed.). Oxford: Routledge.

Tilley, C., & Whitehouse, J. (1992). *Finance and leisure*. London: ILAM/Longman.

Wilson, R. (2011). *Managing sport finance*. Oxford: Routledge.

Winfree, J., Rosentraub, M., Mills, B., & Zondlak, M. (2019). *Sports finance and management: Real estate, media, and the new business of sport* (2nd ed.). New York: Routledge.

CHAPTER 5

PROJECT MANAGEMENT
PLANNING, DESIGN, AND CONSTRUCTION

CHAPTER OUTLINE

- Project management
  - Project life cycles
- Preliminary planning
  - Program analysis
  - Feasibility studies
  - Planning committee
  - Selecting an architect
- Master plan development
- Facility design
  - Facility design basics
  - Timetables
  - Site selection
  - Cost estimate
- Construction
  - Contractor selection process
  - Creation of detailed shop drawings
  - Groundbreaking and actual construction
- Preparation for training and management of facilities
- Chapter review

CHAPTER OBJECTIVES

The objective of this chapter is to explain the important principles of project management required for a sport facility operations manager as related to costs, *scheduling, quality management, and the development and setting of SMARTER objectives. Through the lens of project life cycles, an explanation of task analysis and sequencing, the design of Gantt charts, and use of project management software will be covered. This will then lead to investigating the various stages of the planning, design, and construction processes, including preliminary planning; the development of the design; actual construction; and preparation for training and the management of facilities. By understanding these issues in advance, the reader will have a stronger conceptual underpinning of the management framework applied to sport facilities and be able to connect that knowledge with the implementation processes inherent to the management and operations of sport facilities*

PROJECT MANAGEMENT

Project management deals with planning, scheduling, organizing, and controlling projects. This may be applied across a variety of areas including product development, construction, systems, new business, production layout, and special events. Project management is becoming increasingly more important in today's world. Mastery of key tools and concepts can give you a significant competitive advantage in the management and operations of sport facilities.

A variety of concepts, techniques, and decision tools are available to a sport facility manager. This requires a complete understanding of systems and organizational culture to ensure that an integrative project management approach is taken in the management and operation of sport facilities. This starts with having a clear organizational vision and mission that integrate strategic management processes. The results from this strategy are driven by the prioritization of projects, selecting and activating new projects, and controlling all resources. However, this must be undertaken with a full understanding of the ramifications of these actions on organizational culture. This means that a solid structure needs to underpin an integrated project management process that is clear in scope, has well-defined work breakdown structures, and is measurable through the auditing of controls. This requires implementing networks, planning processes, and scheduling that is appropriate, considers project risks, as well as addresses constraints in a timely manner. It also requires from the sport facility manager quality leadership, as well as solid teamwork among employees and external partners.

In sport facility operations management, there is a multitude of principles of project management that a facility manager needs to understand. These principles are often related to one of four areas: costs, scheduling, quality management, and the development and setting of SMARTER objectives.

The managing of costs is central to any project. Cost management in sport facility operations management focuses on the consideration of logistics and operational costs by optimizing the management structure, ensuring efficiency in systems operations, and managing resources effectively. Most costs are managed through the process of developing and controlling the budget of the sport facility so that the facility manager can efficiently predict expenditures to ensure that the business operation remains in a positive financial position, hence not going over budget. This requires sport facility managers to have a good understanding of financial management, accounting principles, financial ratios, and economic analysis as they will be involved with planning, estimating, financing, funding, managing, and controlling costs.

The Project Management Institute (PMI) has developed the most widely accepted set of global standards that provide guidelines, rules, and characteristics for project, program, and portfolio management that, if applied correctly, helps organizations achieve professional excellence. From a sport facility operations management standpoint, project management focuses on four main areas: resource planning, cost estimating, cost budgeting, and cost control. *Resource planning* involves defining the activities to be created, determining resources needed through a work breakdown structure (WBS), and analyzing historical information of similar projects and facilities. *Cost estimating* involves predicting how much a specific activity will cost. *Cost budgeting*, combined with the project schedule, anticipates the projected costs of each part of a project and allocate in the budget when the cost will be incurred. Finally, *cost control* creates variances to ensure projects stay on target with contingencies built into the budget for errors and omissions so that corrective action can be undertaken.

After managing costs, the next most important function is the scheduling of facilities and the related revenue management associated with sport facility use. Thousands of facilities around the globe, including gyms, health clubs, fitness centers, personal training centers, university athletic/recreation facilities, parks/recreation departments, and multipurpose sport facilities of all types need to implement a scheduling process that manages everything from projects to day-to-day operations. In terms of project management, a quality scheduling process can help streamline all processes related to employee management, resource allocation, and accounting administration. Using project management software is the most effective means of ensuring that scheduling is completed accurately. A number of software packages can be used ranging from generic software such as Microsoft Project to specialized tools stylized for individual organizational use.

Project management costs and scheduling can be maintained only when a process of quality management is overseeing the project. This will be discussed in more details in Chapter 8 about operations management, but from a project management standpoint, a process of continuous improvement needs to be administered to ensure quality implementation through constant refinements based on feedback and observations. This will allow the sport facility manager to better control project quality with the end result being an improvement of all aspects of activity implementation.

All of these areas can be consistently maintained as long as the project management process is framed by setting clear, concise SMARTER objectives. The S can stand for either specific or strategic. Specificity ensures that the objectives are defined clearly and presented exactly, while those choosing to use 'strategic' are identifying the long-term vision for the project and the means of achieving it. The M stands for measurable, meaning that all objectives must produce tangible evidence that the objective has been accomplished. The A can be either attainable or achievable, which, regardless of which term is used, means there needs to be a determination at the start that the objective can actually be reached. The R can focus on being either relevant or realistic. Both are results-focused concepts, with 'relevant' looking at the importance of the objective to the overall attainment of the objective, whereas 'realistic' assesses whether the objective is real versus a wish or something impractical. The T is for time-bound, meaning there need to be a set start and end for the attainment of the objective and the completion of the project. E is for evaluated. As outcomes assessment and accountability are a big part of completing any project, a process of benchmarking and analysis of performance relative to the objective is a critical part of the project management process. Finally, the R is for reviewed, meaning that the sport facility manager and other relevant project management stakeholders actually review the overall process for validation.

Project life cycles

In order to manage costs and scheduling through a process of quality management and the development of SMARTER objectives, an understanding of the development of project life cycles is crucial for sport facility managers to implement a process of project management. Project life cycles are used to map out the starting point of a project (project initiation), organizing and preparing for project implementation (project planning), the actual carrying out of the project (project execution), and the completion of the project (project closure). These distinct stages break down a project to simplify the chronological and developmental process of managing projects, integrate general and specific planning requirements across a time-driven management context, and ensure that each successive activity can be better prepared for and cost-effectively managed within the project. Project life cycles are applied in sport facility management in a variety of ways. The most common is through a process of task analysis and sequencing, the design of Gantt charts, and the use of project management software.

In project management, one of the most basic processes when life cycling a project is conducting a task analysis followed by sequencing of activities. Task analysis involves identifying the processes needed to support the project, while sequencing organizes the tasks into a hierarchal structure based on a progressive order of completion usually based on time to be spent on the task, the difficulty of the task, or the importance of the tasks. Tasks can be broken down into smaller subtasks to provide more detail to accomplish the primary task.

While conducting a task analysis and sequencing is important, a simple listing of these tasks is often not enough. Additional important information must be attached to each task, including the resources needed and a timeline for completion. One of the most common tools utilized by sport facility managers to map projects is a Gantt chart. A *Gantt chart* is a horizontal bar chart that graphically displays the time relationship of the steps of the project, where each step of the project is represented by a line on the chart indicating the time period to be undertaken. When a Gantt chart is completed, the sport facility manager can see the minimum total time for each task, the proper sequence of tasks, which tasks are completed at the same time, and which are connected.

Gantt charts can be created by hand, but the use of a spreadsheet program such as Microsoft Excel can help organize the information so that it can be searched, sorted, and edited. In addition, project management software such as Microsoft Project simplifies the creation of these documents plus makes it easier to make changes during the project. An example is provided in Figure 5.1. There are also numerous companies that design specialized project management software for use by sport facility managers.

The remainder of this chapter will focus on an explanation of the planning, design, and construction project life cycle. This starts with an examination of preliminary planning for the design of a sport facility followed by the actual facility design process. This will be followed by the implementation of construction and finish with the preparation for training and management of facilities.

PRELIMINARY PLANNING

Preliminary planning involves all of the initial tasks that need to be completed in preparation for a specific course of action. A sound preliminary planning process allows the sport facility manager to effectively and efficiently utilize resources to organize, implement, control, and make decisions. Through the preliminary planning process, timelines and standards are established, initial problems are addressed, and strategic, tactical, and operational goals are formalized – working within the philosophy and mission of the organization and toward end results articulated in the vision.

With regard to sport facilities, there are generally six parts to the preliminary planning process: completing a program analysis, conducting feasibility studies, convening a planning committee, selecting an architect, developing a master plan, and creating a program statement.

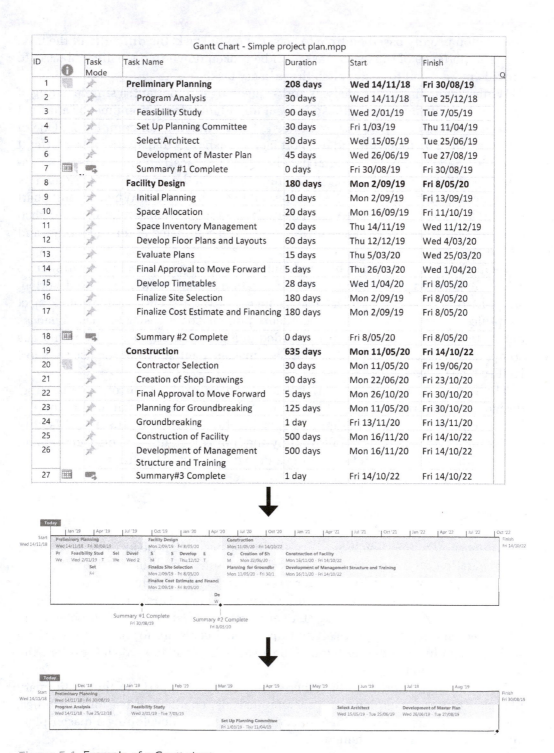

Gantt Chart - Simple project plan.mpp

ID	i	Task Mode	Task Name	Duration	Start	Finish	Q
1			**Preliminary Planning**	**208 days**	**Wed 14/11/18**	**Fri 30/08/19**	
2			Program Analysis	30 days	Wed 14/11/18	Tue 25/12/18	
3			Feasibility Study	90 days	Wed 2/01/19	Tue 7/05/19	
4			Set Up Planning Committee	30 days	Fri 1/03/19	Thu 11/04/19	
5			Select Architect	30 days	Wed 15/05/19	Tue 25/06/19	
6			Development of Master Plan	45 days	Wed 26/06/19	Tue 27/08/19	
7			Summary #1 Complete	0 days	Fri 30/08/19	Fri 30/08/19	
8			**Facility Design**	**180 days**	**Mon 2/09/19**	**Fri 8/05/20**	
9			Initial Planning	10 days	Mon 2/09/19	Fri 13/09/19	
10			Space Allocation	20 days	Mon 16/09/19	Fri 11/10/19	
11			Space Inventory Management	20 days	Thu 14/11/19	Wed 11/12/19	
12			Develop Floor Plans and Layouts	60 days	Thu 12/12/19	Wed 4/03/20	
13			Evaluate Plans	15 days	Thu 5/03/20	Wed 25/03/20	
14			Final Approval to Move Forward	5 days	Thu 26/03/20	Wed 1/04/20	
15			Develop Timetables	28 days	Wed 1/04/20	Fri 8/05/20	
16			Finalize Site Selection	180 days	Mon 2/09/19	Fri 8/05/20	
17			Finalize Cost Estimate and Financing	180 days	Mon 2/09/19	Fri 8/05/20	
18			Summary #2 Complete	0 days	Fri 8/05/20	Fri 8/05/20	
19			**Construction**	**635 days**	**Mon 11/05/20**	**Fri 14/10/22**	
20			Contractor Selection	30 days	Mon 11/05/20	Fri 19/06/20	
21			Creation of Shop Drawings	90 days	Mon 22/06/20	Fri 23/10/20	
22			Final Approval to Move Forward	5 days	Mon 26/10/20	Fri 30/10/20	
23			Planning for Groundbreaking	125 days	Mon 11/05/20	Fri 30/10/20	
24			Groundbreaking	1 day	Fri 13/11/20	Fri 13/11/20	
25			Construction of Facility	500 days	Mon 16/11/20	Fri 14/10/22	
26			Development of Management Structure and Training	500 days	Mon 16/11/20	Fri 14/10/22	
27			Summary#3 Complete	1 day	Fri 14/10/22	Fri 14/10/22	

Figure 5.1 Example of a Gantt chart

Program analysis

A *program analysis* focuses on the need for the facility in terms of the programs that are either already established or are planned to be established. In order to conduct an appropriate program analysis, a sport facility manager must first have a clear understanding of the organizational PMV (philosophy, mission, and vision). The *organizational philosophy* focuses on what is important to the sport facility from the standpoint of business values and beliefs. The *organizational mission* focuses on the reason for the sport facility and the guiding managerial principles. These guiding principles are articulated through the organizational goals – the tasks that need to be completed to achieve the mission – and the organizational objectives – the specific methods to be utilized to accomplish those tasks. These organizational goals and objectives are governed by the policies and procedures set forth by the organization – usually articulated through an operations manual, a human resources manual, and standard operating procedures in the industry. The *organizational vision* focuses on the future and where the sport facility and associated organizations ultimately want to be.

Feasibility studies

The program analysis is usually articulated through feasibility studies. A *feasibility study* is an examination of the likelihood that an idea or concept can be transformed into a business reality. Feasibility studies have a number of components, including the project description and site selection; the scope and constraints of the project; a needs identification; the strategic significance of the project; the sport, economic, and societal impact; capital costs and revenue projections; and timelines. Table 5.1 defines each of these terms.

Table 5.1 Feasibility study components

Component	Explanation
Project description	A general overview of the facility, including square footage, inclusions, and amenities
Site selection	Includes the attractiveness of the location, acreage/hectare available, natural and environmental conditions (weather, soil, grading, wetlands, forestry, rocks/minerals), ease of access, and community support
Scope of the project	The processes required to define and control the work necessary to complete the project
Constraints of the project	Specific restrictions that could have an adverse effect on the scope of the project and related actions

Table 5.1 (Continued)

Component	Explanation
Needs identification/ assessment	The verification process as to whether the facility is essential, including identifying current and future trends, assessing similar facilities/competition, evaluating the relevant social indicators, and determining demand/usage potential
Strategic significance	The potential of having a positive, long-term impact based on the vision of the organization
Sport impact	How the facility will have a direct effect on the future development of sport in the locale
Economic impact	How the facility will directly stimulate the total amount of expenditures in the area
Societal impact	How the facility will directly affect the social fabric and well-being of the community
Capital costs	The expenses incurred on land, buildings, construction, and equipment related to the management and operation of the facility
Revenue projections	The forecasting of sales and other income sources to offset expenses and predict net profit or loss
Timelines	The listing of specific benchmarks, deadlines, and schedules related to effective and efficient management and operation

Most feasibility studies are conducted by hiring a consultant who specializes in this type of analysis. It is important that the sport facility planning committee be actively involved with the feasibility process – from the selection of the consultant through monitoring the progress of the consultant to receipt of the final report. Selecting the right consultant who connects to the project is crucial to the success of the feasibility study process, not only from a logistical standpoint but also as a result of the cost of a good in-depth study. Choosing the wrong consultant can result in having to restart the process, creating delays in the planning process and increasing costs. It is also incumbent on the sport facility planning committee to not try to influence the consultant one way or the other; the best and most truthful feasibility studies are free from bias. However, while the sport facility planning committee should not try to influence the consultant, they definitely should monitor the progress of the study to ensure that it is being conducted properly, provide relevant information regarding the needs for the sport facility, and receive and review periodic reports from the consultant to ensure efficient and effective use of time and to provide further clarity on the project.

Planning committee

Once the feasibility study is completed and a decision to move forward is made, a planning committee is convened to move the project forward. The most difficult part of putting together a planning committee is to limit the size so that work can be accomplished but ensuring that all constituencies and key stakeholders are represented. Individuals who may have a role on a planning committee include the following:

- Initial investors/entrepreneurs in the facility (the individual who most likely conducted or commissioned the program analysis and feasibility study)
- Construction company
- Consultants/experts in the design and construction of sport facilities
- Bank representatives/financiers
- Accountants
- Elected community officials/administration
- At-large community representative(s)
- Representative(s) from the organization(s) who plan to utilize the facility

The purpose of the planning committee is to shape the design of the sport facility. Its major responsibilities include advancing the development of the sport facility efficiently and systematically, establishing an information system about the sport facility, and standardizing the processes of facility use. The three initial responsibilities of the planning committee are selecting an architect, developing the master plan, and establishing the program statement.

Selecting an architect

The main responsibility of an architect is to help design a functional facility. The architect must have a full understanding of the purpose of the facility, be able to visualize the various uses of the facility, and foresee as many issues or problems with the design prior to construction. The communication process between the planning committee and the architect is crucial to the success of the facility – because if the architect does not understand the vision of the planning committee, the appropriate design cannot come to fruition.

In addition to drawing drafts and building scaled models, the architect can serve as a resource when updating site studies, securing zoning and planning approval, obtaining building permits, surveying land, groundbreaking, and any other preconstruction situations that may arise. To that end, there are three key places to look for architects. First is through the construction company that has been selected. Often, as a result of relationships built during previous projects, the construction company can recommend an architect that would fit best for the project. Another way to find an architect is to conduct research on similar facilities or projects and to collect references about the architects used. A third method is to contact the governing body for architects in your area – in the United States, it is the American Institute of Architects – to get a referral list.

The planning committee will publish a request for a proposal from architects, who will then submit their qualifications, references, examples of previous projects, and possibly even a first draft of the project. The planning committee would then review the applications, conduct reference checks, and research previous projects, select their top choices, and bring the shortlisted architects in for a full interview process and presentation. The goal during this interview is to evaluate the knowledge of the architects, assess whether they understand the vision of the planning committee, and determine whether the personalities involved seem to fit. The final determination should be made based on this interview process, the price of the bid, and the perceived quality of work expected to be produced by the successful architect.

MASTER PLAN DEVELOPMENT

After the architect is selected, the next step in the planning process is the development of the master plan, which allows the planning committee to take their vision for the sport facility and plot a path for making it a reality. The main purpose of the master plan is to break down the sport facility project into feasible segments based on numerous factors related to priorities, finances, and time. In addition, the master plan allows the planning committee to begin to contemplate the architectural design of the facility in terms of interior and exterior aesthetics – including look, feel, and appropriate fit within the landscape.

While drawings are often the end result of a master plan, the plan also seeks to answer the who, what, where, when, why, and how much of the sport facility, including:

- Site conditions and environmental/sustainability impact analyses;
- Structural, architectural, mechanical, electrical, and plumbing factors;
- Space requirements and mapping;
- Financial issues;
- Legal parameters;
- Control and management considerations; and
- Provisions for dealing with any potential errors and omissions.

In order to complete an effective master plan, there also need to be facility visits and trend analyses. Facility visits allow the planning committee to look at similar facilities to what they are designing. The function part of the visit involves a features analysis – where the planning committee evaluates the positive and negative aspects of the facilities they visit and then uses that information to incorporate the best functions into their design while avoiding the pitfalls experienced by that facility. Trend analyses also need to be conducted to determine the changes in social, economic, political, or environmental patterns that may have an effect on the design and function of the sport facility.

Once the master plan is completed, a program statement is developed to summarize the major components of the master plan. This program statement will ultimately be used to review the major components of the project, market the project to gain financial and general support for the project, and serve as a framework document for the design and construction of the sport facility. Some of the inclusions within a program statement are:

- Project goals and objectives;
- Basic assumptions about the sport facility – supported through robust research;
- Current trends affecting the planning process;
- A listing of the current and future programs to be a part of the facility;
- Initial specifications/features, space needs assessment, and space allocations;
- Facility usage plans – including auxiliary and service areas;
- Supplies needed – including items such as equipment, furniture, and other supplies; and
- Environmental and sustainability functions.

TECHNOLOGY NOW! AUTOCAD (UNITED STATES)

Regardless of the size or scope of the facility – from Olympics and World Cup venues to secondary school fields and private fitness facilities – there is a demand for quality and impressive building design to provide quality experiences for spectators. In order to create such designs, the latest computer-aided design (CAD) software is needed to shape the vision of these facilities into a visual reality – both two-dimensional (2D) and three-dimensional (3D) – and through both web and mobile technologies.

Major sport entities, ranging from internationally renowned facility design firms Populous to national governing bodies such as Sport England, have utilized AutoCAD software from Autodesk, Inc. For nearly 40 years, Autodesk has provided software solutions to help sport facility designers, engineers, and architects imagine, design, and create the best sport facilities in the world.

A primary architectural tool used is AutoCAD Architecture toolset. This program provides architectural drafting tools that allow users to map out entire facilities such as specific spaces (including walls, doors, and windows) and the size of spaces (both linear and spatial – including elevations and sectioning). It also provides the ability to create and edit drawings throughout the design process, streamlining the information exchange process between those involved with the project. This ability to share and edit designs within the software allows for faster project review cycles among members of the project team and hence shortens decision times – resulting in shorter planning and design timelines and faster movement to the construction phase of the sport facility.

Another program being used by sport facility designers is Autodesk 3ds Max Design software. This takes the visualization of the project off a flat piece of paper and gives it more life in a three-dimensional view. This, in turn, allows for more detailed modeling, animation, and renderings that can address issues that cannot be duplicated on a two-dimensional scale such as daylight access and walkthrough animations.

The use of the Autodesk software is not just a planning and design software; it also plays a crucial role in the construction process. Sport facility contractors are adopting the use of building information modeling (BIM) as part of their construction philosophy. BIM is involved in creating a digital representation of the features of a sport facility, which is then translated into scheduling and coordination efforts during the construction process to know what people and materials are needed when and where.

Source: Autodesk, Inc. (2019). Retrieved May 30, 2019, from www.autodesk.com

FACILITY DESIGN

Once the master plan and program statement have been developed and agreed upon, it is time to design the sport facility. The architect (in partnership with the planning committee) will create drawings and scaled models of the sport facility. As a part of this process, narratives will be written in support of space allotments and utilization plans, atmospheric conditions, environmental issues, and specification sheets – including the types of materials to be used in the construction of the facility.

Facility design basics

When designing a new facility, or modifying an existing one, space allocation and management is a crucial part of the process as it focuses on the planning, projection, allocation, evaluation, and use of space. The goals of effective space management are to ensure that space is appropriately and fairly distributed based on the needs assessment, provides an avenue to establish standards for allocating space, affords the opportunity to determine needs that can be consolidated into the same space to help reduce other costs (utilities, maintenance, and operations), aids with the construction process by reducing the likelihood of errors and omissions, and allows the planning committee to conduct a final evaluation to determine any shortfalls in space inventories (especially prevalent in the area of storage).

94

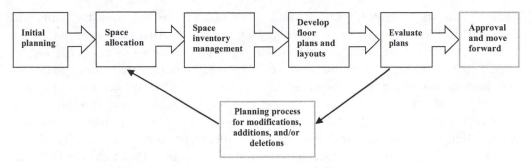

Figure 5.2 Sport facility space allocation and management process

The six-step process that serves as the foundation for the sport facility space allocation and management process is diagramed in Figure 5.2. The initial stage is the planning process, where current and future space requirements are addressed in terms of the needs assessment. Included in this planning are the amount and type of space needed; the configuration of the space including dimensions, square footage/meterage, volume, shape, and location; and space utilization in terms of specific activities, support functions, organizational control, and required adjacencies. Next is the process of allocating space – which must be justified in terms of needs, the footprint of the facility, the organization of the facility in terms of similar require-ments (for example, bathrooms and locker rooms in adjacent zones due to similar plumbing needs), and the flow of the facility (ingress/egress/movement in/around the facility). Third is space inventory management – which allows for keeping track of the types of sizes of space, an identification system for areas, an information database of key features required in specific spaces (utilities, heating, ventilation, air-conditioning, and other special needs/uses), and a diary identifying the eventual uses for spaces. Once spaces are allocated, floor plans and layouts are developed so that the previous information can be transferred from a written form into a visual form. The plans are then evaluated by all pertinent parties with two results – either a return to the planning process for modifications, additions, or deletions from the plan, or approval to move forward.

During this process, a number of considerations, both internal and external to the facility, must be taken into account. First, when spaces are allocated, errors are often made because the focus is only on the specialized spaces within the facility; therefore equal time needs to be spent on shared spaces and flexible-use/multi-purpose spaces to ensure that those needs are met as well. Second, storage space always seems to be the last item on the minds of designers/planners, so it is impor-tant to remember that appropriate storage spaces are designed into the building for equipment, maintenance, custodial, and electronics. Another area of concern is the security and management control of the facility related to the ongoing safety and operation of space. Plans must take into account appropriate ingress/egress (both general and emergency), sightlines and other observatory features for staff, and flow within the facility to ensure safe passage for users. Also important are atmospherics, as sport facility managers must direct considerable attention to the way in which its atmosphere can promote the desired relationship with clientele and the safe and enjoyable participation in specified activities. Atmospherics may include appropriate lighting, flooring/turf, sound/noise levels, temperature, and the general ambiance of the facility. Related to this are concerns related to environmental conditions that may have a direct effect on the proper operation of the facility. Examples include (1) weather and prevalent wind direction may affect how the building faces or where rooms are placed; (2) wetlands and other environmental issues may affect the placement of the footprint and ancillary areas related to the facility; and (3) surrounding communities and the effect that facilities' noise and lighting have on them. Finally, specification sheets (spec sheets) that detail the types of materials to be used in the construction of the facility, including construction materials, paints, and finishes; mechanical, electrical, plumbing, and other utility systems; doors, windows, floorings, ceilings, and wall coverings; appliances, fixtures, and electronics; and furniture and other pertinent equipment, must be completed.

NATURAL GRASS OR SYNTHETIC TURF – WHICH OPTION IS BETTER?

When planning and designing outdoor sport facilities, one of the biggest challenges is deciding whether to use natural grass or artificial turf. This is especially true in areas of drought, where issues of cost, maintenance, water consumption, load, and safety are major considerations when deciding on the type of field surface to use.

Natural grass has traditionally been the surface for sport facilities ranging from grassroots sports to elite events. However, given current climate changes and the vast drought experienced in many parts of the world, the maintenance of natural grass playing fields is becoming more challenging. In addition, in communities where there is a significant load on fields, the 'wear and tear' on natural grass fields makes it difficult to maintain a safe and aesthetically pleasing environment.

Hence, the use of artificial turf surfaces has been utilized as a solution to this problem. Artificial surfaces have been used for many sports worldwide for decades, first seen in 1966 at the Houston Astrodome and branded Astroturf. Second-generation artificial turf systems featured longer fibers and sand infills in the 1980s and 1990s. Since the late 1990s, third generation artificial surfaces made of long and more widely spread fibers of propylene or polyethylene filled with recycled rubber granules or crumbs have been used. These surfaces have proved satisfactory for some football codes and have been accepted by world sporting bodies including FIFA and UEFA (Union of European Football Associations).

Many issues need to be considered prior to the acceptance of artificial turf surfaces for a sport facility, such as the impact on the characteristics of the traditional game, injury risk to participants, benefits to the community, suitability for multisport use, financial considerations, wear and durability of the surfaces, and suitability for use throughout the year.

Some of the facts that have been argued related to the decision-making process of going with natural grass or artificial surfaces center around the concern over an increased risk of injury and illness on artificial turf, especially as related to lower limbs and heat/health effects. Additionally, the utility and maintenance of natural turf versus artificial surfaces have arguments for and against depending on how one interprets research. This extends to the all-important area of water consumption as related to drainage systems, drainage and water collection, water storage and reuse, the costs of watering, and in special cases the potential benefits and deficits to drought locations.

Suggested discussion questions

You have been commissioned to identify the critical factors that can be used to guide a local for-profit sport enterprise to make a decision on the use of artificial turf for their sport programs. At their facility, the owners plan to have six fields for multisport use (lacrosse, soccer, football, athletics/track and field) particularly at the community level but also to have the opportunity to attract a United Soccer League (USL) franchise. The fields could also be used for community events and celebrations.

1   Identify the pros and cons of natural grass versus artificial surface in consideration of the following:

    a   Installation costs
    b   Management and maintenance costs
    c   Water consumptions, collection, and storage
    d   Facility capacity load and play
    e   Societal benefits
    f   Health and safety issues

2   What would your recommendation be? (Defend your response.)

    a   Natural grass for all fields
    b   Artificial surfaces for all fields
    c   A combination of both artificial and natural surfaces (including the breakdown of how many of each and why that breakdown)

Timetables

Once these basics are confirmed, timetables are created to move the project forward effectively and efficiently. *Timetables* are usually created backward from the projected opening date of the facility to the date the timetable is created. The timetable is designed not only to keep the progress of the construction within acceptable parameters but also to provide a framework for the design and implementation of documents related to the management and operations of the sport facility – including the hiring and training of staff, publicity of the facility, and planning for the grand opening. A timetable is a living document – consulted, evaluated, and modified frequently. In general, the architect is responsible for the creation and management of the timetable – but the owners, planning committee or the architect may 'fast-track' certain parts of the project based on needs, environmental situations, or delays. While these fast-tracks may be more expensive initially, they are often needed to speed up the completion time of the facility to ensure that other problems or issues do not occur.

Site selection

As described earlier in the chapter, *site selection* is defined as the process of choosing a location for the facility – taking into account such considerations as the attractiveness of location, available acreage/hectare, natural and environmental conditions (weather, soil, grading, wetlands, forestry, rocks/minerals), ease of access, and community support. It is possible at this point in the process that a site has already been selected. If so, the planning committee will confirm if the site is appropriate for the facility designed, and determine if modifications are necessary. However, in some cases, planning committees will wait until this time to select a site based on the facility they have designed. In either scenario, an analysis of the site in terms of numerous factors needs to be conducted at this time, including internal and external access, utilities, availability of space for adequate parking, environmental issues, community and political issues, and economic issues.

Cost estimate

There are multiple purposes for creating a cost estimate ranging from determining whether the planning committee can afford the facility they want to build – to securing public and/or private financing.

The first part of the cost estimate is the building cost review. This major capital expenditure includes general construction costs for materials, personnel, and equipment; site works; fit-out (the cost of the shell without adaptations for a specific use – partitions, floors, ceilings, walls, mechanical, electrical, environmental); specific activity and ancillary area costs; car parking; contingencies; insurance; security; landscaping; and consultancy/project management fees. Another major cost is the acquisition of land. Fees over and above the purchase price include potential easements, appraisals, the purchase price, and attorney fees. Other possible fees may be related to zoning requirements, conveyancing, the filing of deeds, stamp duties, banking/mortgage loans, and environmental issues. A final major cost is for support needs in the facility including furniture, equipment, communications, and supplies.

FACILITY FOCUS: RECYCLED STADIUM CONSTRUCTION: RAS ABU ABOUD STADIUM, DOHA, QATAR

One of the most innovative and sustainable design models for sport facilities today is being constructed as part of the 2022 FIFA World Cup. In Doha, Qatar, the Ras Abu Aboud Stadium is a new 40,000-seat stadium being built on an artificial promontory. While the building of a stadium as part of a mega event is not new, the concept of using a modular design using recycled shipping containers is. The concept is to modify the shipping containers with removable seating, set them up in a building block concept around a frame, and then it can be dismantled and repurposed after the tournament, which will also allow for the development of the waterfront on the promontory for community use.

The innovation in using this type of modular design reduced the quantity of building materials needed as compared to a traditional sport venue, which in turn should reduce construction costs. From a sustainability standpoint, the ability to reuse components of the modular stadium means the impact of the utilization of the stadium will be ongoing well beyond the World Cup.

The concept of modular sport facilities has the opportunity to provide short-term impacts and sustainable long-term legacies for communities. Furthermore, these types of venues have the opportunity to become part of the mainstream in strategic event planning, with the potential for revolutionizing the sport facility design and construction industry.

For more information about the Ras Abu Aboud Stadium, go to www.sc.qa/en/stadiums/ras-abu-aboud-stadium

CONSTRUCTION

Once the design phase is completed, it is time to break ground and construct the facility (or in the case of an existing facility, start renovations). In order to initiate this process, a contractor needs to be chosen, detailed shop drawings need to be created, and groundbreaking and actual construction started – including securing necessary building permits. This section of the chapter takes you through this process.

Contractor selection process

The main responsibility of a contractor is as the main builder for the sport facility. While the overall responsibility of the project falls on the contractor, work is usually completed in coordination with subcontractors for specific tasks.

Many times a contractor will actually be a subcontractor to an architect. In many cases, this is the best scenario for a planning committee, as the contractor knows the work of the architect, and there is usually a more seamless transition through the construction process. While this may seem like the easiest and best route to take for the project, it is imperative that the planning committee carries out due diligence and conducts a thorough bid process for the contractor.

As with the architect, the planning committee will publish a request for proposal from contractors, who will then submit their qualifications, references, and examples of previous projects. The planning committee reviews the applications, conduct reference checks, researches previous projects, selects their top choices, and brings the contractors in for a full interview process. The architect should be a part of the interview process to help in evaluating the knowledge of the contractor, assessing whether the contractor understands the vision of the planning committee and in determining whether the architect and contractor can effectively work together. The final determination should be made based on this interview process, the price of the bid, and the perceived quality of work expected to be produced by the contractor. Once the contractor is selected, contracts are negotiated, and the construction process is put into action.

Creation of detailed shop drawings

One of the first responsibilities of the contractor is to create a detailed set of shop drawings from the architect's renderings. The architect needs to work closely with the contractor during this phase to ensure that all essential parts of the facility are included. The shop drawing will address all aspects of the facility including appearance, performance aspects, and governing principles. Also noted on the shop drawings are any modifications, additions, or deletions that have been made based on the recommendations of the architect and/or contractor. This information is extremely detailed to ensure that the project is totally clear and complete so the planning committee can get a full visual of what the project will eventually look like. One of the issues a planning committee must look out for with regard to these changes is that they need to ensure that the changes do not represent a compromise that gives up essential aspects addressed in the original needs assessment. In addition, the planning committee needs to be open-minded to concepts brought forth at this stage, because this is the final change to make any significant changes before ground is broken on the project. This is very important because any changes made once construction has started often will result in delays to the overall project and increased costs.

Groundbreaking and actual construction

In preparation for groundbreaking, the contractor will secure all building permits. Usually this process involves filing for a building notice with the municipality, having the site approved by the municipality (which may also involve town meetings for the community to speak on the project), plans and detailed shop drawings are evaluated and approved, zoning issues are addressed, and finally the application will be accepted and the permits issued.

The groundbreaking is an exciting time for all involved because it brings all the hard work through the planning and design process from concept to reality. As such, it is appropriate at this time to celebrate, and hence a groundbreaking ceremony should be scheduled. The first step is to select a date for the groundbreaking – one that can bring together the best audience. This audience usually includes owners, municipality officials, chamber members, and the community. Early afternoons during the week (Monday–Friday) have shown to be the best time for a groundbreaking – and also are a great time to entice the media to cover the event. Also, it is important to make sure that your groundbreaking does not conflict with other activities in the area, as you would like to maximize attendance, and that you plan for inclement weather in your planning process.

Invitations should be sent to all pertinent individuals who were integral to reaching the groundbreaking stage. This should include planning committee members, architects, contractors, business associates (bankers, consultants, and project managers), local businesses near your construction site, volunteer associations in the area, community leaders, elected officials, and the media. A master of ceremonies, or emcee, should be chosen for the event to welcome guests and introduce dignitaries. In addition, choose appropriate guest speakers for the groundbreaking – giving those individuals enough advanced notice about their participation and how long they will speak (two to three minutes is the standard).

Groundbreaking ceremonies should be between 20–30 minutes. Activities in addition to speeches that may be included during the groundbreaking would include having a plot of dirt with ceremonial shovels to enact the first dig on the site involving all pertinent dignitaries, tours of the site, exhibits of the shop drawings, music and/or entertainment, raffles, and refreshments. It is also important to have literature about the facility available for all that attend.

After the groundbreaking, there are two important steps. First is to contact all pertinent media with a summary of the groundbreaking and pictures from the event. Second is to send out thank-you notes to all speakers, sponsors, and other dignitaries. Once this has been passed, the construction process will start. During this phase of the project, it is important that there is open communication between designated planning committee members, owners, architects, and contractors. Depending on the scope of the project, it can take anywhere from 4 to 18 months to fully construct a sport facility.

PREPARATION FOR TRAINING AND MANAGEMENT OF FACILITIES

Throughout the construction process, and especially when construction is nearing completion, the focus turns to the management and operation of the sport facility. Included in this process is preparing the facility management infrastructure, attracting events to be staged in the facility, and then preparing an event management infrastructure.

The following chapters in this textbook will take you through a series of concepts that will aid in the preparation for training and the management of facilities. Each of these areas is crucial to the understanding of global sport facility management and will serve as a framework for realizing the scope of responsibilities involved in the implementation of management and operations.

- *Organizational and human resource management* (Chapter 6) – the processes involved in understanding human and organizational behavior, leadership and governance methodologies used to improve organizational performance and effectiveness within the sport facility, and the practices and procedures focused on managing sport facility personnel.
- *Financial management, budgeting, and operational decision making* (Chapter 7): The basic fiscal and economic skills that are an important part of the sport facility manager's overall portfolio of management skills leading to the efficient and effective management of facility-related costs and the knowledge necessary to improve the financial performance of a facility
- *Operations management* (Chapter 8): The general functions that are integral to the production of quality programming and services within a sport facility including operational structure, processes of continuous improvement, operations procedures for various areas, and managing associated services
- *Implementing sport facility operations management* (Chapters 9–13): Includes the relationship of multichannel marketing, communications, customer experiences, event planning and activation, legal issues, risk assessment, and security planning to sport facility operations management
- *Effectiveness of sport facility operations management* (Chapter 14 *and Epilogue* Chapter 15): Focuses on the importance of benchmarking and performance management using analytics to evaluate the efficient and effective operation and management of sport facilities leading toward providing sustainable short-term impacts and long-term legacies for society

CHAPTER REVIEW

The purpose of this chapter was to introduce the important principles of project management required for a sport facility leading to the planning, design, and construction processes – all of which are integral to the management and operation of a sport facility. Project management deals with the planning, scheduling, organizing, and controlling projects and is directly related to the processes of cost management and scheduling through a process of quality control. This requires the development of SMARTER objectives (specific/strategic, measurable, attainable/achievable, relevant/realistic, and time-bound) that lead to efficiently managing project life cycles through appropriate task analysis and sequencing reported via Gantt charts and/or the use of project management software.

The first stage in the management of any project is a preliminary planning process, which encompasses program analysis, a feasibility study, convening of a planning committee, selecting an architect, and development of the master plan and program statement. Program analysis focuses on the need for the facility in terms of the programs that are either already established or are planned to be established. The feasibility study serves to determine the likelihood that the facility concept can be transformed into a reality through the creation and evaluation of program descriptions; conducting project scope/constraint, site, needs, and impact analyses; and forecasting strategic significance, cost and revenue projections, and timelines. The planning committee is convened and represents all key constituencies and stakeholders in the facility project and will shape the design of the sport facility. A key member that will be added to the committee through a bid, interview, and selection process is the architect, who will be the key individual in designing a functional facility. Eventually, the development of the master plan and program statement serves as the blueprint to take the vision for the sport facility and make it a reality.

The second phase is the actual design of the facility. Facility basics involve implementing a space management plan, which involves ensuring space is appropriately and fairly distributed, establishes standards for allocating space (including consolidation to reduce costs), reducing the likelihood of errors and omissions, and conducting final evaluations to determine any shortfalls in space inventories. As a part of this phase, timetables are created, sites are selected, and costs are estimated.

Phase three is the actual construction process. The initial step in this process is to select a contractor through a bid, interview, and selection process. Many times, the contractor may actually be a subcontractor of the architect to have a more seamless transition from planning and design to construction. Once the contractor is selected, detailed shop drawings are then created to address all aspect of the facility including appearance, performance aspects, governing principles, modifications, additions, and deletions. Once these plans are finalized, groundbreaking is scheduled and construction is started.

The final phase is the preparation for training and management of facilities. Although much of the focus is on the actual construction process, which can take anywhere from four to 18 months to fully construct a sport facility, it is important that plans are implemented in preparation for the opening of the facility. The organizational structure of the facility must be created, human resource and operations manuals designed and implemented, financial plans and budgets evaluated and finalized, and operational management processes developed and implemented. Furthermore, projections need to be made related to how the management and operational structure will look once implemented, and a procedure for evaluating efficiency and effectiveness needs to be established. These concepts are the framework for the rest of this textbook.

IN THE FIELD . . .

With Ronnie Hurst, project director of Optus Stadium, Perth, Western Australia

Ronnie Hurst was the project director responsible for the $1.3 billion project to bring a new 60,000-seat stadium to Perth in Western Australia (WA). Previously, he was involved with Perth's bid to host matches as part of the 2018/2022 FIFA World Cup bid for Australia and was the lead negotiator for the redevelopment of NIB Stadium in Perth.

With naming rights sold to telecommunications company Optus, the venue is the home to cricket and Australian Rules football in WA and also hosts other major sporting events (international soccer, rugby) and concerts. It took nearly ten years from project inception (2008) to doors opening (2018).

According to Ronnie, '[A] project of this magnitude is a once in a career opportunity.' The consortium to build the stadium, Weststadium, started with team building activities to get to know one another and to have everyone involved in the development of a team charter. This joint leadership commitment was key to the success of the project – getting all stakeholders on the same page from the start with a 'one-team approach.' The overarching values statement that drove all decisions and communications centered on 'respect, trust, collaboration and integrity; and the principle of no surprises.' In addition, since it was a high-profile project, the importance of having all stakeholders located in the same place to ensure comradery, direct communication, and quick conflict resolutions was vital to the success of the project.

Ronnie also commented on the philosophy of 'fans first all the way through.' Ultimately, the most important stakeholders would be the users, and the largest group of users would be spectators. Hence, it was important in a project this size to have 'a reference group of fans to bounce ideas off and get their views.' Another important group is event promoters to understand the infrastructure involved and the ingress and egress needed to ensure optimal event implementation.

Source: Excerpt from L. Hambly. (2019, March). How to manage a mega project. Retrieved March 18, 2019, from https://aussieprojects.com/how-to-manage-a-mega-project

BIBLIOGRAPHY

Cressley, G. (2016). Involving stakeholders in the facility design process. *Athletic Business*, *40*(5), 146–147.

Drury-Grogan, M. L. (2014). Performance on agile teams: Relating iteration objectives and critical decisions to project management success factors. *Information and Software Technology*, *56*, 506–515. https://doi.org/10.1016/j.infsof.2013.11.003

Geraint, J., Sheard, R., & Vickery, B. (2013). *Stadia: The populous design and development guide* (5th ed.). London: Routledge.

Ming, L., Yang, Z., Jianping, Z., Zhenzhong, H., & Jiulin, L. (2009). Integration of four-dimensional computer-aided design modeling and three-dimensional animation of operations simulation for visualizing construction of the main stadium for the Beijing 2008 Olympic games. *Canadian Journal of Civil Engineering*, *36*(3), 473–479. https://doi.org/10.1139/l08-145

National Intramural-Recreational Sport Association. (2009). *Campus recreational sports facilities: Planning, design, and construction guidelines*. Champaign, IL: Human Kinetics.

Project Management Institute. (2017). *A guide to the project management body of knowledge (PMBOK)* (6th ed.). Newtown Square, PA: Project Management Institute.

Roper, K. O., & Payant, R. P. (2014). *The facility management handbook* (4th ed.). New York: Amacom Books.

Sangree, D. J. (2012). Perform market analysis with a feasibility study for indoor waterpark resorts and outdoor waterparks. *Appraisal Journal*, *80*(2), 149–156.

Schwarz, E. C., Westerbeek, H., Liu, D., Emery, P., & Turner, P. (2016). *Managing sport facilities and major events* (2nd ed.). London: Routledge.

Stice, S., & Stice, W. (2007). A good design is no accident. *Athletic Administration*, *33*(3), 18–19.

Tompkins, J. A., White, J. A., Bozer, Y. A., & Tanchoco, J. M. A. (2010). *Facilities planning* (4th ed.). Hoboken, NJ: John Wiley & Sons.

Torkildsen, G. (2010). *Leisure and recreation management* (6th ed.). London: Routledge.

Veal, A. J. (2017). *Leisure, sport and tourism: Politics, policy and planning* (4th ed.). Wallingford, Oxfordshire: CABI Publishing.

SECTION II

APPLICATION OF MANAGEMENT AND OPERATIONS PRINCIPLES FOR SPORT FACILITIES

CHAPTER 6

ORGANIZATIONAL LEADERSHIP AND HUMAN RESOURCE MANAGEMENT

CHAPTER OUTLINE

- Introduction to organizational leadership and management
- Leadership
  - Contingency theories of leadership
  - Transformational and charismatic leadership
- Organizational culture and change
  - Cultural diversity and global organizational behavior
- Managing human resources in a sport facility
  - Professional staff
  - Volunteers
  - Customers and clients
  - Individual behavior in the workforce
- The employment process
  - Job analysis and design
  - Recruiting and selecting personnel
  - Orientation, training, and development of new personnel
- Performance Management
  - Appraisal systems
  - Reward systems
  - Promotions and succession management
  - Termination processes
- Creating human resource manuals for sport facilities
- Chapter Review

CHAPTER OBJECTIVES

The purpose of this chapter is to articulate the important concepts of organizational leadership and human resource management. From an organizational perspective, the reader is introduced to the functions and roles inherent to organizational management and leadership through the lenses of behavioral and contingency leadership theories and practice. The integration of these concepts into the implementation of organizational culture and change is also be discussed. Of the utmost importance for a sport facility is the application of these concepts through interactions with the most important resource a sport facility has: human resources. Readers will gain an understanding of the growth, interest, and complexity of human resource management in sport facilities through an explanation of the various types of human resources for sport facilities, the hiring process, and employee performance management. The chapter will conclude by highlighting the critical components of a human resource manual.

INTRODUCTION TO ORGANIZATIONAL LEADERSHIP AND MANAGEMENT

The job of a facility manager is best described in terms of management functions and roles. The four major functions of management are planning, organizing, leading, and coordinating (or controlling). *Planning* involves selecting and prioritizing goals and objectives and the methods to be used to achieve desired results. There are various types of planning, for example, strategic planning, business planning, project planning, and staff planning. *Organizing* is simply identifying resources and allocating those selected resources to meet specific goals and objectives established during the planning stage. Sport facility managers may organize their staff, teams, and events, or sponsoring agencies. *Leading* entails providing direction for the sport organization and its staff and influencing staff to follow the desired direction. *Coordinating*, or controlling, activities include monitoring resources and processes to achieve goals and objectives in an efficient manner.

The most important resource for a sport facility is the human resource. Individual and group interactions in human resources are found across three categories: interpersonal roles, informational roles, and decision-making roles. *Interpersonal roles* are social in nature and include serving as a figurehead or 'face' of the sport organization. *Informational roles* include disseminating pertinent information to staff members and acting as a spokesperson to external constituencies. The facility manager also assumes a *decision-making role* that includes initiating change, resolving disputes, and conducting negotiations with internal and external entities. In all of these roles, the integration of leadership principles in combination with management principles is crucial to the successful operation of a sport facility.

LEADERSHIP

Leadership is the process of influencing followers (employees) to attain organizational goals. Leaders provide direction, generate trust, take risks, and reinforce the belief that success will be attained. Leadership traits and personal characteristics have been researched since the early 1900s. Specific traits and characteristics of effective leaders include self-confidence, trustworthiness, emotional intelligence, desire for power and achievement, and a sense of humor. A self-confident leader has the potential to instill confidence among his or her staff. Trustworthiness is critical to leadership effectiveness and is exhibited through behavioral consistency (being reliable and predictable) and integrity (telling the truth and keeping promises). Having a passion for the work and the people is an important aspect of emotional intelligence in order to inspire others about their work duties.

Studies conducted at The Ohio State University and the University of Michigan originated much of the theory underlying leadership styles. The Ohio State researchers concluded that employees conceptualized their leaders' behavior on two leadership dimensions: consideration and initiating structure. Consideration is concerned with the degree to which a leader creates an environment of warmth, friendliness, trust, and support through leader behaviors such as being friendly, being concerned about the personal welfare of employees, and informing staff of new developments. Initiating structure describes the degree to which the leader establishes a structure for staff members through activities such as assigning specific tasks, establishing procedures and protocols, scheduling workloads, and clarifying expectations. The Ohio State Leadership Studies found that employee turnover was lowest and job satisfaction highest under leaders rating high in consideration.

The University of Michigan researchers studied the differences in employee-centered and production (job)-centered leaders. *Employee-centered leaders* focus on employees by delegating decision making and creating a supportive work environment. They are concerned with employees' personal advancement, growth, and achievement. *Production-centered leaders* focus on completing tasks and closely supervise employees to ensure work is completed using stated procedures. They use coercion, rewards, and positional power to influence behavior and performance. It has been reported that most productive work teams had leaders who spend time planning, are employee centered, and not engaged in close supervision of employees.

Contingency theories of leadership

Based on the concepts inherent to the behavioral theories of leadership, researchers attempted to identify which leadership style would produce the best results. The contingency theory of leadership explains that the most effective style of leadership is dependent on factors relating to employees' and the work environment itself.

The two contingency theories of leadership that we will discuss are the Path-Goal theory of leadership and the Situational Leadership model.

The *Path-Goal* contingency theory focuses on how leaders influence employee perceptions of work goals, self-development goals, and paths to goal attainment. The model explains what effects different types of leader behavior will have on employee morale (satisfaction) and productivity (performance). The four primary types of leader behavior are directive leadership, supportive leadership, participative leadership, and achievement-oriented leadership. *Directive leadership* involves setting standards and communicating expectations to workers. *Supportive leadership* emphasizes concern for the well-being of the workers and developing mutually satisfying relationships by treating workers as equals. *Participative leadership* involves consulting with workers to solicit suggestions and including them in the decision-making process. The *achievement-oriented leader* expects workers to assume responsibility and implement the challenging goals set by the leader at a high level of performance.

Contingency variables considered in this theory are the personal characteristics of workers and the environmental pressures and demands that the worker must cope with to accomplish goals and satisfaction. Personal characteristics include a person's locus of control, experience, and ability and skill level. Environmental factors are not within the control of the worker and may include work tasks, the authority system of the organization, or the working group itself. Any of these variables can motivate or constrain the worker.

Individuals with a higher perceived level of ability to perform task demands would not be suitable for a directive style of leadership. Additionally, individuals with an internal locus of control (believe rewards are contingent on their efforts) are more satisfied with a participative style of leadership. Individuals with an external locus of control (believe rewards are beyond their control) are more satisfied with a directive leadership style.

Paul Hersey and Kenneth Blanchard developed the Situational Leadership Model (SLM) to assist leaders in selecting their leadership styles based on the readiness of employees. The SLM is based on two types of leader behavior: task behavior (similar to initiating structure) and relationship behavior (similar to consideration). The situational variable between the task and relationship behavior and leadership effectiveness is the worker's maturity level (or readiness). Readiness is defined as the ability and willingness or confidence of the worker to accomplish a specific task. Two dimensions measure worker readiness: job maturity (technical ability) and physiological maturity (level of self-confidence and self-respect). Hersey and Blanchard developed four styles of leadership styles for managers to utilize depending on the readiness level of the employee:

1   *Telling*: The leader defines roles and tells employees what, where, how, and when to perform specific tasks.

2 *Selling*: The leader provides employees with instructions and is supportive.
3 *Participating*: The leader and employees share in the decision-making process to complete a quality job.
4 *Delegating*: The leader provides little instruction, direction, or personal support to employees.

The key point to situational leadership is that, as the employee's readiness level increases, the leader should focus more on relationship behavior and less on task-oriented behavior. As an individual matures (becomes more skilled), they need less direction, although they may still need some motivation and encouragement. When an employee becomes self-sufficient, a minimum of task and relationship behavior is needed. Suppose that a sport facility manager determines that a new employee has low self-confidence and is insecure about performing job duties. The sport facility manager would exercise a 'telling' style of leadership to provide specific instructions and closely monitor performance. However, as the employee grows personally and professionally in the job role, the leadership style may be adapted to meet the individual's current needs. For employees who are considered to be self-sufficient or provide an area of expertise, the sport facility manager would exercise a delegating style of leadership.

Transformational and charismatic leadership

Leaders are continuously forced to make changes in their organizations to address the evolving and highly competitive global nature of the business world. Transformational leaders are capable of influencing major changes in the organization's objectives, strategies, culture or philosophy. Transformational leaders go beyond the routine transactional leader who is concerned with only exchanges between the leader and employee to achieve a set of goals. The transformational leader can develop new visions for the organization and inspire followers to attain these new visions. Transformational leaders exhibit several key characteristics. They have the ability to clearly communicate a positive vision of the future. They support and encourage staff development and treat employees as individuals. They provide encouragement and recognition to employees and empower their staff by fostering trust and involvement in decisions. Furthermore, they encourage innovative thinking, leading by example, and exuding charisma to inspire staff to be highly competent.

Charisma is a major contributing factor to transformational leadership. Charismatic leaders possess several key characteristics. Charismatic leaders provide vision to the organization that extends beyond organizational goals. They are effective communicators and formulate achievable dreams and vision for the future. Inspiring trust is also critical in order to get followers to share their vision and make sacrifices up front with the potential for future success. Charismatic leaders are also very energetic and action oriented, and they serve as a model for getting tasks completed on time. Additionally, they are able to manage their impression well through physical appearance.

ORGANIZATIONAL CULTURE AND CHANGE

Culture influences management and leadership styles implemented within an organization. *Organizational culture* is a system of shared values, beliefs, assumptions, and understandings that influence worker behavior. Employees sharing the same core values characterize a strong (thick) organizational culture. A weak (thin) organizational culture is one in which employees do not possess common values. Organizational culture has the potential to affect organizational effectiveness. Managers can create an appropriate organizational culture by setting a vision and getting employees excited about the fundamental purpose of the organization. Secondly, they can help develop the culture by taking action, for example, the NFL's partnership with United Way promotes to all NFL stakeholders their goal of assisting youth development and giving back to the community. Once a culture is created, it must be maintained (or changed if it is not working). Leaders pay attention to, measure, and control an organization's culture through various actions ranging from comments to rewards. In addition, how a leader handles critical incidents and organizational crises through role modeling, teaching, and coaching sets the example for the rest of the organization and directly influences its culture.

If the current culture is not appropriate then the manager is faced with the task of *changing the culture*. First, the manager must gain support for this change. Methods to gain support for change include education and communication. This allows for the discussion and negotiation of aspects involved in the change process. Participation and involvement of employees provide an opportunity to have a say in the change that affects them, also helping to increase compliance. Financial benefits of the change should be openly communicated. An increase in salary could be an advantage. The change process should not be too overwhelming at first. Avoid change overload, and try to make small changes over a period of time instead of sweeping changes overnight.

Cultural diversity and global organizational behavior

Cultural diversity in the workforce is important in today's global economy. To value diversity, one must value a wide range of cultural and individual differences. A truly diverse organization is one where all employees, regardless of cultural backgrounds, achieve their full potential. Diverse organizations have a competitive advantage potential and offer benefits in various ways. A multicultural workforce enhances the ability to reach a multicultural client base, and this marketing advantage leads to increased sales and profits. Effectively managing a diverse working group can prevent turnover and absenteeism. Furthermore, it reduces the likelihood of discrimination lawsuits, thereby reducing costs. Organizations with a history of employing and effectively managing a diverse workforce have an advantage in recruiting top talent from minority groups. Workforce heterogeneity also offers the organization a creativity advantage. Diverse groups are more likely to develop creative solutions to problems. To understand how to work well with diverse groups, one must first examine different cultural values. Table 6.1 describes various cross-cultural values.

Table 6.1 Cross-cultural values

Individualism versus collectivism
Individualistic cultures are made up of people who are concerned for their own interests first. They tend to be more concerned with their own careers than the good of the organization (for example, the United States, Canada, United Kingdom, and Australia). Collectivism is a feeling that the group or organization receives priority over individual interests (for example, Japan, Mexico, Greece, and Hong Kong).
High-power distance versus low-power distance
Power distance is the extent employees accept the idea that members of the organizations have different levels of power. In a high-power distance culture, employees willingly comply because they have a positive orientation toward authority (for example, France, Spain, Japan, Mexico, and Brazil). In a low-power distance culture, employees only accept directions when they feel the superior is correct. They do not willingly recognize a power hierarchy (for example, the United States, Ireland, Germany, and Israel).
High-uncertainty avoidance versus low-uncertainty avoidance
High-uncertainty avoidance cultures contain a majority of people who do not tolerate risk and want predictable and certain futures (for example, Japan, Italy, Argentina, and Israel). Low-uncertainty avoidance cultures contain people who are willing to take a risk and accept the unknown (for example, the United States, Canada, Australia, and Singapore).
Materialism versus concern for others
Materialism refers to the acquisition of money and material objects and a de-emphasis on caring for others (for example, Japan, Austria, and Italy). A concern of others means building personal relationships and having a concern for the welfare of all (for example, Scandinavian countries).
Long-term orientation versus short-term orientation
Employees from a long-term orientation culture believe in planning for the long term and not demanding immediate returns on investments (for example, Pacific Rim countries). Short-term orientation cultures demand immediate results and have a propensity not to save (for example, the United States and Canada).
Formality versus informality
Cultures high on formality respect traditions, rituals, and ceremonies (for example, Latin American countries). Informality cultures have a casual attitude toward tradition, social rules, and rank (for example, the United States, Canada, and Scandinavian countries).
Urgent time orientation versus casual time orientation
Some cultures perceive time as a scarce resource and are impatient; they tend to have an urgent time orientation (for example, the United States). Other cultures tend to view time as an unlimited resource and are more patient and have a casual time orientation (for example, Asians and Middle Easterners).

Source: A. J. DuBrin. (2002). *The winning edge: How to motivate, influence, & manage your company's human resources.* Cincinnati, OH: South-Western College Publishing, pp. 282–285.

Research conducted by Geert Hofstede revealed national stereotypes of management styles. German managers are technical experts who assign tasks, solve problems, and are primarily authoritarian. Japanese managers tend to rely on group consensus for decision making. French managers of major corporations are considered part of an elite class and exhibit superior and authoritarian characteristics. Dutch managers believe in quality and group problem solving and do not expect to impress employees with their status. Chinese managers often have one dominant person who is often over the age of 65, who maintains a low profile, and who makes major decisions for the organization.

MANAGING HUMAN RESOURCES IN A SPORT FACILITY

As noted earlier, the most important resource within a sport facility is the human resource. Human resource management is the function within an organization that is responsible for the recruitment, training, and retention of personnel but goes much more in depth in an effort to strategically move the organization forward toward a vision. The primary human resource categories for a sport facility include professional staff, volunteers, and clients.

Professional staff

Professional staff are the employees of a sport organization who are hired to perform specific jobs/tasks in exchange for some form of remuneration. There are usually four levels of professional staff: executive, administrative, supervisory, and general. Regardless of the level of professional staff, ultimately each is responsible for ensuring that the planning, organizing, and controlling of the sport facility is appropriately administered through proper direction and adequate staffing. However, each level has additional specific responsibilities within the organization.

The *executive level* has the most power and authority. It is made up of senior or top managers who are usually responsible for the majority of the management and operations of the overall sport facility. Typical titles of professional staff at the executive level include presidents, chief executive officers (CEOs), vice presidents of various operations, and general managers. The professional staff at the top levels are mostly responsible for the conceptual management of a sport facility.

Administrative-level professional staff, also known as middle managers, are accountable for the day-to-day operations of specific departments or operations within a sport facility. These staff members have a unique position within the organization since they connect both the upper and lower levels of management. Therefore, they must balance the leadership of lower professional staff with managing the tasks set forth by upper management. In sport facilities, these individuals are usually directors or coordinators of various departments such as marketing, facility operations, business operations, sport programs, and food and beverage services.

Supervisory level professional staff are responsible for the day-to-day operations within a specific unit in a department. These assistant or associate-level managers are responsible for ensuring that the specific tasks within their unit are completed based on the directives from their middle manager and are the connection between the specialists working in each unit. For example, within the department of sport programs, there may be assistant directors for boys/men's programs, girls/women's programs, kids programs, and camps/clinics. These managers have little authority in the grand scheme of the overall sport facility but are the ultimate authority that general staff answer to. Middle managers are accountable for the highest levels of interpersonal skills by ensuring concepts are communicated to general staff while at the same time technical issues are articulated to upper management.

General staff are the specialists within individual units who complete the tasks as assigned by the management structure within a sport facility. In other words, they are in charge of conducting the technical aspect of running a sport facility. These professional staff are specialists in their area of employment – such as coaches, custodial staff, front office staff, security, and officials.

FACILITY FOCUS: HIRING, TRAINING, AND RETENTION: MERCEDES-BENZ STADIUM, ATLANTA, GEORGIA, UNITED STATES

AMB Sports & Entertainment manages the Mercedes-Benz stadium, and according to its vice president for security Joe Coomer, one key factor to ensuring a quality fan experience and becoming an elite venue is the game day associates – parking attendants, ushers, beer vendors, concessionaires, and security staff. Coomer surveyed security staff and found the three main drivers for retention included pay, parking, and food. As a result, AMB Sports & Entertainment adjusted their security officer pay scale, making it highly competitive in the Atlanta area. This, in turn, drew the attention of new prospects, many of whom had professional careers elsewhere and who could bring those skills to their jobs at the stadium.

The State of Georgia requires 24 hours of training for security officers who serve as a baseline for incoming officers; in addition, customer service training and on-site walkthroughs are provided. On an ongoing basis, a third-party company conducts background checks on the officers. Incentives such as free parking, free food before a shift starts, and half-off stadium pricing during the event, as well as bonuses for the more hours and events you work at the stadium, are effective ways to increase morale. A quality control program is also utilized to test processes, such as the use of fake credentials. An officer who does catch a phony document gets a reward. The investment in staff is paying off as a third-party fan survey ranked the Mercedes-Benz Stadium as number 1 for security overall.

Source: C. Meyer. (2018, July). Training for better sports security: See something, say something, do something. *Security Magazine*. Retrieved May 28, 2019, from www.securitymagazine.com/articles/89185-training-for-better-sports-security-see-something-say-something-do-something

Volunteers

One of the challenges sport facilities face is appropriately staffing events and budgeting for the associated costs. Sport facility managers need to ensure that all laws and regulations are followed pertaining to the number of staff members who need to be present in various areas to ensure the safe and enjoyable experience of guests. The cost to staff the required number of people at hallmark events such as Super Bowl and World Cups or regional events such as marathons, triathlons, bike tours, and the like has led to the significant growth of volunteers working events.

A *volunteer* is a nonemployee who willingly becomes involved with an organization or event for no compensation to assist with a need that could not otherwise be offered. This definition is generic in nature, as there is truly no universally agreed upon description, and it depends on the viewpoint. Those who volunteer believe volunteerism is giving time, effort, and expertise to an organization with a need for either socially responsible or altruist reasons, whereas those who recruit volunteers look to accomplish the goals and mission of the organization by securing individuals who have the expertise to meet the need without having to put them on the payroll.

GLOBAL VOLUNTEERISM

Sports, no matter what the event, are always in need of volunteers, and hence sport facility professional staff members must recognize their importance. Volunteers are imperative to the success or failure of an event and hence to the positive or negative image of a sport facility. Sport facilities that hold events ranging from the small local recreation basketball tournament to the Olympics need volunteers to succeed. These organizations usually will consider any volunteers they can get their hands on, regardless of their professional background.

As the volunteer concept has many definitions globally, a sampling of the volunteer concepts from around the world are presented here.

Volunteering Australia

In Australia, Volunteering Australia is the national body charged with overseeing and advancing volunteerism across the country. With a mission 'to lead, strengthen, promote and celebrate volunteering in Australia' and a vision of 'a stronger, more connected and resilient Australian communities through volunteering,' they seek to offer opportunities that are 'collaborative, accessible, inclusive, innovative, flexible, proactive, transparent, and accountable' (Volunteering Australia, 2019).

Their overall values focus on the privilege of leadership and working together to provide reliable information and being an organization that the community can trust and rely on. Their strategic focus areas include national leadership and advocacy, creating informative and useful research, providing effective communication, engaging with stakeholders, and having collective viability. They seek to create formal volunteering as an activity that takes place through not-for-profit organizations or projects and is undertaken (1) to be of benefit to the community and the volunteer, (2) of the volunteer's own free will and without coercion, (3) for no financial payment, and (4) in designated volunteer positions only.

Volunteer Canada

For over 40 years, Volunteer Canada has been the peak body to increase and support civic participation and volunteerism through centers, local organizations, and national corporations. Their mission is to provide 'national leadership and expertise on volunteerism to increase the participation, quality, and diversity of volunteer experiences' through various programs, research, training, resources, and national initiatives. Their vision states that 'involved Canadians build strong and connected communities to create a vibrant Canada.'

The Canadian Code for Volunteer Involvement includes values for volunteer involvement, which are core statements on the importance and value of volunteer involvement in voluntary organizations and Canadian society. They are:

- Volunteer involvement is vital to a just and democratic society, as it fosters civic responsibility, participation, and interaction.
- Volunteer involvement strengthens communities, as it promotes change and development by identifying and responding to community needs.

- Volunteer involvement mutually benefits both the volunteer and the organization, as it increases the capacity of organizations to accomplish their goals and provides volunteers with opportunities to develop and contribute.
- Volunteer involvement is based on relationships, as it creates opportunities for voluntary organizations to accomplish its goals by engaging and involving volunteers, and it allows volunteers an opportunity to grow and give back to the community in meaningful ways through voluntary organizations.

The code also provides guiding principles for volunteer involvement, which detail the exchange between voluntary organizations and volunteers. These include:

- Volunteers have rights – hence voluntary organizations must recognize that volunteers are a vital human resource and will commit to the appropriate infrastructure to support volunteers. This includes ensuring ensure effective volunteer involvement and providing a safe and supportive environment for volunteers.
- Volunteers have responsibilities – therefore must make a commitment and are accountable to the organization. This includes volunteers acting responsibly and with integrity and respect for beneficiaries and community.

National Council for Voluntary Organisations (United Kingdom)

In 2013, Volunteering England merged with the National Council for Voluntary Organisations (NCVO) to create the largest volunteering body in the United Kingdom. The NCVO has over 14,000 member organizations focused on strengthening volunteerism and civil society ranging from small community organizations to large multinational charities. With a mission of 'helping of members make the biggest difference' and a vision of creating 'a society where we can all make a difference to the causes that we believe in,' the NCVO seeks through research, innovation, collaboration, inclusiveness, and integrity to meet the needs of civil society in the United Kingdom (National Council for Voluntary Organizations, 2019). Their overarching goal is to bring ideas and people together, develop better networks and structures, and initiate projects to support volunteering in a wide range of fields, such as health, social care, sport, and employer-supported volunteering.

Sources

National Council for Voluntary Organisations. (2019). *About us*. Retrieved January 11, 2019, from www.ncvo.org.uk/about-us

Volunteer Canada. (2014). *About us*. Retrieved January 11, 2019, from https://volunteer.ca/index.php?MenuItemID=317

Volunteering Australia. (2019). *About us*. Retrieved January 11, 2019, from www.volunteeringaustralia.org/about/

Suggested discussion topics

1   In December 2018, the United Nations General Assembly adopted a resolution encouraging volunteerism in order to advance the global body's sustainable development agenda. The resolution was sponsored by four nations – Brazil, Chile, Russia, and Japan. How has Japan integrated this into their facilities and event development strategies, plans and policies to help mobilize volunteers for the 2019 Rugby World Cup and the 2020 Summer Olympic Games?

2   What concerns should organizations and volunteers have from a legal and risk management standpoint? How would you address these concerns as a sport facility manager and as a volunteer?

Customers and clients

Customers and clients are a unique human resource for sport facilities because of the service orientation involved. These individuals are often participants and/or are involved in sport events that take place in sport facilities. Sport, in general, is in the position of producing services and consuming services simultaneously. Since the customers or clients of a sport facility provide both inputs and outputs, they must therefore be considered a human resource.

Similar to the volunteer, the customer/client as a human resource provides the opportunity for a sport facility to offer a service through the events it hosts, while at the same time lowering the expense of paid staff by having customers and clients help staff the events. Examples might include scorekeepers and secondary officials for games, completing registration and waiver forms on behalf of the facility, as greeters to give directions to other guests and customers of the sport facility, and as extra security to help control crowds.

Individual behavior in the workforce

Individual worker differences are based on personal characteristics. Workers may differ regarding demographic factors such as gender, age, socioeconomic background, education level, race, and ethnicity. Additionally, the presence of various levels of abilities and skills is directly related to job performance. It is the facility manager's job to align a person's abilities and skills to the appropriate job requirements. Job analysis is a common technique used to help a manager match the individual to a specific job. Job analysis involves identifying tasks and behaviors associated with the position, as well as the responsibilities, education, and training required to successfully perform the job's requirements. Personality characteristics play a major role in job success or failure. Many successful managers are extroverted or outgoing and are social, assertive, and active. Emotional stability also affects job performance. Positive emotional traits include being calm, enthusiastic, courteous, and friendly, all of which are necessary when dealing with facility patrons. The facility manager must be an effective planner, as well as dependable, responsible, and organized.

Perceptions of the job are significant. Employees who perceive their job to be challenging and interesting have high job satisfaction and motivation, which results in better performance. Attitudes are also determinants of job behavior. An attitude is a mental state of readiness that is learned and organized through experience. Facility managers are sometimes required to change the attitude of workers to enhance job performance. To change a worker's attitude, three factors must be considered: trust in the facility manager, the message being communicated, and the situation itself. If the manager is not trustworthy, it is highly unlikely that the employee will change his or her attitude. Likewise, if the message being communicated is not convincing, it will not be accepted. The facility manager must gain the respect of his or her staff to successfully initiate change in job behavior and performance.

The values and beliefs of employees influence job performance. In an ideal situation, the values of employees match the values of the job and organization, thereby leading to higher job performance. Typical values sought by organizations include respect, uncompromising integrity, trust, credibility, and the desire for continuous improvement. Personal ethics (individual beliefs on what constitutes right and wrong or good and bad) is another key factor for understanding individuals in organizations. The ethical behavior of organization members can have an impact on the public's perception.

THE EMPLOYMENT PROCESS

In order to most effectively hire the best and the brightest, job tasks need to be analyzed and appropriate positions designed. This also requires the quality recruitment and selection of new personnel, followed by the implementation of an orientation, training, and development program.

Job analysis and design

Job analysis is the process of examining and evaluating the specific tasks to be completed within an organization and determining the best way to design a method for completing them in the most timely and relevant way. Usually, job analysis for a sport facility requires understanding the current organizational structure, the work activities that need to be accomplished, and the knowledge and informational content present within the organization at present. Once this information is compiled, tasks are grouped, positions are determined, job titles are assigned, and organizational charts are modified as necessary. The process of designing a job description is then undertaken.

The main purpose of the job description is to articulate the job responsibilities of the position opening and the expected competencies of candidates for the position. Here is a sample job outline:

- Job title
- Commitment required
  - Usually articulated in hours per week
- Salary
  - Including rewards and incentives available over and above the salary
- Summary of the job
  - Duties and responsibilities
  - Authority and reporting structure
  - Performance standards
- Knowledge
  - Education requirements
  - Experience requirements
  - Skills and abilities desired (including qualifications)
- Contact information
- Application deadlines
- General information about the sport organization/facility
- Any required legal or governmental statements
  - Equal Employment Opportunity statements
  - Background/criminal checks (especially when working with children in sport facilities)

The job description is used to standardize the information about a specific task or group of tasks, including the essential duties of personnel working under that description. This is important in standardizing and balancing the work assignments between employees in the organization and can be effectively used to stylize the training and quality assessment programs, as well as to assure compliance with industry standards and legal responsibilities. Another major use of job descriptions is in the creation of job announcements to recruit new personnel. The job announcement also provides parameters for managers to do quality searches for employees, helps formulate questions during the interviewing process, and provides the most important information to potential job candidates.

Recruiting and selecting personnel

The recruitment and selection of personnel occur for one of two reasons: a new position has been created, or an individual has left a position because of termination, temporary leave, or job change. Regardless of the reason, the sport facility manager must engage in the recruitment and selection process, which involves submitting recruiting documents, engaging in the actual selection process, empowering a search committee, conducting interviews, carrying out reference checks, making the hiring decision, and documenting the entire process.

The recruitment and selection process starts by submitting recruiting documents, which usually includes a 'request to hire' memorandum explaining the need for the hire accompanied by an updated position description. Once approved, a job posting is created to be published in newspapers, on websites, and with job listing services.

Applications are screened to select the most qualified candidates for the position. It is important to review the position description point by point to ensure your understanding of all requirements and then develop a plan to most effectively identify and assess the candidates. As a part of the selection process, depending on the number of applicants, there may be multiple levels of assessment. For example, assume there is a pool of 100 applicants, and eight are deemed most qualified. Phone interviews may be the appropriate next step to further assess the candidates and determine the most appropriate candidates to bring in for face-to-face interviews.

TECHNOLOGY NOW! TEAMWORK ONLINE (UNITED STATES)

Finding the right employee is always a challenge. Whether it is for an internship or a full-time job, sport facility operations managers are on the lookout for the best employees to help their venue run smoothly and meet the needs of their guests.

One of the best tools online for posting positions and finding employees is TeamWork Online. Ranging from hundreds of individual facilities, to networks of facilities such as Arena Network and Delaware North Sportservice, to merchandising and food service companies such as Gameday Merchandising and Legends, and to global facility management companies, including SMG, all of these entities use TeamWork Online to find their employees and streamline their human resource process.

TeamWork Online is an online sport and live events job matchmaking engine that connects applicants with employers – and employers with the right candidates. The service provides an online job application process that networks the employment pages of their member employers. For over 15 years, Team-Work Online has provided employers with a talent management network, and the best pool of qualified candidates interested in all aspects of sports, including sport facility operations management. The daily average of open jobs is greater than 2,500 with over 1,100 organizations participating and 120,000 candidates successfully being hired. TeamWork Online goes beyond being a job posting service; it also provides face-to-face interactions through job and career fairs, and networking events with over 70 events conducted annually.

Source: TeamWork Online. (2019). Retrieved May 28, 2019, from www.teamworkonline.com

The direct supervisor who is conducting the hiring process may be the only one to assess applicant pools, but it is recommended that a search committee conduct applicant assessments. A search committee is a group of individuals who evaluate, screen, and interview individuals seeking employment. This often is a mix of direct supervisors, potential coworkers, and outside-of-the-department employees and can give additional perspectives on the selection process of employees for the sport facility.

Once the applicant pool is reduced to the final candidates, interviews take place. The purpose of an interview is to elicit information from an applicant to determine the individual's ability to perform the job. Successful interviewers learn how to ask the right kind of questions, how to keep the applicant talking about relevant information, and how to listen – because much of what is learned about applicants in an interview is based on their experiences, and past performance is a primary indicators of future performance.

When conducting interviews, there are two types of questions – nondirective and directive. *Nondirective questions* do not give the applicant any indication of the desired answer, are usually phrased in the news reporter's style of who, what, when, where, and how, and often they begin with the words 'describe' or 'explain.' Examples of nondirective questions are:

- Describe your experiences working as a scheduling manager for a sport facility?
- Explain what you consider are the most important responsibilities of a sport facility manager?
- Why does this position interest you?
- How has your background prepared you for this position?

It is also important to ask follow-up questions if the response is unclear or incomplete. Clarify and verify any piece of information by asking the candidate to explain the answer again or to elaborate on the given answer.

Directive questions are useful for drawing out specific information, as opposed to indirect questioning, where the interviewer asks, directs, or guides the applicant to specifics. Often, directive questions result in a 'Yes' or 'No' response. Examples of directive questions include:

- Do you have experience running a specific type of scheduling software?
- Are you still employed at your current job?
- Do you have certifications in pool and spa operations?

In addition to nondirective and directive questions, interviewers often develop special questions that are unique to the specific candidate either because of the individual's education or experience or as a result of a previous answer during the interview. One type of question format is using self-evaluation – where the interviewee is asked to provide personal perceptions and beliefs. Many times, this type of question focuses on asking about an applicant's likes and dislikes or strength and weaknesses.

Another type of question may be behavioral and/or experience focused. This type of question asks the applicant to describe as closely as possible the actual behavior that went on in a particular situation. The use of superlative adjectives such as most/least, best/worst, and toughest/easiest tends to stimulate specific events in the mind of the interviewee and therefore makes it easier to respond. Here is an example:

- On your resume, you noted that you were the director of scheduling at XYZ Facility. Can you share with the committee a time when you had a double-booking scenario and how you dealt with the situation?

Another method for developing special questions is by using a problem solving/judgment–type question involving a scenario that might be common on the job. An example is as follows:

- You are the facility supervisor on a Friday night when you are called to the basketball court where a person is lying on the ground under the basket unconscious. You hear from the other individuals on the court that the player went up for a dunk, got undercut by another player, and came down back and head first on the floor. How would you handle this situation?

Once all candidates have been interviewed and evaluations collected from all members of the committee, usually candidates are rank-ordered in preference of selection. At that point, the top candidate is pursued. The first step in this process is to conduct reference checks. It is important to remember that information received in an interview is biased and typically includes only what the applicant wants to share. A thorough reference check may produce additional information to help ensure that the most suitable candidate is hired. It is a way to clarify, verify, and add data to what has been learned in the interview and from other portions of the selection process. The best source of information on any candidate is a current or former employer, especially the direct supervisor if possible. On-the-job performance is the most useful predictor of future success. The supervisor can specify the quality and quantity of work, reliability, potential problem areas, and job behaviors. It is better to do phone reference checks rather than utilize written references provided by candidates – the validity of written references cannot often be verified. It is also important to contact multiple references (usually a minimum of three is a good standard) to verify that the information about the candidate is consistent.

Assuming all reference checks go well, it is time to offer the position. However, this is not the end of the recruiting and selection process. Many things can happen at this point.

- The person is offered the position and, after negotiation, accepts the position.
- The person is offered the position and, after negotiation, declines the position.
- You offer the person the position, and your offer is turned down.

If they turn down your offer, you need to start the reference check process on your next choice, and depending on the results:

- The individual is offered the position and either accepts or declines the offer.
- The individual is deemed not appropriate for the position.

Should the latter happen, the following process takes place:

- The re-review of applicants who were not offered interviews in the first round to determine whether any of them are qualified for an interview
- If so, the interview process starts again. If not, either:
  - The position is re-posted for new applicants;
  - The need within the sport facility is reevaluated to see whether current employees might be able to cover the responsibilities in-house, and hence their positions can be adjusted accordingly.

If selected for a position, a person often needs to come into the human resource office to complete paperwork. This may include:

- Contracts;
- Personal demographic data;
- Tax and work verification paperwork;

- Payroll and benefits paperwork; and
- Verification of receipt of human resource and operations manuals.

They may also need to bring in updated or additional paperwork such as updated resumes, education transcripts, and medical clearance forms. In some cases, this paperwork process is conducted in coordination with the orientation of the new employee.

Orientation, training, and development of new personnel

Orientation involves introducing new employees to the organization, *training* is the education of the employee in the job tasks, and *development* is the further education of the employee to further personal skills and value to the sport facility. Each of these processes is integral to the proper management of human resources.

New employee orientation is the first step in integrating personnel into the sport facility. Effectively orienting new employees to the sport facility and to their positions is critical to establishing successful, productive working relationships. The employee's first interactions with you should create a positive impression of the sport facility. The time you spend planning for the new person's first days and weeks on the job will greatly increase the chance for a successful start. An effective orientation program:

- Fosters an understanding of the organizational culture;
- Helps new employees make a successful adjustment to the new job;
- Helps new employees understand their role and how they fit into the total sport facility operation;
- Helps new employees achieve objectives and shortens the learning curve; and- Helps new employees develop a positive working relationship by building a foundation of knowledge about facility philosophy, mission, objectives, policies and procedures, rules and regulations, organizational structure, and vision.

Depending on the education and experience of the new employee, training may be extensive or specialized. Extensive training may be for a new employee who has little education or experience or who has shifted into a new area of responsibility. Specialized training may be for a new employee with many years of experience in the field but in need of specific knowledge particular to the sport facility. Training should be an ongoing process to help employees advance their knowledge and skills and therefore advance the operation of the sport facility. Some of this training may be in the form of development and certification programs. These may include attending seminars, trainings, conferences, or even classes offered at a local educational service or college/university.

PERFORMANCE MANAGEMENT

Performance management is the process of evaluating the past and current performance of employees. This evaluation is usually conducted by the immediate supervisor of the employee and is kept on file by the human resource coordinator. The process of performance management usually involves three ongoing stages. First is the planning of performance and development metrics, where goals are set and measurement parameters are agreed upon. Second is the managing of performance throughout the employment process, where the supervisor and the employee gauge the successful attainment of goals. The final stage is a performance review, where the supervisor (at a predetermined time – 90 days, six months, or annually) assesses progress and accomplishments to determine exceptional, acceptable, or nonacceptable performance. These performance reviews are governed by the appraisal system set forth by the individual sport facility.

Appraisal systems

Employee performance appraisals systems are crucial to the successful administration of a sport facility. It is an important tool for making decisions about employee advancement, retention, and termination; salary increases; and employee improvement. Appraisal systems usually include three basic steps: collecting data; evaluating performance based on the data; documenting the evaluation in writing. In collecting the data, immediate supervisors should assess behaviors of the employee and avoid personality issues and differences unless they impact performance. The evaluation is about the employee's performance and not their personality. Once the data is collected and evaluated, it can then be utilized to measure performance and appraise the employee's value to the sport facility.

A performance appraisal should be seen as a way to maximize performance for the employees and the overall organization in the future instead of focusing on what has happened in the past. The ultimate goal of performance appraisals is to enhance the career building of the employee and advance the operation of the sport facility. At times, this is not possible, which may result in the termination or voluntary separation of the employee from the organization. All performance appraisals should be done in writing and verbally reviewed with the employee. Employees should be given an advanced warning when the evaluation meeting will occur. A good practice is to have the employee do a self-evaluation prior to the meeting so that discussion points can be created.

Appraisal processes can be both a very exciting yet stressful time for an employee, as there is always fear that the employee's belief of their performance is not the same as the supervisor's. However, if there has been regular discussion and evaluation throughout the year, rewards have been provided upon attaining a certain level of performance, resources have been provided to the employee to succeed such as proper training and development to do the job, and clear organizational and personal goals have been articulate and agreed upon, there should be no surprises during the appraisal process. Therefore, a quality appraisal system explores the past, accurately examines the present, and creates a plan for the future – hence enhancing retention and personnel relations.

Reward systems

Reward systems are the policies and strategies of a sport facility that focuses on compensating employees in a fair, equitable, consistent, and transparent manner. There are numerous reasons for rewarding employees, including:

- The added value they create for the sport facility;
- The exhibiting of appropriate behaviors or of meeting the desired outcomes;
- The development of a performance-based organizational culture where accomplishment is rewarded;
- The motivation of people to be committed and engaged with the organization;
- The retention of high-quality employees; and
- The development of positive employment relationships.

The most basic of rewards is a financial reward, such as an increase in base salary or basic pay. Other monetary rewards may include bonuses/additional commissions, long-term incentives (such as pensions), shares in the organization, profit sharing, and other incentives such as company cars and use of company-owned property/equipment. Nonfinancial rewards may include flextime (partial days off), holidays, and memberships (such as in a country club or sport facility). One of the most significant nonfinancial rewards is earning a promotion – an important element of succession management.

Promotions and succession management

Succession management is the process of making provision for the development, replacement, and strategic application of key people over time. It is inevitable that people will retire, leave an organization, or be promoted to another position; hence, a succession plan must be in place. In some cases, succession will come from within via a promotion. In other cases, it requires hiring a new employee. Regardless, succession management requires the identification of the organization's values, mission, and strategic plans in a proactive manner that ensures continuing leadership within the sport facility by cultivating talent, preferably from within the organization, through planned development activities.

Termination processes

While the overriding goal of sport facility managers is to hire, cultivate, and retain the best employees, it is probable that a manager will have to terminate an employee at some point in time. The process starts by documenting all the reasons for terminating the employee and then setting up a meeting with that employee to discuss the following:

- Explain to the employee how and why they will be no longer working at the company. It is important to tell the truth, including such facts as the employee's poor performance, regardless of how uncomfortable it is. It is also crucial that the discussion is based solely on the performance – do not make remarks about an employee's personal character.
- Let the employee know that the decision is final and when the termination will be effective:
  - If for poor performance, normally immediately;
  - If because of a layoff; the date in the near future.
- Inform the employee what benefits are still available, if any. This may include unemployment compensation, health insurance, and severance pay. Each municipality has laws that govern how and when final pay and vacation pay are handled.
- Provide the employee with a written termination notice. If the employee does not show up for the meeting or is being terminated for failing to show up for work, send the termination notice via certified mail.
- Collect any keys, access cards, uniforms, equipment, and/or any other property that is owned by the sport facility.

With regard to the last bullet point, certain employees may have access to confidential material, such as access codes and computer files, that needs to have access denied to prior to the termination meeting. In some cases, this confidential material may go with the employee and be used against your facility during employment with a competitor or another company where their knowledge of your company may put you at a competitive disadvantage. To prevent such a problem, there are two courses of action. One is to have a company employee be with the terminated employee after the termination meeting to observe them 'cleaning out their desk' and escort them off the premises. Another course of action is to have an employee sign an agreement upon being hired (usually found in the human resource manual) that seeks to ensure the preservation, protection, and continuity of the confidential business information, trade secrets, and goodwill of the sport facility.

CREATING HUMAN RESOURCE MANUALS FOR SPORT FACILITIES

The purpose of creating a human resource manual is to have a central document that articulates accurate and current information regarding the policies and procedures of the sport facility as they relate to employees/personnel/volunteers/other associated human resources. The information provided usually includes but is not limited to employment and employee relations, benefits and compensation, general information about the sport facility, and policies/procedures of the sport facility.

A human resources manual for a sport facility usually has three sections. The first section presents the philosophy and expectations of human resources, which is a compilation of information to introduce the sport facility to the employee. This usually starts with a welcome to the employee and an articulation of the sport facility's philosophy, mission, and goals. This is followed by an explanation of the purpose of the manual – which usually focuses on the manual as an operational and reference guide for the employee. The rest of this section usually focuses on general statements deemed important by the owners of the sport facility. These statements may include general information about ethics and conduct, the pride of ownership, owner expectations, daily routines, attendance, scheduling, job descriptions, and contact information.

The policies and benefits section is the meat of the human resource manual. This section itemizes each of the human resource policies that should be understood by an individual working with or in a sport facility. The following would be a sample of the inclusions within a human resource manual:

- A general statement articulating that the human resource manual is a living document, that changes will be made as needed, and that notification will be provided within a reasonable amount of time.
- Policies whose offenses may result in sanction or termination, including equal employment opportunities, sexual harassment, and smoking/substance abuse.
- Employment policies including types of documentation needed and confidentiality and privacy statements.
- Employee compensation and work information such as anniversary dates, evaluations, workday, pay information, overtime, and gratuity allowances.
- Benefits information related to payroll deductions, insurance, retirement plans, reimbursements, and leave allowances (holiday, vacation, illness, medical, funeral, jury duty and other legal obligations, personal time, and leave of absence).
- Performance-related policies including performance reviews, merit increases, performance improvements, separations, and severance.

- General sport facility policies as related to dress code, the upkeep of facility and offices (including common areas, infrastructure, equipment, and appliances), and use of facility-issued utilities (electronic communication devices, keys, lockers, computers, phones).
- An employee agreement form that seeks to ensure the preservation, protection, and continuity of confidential business information, trade secrets, and goodwill of the sport facility. Concepts included in this agreement may include employment issues, no-solicitation obligations with respect to employees and customers, nondisclosure obligations, possession of company information and materials, the absence of conflict agreement statements, remedies should there be a breach of the agreement, and any additional miscellaneous information deemed important to the sport facility.

CHAPTER REVIEW

A key difference between managers and leaders: Managers preserve order and consistency, whereas leaders deal with change in a rapidly changing competitive environment. Four types of leader behavior are directive leadership, supportive leadership, participative leadership, and achievement-oriented leadership. Hersey and Blanchard developed four styles of leadership for managers to use depending on the maturity level of the follower: telling, selling, participating, and delegating. Organizational culture is a system of shared values, beliefs, assumptions, and understandings that influence worker behavior. Diverse organizations have a competitive advantage potential and offer benefits in various ways (e.g., a marketing advantage with a multicultural client base, lower turnover and absenteeism, reduction in the likelihood of discrimination lawsuits, and advantages in recruiting top talent from minority groups).

Human resource management is the function within a sport facility that is responsible for the recruitment, training, and retention of personnel but goes much more in depth in an effort to strategically move the organization forward toward a vision. Typically, in a sport facility, there are three types of human resources: professional staff, volunteers, and customers/clients. The hiring process includes a job analysis, job description, application and screening, interviewing, and training. Once individuals are hired and trained, it is important to assess performance through appraisal systems and reward employees (financial or nonfinancial) as appropriate. All the information about human resources is usually documented in a human resource manual. Its purpose is to have a central document that articulates accurate and current information regarding the policies and procedures of the sport facility as they relate to employees, personnel, volunteers, and other associated human resources.

IN THE FIELD . . .

With Kristin Houston, director of human resources, Tampa Bay Buccaneers, Tampa, Florida, United States

As director of human resources, Kristin Houston reports to the general counsel for the Tampa Bay Buccaneers and is responsible for a multitude of functions. The role of human resources must be in alignment with the needs of the organization. When HR professionals are aligned with the business, they are thought of as a strategic contributor to business success in terms of diversity and inclusion, employee culture, change management, organization development, employee and labor relations, and employee benefits.

She manages the recruitment efforts for the organization, including maintaining and monitoring all job vacancies, scheduling prospective candidate interviews, coordinating and implementing all aspects of the new hire process, conducting criminal background investigations, and auditing and verifying that employee forms are completed. This includes overseeing the internship program, career fairs, recruiting efforts, and learning series

She responds to and monitors all unemployment notices and potential charges, including guiding management through the hearing process prior to attending the hearing and attending hearings as required. In addition, she monitors and maintains work eligibility for all employees, while ensuring federal compliance is consistently maintained in anticipation of potential agency audits. Inclusive of these responsibilities is the maintenance of job descriptions, including assisting management with updates and creating new descriptions when vacancies occur.

Another major responsibility involves acting as the primary contact for the health and welfare benefit plans for the employees, which include addressing questions, resolving issues, providing resources, and handling benefit inquiries and complaints to ensure quick, courteous resolution. Furthermore, she coordinates with third-party benefit vendors to resolve insurance issues, conducts new hire orientation to ensure that employees complete mandatory new hire paperwork and are properly enrolled in benefit plans, and coordinates COBRA activities including eligibility to vendors and communication with employees regarding COBRA events. She also completes and maintains life insurance and long-term disability underwriting applications and related status updates, maintains updated benefits-related information on the intranet, completes monthly invoicing and billing for health and life insurance plans, conducts the annual benefits renewal process to include outside benefit comparisons, and administers the annual open enrollment period.

She also assists employees with any personnel-related issues, including coaching management and executives on best practices in adhering to local and federal employment laws. This also includes guiding management through the employee termination process in compliance with local and federal laws, including conducting termination meetings; preparing, administering and monitoring severance packages; as well as coordinating payments through payroll.

Finally, as related to performance management, she works with outside auditors to complete the annual plan audit, oversee and manage the annual tax filings for all benefit plans, ensure the timely filing of extensions and submissions with the federal government, manage federally required reporting and submission, and maintain confidential record keeping and reporting within the human resource information systems (HRIS). This also results in assisting with the annual employee handbook review and coordinating the production and distribution of revised policies and handbooks and, if needed, the development of and revisions to the organizational chart.

BIBLIOGRAPHY

Armstrong, M., & Taylor, S. (2017). *Armstrong's handbook of human resource management practice* (14th ed.). London: Kogan Page.

Case, R., & Branch, J. (2003). A study to examine the job competencies of sport facility managers. *International Sports Journal*, 7(2), 25.

Chelladurai, P., & Kerwin, S. (2017). *Human resource management in sport and recreation* (3rd ed.). Champaign, IL: Human Kinetics.

Hersey, P., Blanchard, K. H., & Johnson, D. E. (2012). *Management of organizational behavior: Utilizing human resources* (10th ed.). Englewood Cliffs, NJ: Prentice Hall.

Meng, X., & Minogue, M. (2011). Performance measurement models in facility management: A comparative study. *Facilities*, 29(11/12), 472–484.

Slack, T., & Parent, M. M. (2006). *Understanding sport organizations: The application of organization theory* (2nd ed.). Champaign, IL: Human Kinetics.

Vos, S., Breesch, D., Késenne, S., Lagae, W., Hoecke, J. V., Vanreusel, B., & Scheerder, J. (2012). The value of human resources in non-public sports providers: The importance of volunteers in non-profit sports clubs versus professionals in for-profit fitness and health clubs. *International Journal of Sport Management and Marketing*, 11(1), 3–25.

CHAPTER 7

FINANCIAL MANAGEMENT, OPERATIONAL DECISION MAKING, AND BUDGETING

CHAPTER OUTLINE

- Introduction to sport facility financial management
- Cost behavior
- A costing matrix
- Practical applications of costing
- Financial planning
  - The budgeting process
- Chapter review

CHAPTER OBJECTIVES

This chapter provides readers with an overview of why financial skills and their application to decision making are an important part of the sport facility manager's portfolio of management skills. A key skill in managing sport facilities is the ability to contribute to the budgeting process, which can be said to be an expression of the organization's business goals in financial terms. In this chapter, we examine the nature of costs and the importance of key concepts such as break-even analysis and the modeling of what-if scenarios. By using these techniques, you will be able to understand how managers use knowledge of cost behavior to inform their decision making and to derive budgets, which in turn will help in assessing how actual performance compares with projected performance. Finance has often been described as the 'language' of business. People who wish to progress their careers need to be fluent in this language *in terms of both understanding it and being able to communicate in it. By reading this chapter, we hope you have been pointed in the right direction and have the confidence to develop your financial skills further. The important point that this is a logical and systematic process that anyone can learn with the correct application.*

INTRODUCTION TO SPORT FACILITY FINANCIAL MANAGEMENT

For all sport facilities, whether they are iconic stadia played in by professional teams, municipal facilities for public use, or a local recreational rugby club field, it is essential that sound financial management underpins the overall governance of the organization. A key question to answer would be, 'Is the selling price higher than the cost?' In other words, is the organization making a profit? For nonprofit-making organizations such as members' sports clubs and municipal facilities, we can modify the question: 'Is the organization operating within the resources allocated to it?' If facilities are not profitable or do not operate within their resources, then problems will follow. In the context of our own lives, if we live beyond our means, then varying degrees of problems will occur. Initially, we may experience a cash flow problem, next we might incur interest payments we are unable to meet, and potentially we may end up declaring bankruptcy. The same analysis is applicable to sport facilities and teams that do not operate within their resources.

HIGHMARK STADIUM AND THE PITTSBURGH RIVERHOUNDS

In the second edition of this book, we told the story of the Highmark Stadium and the Pittsburgh Riverhounds. The Highmark Stadium opened in 2013 at cost of some $10.2 million with what was described at the time as 'top-notch' facilities and an excellent view of the field of play. The chief executive of the team went on record to say that by 2023 the Riverhounds would make it all the way to Major League Soccer. However, in March 2014, just days before the start of the soccer season, the companies behind the stadium and the team filed for what is known as Chapter 11 bankruptcy protection. Chapter 11 is a situation in which a failing business tries to work out a plan to return to profitability while paying back its creditors. The truth appears to be that the construction costs got out of control and were higher than expected. This, in turn, meant that even more revenue had to be generated from soccer matches and other events to service the additional loans and interest that built up.

What happened in the interim? In 2019, the Highmark Stadium is thriving, and the Hounds had a winning record in 2018 and reached the quarterfinals of the conference playoffs with average crowds of around 2,400. The stadium's pitch has the highest rating possible from FIFA (the world governing body for soccer), and local colleges and schools use it extensively for soccer, rugby union, and lacrosse. This strategy of 'sweating the asset' by allowing college and school use is a classic example of how businesses should respond positively to the challenge of income from the core product (home matches of the Hounds) being insufficient to cover operating costs. By extending the use of the facility to other users, there are now new income streams for the stadium, as well as more football that in turn can drive increased revenue on secondary spend such as catering. Should the Hounds make it all the way to Major League Soccer, the stadium is flexible enough to be adapted into an 18,000+ seater, which would be in line with League requirements.

Source: Adapted from http://pittsburgh.cbslocal.com/2014/03/27/highmark-stadium-riverhounds-owners-file-for-chapter-11-protection/

Suggested discussion questions

Try these two questions before reading the chapter in full, and then revisit them after you have read it. Are your answers any different?

1   Why is increasing the revenue streams at the Highmark Stadium a more logical strategy than cutting costs?
2   The 2018 average attendance of 2,400 is well short of maximum capacity. What strategies would you use to increase average attendance?

How many 'one-man band' gyms have you seen that have been opened by a bodybuilding enthusiast that are here today and gone tomorrow? Why do these businesses fail? The simple answer is that selling price is not higher than the cost; the business gets into financial difficulty and dies. By contrast, why do the iconic sport stadia survive? The simple answer is that they are profitable, or the selling price is higher than the cost. When profits are made, they can be reinvested in the business to improve it, to develop new products, and to keep ahead of the game.

In the remainder of the chapter, we will examine operational finance issues such as cost behavior, break-even analysis, and budgeting. Every sport facility manager dreams of the day when he or she will be involved in a new build project. The challenge of opening a new venue, the appeal of brand-new fixtures and fittings, and the smell of fresh paint and a new carpet can all be career-defining moments. The extent to which you will get to enjoy such moments may well boil down to how good your financial skills are and the extent to which you can ensure the sport facility you run is managed profitably or at least within its available resources.

COST BEHAVIOR

Everything in business life has a cost; for example, sport facilities need staff, insurance, electricity, water, marketing, and maintenance expenditure. These costs will behave in different ways depending on the courses of action (or strategies) being implemented. It is therefore essential that we know about cost behavior and can model it accordingly. A new question to consider, then, is, 'How much do I need to sell in order to break even?' To begin to answer this question, we need to know about the types of cost that exist, as well as how they behave under certain business circumstances. The most basic type of cost is the *fixed cost*, which is a form of expenditure that does not vary in the short term relative to the level of activity. A lot is going on in this definition, so we can unpack it by using an example. Consider the case of a stadium manager of a professional soccer club who earns $100,000 per year. At this stadium, there might be 20 home games per season plus any number of extra events such as exhibition matches, private hires, and conferences. Over the duration of a financial year (12 months), the salary of the manager will not change, nor will it change if there are 25 home matches or 15 home matches or any variation in the number of other events staged. Therefore, in the context of looking at the cost of the stadium manager, we can say that, over the next year, the salary of $100,000 is a fixed cost relative to the level of activity taking place.

An important learning point for facility managers is that in real life, the majority of costs you encounter will be fixed, and therefore there is a strong incentive to increase activity levels because this dilutes fixed costs over a greater level of activity and therefore creates more opportunities to generate revenue and ultimately profit. Modern stadia face the problem that there are relatively few days out of 365 when the core product is available to sell. What this means in financial terms is that a considerable amount of fixed cost is being spread over relatively few days. Managers will therefore stage other events such as concerts, boxing matches, and other sports to give themselves more opportunity to recover their fixed costs and to put a stadium's facilities to good use. Accountants have been known to use the term 'sweating your assets' to describe the process of making the assets of a business work hard to generate income and profits.

While most of the costs of operating a stadium might be fixed, we will find that in the catering and merchandising outlets within the stadium, there are numerous examples of costs that vary in line with changes in levels of activity. For example, the more hot dogs or bottles of beer we sell, the more costs we incur; these expenses are also known as the *cost of goods sold*. Similarly, in the merchandise shops, the more replica kits that are sold, the greater the cost of goods sold in buying those kits in the first place. If a case of 24 bottles of beer costs $48, then if we sell one case, the cost to us is $48, and if we sell 10 cases, the cost will be $480. Variable costs react very differently to changes in the level of activity than do fixed costs, that is, variable costs vary and fixed costs remain fixed. Understanding this point is fundamental to being able to use these principles to make operational decisions in sport facility management.

As a logical consequence of identifying fixed and variable costs, it follows that total costs are the sum of the two. We started this section by saying that those people who advance in their careers as facility managers are the people who can use their knowledge of cost behavior to maximize profits. Now that we have acquired an understanding of the nature of cost and its relationship to activity, it is time to put it all into practice by looking at how such information is used in real life.

A COSTING MATRIX

In this section, we use a series of different scenarios to model cost behavior, which in turn can be used to evaluate business decisions. We start by introducing the notion of contribution. The term *contribution* is used to describe what is left as a contribution toward fixed costs once the variable costs have been paid for. Sport stadiums are often used to stage rock concerts, and the deal between the promoter of the band and the venue might be that the band receives 70% of the revenue generated by ticket sales. If budgeted ticket sales are 50,000 and the price per ticket is $100, then we can model how this will look in financial terms as shown in Table 7.1.

Table 7.1 Costing matrix to show contribution

Quantity	Selling price	Sales	
50,000	$100.00	$5,000,000	
	Variable cost	Total variable cost	
	$70.00	$3,500,000	
	Contribution	Total contribution	C/S ratio
	$30.00	$1,500,000	30%

Assuming the concert sells out the 50,000-seat stadium at $100 per ticket, then, this will generate revenue of $5 million, of which 70% (or $3.5 million) will be paid to the band, and the remaining $1.5 million will be a contribution toward the fixed costs of the stadium. Note how contribution can be expressed in three ways:

- Contribution per unit, $30 per ticket sold;
- An absolute amount, $1.5 million (number of tickets sold × contribution per ticket); and
- A percentage, in this case 30% of the ticket price (or 30% of total sales), is a contribution toward fixed costs, which is known as the *contribution-to-sales* (C/S) *ratio*.

The stadium manager is now faced with an important question: If we can generate a contribution of $1.5 million from this event, how much money will be left over once we have paid for the fixed costs? This is a real-life application of the question, 'Is the selling price higher than the cost?' If we assume that the fixed costs for the event are $900,000, then we can complete the costing matrix as shown in Table 7.2.

As the concert generates a contribution of $1.5 million and the fixed costs are $900,000, then the event generates a net profit, or surplus, of $600,000, as shown in Table 7.2. This looks like good business at face value because, if nothing else, the selling price or revenue of $5 million is greater than the sum of the total costs of $4.4 million (variable plus fixed costs). So assuming that all other operational

Table 7.2 Complete costing matrix

Quantity	Selling price	Sales				
50,000	$100.00	$5,000,000				
	Variable cost	Total variable cost				
	$70.00	$3,500,000				
	Contribution	Total contribution		C/S ratio		
	$30.00	$1,500,000		30%		
	Fixed costs	$900,000	Break-even units	30,000	Break-even sales	$3,000,000
	Net profit	$600,000	Margin of safety units	20,000	Margin of safety	$2,000,000

issues fell into place and that the stadium was not missing out on a better opportunity, the wise decision here would be to accept the deal offered by the promoter
and to stage the concert.

At this point, good managers would realize that they had taken on a degree of risk
and would ask a couple of questions. First, 'How many sales do we need to make
in order to break even?' Second, 'How many sales can we afford to lose from our
planned level of sales to the point at which we start losing money?' The answer to
the first question can be found in 'break-even' analysis and the answer to the second
in 'margin of safety' analysis. These concepts are shown to the right-hand side of
Table 7.2 and are worthy of further explanation.

If the fundamental question of business is if the selling price higher than the
cost, then break-even analysis is concerned with the point at which the selling
price equals the cost. That is, we do not make any money, but nor do we lose any.
If we look at Table 7.2 and think about the break-even point, it should become clear
that the break-even point is the point at which total contribution equals fixed costs.
So in our concert example, at what level of sales is a contribution of $1 million
achieved? We can now use some simple logic to tackle this question. If each ticket
sold generates a contribution of $30 and to break even we need to generate $1 million, then the number of ticket sales required to achieve this is simply total fixed
costs divided by the contribution per ticket.

Breakeven = Fixed costs $900,000/Contribution per unit $30 = 30,000
Admissions

So at 30,000 admissions, the event reaches the point at which all costs are covered
but no profit is made. However, as the event is budgeting for 50,000 admissions,
we have a *margin of safety* of 20,000 admissions. That is, if we budget for 50,000
admissions, we can afford to lose 20,000 of these before we would actually lose any
money. The margin of safety is simply the difference between the planned level of
activity (50,000) and the breakeven point (30,000). However, we can also derive this
logically as we did for the breakeven point.

Margin of safety = Net profit $600,000/Contribution per unit $30 = 20,000
Admissions

This analysis enables us to bring together the cost data with the income data to produce a chart that shows all of this in one place, as shown in Figure 7.1. In Figure 7.1
the total cost line begins on the *y*-axis from the fixed costs of $900,000, and the total
revenue line starts at the origin to reflect the situation that no sales equals no revenue.
The two lines have different gradients, meaning that at some point, they will intersect,
and where the intersection occurs is the breakeven point. At all points before this,
costs are higher than revenues, and a loss is incurred. At all points after breakeven,

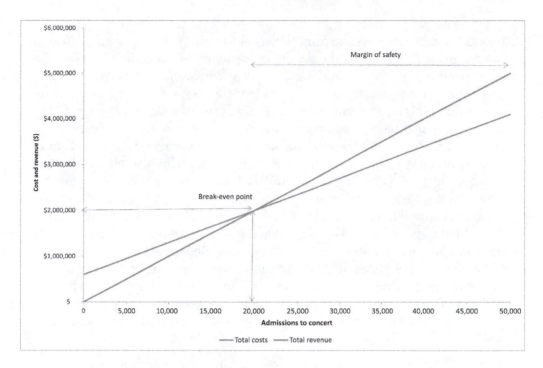

Figure 7.1 Cost, revenue, and break-even chart

revenue is higher than costs, and a profit is made. The gap between planned-for sales (50,000) and break-even sales is the margin of safety. Note how for both break-even sales and the margin of safety, we can derive an answer in both units (x-axis) and revenue (y-axis). The ability to represent data either in the form of the costing matrix (Table 7.2) or in the form of a graph (Figure 7.1) is a useful skill for facility managers in sport. More important, however, is the ability to understand what it all means and to use it to support sensible decision making.

TECHNOLOGY NOW! SIVTICKETS.COM (UNITED KINGDOM)

The city of Sheffield in England is home to the largest complex of sporting and theater facilities outside of the capital, London. Sheffield International Venues Ltd (SIV) has established SIVTickets.com, which is an online system that integrates ticket sales data across different venues and different organizations. The system has helped to reduce the costs of administrating ticket sales because with the option to print your ticket at home or have an e-ticket on your phone, there is no longer any need to print tickets or to send them out by mail. Tickets that are printed at home and e-tickets are scanned by barcode readers at the venues and provide access in the same way as conventional tickets.

For senior managers, the system gives real-time access to how many tickets have been sold and how much revenue has been generated. Revenue is the most important financial measure in this context because the managers know what their costs are, and therefore the key piece of missing information is how much revenue will be contributed toward the costs. This knowledge enables managers to take timely action to control their business. For example, if a show is not selling as well as anticipated, it is possible to communicate with known ticket purchasers who have a history of attending similar events and to make them a special offer. This type of business control is a practical example of the key business question, 'Is the selling price higher than the cost?' Clearly, it is unsustainable to put on sporting and theatrical events unless the cost of buying in and staging the shows is worthwhile. Where technology has helped in this goal is to reduce barriers to accessing tickets, stripping out costs in the booking process, and providing managers with real-time information that enables them to take corrective action where possible.

Source: Sheffield International Venues. (2019). Retrieved March 23, 2019, from https://buy.sivtickets.com/Online/default.asp

PRACTICAL APPLICATIONS OF COSTING

Business is often unpredictable, and often reality turns out differently from what was planned. The difference between the proactive manager and the reactive manager is the skill to use information wisely in the way in which you run your business. As a result of the difference between planned and actual outcomes, an important skill for managers is being able to model what-if scenarios. We know in our concert example that we can sell out a 50,000-seat stadium if the tickets are $100 each. What if we increased the prices to $120 and sacrificed 10,000 sales so that the attendance was 40,000? Would this be a good decision in financial terms? To answer the question, we can adapt the costing matrix in Table 7.2 to show the outcome of the two different scenarios on our bottom line (net profit) in Table 7.3.

The idea of charging higher prices in return for a lower audience does not work in purely financial terms as shown by the reduction in net profit of $60,000 ($600,000 – $540,000). The first clue that this is not a good idea can be seen by the fact that it delivers a lower contribution than selling 50,000 tickets at the lower price of $100. Lower contribution equals lower profit because the fixed costs remain the same.

Table 7.3 What-if scenario

Quantity	Selling price	Sales					
50,000	$100.00	$5,000,000					
40,000	$120.00	$4,800,000					
	Variable cost	Total variable cost					
	$70.00	$3,500,000					
	$84.00	$3,360,000					
	Contribution	Total contribution		C/S ratio			
	$30.00	$1,500,000		30%			
	$36.00	$1,440,000		30%			
	Fixed costs	$900,000	Break-even units	30,000	Break-even sales	$3,000,000	
		$900,000		25,000		$3,000,000	
	Net profit	$600,000	Margin of safety units	20,000	Margin of safety	$2,000,000	
		$540,000		15,000		$1,800,000	

The only positive is that it would reduce the number of sales required to breakeven from 30,000 to 25,000. Other considerations also need to be taken into account that requires managerial judgment. By having 10,000 fewer admissions, it might be possible to save a bit of money on staffing levels, but at the same time, there are negatives. First, if there are 10,000 fewer spectators, then there are 10,000 fewer people to pay for car parking, food, drinks, programs, and merchandise, which may be a huge missed opportunity in terms of secondary spending at the event. Second, fewer people in the audience may mean less of an 'atmosphere,' which has the effect of reducing the quality of the experience for those who are there, particularly the people near the empty seats. Third, empty seats do not look good, especially if an event is being broadcast beyond the venue. Managers need to evaluate all of the influences that affect an event to implement a strategy that gives the optimum outcome. In this context, an optimum outcome is achieving financial objectives, giving customers a good experience so they will come back again, and delivering an event that looks good. Using techniques like the costing matrix and a what-if scenario then provides managers with the tools to be able to make decisions supported by information rather than relying solely on guesswork or intuition to deliver the optimum outcome.

A useful application of what-if analysis is *sensitivity analysis*, whereby managers model how sensitive their cost assumptions are to changes in some of the key variables in the costing matrix. For example, the promoter of the concert in our stadium example comes back to us and says that the finances will not work unless he is guaranteed $77 per seat instead of $70. This is an increase in the variable costs of 10%, which will therefore lead to a reduction in contribution and a reduction in profit. At this point, the question that the good manager would ask is, 'How sensitive is my bottom line to an increase in variable costs of $7 per seat?' Using the costing matrix, we can model this easily, as shown in Table 7.4.

The effect of a $7 (or 10%) increase in variable costs has a dramatic effect on the net profit of the concert, which as a result falls from $600,000 to $250,000 – a reduction of 58%. Aware of this sensitivity between increases in variable cost and reduced profit, the proactive manager now has the information readily available to negotiate hard that this is not an attractive proposition and should be resisted strongly. In addition to delivering an inferior financial outcome relative to the original deal, it also means that the venue bears an increased level of risk as

Table 7.4 Sensitivity analysis

Quantity	Selling price	Sales					
50,000	$100.00	$5,000,000					
50,000	$100.00	$5,000,000					
	Variable cost	Total variable cost					
	$70.00	$3,500,000					
	$77.00	$3,850,000					
	Contribution	Total contribution		C/S ratio			
	$30.00	$1,500,000		30%			
	$23.00	$1,150,000		23%			
	Fixed costs	$900,000	Break-even units	30,000	Break-even sales	$3,000,000
		$900,000		39,130		$3,913,000
	Net profit	$600,000	Margin of safety units	20,000	Margin of safety	$2,000,000
		$250,000		10,870		$1,087,000

demonstrated by the break-even point rising from 30,000 to 39,130 sales and the margin of safety falling from 20,000 sales to 10,870 sales. These are much better arguments to counter the promoter with than simply saying 'No' or shouting and becoming aggressive.

Unfortunately, not all events sell out, and in the case of facilities such as swimming pools and gyms, it is unlikely that operating at 100% capacity is feasible or realistic. Therefore, this means that once unsold capacity is lost, it is lost forever and cannot be recovered. To counter this problem of the perishable nature of services such as sport spectating and sport participation, managers can use their knowledge of costing to make additional sales. If we continue the example of the 50,000-seat stadium, imagine that it is staging a football match and that two days before kick-off, several thousand seats, which normally sell for $80, are unsold. As the venue manager, you are faced with a choice. You can leave the seats to see whether there any walk-ups on the day, or you can show some initiative and try to recover some revenue from them. For example, assume that at the time of the match there was a conference in town with 2,000 delegates. It would be a good strategy to contact the conference organizers and offer to cut them a deal. We know that our cost base is fixed and will not change. We also know that under these conditions any extra contribution equals extra profit. Assuming we cannot sell the tickets anywhere else, we could say to the conference organizer as a special offer we can let you have 1,000 tickets at say $50 instead of $80. This would generate a further $50,000 in revenue, it would help with secondary sales, and it would reduce the number of visibly empty seats. So faced with taking a risk on trying to get $80,000 for 1,000 seats and possibly getting nothing or reducing your risk by going for $50,000, what would you do? Much would depend on your attitude to risk and the financial targets that have been set. Nevertheless, in a business like sport facility management where the majority of costs are fixed, then some contribution is better than no contribution. Therefore, there is a place for special deals and discounts so long as they make a positive contribution to the bottom line. However, steps such as these group discounts should be used sparingly because there is the danger that you end up devaluing the product, and your regular customers, who were previously prepared to pay your original prices, might start to demand discounts as well. These are the techniques to be used in the push for full capacity beyond the way you go about selling tickets from the outset.

One of the most important applications of knowing about costs and cost behavior is setting prices. This is one of the defining skills of a true manager compared with operational staff. If you were the manager of a swimming pool, how would you go about setting the price of admission to the pool? In practice, there is a variety of methods, but the ones most likely to succeed are those that are at least in part based on knowledge of cost and cost behavior. There are in practice three main methods by which prices for activities can be set. The first is *cost-based pricing*, whereby the costs of providing a service are analyzed and managers work back from these to arrive at the desired outcome such as break-even or a specified level of profit. The second is known as *copycat pricing*, whereby managers simply copy the prices being charged by comparable facilities. The third is *market-based pricing*, which takes into account what the market will bear for a service rather than basing prices on the costs of provision. All of these methods have their strengths and weaknesses; however, the confident manager will realize that the methods are not mutually exclusive and that, by using some or all of them simultaneously, it is possible to make pricing decisions that are informed by a broad rather than a narrow range of influences.

Table 7.5 represents the budgeted costs for a community swimming pool for which the financial objective is to break even. The facility will be open for 50 weeks of the year and will generate 1,000 admissions per week. Given the cost base, what should the price per swim be?

If the throughput to the swimming pool is 50,000 admissions per year and the running costs are $500,000, it follows that in order to break even, the cost per swim must be $500,000/50,000 admissions, which equates to $10 per swim. This, if you like, is the *cost of production* of one swim. However, there is no guarantee that people will be prepared to pay $10 to use a municipal swimming pool because it may be perceived as being a price that is too high. As a test of reasonableness, then, the manager might visit other pools either in person or via their websites to assess what comparable facilities are charging. If they are charging less, it may well be because their cost base is lower and that to be competitive, our manager needs to find some economies. It may also be the case that $10 is relatively cheap for the locality and that there is room to increase prices. Hopefully, it is at least implicit that simply copying the prices of another facility is not a good strategy for the proactive facility manager. The reasons for this view are as follows: First, we do not know the cost base of rival facilities; second, we do not know the financial outcomes required of our rivals; and, third, we ignore considerations such as what the market will

Table 7.5 Swimming pool annual running costs

Expenditure	
Staff costs	$ 275,000
Premises	$ 125,000
Energy	$ 75,000
Water	$ 25,000
Total expenditure	$ 500,000
Required profit	—

bear. The third method of pricing, 'What the market will bear,' is perhaps the most sophisticated and therefore reliable basis from which to work. We can find out in general terms what the market will bear by looking at rival facilities, which might give us some ballpark figures that the price of most swims is somewhere between, say, $5 and $15. However, what is the right price for a specific facility? This is often achieved via market research, whereby the developers of a new facility will interview people and take the opportunity to explain the facility to them. An example of a question, 'Would you use this facility?' If the response is yes, the follow-up questions are, 'How often would you use it?' and 'What price would you be willing to pay to use it?' If this type of market research is done properly and with a sufficient sample, it is possible to generalize that from a population of, say, 500,000 people, we might be able to generate 50,000 swims per year at an average price of $10. If we achieve this, then we will break even and thereby achieve a situation whereby the selling price is at least equal to the cost.

It is important to realize that when we produce models of cost behavior and build up what-if scenarios, we are using these tools as decision support systems, not as decision-making systems. Take, for example, the case of a swimming pool, for which the costs are essentially fixed for a given level of output, namely opening hours. If the pool is open for 40 hours per week, what would be the cost of opening it for an extra hour so that a triathlon club could have exclusive use of the facility one evening? The premises, water, and energy costs would not change, but there would be an increase in staff costs to cover the extra hour. If we said that an extra hour of staff costs and any other variable costs were $20, what would we charge the triathlon club? We could charge $20 and in so doing would put the facility in a position whereby it incurs no additional cost or makes no extra profit, that is, it breaks even. Intuitively, you should be able to realize that charging the marginal cost of an extra hour of swimming is missing a commercial opportunity. We know that the market will bear $10 per swim, and if 20 members use the exclusive club time, we could generate up to $200. This might be too much for the club, but it would certainly be possible to agree on a price at around $100 to $150 for the extra hour, which would show the club that they were getting the pool at a cheaper price than usual and also make more than the extra costs incurred for the swimming pool. This sort of thinking forms the art of operational decision making to go alongside the science that underpins decision support systems. Art and science go hand in hand when managing facilities. We can acquire the science from books such as this, but the art comes from experience, gut reaction, and instinct. Used in tandem, art and science are more powerful than relying on art only or science only.

Having looked at the nature of cost and cost behavior in the context of modeling the finances of specific scenarios such as staging a concert, varying the price of tickets, and the impacts of changes in variable cost, we move on to look at setting the budget for the entirety of a business.

FINANCIAL PLANNING

For managers of sport facilities, the most likely way in which you will experience the pressures of financial management is through the process of compiling and being held accountable to the budget. Businesses do not lurch from year to year and hope that their finances show a favorable outcome. Facilities that are managed well are continually monitoring their financial performance on an ongoing basis. Questions we need to answer include:

- How many admissions did we achieve today?
- How does this compare with the target?
- How much did we sell to our customers when they were on site?
- How does this compare with the target?
- How many staff hours did we use?
- How did this compare with the target?

Financial performance needs to be managed so that you achieve what you set out to achieve. In this regard, the budget can be said to be the objectives of an organization expressed in financial terms.

You will discover if you work in sport facility management that one of the key differences between a routine job and a long-term career is that people who have careers also have responsibility for budgets and are successful in achieving them. In the remainder of this section, we will look at the budgeting process, the format for an operating budget, and how budgets can be used to monitor performance.

The budgeting process

The most frequently used budgeting process is *continuation budgeting*, which refers to situations in which the business objectives of an organization continue from one financial period to the next. Under these conditions, it is sensible to continue with the same approach to budgeting. An example of a continuation budget might be a health and fitness club whose main aim is to make a profit for the owners of the business who will pursue the same approach to running their business as they have in the past. If the club's basic operations led to a situation whereby the selling price is higher than the cost, then besides increasing the number of members of the club or how much they are charged for their memberships, there is no point wasting time and resources on a more complicated approach to the club's finances.

An important point about budgeting, when it is done well, is that it is an ongoing process rather than a one-off event. The actual mechanics of collating the numbers involved in a budget are a small part of the overall budgeting process. By bearing in mind that budgeting is designed to help an organization with planning, decision making, and control, it is possible to appreciate that budgeting is a continuous part

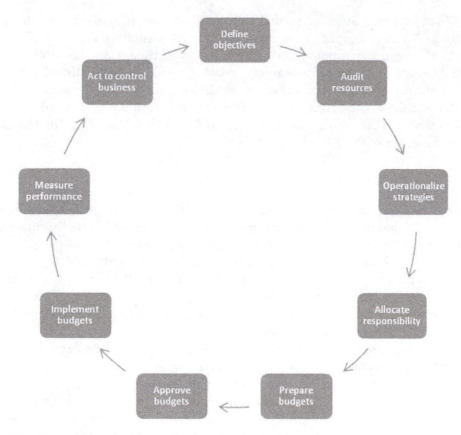

Figure 7.2 *Budgets as steps in a logically sequenced planning process*

of business life. This point can be reinforced by viewing budgeting as steps in a logically sequenced planning process as shown in Figure 7.2, with each stage discussed in turn afterward.

Define objectives

The first question to ask when involved with any financial business planning is, 'In monetary terms, what are we trying to achieve?' This question should provide a clue that most sane businesspeople would not answer by saying 'Making a loss.' Losses are made in business, but it is inconceivable to imagine that managers set out deliberately to lose money. Losses normally occur when there is a mismatch between what was planned and what happened in reality. Organizational objectives will vary according to the nature of the business. A community sports club that exists for the benefit of the members may desire nothing more than to break even or to make a small surplus to maintain its existing facilities. A more complex organization such as Manchester United needs to balance the requirements of producing a successful team on the pitch (utility maximization) with the requirements of being a stock market–listed company with multimillion-dollar commitments to the providers of funds such as banks and shareholders. The banks want the interest on their loans to be paid securely, and the shareholders want a share of the profits in the form of dividends and a rise in the value of their holdings.

Audit resources

The audit of resources is a reality check on objectives. Its purpose is to ensure that the objectives and the resources required to achieve them are internally consistent. As an example, Sheffield United Football Club needs around 15,000 spectators per home match to break even. With a stadium capacity of nearly 31,000, it is clear that 15,000 people can be accommodated at a home match so long as they can be attracted to the match in the first place. The term 'resources' should be used in the widest sense to include personnel and the skills required to ensure that those running the business are 'fit for purpose.'

When there is a discrepancy between the objectives and the resources available to achieve them, two courses of action are possible. One course of action is to change the objectives so that they are compatible with the resources. The other course of action is to identify the gap between the resources available and the resources required to form the basis for prioritizing capital investment such as increasing the capacity of a stadium or identifying training and development needs to ensure that staff has the skills to deliver what is required of them.

Operationalize strategies

Having defined objectives and confirmed that you have the resources to deliver them, the model proceeds to consider the day-to-day actions to be used to deliver the required performance. In a health and fitness club, these might include marketing plans, pricing policies, customer care protocols, and hours of business. If organizational objectives can be regarded as 'what' we wish to achieve, then operational strategies can be regarded as 'how' we plan to achieve the objectives. For example, a swimming pool manager aiming to achieve a turnover of $1 million per annum from an annual throughput of 100,000 admissions needs to think carefully about how to convert every click on the turnstile into an average of $10 in the cash till. This will probably be via a combination of parking fees, admission costs, secondary spend on food and drink, locker hire, use of drying machines, and the sale of items such as goggles and armbands.

FACILITY FOCUS: INCREASING INCOME VIA FACILITY HIRE: HATHERSAGE SWIMMING POOL, UNITED KINGDOM

Hathersage Swimming Pool is an open-air swimming pool located in the Peak District National Park. It ranks as one of the most beautiful settings for a swim anywhere in the UK. Business hours are seasonal with a low season from March until May and a high season from June until September. As an innovative approach to generating extra income in the high season, the pool is available for private hire for 90 minutes at a time in three time slots:

- Friday: 18:00–19:30
- Saturday: 17:00–18:30
- Sunday: 17:00–18:30

For a cost of £225, hirers can have lane swimming, fun floats, or, for an additional £25, the Challenger Aqua Run, which is a large inflatable assault course. Availability of the slots is maintained in real time on the website. The relevance of enabling the facility to be hired is that it is a relatively risk-free approach to increasing revenue. The risk is in effect transferred to the hirer, and the pool management knows that if the pool is hired, they will receive £225 to £250, and if it is not, they will not lose anything. From the hire fee, the only additional cost to the pool is the marginal cost of staff time to keep it open for the extra 90 minutes, and the vast majority of the income received will be a contribution toward fixed costs. This example is a classic demonstration of how a facility with predominantly fixed costs should take advantage of the opportunity to increase revenue. Perhaps not surprisingly, Hathersage Swimming Pool is particularly popular with groups such as Scouts and Guides, who often camp nearby and then have exclusive use of Hathersage Swimming Pool as one of the highlights of their day. Not only is the location beautiful, but the business model is too!

Source: Retrieved May 28, 2019, from www.hathersageswimmingpool.co.uk/

Allocate responsibility

The successful delivery of financial objectives does not happen by accident or as the result of simply compiling a spreadsheet. Facility management in sport is primarily a service industry, and the key people who determine the extent to which objectives are delivered are the facility's staff. So that people can see where their efforts and talents fit into a business's overall plan, it is good practice for staff to have an understanding of their responsibilities for their particular areas of work. Agreed responsibility is particularly important in situations where staff can be rewarded or indeed sanctioned based on their performance. For example, basic performance for a fitness consultant in a health club might be 20 new peak time members per month, with financial incentives on offer if the agreed-on target is exceeded. If who is going to do what and by when is known and clearly stated, then there is the basis for a meaningful comparison of actual performance compared with planned (or expected) performance. It is important to note that budgeting does not occur in a vacuum and that it has a human dimension as well. Everyone involved in delivering the budget needs to own his or her share of it and be willing to be held accountable for it. The art of good management is the ability to motivate your staff to take ownership of the budget and accountability for it.

Prepare budgets

It is worth noting that the actual preparation of budgets, that is, the 'mechanics,' does not occur until the midpoint of the budgeting model just shown. This is important because it makes the point that budgeting is not some isolated or abstract process but is actually integral to the way an organization approaches business planning. When preparing a budget, there are two important considerations to address, namely how much income or expenditure will there be, and when will the expected income or expenditure occur? To illustrate the point, if a swimming pool is expecting 100,000 admissions per year at an average admission price of $7.50, then the answer to how much income will be generated is $750,000. However, it is unlikely that a pool will average nearly 2,000 admissions per week for 52 weeks of the year. There will be peak times such as during school holidays and off-peak times such as during the winter when it is cold. Hence, to make sure that the appropriate level of a resource such as staff is in the right place and at the right time, it is necessary to plan the predicted level of activity on a week-by-week or month-by-month basis. Conducting such an exercise enables managers to plan for situations where expenditure may be greater than income and there is insufficient cash to meet the shortfall. Having identified situations requiring management action, strategies can be put in place to deal with them such as negotiating an overdraft facility at the bank, rescheduling capital expenditure, or imposing an expenditure embargo on nonessential revenue items. The important point of note is that the process of budgeting identifies potential problems in advance so that appropriate action can be taken to avoid them or to mitigate their consequences.

It is more likely to be good fortune rather than good planning that the first draft of the budget will deliver the financial outcomes required. As a result, managers may need to revise their budgets so that the desired outcomes are achieved. In practice, a budget can be revised in five ways. The first is to increase revenue while keeping costs constant, for example by increasing prices, increasing throughput, or a combination of the two methods. Note the assumptions underpinning the thinking here. In the case of deciding to increase prices to balance the budget, there is the assumption that the market will bear such an increase and that revenue will increase despite the likelihood that some people may either stop participating or take their business elsewhere.

A second method is to decrease expenditures while keeping income constant, for example by making savings on expenditures or reducing the amount of the service on offer (e.g., reducing operating hours). Remember, though, that the majority of costs in sport facility management are fixed. Thus if you run a 'tight ship' and there are no obvious excessive or wasteful expenditures, then the most logical course of action to improve financial performance is to increase income.

A third way is to increase income while decreasing costs, as the first two options are not mutually exclusive. Alternatively, a fourth method would be to alter the financial outcome required. It may be that it is not possible to bring the required outcomes and the budget into line by using any of the three methods previously discussed. Rather than altering income and expenditure, management may decide to alter the financial outcome required. This approach can work both positively and negatively. If staff provide managers with a budget that exceeds the required bottom line and the assumptions underpinning the budget are correct, then it would make sense to increase the overall budget target accordingly. Alternatively, imagine that the targeted outcome cannot be met by revisions to income and expenditure as a competitor has recently opened a new facility nearby and is poaching some of your customers. Under these conditions, managers might agree to settle for a reduced financial outcome, for example, an annual profit of $0.45 million rather than $0.50 million, which in turn would require a reworking of the budget.

A final method is to alter the overall business objectives. It may be the case that it is impossible to arrive at an acceptable solution to a budget using any of the methods previously discussed. Under these conditions, it may be that the required outcomes and the organization's capabilities are not compatible. The only remaining alternative is to change the organization's objectives. As an example, it is often the case that municipal sport facilities are required to meet social as well as financial objectives. On occasion, the pursuit of these differing aims may be incompatible in the sense that programming activities for target groups prevent revenue maximization. Every use of a resource has an opportunity cost, that is, the price of the best alternative foregone. In order to make the budget balance, it may be that some of the desired priorities have to be sacrificed to protect more important business interests.

The relevance of preparing a budget, comparing it with business objectives, and taking corrective action where appropriate indicates the importance of achieving so-called internal consistency. If potential problems can be identified at the planning stage, appropriate action can be taken by devising strategies to deal with adverse circumstances. This type of approach has a far greater chance of success and is more desirable than trying to deal with situations reactively as they occur without warning.

Approve budgets

When an acceptable balance has been achieved between an organization's business objectives and the subsequent financial consequences, then the preparation of budgets is complete. From this point, the budget should be approved formally. It is recognized good practice for the approval of a budget to be formalized in the official records of a business such as the minutes of a board or committee meeting. In an ideal world, budgets should be approved in advance of the financial period to which they relate. This process ensures that those who have compiled the budget and those whose performance will be judged by it have a clear picture of their responsibilities. This clarity has two benefits. First, if you know what is expected of you, then the evaluation of your performance can be based on facts rather than on personal opinions. Second, expectation creates accountability, which provides managers with the focus to concentrate their efforts on those things that are important to meet the key business objectives.

Implement budgets

Once a budget has been approved, it can be implemented with effect from the date to which it applies. For example, if an organization's fiscal year operates from April 1 to March 31, then it would be a reasonable expectation for the budget to be approved at least a month before the start of the new financial year. A less than ideal situation is an organization entering a new fiscal year without an approved budget, as this would in effect be an admission that the business had no financial direction.

Measure performance

To reinforce the point that budgeting is integral to overall business planning, it is important to realize that the budgeting process does not end once the process of getting a budget to the implementation phase is complete. Once a budget is operational, it is good practice that periodically, a check is made between how the business is actually performing compared with how it planned to perform. For operational issues such as admissions and staff hours used, there might be a daily or weekly check, whereas for overall business performance, monthly and quarterly checks are the conventional norms. Measurement of performance is not an end in itself and is valuable only if it is used to add value to the process of management of a business by being the basis for subsequent action where necessary.

Act to control business

Decision making should be made based on the best information available to help those making the decisions. It is rare that there will be a perfect match between budget and actual comparisons, so the first decision to make is whether variances are within a tolerable range. If variances are tolerable, then major changes in policy are not necessary. By contrast, if variances are considered to be so large that proactive management action is needed, then this is when good managers show their worth. Of course, variances can be positive, such as when a business is considerably ahead of its target. The only management action required here might be to continue with the same policies and to revise targets upward. By contrast, if actual figures compared with budgeted figures reveal a significant shortfall in performance, then more proactive corrective action may be needed. Such action might include extra marketing efforts to increase sales, reducing prices to stimulate sales, or reducing costs in an attempt to maintain profit margins.

In concluding this section, it is worth reiterating two key points about budgeting being a logically sequenced planning process. The first is that budgeting is a process designed to help managers make sensible decisions about running and controlling their businesses. The ability to contribute fully to the budgeting process and to be held accountable for it is one of the key differences between managers and the staff they manage. The second point is that compiling a budget is an iterative process. It is unlikely that the first draft of a budget will produce an acceptable result. Various scenarios will be modeled and differing assumptions will be tested until an acceptable solution is found. The basic point is that each step of the model is a reality check on the previous step. The end game is to ensure that an organization's overall plans and the financial consequences of those plans are internally consistent.

CHAPTER REVIEW

In this chapter, we have examined some of the skills that managers working at higher levels of responsibility within a sport facility are faced with as integral parts of their job. Lifeguards in a swimming pool ensure public safety, but they do not set the prices of swims or venue hire. Staff who work in the concession stands of a stadium sell hot dogs and beer but do not negotiate the price at which these are purchased and sold. This type of operational pricing decision is the domain of the manager and requires some specific skills. The first of these skills is to know about the nature of costs and the way in which costs behave in response to changes in levels of output. A feature of sport facilities is that, regardless of the type of facility, the majority of costs are fixed for any given level of output. This means that the only logical strategy to pursue is income generation to make sure that we are pulling in enough money to contribute toward fixed costs. To help make sensible decisions, managers should use decision support systems such as the costing matrix to quantify the cost behavior of their business. A very important skill set to have is the ability to use a spreadsheet to create costing models that are specific to a given set of circumstances. From here, it then becomes possible to model what-if scenarios and to conduct sensitivity analyses. These sorts of methods give managers an idea of what is important when certain assumptions are modeled. As an absolute minimum, we need to be clear about what our breakeven position is and the extent (if any) of our margin of safety. Our models and spreadsheets are only as good as the data that drives them.

Finance or finance professionals who seem to wield a disproportionate amount of power in some businesses should not intimidate aspiring managers. The vast majority of finance is little more than addition, subtraction, multiplication, and division plus the ability to use spreadsheets (which, of course, will do all of the number crunching for you). Furthermore, finance is intuitively logical. Once you understand the logic, there will be no more smoke and mirrors to confuse you. What this chapter has shown is that even for simple day-to-day operations, finance and financial skills are an important part of the knowledge base of a sport facility manager. Each scenario you face as a manager has its own particular challenges, and thus there is no one-size-fits-all approach. However, what you can do is to learn from more experienced people as you progress through your career. If you treat your bosses as mentors, you can ask them questions such as: 'How many admissions did you think we could achieve?' 'Why did you choose that particular price?' 'To what extent have we achieved what we set out to achieve?' Inevitably, along the way we all make mistakes, this is all part of the learning process and can be forgiven so long as we do not make the same mistake twice. Using the tools and techniques outlined in this chapter will help to minimize the likelihood of error by underpinning the art of operational decision making with science.

IN THE FIELD . . .

With Steve Brailey MBE, former chief executive officer, Sheffield International Venues Ltd (SIV), Sheffield, United Kingdom

The Sheffield City Trust (SCT) and its operating company SIV manage 18 sport, leisure, and entertainment venues including the flyDSA Arena, the English Institute of Sport Sheffield, Ponds Forge International Sports Centre, iceSheffield, Sheffield City Hall, nine leisure centers, and four public golf courses. The company employs over 1,200 staff (800 FTEs) and attracts over 5.5 million customers every year.

Steve's expertise in building positive relationships with a wide range of stakeholders and partners has delivered outstanding results for the city and the region. He led a team that has enjoyed numerous awards for the excellence of its service. SIV's sport facilities have attained some of the highest Quest management scores in the country while its Fitness Unlimited gym membership is an unprecedented quadruple winner of the Fitness Industry Association's award, Centre of the Year. Through strong leadership, innovation, and a forward-thinking approach, Steve was instrumental in transforming Sheffield's underused and closure-threatened sports facilities built for the 1991 World Student Games into highly sought-after, modern venues for the whole community – leaving a legacy for future generations.

Steve has some advice for those who aspire to work in the industry:

- Ensure you experience a wide variety of different roles in different organizations while in education and in the early stages of your career.
- Pay attention to leadership styles during your early career, and note the good and bad points in different leaders. It is as important to learn what not to do, as it is to learn what you should do.
- Enjoy your work. You spend more time at work than anywhere else – and life is too short for work to be a chore. Be able to laugh at yourself.
- Better to try and fail than not to try at all. Encourage your team to take some risks and try different ideas. Reward success, but do not flog an employee for trying to improve your business.
- Be positive. Negative people do not get promoted.
- Encourage a can-do attitude among your employees.
- Demonstrate a consistent temperament. Staff do not respond well when their leader is moody and unpredictable.
- Treat people fairly and in the manner you would expect to be treated.
- Be honest with yourself and your colleagues. People respect honesty even if told difficult or disappointing news.
- Team building is critical. Construct a team with similar core values but with different skills and strengths. You do not need a team of people who mirror your own strengths.
- Commit to continuous improvement. Always seek to develop your skills and experience. Do not stand still.
- Work hard. As the famous film producer Samuel Goldwyn once said: 'The harder I work, the luckier I get.'

BIBLIOGRAPHY

Beech, J., & Chadwick, S. (Eds.). (2013). *The business of sport management* (2nd ed.). London: Pearson United Kingdom.

Brown, M., Rascher, D., Nagel, M., & McEvoy, C. (2017). *Financial management in the sport industry* (3rd ed.). Oxford: Routledge.

Fried, G. (2015). *Managing sport facilities* (3rd ed.). Champaign, IL: Human Kinetics.

Naylor, D. J. (2001). *Managing your leisure service budget*. London: Ravenswood Publications Limited.

Robinson, L. (2004). *Managing public sport and leisure services.* London: Routledge.

Robinson, L., Chelladurai, P., Bodet, G., & Downward, P. (2012). *Routledge handbook of sport management.* Abingdon: Routledge.

Russell, D., Patel, A., & Wilkinson-Riddle, G. J. (2002). *Cost accounting: An essential guide.* London: Pearson Educational.

Shibli, S. (1994). *Leisure manager's guide to budgeting and budgetary control.* London: ILAM/Longman.

Stewart, B. (2017). *Sport funding and finance* (2nd ed.). Oxford: Routledge.

Trenberth, L., & Hassan, D. (2012). *Managing sport business: An introduction.* Oxford: Routledge.

Wilson, R. (2011). *Managing sport finance.* Oxford: Taylor & Francis.

Wilson, R., & Joyce, J. (2008). *Finance for sport and leisure managers.* London: Routledge.

Winfree, J., Rosentraub, M., Mills, B., & Zondlak, M. (2019). *Sports finance and management: Real estate, media, and the new business of sport* (2nd ed.). New York: Routledge.

CHAPTER 8

OPERATIONS MANAGEMENT

CHAPTER OUTLINE

- Operational structure and procedures
- Sport facility operations
  - Plant and field operations
  - Maintenance and cleaning
  - Waste and recycling
  - Utilities
  - Safety
  - Alterations
  - Inventory
- Sport facility services
  - Security
  - Ticketing
  - Parking
  - Concessions
  - Customer service desk
  - Event management
- Principles of continuous improvement
  - Total quality management (TQM)
  - ISO 9000 standards
  - Six Sigma
  - Risk management
  - Creating an operations manual for sport facilities
- Chapter review

OPERATIONAL STRUCTURE AND PROCEDURES

For any sport facility to run efficiently and effectively, there must be a strong operational structure and appropriate operational procedures. From a structural standpoint, many of the previous chapters articulate the various structures that must be in place. Chapter 2 on ownership structures covered the various legal business structures of a sport facility, and the operational framework that each allows is crucial to the operations and management of a sport facility from a legal and functional standpoint. In addition, there was an explanation that to appropriately govern a sport facility, a manager must have a clear understanding of the concept of organizational effectiveness, which is the concept of how efficient a business is in achieving the outcomes set forth in the planning processes. Chapter 6 introduced the concept of organizational behavior as the study of human behavior in the work environment including how leadership and organizational culture are crucial to the management of sport organizations. The chapter also covered the topic of human resource management in terms of the recruitment, training, and retention of personnel, as well as its role in strategically moving sport facilities forward toward a vision. This included how the organizational chart is utilized to integrate operations in the sport facility, along with the job descriptions that articulate the responsibilities of personnel. The financial management, budgeting, and operational decision-making chapter (Chapter 7) focused on why financial skills are an important part of the sport facility manager's overall portfolio of management of skills. Understanding each of these areas in detail serve as a framework for developing the operational structure of a sport facility.

Beyond these important concepts, there also needs to be a clear understanding of the history and philosophy attached to the sport facility. From a historical perspective, by knowing about what has happened in the past with regard to a sport facility, a manager can see why things are the way they are as of now, what potential there is in the future, and how the organization has functioned. Without knowing what has happened in the past, a sport facility manager cannot truly understand the organization or the current situation of the operation of the sport facility. In addition, by understanding what happened in the past and the current situation of today, the sport facility manager can better project the future because they can understand what should be avoided and what can be accomplished to move the sport facility forward toward a higher level of success. From a philosophical standpoint, understanding the values and beliefs of the sport facility organizational structure provides a framework and reasoning for why operations are conducted. The philosophy also serves as a framework for the mission of the sport facility (the purpose of the organization), the vision (where the organization wants to be in the future), and the action plan (what the organization wants to accomplish – articulated through goals, objectives, and strategies and within the parameters of policies and procedures).

All of these components drive the development and application of the operating procedures for the sport facility. These are implemented to provide a safe, efficient, and equitable functioning of a sport facility through a commitment to the provision and maintenance of appropriate physical facilities that contribute to a comfortable and conducive sporting and work environment. In sport facilities, a range of general operating procedures must be considered, including hours of operation, user categories, fees and rates, outsourcing of services, procurement practices, reservation procedures, and space allocation. The most challenging of these is often the reservation and space allocation processes, which includes programming, scheduling, and prioritization of both the use and maintenance of the facility. Each sport facility will have a different scheduling and prioritization process based on the type of users, the programs that utilize the facility, the different facility spaces, and the day and time activities take place. Adding to the challenge is that it is entirely feasible to have multiple prioritization schedules based on each part of the sport facility and at different days and times. Table 8.1 provides an example of a prioritization chart for the main gymnasium in a university sports complex.

With regard to the scheduling and organizing of maintenance, the general premise is to conduct the majority of this work during off-hours, which may include overnight, between activities, or after major events. For sport facilities, off-hours are not always the typical overnight because of the type of activities that take place and the late hour some activities or events may end. This, in addition to many other functions, falls under the category of facility operations.

Table 8.1 Prioritization chart for the main gymnasium – university sports complex

Priority	Monday–Friday 8 a.m.–3 p.m.	Monday–Friday 3 p.m.–8 p.m.	Monday–Friday 8 p.m.–12 a.m.	Saturday–Sunday all day
1	Physical education classes	University-sponsored sports teams	Campus recreation/intramurals programs	General open recreation time
2	University-sponsored sports teams	Campus recreation/intramurals programs	Student-sponsored clubs/organizations	Special events
3	Campus recreation/intramurals programs	Student-sponsored clubs/organizations	General open recreation time	Campus recreation/intramurals programs
4	Student-sponsored clubs/organizations	Physical education classes	Special events	Student-sponsored clubs/organizations
5	General open recreation time	General open recreation time	University-sponsored sports teams	University-sponsored sports teams
6	Special events	Special events	Physical education classes	Physical education classes

SPORT FACILITY OPERATIONS

Now that we have a basic overview of operating procedures, it would be important to recognize the various areas of operation within a sport facility. Sport facility operations can be divided in many different ways, based on the operational structure of the individual organization. For the purpose of this chapter, we will divide facility operating into the following categories: plant and field operations; maintenance and cleaning; waste and recycling; utilities; safety; alterations; inventory; and environmental issues including greening and sustainability.

Plant and field operations

Plant and field operations include managing the physical plant, including natural and artificial surfaces. Plant operations are the necessary infrastructure used in the support of facility operations and maintenance. Generally, the plant operations for a sport facility fall under five systems: (1) heating, ventilation, and air-conditioning (HVAC); (2) mechanical and electrical transportation (elevators); (3) major electrical systems; (4) plumbing; and (5) emergency power/generators. Additionally, there are numerous types of specific plant infrastructure for specialized facilities – such as

164

refrigeration and ice systems for ice arenas; filtration and chemical systems for swimming pool facilities; and watering systems for outdoor fields and artificial surfaces.

Today, the expectation of facility managers in their role as plant operators is to be a technician with mechanical competence. This expectation is verified by the numerous examinations and certifications that test for technical knowledge and interpersonal skills that most sport facility plant operations require. The reason for this necessary competence is that the facility manager is responsible for expensive equipment, proper operating conditions, quality control and improvement, profits and losses, problem solving, community involvement, and the environment, among many other things. The sport facility cannot survive without quality management of plant operations because the lack of skills operating these functions will result in significant risk, damage, and cost to the sport facility. Therefore, facility managers must understand the unique plant within their sport facility, must be secure and keep up-to-date about the technical skills and knowledge related to the sport facility, must operate in a safe manner with quality consciousness, and must possess the effective communications skills required to ensure proper operations by all staff.

Maintenance and cleaning

All infrastructural problems and damages to facilities and equipment are detrimental to the continued operation of a sport facility. Shutting down facilities disrupts customers' use and can be perceived as incompetence on the part of those running the sport facility. Hence, proper coordination of maintenance and cleaning is crucial to operational success.

In general, all maintenance and repair needs that are discovered by staff should be communicated to the facility or operations manager responsible for this area and be documented on a maintenance form. In addition to reporting maintenance and repair, managing staff should regularly conduct an evaluation of all infrastructure and equipment to determine the status of its condition and organize and coordinate appropriate remedies. Based on the severity of the problem or damage, the remedy will take one of three courses. First is general maintenance, which is the work necessary to maintain the facilities and equipment. *Maintenance* includes periodic or occasional inspection, adjustment, lubrication, cleaning, painting, replacement of parts, minor repairs, and other actions to prolong service and prevent problematic breakdowns. *Repair* refers to restoring damaged or worn-out facilities and equipment to a normal operating condition. Repairs are curative, whereas maintenance is preventive. A repair can be classified as minor or major. Minor repairs are those associated with maintenance activities that do not exceed one to two workdays per task. Major repairs are those that exceed two workdays per task or are beyond the capability of existing maintenance personnel. If the facility and equipment components or systems cannot be repaired, this leads to the need for replacement. This is the exchange or substitution of one fixed asset for another having the capacity to perform the same function. Replacement arises from an asset becoming obsolete, having excessive wear and tear, or being damaged beyond repair.

To limit the need for maintenance and repair, as well as to provide a pleasant environment for all stakeholders, it is important for a sport facility to be clean and functional. This is where custodial and housekeeping services come in. Patrons do not want to come to a facility that is dirty or where simple items such as soap, paper towel, and toilet paper are not readily available. As with almost any other service, custodial and housekeeping can be outsourced or kept in-house. In-house offers more control over keeping the facility clean; however, depending on the size of the facility and the scope of the events, outsourcing may be inevitable. Ultimately, the goal is to provide responsive service to meet the needs of the visitors and the facility and to enhance the quality of the experience of facility users.

Waste and recycling

One of the most overlooked costs of a sport facility is the result of the trash that it puts out. While a sport facility's main objective for reducing the contribution to the local landfill is to cut costs, the social importance of environmentally friendly business operations cannot be understated. Recycling mandates seem to be a trend that is starting to affect sport businesses everywhere. Some mandates are coming from city governments, while others come from within the sport business itself. In addition to typical waste, sport facilities, as a result of general operations, often have a multitude of recyclables including paper (newspaper, white paper, all other); aluminum cans; glass bottles and jars (clear, green, brown); scrap metal; Styrofoam; and cardboard. To deal with this, many sport facilities have segregated recycling bins at the rear of the complex.

The only way to reduce costs related to waste management is to reduce the amount of trash going to landfills, whose costs are determined by quantity. One of the biggest problems in trying to implement recycling as part of a waste management reduction program is getting customers to recycle. Having recyclables mixed in with the trash results in additional costs for the facility. Although the sport facility managers and staff are not in direct control, a number of things can influence visitors to recycle. The first way to raise awareness of recycling is through video messages that are displayed during an event. Another important part of recycling awareness has to do with both the visual appeal and the prominence of the recycling bins that are located in the facility. Improving that ratio of bins to seats would make it much easier for people to recycle.

Utilities

The two major utilities for a sport facility are electricity and water. Energy management is a function that spans all aspects of a sport facility. Some of the traditional energy management measures include thermostat regulation and investing

166

in energy-efficient capital equipment. While electrical consumption control is the responsibility of all employees of a sport facility, it is important for sport facility managers to conduct regular energy audits and implement energy improvement initiatives such as the lighting in offices being turned off when not in use. Other initiatives may include lighting in courts, spectator areas, and other activity areas being dimmed or turned off when not in use; thermostats being lowered during downtime and closed time (turned down one hour before closing and turned up to two hours before opening); and computers and other electronics being turned off when not in use. Furthermore, sport facility managers should review the energy efficiency of all parts of the infrastructure to see where retrofits may be appropriate to reduce energy costs in the long term. Energy costs are among the biggest expenses for a sport facility (usually second to staffing). Taking steps to reduce these costs can significantly improve the operation of a sport facility by increasing the financial resources available for other areas.

Equal in importance is water management. This is especially true in climates where rainfall is limited. Water efficiency in terms of consumption is not only a key indicator of quality facility management; it can provide significant financial savings. Good water management principles can range from installing efficient toilets, faucets, and showerheads in locker rooms and lavatories to implementing procedures as part of a daily security check to include monitoring these spaces to ensure that taps have not been left on or that there are no other issues such as leaks or faulty plumbing.

Water management also extends outside the facility. The ability to capture natural rainfall to reduce stress on water management systems is becoming a standard procedure in sport facilities. From a landscaping perspective, native and indigenous plants tend to use less water than exotic species. The use of mulch to prevent water loss means less watering. Treating irrigation systems in the same manner as internal plumbing with flow restrictors and daily inspections can prevent significant water loss. In addition, water harvesting using water collection tanks to capture water from natural rainfall and runoff from roofs and balconies is being widely utilized. In fact, many sport facilities are now connecting their rainwater collection tanks to general facility plumbing to reduce the need for and cost of traditional water utilities.

Safety

Another important area of sport facility operations is safety ranging from general safety to specific issues related to health, emergencies, fire, and handling dangerous goods. In terms of general safety, sport facility managers and owners have both a legal and a moral obligation to provide a safe environment for all stakeholders including users and employees. This extends to the duty of care owners, managers, and employees in the undertaking of all responsibilities and tasks. Beyond identifying and mitigating safety hazards, managers are responsible for safety planning, systems enhancements, and application processes to deal with a risky and dynamic environment such as a sport facility. Hence, sport facility managers must understand legislative issues governed through codes of practice, industry standards, and alerts from many sources ranging from equipment manufacturers to government authorities. In addition, implementing appropriate safety policies that include training employees, conducting safety audits, implementing emergency action procedures, and maintaining occupational health and safety (OH&S) standards are also part of the responsibilities of a sport facility operations manager.

In terms of these safety policies, those related to health, emergencies, fire, and handling of dangerous goods requires additional rigor. From a health standpoint, this may include ensuring appropriate indoor air quality with suitable ventilation systems; proper lighting, acoustics, and temperature control; and space management ensuring activities taking place are not overcrowded or impinge on other activities. Emergencies and fire require an appropriate emergency action plan that should include evacuation plans posted in all major areas with clear signage for users to follow. The plan should also encompass relevant documentation including an emergency contact list, a list of facility safety features, floor plans for all parts of the sport facility, a list of responsibilities and evacuation procedures, and a safety checklist to be completed prior to reentering the facility. Beyond the emergency action plan, there also needs to be ongoing procedures for ensuring that safety systems such as fire doors, fire extinguishers, hydrant pumps and valves, smoke detectors and alarms, sprinkler systems, and emergency announcement systems are all in operating order.

Another important issue of safety in sport facilities is the handling of dangerous goods, including hazardous materials (HAZMAT). Storage and usage of these types of materials are commonplace in sport facilities, ranging from cleaning materials to fuel for machinery to chemicals for swimming pools and grounds to paint for facility upkeep. Implementing policies and procedures for the proper storage of these materials may include suitable containers, temperature-controlled facilities, and handling instructions. Hence, sport facility operations managers must have a clear understanding of what materials are being used and stored in the facility, the disposal requirements for each, and procedures for dealing with spills and contamination. This requires having material safety data sheets (MSDS) available in the areas where the materials will be used.

Hazardous materials (HAZMAT) are classified under this category due to the health risk to humans if they are exposed to these materials. While most new facilities do not contain HAZMAT materials, older sport facilities may. Sport facility managers of older facilities must understand these materials both in terms of their existence in the facility as well as dealing with them during alterations or renovations. The most common HAZMAT materials seen in sport facilities include asbestos-containing materials (ACM), lead-based paint polychlorinated biphenyl compounds (PCB), ozone-depleting substances (ODS), synthetic greenhouse gases (SGG), and synthetic mineral fibers (SMF) including fiberglass.

Alterations

While all sport facilities are designed with space and needs in mind, it is inevitable that certain alterations need to take place. Many times these alterations are needed for three main reasons in a sport facility: (1) the need for additional storage, (2) the need for modified spaces for new programming, and (3) the need for additional office space for expanding staff. These alterations can be infrastructural (examples: building new spaces, splitting spaces by adding walls) and/or operational (examples: the need for additional electrical outlets, plumbing, or communications). Many sport facilities are designed with the potential for alterations in the future, which in the end reduces the costs of alterations. Alterations that are unplanned usually have a higher cost – as much as two to three times more than if they were planned for in the design of the sport facility. In some cases, alterations are temporary – usually because of a special event. In any case, to ensure that alterations are an appropriate outlay of money, sport facility managers should engage in a cost-benefit analysis to determine whether the benefit of the alteration is worth the money being spent.

FACILITY FOCUS: CUSTOMIZED CORPORATES BOXES: SANTIAGO BERNABÉU STADIUM, MADRID, SPAIN

The evolution of hospitality and VIP management continues in sport facility management. Corporate boxes offer value-added experiences and amenities to the highest-end users during events at the stadium that traditionally may include specialized catering areas and hosted experiences. Area VIP at the Real Madrid Football Club in the Santiago Bernabéu Stadium in Spain has taken it one step further – customizable corporate boxes and suites.

One of their key performance indicators for hospitality and VIP management is the continuous adaptation and improvement to meet the ever changing client needs and climate conditions through new products, visual changes, new services, catering enhancements, and top-quality customer service. One of those innovations is allowing clients to customize their suite. Architectural drawings can be submitted to Area VIP for approval, and then at the expense of the client, contractors can be brought in to modify the suites with everything from custom flooring and seating, merchandise displays, food and beverage kiosks, specialized sounds systems, and the latest technology.

This is a win-win for the client and the stadium. Clients can further personalize the experience for the users of their suites during events. For the stadium, it is an opportunity to lock in clients for longer and to increase revenue via new annual contracts at a higher rate. The odds that a client will not renew is limited because of the additional investment made in the suite, as well as the additional cost incurred reverting the suite back to its original condition should they not renew.

Inventory

Traditionally, we think of inventory management in terms of having available the products that customers' desire, such as merchandise, food service, and concessions. While these are concerns for the sport facility manager, those individual tasks fall under the management of those ancillary areas and are discussed later in this chapter. Inventory management as related to facility operations involves two distinct areas. First is the inventory of available spaces in the facility and how those spaces are reserved, scheduled, and allocated. Second is the procurement process related to the inventory of equipment and supplies used in the various areas of the facility. Some of this inventory includes light bulbs for a gymnasium or arena, tools and supplies for conducting maintenance, cleaning supplies for custodial crews, and tables/chairs/and barricades for event setup.

SPORT FACILITY SERVICES

All sport facilities are engaged in the service industry. As such, there is a need to provide a number of facility services over and above the general facility operating procedures. While the purpose of this section is not to delve into every aspect of facility services in detail, it is to provide information about the major services in sport facilities. Again, as with operations, there will be specialized services unique to specialized facilities, but the focus for this chapter will be on security, ticketing, parking, concessions, customer service, and event management.

Regardless of facility service, there are general rules and regulations followed by most, including standards of conduct, general guidelines, and appearance. Standards of conduct focus on providing users of the sport facility (members, guest, visitors, and spectators) the best possible examples of conduct, decorum, and good citizenship. The behavior of employees sets the example for all to follow. The care, safety, and welfare of all are paramount, and it is important that any situations endangering the health, safety, or well-being of people be dealt with immediately.

Security

Security in a sport facility can range from in-house staff at a small recreational facility to professional staff from global companies (Contemporary Services Corporation, www.csc-usa.com/home), local companies (Sentry Event Services in Florida, https://sentryeventservices.com/) or league/event-based (SAFE Management, the NFL's security company for the Super Bowl, www.safemanagement.net). Regardless of the level of security, all sport facility managers must recognize some important features when working with security. While a more detailed look at security planning and management will be provided later in this book (Chapter 13), we will introduce some basic concepts important to facility operations and providing service here.

The director of security (or the authorized management member overseeing security) is the point person who is directly responsible for security procedures and systems. The head of security also provides liaison between the sport facility and the appropriate local law enforcement authorities. The head of security and other security personnel are not sworn peace officers or law enforcement officers and are not authorized to carry firearms in most cases but are authorized by the owners of the sport facility to enforce all rules and regulations.

While specific staff members are hired to work as security, generally all employees of a sport facility act as members of the security team. Employees are the eyes and ears of a sport facility and should report criminal activities or rule violations occurring as soon as possible to security, who then will respond as required. This response can range from internal disciplinary action to a notification to the proper local law enforcement authorities.

Ticketing

The ticketing operation at a sport facility can range from a small box office of one person selling tickets for general admission to an event (such as a secondary school basketball tournament) to a full-service box office with a separate manager, paid staff, and relationships with secondary and tertiary ticketing services. Ultimately, whether it is the facility manager at a facility holding a small sporting event or a full-time box office manager, both have the role of selling tickets and controlling admissions to events.

In order to conduct a ticketing operation effectively, the facility manager/box office manager must know the inventory – or the number of seats available for a specific event. Seating capacities vary based on the type of event. For example, certain shows may only require 180-degree seating (for example, a concert), others 260-degree seating (for example, a World Wrestling Entertainment event), while others need full 360-degree facility seating (most sporting events). This information is then put into a manifest, which gives every seat in the facility a section/row/seat number and attaches the price of the ticket. This pricing can range from one price for all tickets (general admission or festival seating for all) to multiple pricing levels based on closeness to the field of play, location in proximity to the center of the field of play, amenities offered in conjunction with the seat, among other factors.

With larger events, full-service ticket offices (such as for large stadiums and arenas) take on extra responsibilities. In addition to overseeing general operations, hiring staff, training staff, and operating computer systems where manifests are stored for issuing tickets, the box office has to initiate on-sales events (the first day tickets are on sale) and operate a will call window (a place when tickets purchased in advance can be picked up by attendees to events). In addition, box office managers need to coordinate operations with secondary and tertiary box offices. As an example of a secondary box office, individual teams might sell tickets in addition to the box office. The box office is the place that issues these tickets to the teams, usually through secure access to the manifest in the box office's computer system. Similar processes are utilized for tertiary box offices, which would include online ticketing companies such as Ticketmaster and StubHub.

Parking

A sport facility should offer enough parking for spectators, members, guest, employees, and management. The usual standard for a sport stadium or arena is one parking spot for every four seats if there is no mass transit to the facility and less if mass transit is available (dependent on the quantity of transit and location). For a smaller facility, it really depends on projected usage. For example, a recreational facility with a fitness center and four basketball/volleyball courts may only need 30–40 spots, but if they plan to hold weekend tournaments, the need probably will blossom to 200 spots. Therefore, a parking plan integrated into the entire facility and event planning process is crucial for offering this service.

Sport facilities have a choice to keep parking services in-house, outsourced, or not offered. *In-house* ownership of parking services offers the opportunity for maximum financial benefits, security, and service. Especially for larger events, parking revenues can be significant. In addition, by owning the parking, the sport facility is providing a direct service to their customers. However, by retaining responsibility, the sport facility operator also incurs the responsibility for security. The cost associated with staffing and securing a parking area, along with the responsibility, sometimes outweighs the revenues that can be earned. In these cases, parking services are *outsourced* to parking management companies – where the sport facility receives a very small percentage of parking revenue but transfers all risks associated with security to the parking management company. Another type of outsourcing is *offering* limited or no parking services. This often takes place in larger cities where there is ample public parking. The sport facility receives no revenue from parking but also does not have to worry about this service because the municipality covers it.

Concessions

Concessions are defined as a secondary business under contract or license from a primary business to exclusively operate and provide a specialized service. In sport facilities, the main two concessions areas are merchandising and food service. As with any other service, concessions can be outsourced or kept in-house. Most often, merchandising is an in-house function, where a majority of food service is outsourced – mainly because of the significant liability.

The major goals of both merchandising and food service are to create a market demand for the products and services offered and to increase the profitability and financial health of the entire sport facility. One of the major duties of a concessions manager is inventory control including turnover, inventory management, shrinkage, and point-of-sale systems. Managing inventory also includes having a diverse product offering including a variation of sizes, inventory on hand, management of exclusive brands, and offering a variety of accessories. Concessions managers are also responsible for marketing and promoting product offerings through creating displays, managing an effective website, and determining appropriate price points. They also coordinate with human resources to hire and fire staff, as well as train the staff in the procedures of running the operation and offering high-quality customer service. Furthermore, they must secure the appropriate licenses and municipal approvals to operate a concessions operation; complete all associated accounting, billing, payments, bookkeeping, and payroll for the concessions operation; and maintain all equipment including displays, kiosks, computer systems, and appliances.

Food and beverage services offer some additional challenges, which often involve implementing an additional planning process for safety. The purpose of this plan is to identify and prevent possible food-related problems in order to enhance food safety. The problems may relate to the purchase, receiving, storage, preparation, cooking, packaging, transport, or display of food. Especially important in ensuring food safety and management are cleanliness and sanitation. Food preparation areas, facilities, equipment, and all food contact surfaces should always be kept clean because food residues and dirt may act as contaminants, resulting in food poisoning. A cleaning program should be developed to ensure that cleaning and sanitizing be carried out systematically, regularly, and effectively. In addition, good personal hygiene is essential to ensuring food safety. Food poisoning bacteria may be present on the skin and in the noses of healthy people. All food handlers should therefore maintain a high standard of personal hygiene and cleanliness in order to avoid transferring food poisoning microorganisms to food.

Customer service desk

The kiosk at the entrance to the facility. The customer service desk. The main office. These areas, as well as almost everything implemented at a sport facility, needs to have customer service in mind at all times. However, these areas are possibly the most important because here is where first impressions are created on members and guests. The employees working in these areas have an important responsibility to project a positive image for the sport facility, to help maintain the security of the sport facility by controlling ingress and egress, and to truly set the tone for each person's visit to the sport facility.

Each individual facility will have their own policies and procedures for managing the customer service desk, however, most will incorporate admission and front desk policies. In terms of admissions, every individual who comes in the door must have proof of entry. For larger events such as concerts and professional sport games, this is either in the form of a ticket or a credential. For a facility such as a recreational facility, it may be a card. If there is an allowance for nonmembers and guests, there should be a policy for signing in, completing appropriate paperwork, and/or paying a fee. In addition, individuals restricted from entry to the sport facility should never be allowed to enter without the express permission of management or ownership. For the front desk area, policies need to be in place to ensure cleanliness and organization at all times, restrictions are needed on who is authorized to be in the front desk area, and customer service desk employees must be readily accessible and willing to help members and guests.

Event management

While all of the services just described are important to the operation of a sport facility, the single most important is event management. Without events, there would be no need for a sport facility. There are two categories of events in a sport facility: events that are offered through and by the sport facility and those offered by outside entities that rent or lease the facility. In both cases, coordination between facility managers and event managers is crucial to success on both sides. However, there are usually issues between the managers because the event manager is mainly concerned about a successful event, and the facility manager is concerned with operating the facility safely with no damage. These missions often clash, and compromise and teamwork often need to be implemented.

Chapter 11 of this text will discuss in detail event planning and activation from a facility perspective. It is important to recognize at this point that the role of facility operations is not to run an event; hence, there will be little discussion about actual event management. From a facility operations standpoint, there are three major service roles, including synchronizing event ingress and setup, providing support during the event, and coordinating event breakdown and egress.

TECHNOLOGY NOW! AWAREMANAGER (UNITED STATES)

AwareManager is one of the foremost sport facility operations software being used by some of the most recognized facilities in the world. The goal of AwareManager is to optimize operations within sport facility management with the most current mobile, database, and business intelligence solutions.

Sport Authority Field at Mile High Stadium is the home of the Denver Broncos of the National Football League (NFL). In order to manage the wide range of data across multiple operational functions including event incidents, insurance documentation, preventive maintenance, purchase orders, and work orders, the venue needed four different programs to analyze and integrate the data. The director of stadium operations sought a single system to integrate all of these functions allowing for a streamlined tracking process. The system developed by AwareManager phased out the old systems, integrated all of the operations, and provided an integrated approach to analyzing key performance indicators to ensure that the needs of customers and clients were being met. A similar system has also been implemented with the Maryland Stadium Authority, who oversees the management and operations of M&T Bank Stadium, home of the NFL's Baltimore Ravens, and Oriole Park at Camden Yards, home of the Baltimore Orioles of Major League Baseball (MLB).

At Phillips Arena, home of the Atlanta Hawks of the National Basketball Association (NBA), significant changes were made in the antiquated systems being used for guest services staffing for events – so much so that they abandoned the systems and went back to paper and e-mail scheduling. To solve this problem, AwareManager introduced their Gunner platform for event operations to manage human resource needs. Event templates were created for each event type, with staffing needs and locations included and the ability to produce visual representations of those needs. AwareManager also introduced a human resource profile database that included staff contact information, availability, qualifications, and certifications, which was then integrated with the event templates to more efficiently schedule staff for events.

The flexibility of integration with other venue management software systems is also a key ability of AwareManager. For instance, Gillette Stadium, home of the NFL's New England Patriots and Major League Soccer's (MLS) New England Revolution, integrates AwareManager with Vizsafe Geoaware Services Platform for facility maintenance and incident management for events. The Vizsafe software is a platform that provides security and safety functionality within venues using visual communications, mobile reporting, and mapping/permission-based sharing used as a technology for everything from minor incidents to antiterrorism management.

Source: AwareManager. (2019). Retrieved May 28, 2019, from www.awaremanager.com

PRINCIPLES OF CONTINUOUS IMPROVEMENT

The integration of facility operations and services into a single framework of sport facility operations management requires a comprehensive and organized approach in order to succeed. This is where the principles of continuous improvement can be a significant asset to the sport facility manager.

The concept of continuous improvement is crucial to the success of sport facility operations management. With a constantly changing environment ranging from customer needs to external factors such as the economy and social norms, sport facility operators must recognize these changes quickly and determine how they may affect the operation of the sport facility. The foundation of the philosophy of continuous improvement comes from the Japanese concept of *Kaizen*, meaning good change. The goal of *Kaizen* in terms of sport facilities involves engaging in business activities that continually improve all functions of operations and that strives to involve all employees in the process through a process of feedback, efficiency, and evolution. In sport facility operations management, the principles of continuous improvement commonly implemented include total quality management (TQM), ISO 9000 standards, Six Sigma, risk management policy implementation, and the creation of operations manuals for sport facilities.

Total quality management (TQM)

TQM is a comprehensive, structured approach to operations management that was first prevalent in the 1980s and 1990s but is still one of the most widely used continuous improvement principles in sport facility management. TQM seeks to improve the quality of facility services through constant refinements in response to feedback from users and staff. The main purpose for implementing a quality TQM program for a sport facility is to control operational and service quality with the result being an improvement of all aspects of activity implementation.

TQM processes are divided into four sequential categories: plan, do, check, and act (the PDCA cycle). The *planning* phase involves defining the problem to be addressed, collecting relevant data, and determining the main cause of the problem. The *doing* phase entails implementing a solution and choosing the best measurement to gauge its effectiveness. The *checking* phase is an evaluation of the results to confirm success or failure. The *acting* phase is the documentation of results, the articulation of process changes to the entire organization, and making recommendations for the problem to be addressed in the next PDCA cycle.

A sport facility manager implements a TQM process for four key reasons: (1) measure and analyze how tasks are being accomplished, (2) eliminate procedures that are not working, (3) allow for input from all employees within the sport facility based on their areas of expertise, and (4) eliminate stereotypical thinking and replacing it with visionary thought processes. This measurement and analysis process is most often implemented through the process of benchmarking. *Benchmarks* are individual management tools used by a sport organization to plan for evaluation, measurement, and improvement. Benchmarking is an important concept to sport facility managers to implement for three key reasons. First, they help facility managers to achieve better results by enabling them to understand and influence the drivers of performance. Both data benchmarking (comparing statistical performance with others) and process benchmarking (comparing the key decisions made to achieve good performance) achieve this. Second, benchmarks provide much more authoritative reporting of performance than an organization's performance reported in isolation. Third, when benchmarking techniques become established as part of organizational culture, they provide the basis for a clear focus on the business essentials as well as the direction for continuous improvement. We will revisit this concept in the performance analytics chapter of this book (Chapter 14), where we will bring together various concepts from the entire book and show how all aspects of sport facility management effectively interact with one another.

However, focusing specifically on operations management, their major goal is to ensure quality control through TQM. One of the most widely used models of quality control to measure business effectiveness used in sport facility management is Deming's 14 Key Principles of Points for Management. In brief, the principles are:

1 Create constancy of purpose toward the improvement of products and services.
2 Adopt the new philosophy.
3 Eliminate dependence on mass inspection and require statistical evidence that quality is built in.
4 Do not award business on the basis of price – quality is much more important.
5 Find problems and continually improve the quality control system.
6 Institute the most current methods of on-the-job training.
7 Implement the most current methods of supervision of employees to ensure maximum quality of operation and services provided.
8 Eliminate fear to increase the level of employee effectiveness.
9 Break down barriers between departments/work areas.
10 Get rid of numerical goals and replace them with quality goals.
11 Eliminate work standards and quotas.
12 Remove barriers that prevent part-time, hourly, and volunteer workers from having pride of ownership in the work produced for the sport facility.
13 Institute an efficient and effective program of education and retraining.
14 Create an operational structure in top management that forces the implementation of the preceding principles on a regular basis.

(Adapted from Ross, 2017)

For a sport facility, managers should be concerned with four major areas of TQM: customer service, empowering employees, human resource management, and media/

public relations. Probably the most important is customer service because without customers, there would be no purpose for the sport facility. Five pillars of quality are integral to customer service and the TQM process:

1   Quality services start with customer service because only the customer can define whether the right service is being offered and the quality of its offering.
2   There must be a commitment to continuous improvement.
3   There must be the ability and a willingness to be measured and evaluated.
4   Employee and staff must be empowered, be held responsible for their actions, and view themselves and their jobs as an integral part of a quality sport facility operation.
5   Quality service should be both recognized and marketed inside and outside the company

(Adapted from Friday & Cotts, 1994)

As related to the empowerment of employees and overall human resource management, it is important to remember that the job of all within a sport facility is ultimately to sell its image. Therefore, employees must do their job, as well as other duties as assigned by supervisors and ownership, in line with the guidelines of the human resource and operations manual. However, to sell the image, empowering employees with authority and power is integral to the process. Employees need to have an active role in the administration of the sport facility because employees bring to the table a unique set of qualities that will allow any sport facility to operate at an optimal quality level. Management provides training, resources and a safe work environment for employees; employees work together with management to control processes, identify problems, and be a part of the solution to improve performance with the ultimate goal of effectively and efficiently serving customers.

Media and public relations are the foremost means by which a sport facility seeks to control public opinion regarding its products and services. At times, information will need to be released to the customers, the media, and the public regarding situations, problems, opportunities, and event results at a sport facility. The release of this information needs to be controlled; therefore, unless specifically authorized by the operational structure of a sport facility, employees should never release information about the operations, policies, procedures, and actions associated a sport facility to the public (customers, the press, or the public). Quality control also involves the proper release of information by the appropriate authorities within a sport facility and in a voice shared by all members of the facility's organization. From a TQM standpoint, if unsure what to say – say nothing, 'no comment – or direct the individual to the person within the organization who is authorized to speak.

ISO 9000 standards

As TQM was being implemented in businesses across the United States, another set of international standards were developing and are now being utilized globally. The International Organization of Standards (ISO), an independent, nongovernment agency from Geneva, Switzerland, is the leading developer of voluntary international standards in the world. Of the nearly 20,000 standards they have developed over time, ISO 9000 has gained traction in the realm of business operations and has spilled over into the area of sport facility operations.

ISO 9000 was first published in 1987, designed to assist organizations in ensuring they were meeting the needs and wants of all stakeholders of a business within the legal and regulatory standards set within a specific industry. ISO 9000 focuses on the fundamentals of quality management, and the original version in 1987 focused on three main models. The first (ISO 9001) focused on quality assurance in design, development, production, installation, and servicing. This was developed for organizations that created new products, such as equipment and apparel companies. The second (ISO 9002) was dedicated to quality assurance in production, installation, and servicing for organizations that were not developing new products. Hence, those with established businesses that were not developing new functions fell under this standard. The third (ISO 9003) was directed toward quality assurance in final inspection and testing, where the production process was not examined – only a look at the final product.

Over the years, ISO 9000 has evolved to address the evolution of industries. In 1994, an update of the standards was produced to include quality assurance via corrective and preventive actions (CAPA). However, the most significant change came in 2000, where the three ISO 9000 standards were replaced with a new ISO 9001. In this iteration, the concepts of design and development procedures were applied only to those creating new products, and a significant change across other areas focused on the concept of process management. The aim of process management includes (1) standards for monitoring and optimizing all activities of a business, (2) the oversight of standards involving top management – where in the past it was acceptable to delegate to middle and lower management, (3) the incorporation of benchmarking and performance metrics as part of the quality management process, and (4) the need to strive for continuous improvement through the tracking of customer satisfaction. More about benchmarking and performance management will be discussed in Chapter 14 of this book.

After this modification, ISO 9001 was able to be more widely used across all aspects of the business industry and was especially welcomed by sport facility operators across the globe. It provided them with standards of operation that examined processes involving all levels of management and ownership, included analytics and metrics for feedback from customers, and created a continual process loop connecting development and implementation to evaluation and feedback. ISO reviewed their standards in 2008 with little change other than a clarification of requirements. In December 2015, a new version of the standards was published (ISO9001: 2015), embedding the process approach more clearly within all requirements, with clarifications provided in the areas of structure, context, documentation, and terminology. However, the most significant and welcome change for sport facility managers was the elimination of preventive action and replacing it with a complete risk management process.

Six Sigma

Six Sigma is another continuous improvement process that is an evolution of TQM and Deming's Principles and is gaining some traction in the sport facility operations industry. The goal of Six Sigma is to reduce variability in business processes and hence improve the quality of business operations by identifying and eliminating mistakes. This is usually accomplished through quality policies and procedures in place through an operations manual; using appropriate benchmarks, analytics, and metrics to evaluate and make positive changes; and creating committees or groups of employees to oversee and evaluate the operations process. The Six Sigma process is more of a statistical, analytics-based examination of operations processes, as the result should effectively be a sigma rating for the process, where the effectiveness and efficiency levels of operations are at 99.99966%. As the evolution of analytics-based analysis continues to grow, the evolution of TQM toward Six Sigma will be inevitable.

Risk management

Risk management is the process of attempting to prevent the possibility of loss from a hazard such as personal injury, property damage, or economic loss. Risk cannot be eliminated from the environment, but with careful planning, it can be managed. Appropriate risk management practices are crucial to reduce legal exposure, prevent financial and human loss, protect facility assets, ensure business continuity, and minimize damage to the sport facility's reputation. All members of the sport facility management team – from ownership to hourly staff and volunteers – have a duty to act in a prudent manner and a duty of care to provide a reasonably safe environment for users of the sport facility.

While this topic will be covered in more detail in Chapter 12, it is important to recognize that from an operational standpoint, the major areas of concern within risk management involves dealing with noncritical injuries/illnesses to be addressed internally and critical injuries/illnesses requiring emergency medical personnel. It also includes the appropriate use of alarms and warning signals, the implementation of general emergency evacuation procedures, and dealing with issues including electrical power failure, elevator entrapment, and natural disasters.

Creating an operations manual for sport facilities

The purpose of creating a facility operations manual is to have a central document that articulates accurate and current information regarding the operational policies and procedures of the sport facility. The information provided usually includes the majority of the concepts provided in this chapter and often more. The operations manual is often connected to the human resource manual (Chapter 6) because it builds on the concepts embedded in the human resource manual, including how operations interact with employment/employee relations. It also connects operations with the general information and policies/procedures of the sport facility. A sample of a sport facility operations manual as just described can be found in the online resources for this book.

PANORAMA STADIUM

You have just been hired as the facility manager for Panorama Stadium, a renovated 69,000-seat natural grass stadium originally built in 1994. The stadium will be the home for both a new professional soccer expansion team and a relocated rugby club. The chief executive officer (CEO) of Panorama Stadium wants you to create an operations manual that will help the building run efficiently while making your job easier. The following is a list of priorities given to you by the CEO:

1 *Operations management*: The CEO wants you to describe and diagram the optimal organizational structure and position descriptions with projected salaries.
2 *Risk management*: The CEO is very concerned with this area. Describe the overall function of risk management within the facility for a multipurpose stadium whose primary sport is football but need to host a multitude of events to be profitable.
3 *Marketing*: The CEO wants a marketing plan developed for the facility that will attract new clients and customers.
4 *Event management*: The CEO wants a new event management process across all areas including parking, ticketing, security, and game day management.
5 *Concessions*: The CEO is not satisfied with the revenue generated from concessions (food service and merchandising) and wants the pros and cons of owning versus outsourcing.

Suggested discussion topics

1 Where would you start with this operations plan? Identify the steps you will take to create a comprehensive, functional operational plan.
2 What special operational needs will be necessary because of the opening weekend for Panorama Stadium, where there will be a Friday night football match followed by a Saturday night concert and a Sunday afternoon open community event? What special considerations need to be in place (for example, environmental factors such as weather)?

CHAPTER REVIEW

The role of sport facility operations is to maintain quality visitor experiences consistently without the depletion of resources. Good sport facility operations start with a functional organizational structure that allows for the quality legal and financial management of the sport facility. It is followed by the implementation of general sport facility operating procedures that provide a safe, efficient, and equitable functioning of a sport facility through a commitment to the provision and maintenance of appropriate physical facilities that contribute to a comfortable and conducive sport and work environment. While there are numerous categories of operating procedures, among the most important is how space is reserved and allocated and what the user prioritization process is.

Operating procedures may differ based on the various operations and services provided within a sport facility. Major facility operations inherent in most sport facilities include plant and field operations, maintenance and cleaning, waste and recycling, utility management, safety, alterations, inventory management, and environmental management including greening and sustainability. Facility services, which may be outsourced or kept in-house, include security, ticketing, parking, concessions, customer service, and event management. Each of these services will have their own general rules and regulations that must be followed including standards of conduct, general guidelines, and appearance.

The implementation of these concepts in the operation of a sport facility can be best articulated through various principles of continuous improvement. One such principle is the process of total quality management (TQM) – a comprehensive, structured approach to operations management that seeks to improve the quality of facility services through constant refinements through the PDCA cycle (planning, doing, checking, acting). The TQM process works well for sport facilities because it measures and analyzes how tasks are being accomplished; eliminates procedures that are not working; allows for input from all employees within the sport facility based on their areas of expertise; and eliminates stereotypical thinking and replacing it with visionary thought processes. Sport facility managers are most concerned with the TQM process as it relates to customer service, employee and human resource management, and media/public relations. Internationally, ISO 9000 standards comprise another principle for continuous improvement utilized to monitor and optimize business activities, involve top management in the improvement process, incorporate benchmarking and performance metrics as part of the quality management process, in addition to striving for continuous improvement through the tracking of customer satisfaction.

A more recent application of performance improvement is the Six Sigma process – an evolution on TQM and Deming's Principles that focuses on reducing variability in business processes and improving the quality of business operations by identifying and eliminating mistakes through the use of appropriate benchmarks, analytics, and metrics to evaluate and make positive changes.

Part of continuous improvement also includes the implementation of risk management principles, which involves the process of attempting to prevent the possibility of loss from a hazard such as personal injury, property damage, or economic loss. Risk cannot be eliminated from the environment, but with careful planning, it can be managed. The best way to reduce the amount of risk is to articulate all policies and procedures, rules and regulations, and philosophies and missions in one document. The facility operations manual is the central document that articulates accurate and current information regarding these areas. The operations manual is often connected to the human resource manual because it builds on the concepts embedded in the HR manual and connects operations with the general information and policies/procedures of the sport facility.

IN THE FIELD . . .

With Charlotte Jensen-Murphy, senior vice president, sports and entertainment, ABM Industries, New York City, United States

One of the biggest challenges today for sport facility operations managers is to offer services that will entice fans to come to the venue. With the continued evolution of technology, the ability to watch sports from home on high-definition televisions and from multiple camera angles of the viewer's choice can potentially take away from placing 'bums in seats' at the venue.

Charlotte Jensen-Murphy, a senior vice president of sports and entertainment at ABM industries, provides innovative facility solutions across the United States and multiple locations. She explains that operations managers can improve upon many areas to enhance the management of a stadium and create value-added customer experiences.

1 Improving parking management by including shuttle service to and from parking lots, VIP parking areas for suite and season ticket holders, valet parking as an option for all, and even a parking app to tell customers where parking is available.
2 Cleanliness! While this seems to be obvious, operations managers need to ensure that maintenance and cleaning in seating areas, concourses, food areas, and restrooms are of the highest priority. This includes having the proper equipment, using environmentally friendly cleaning products, and incorporating a communication process that deals with issues promptly when they happen.

3 Aesthetics of the green areas such as landscaping on the approach to the stadium and within the facility creates a more pleasant atmosphere and the image of paying attention to details.

4 Build on the concept of aesthetics and atmospherics by making sure properly designed and maintained HVAC and lighting systems are incorporated into the facility operation. Everything from well-lit areas walking to and from the venue to having the appropriate temperature in facility spaces is vital to a quality experience for customers.

5 Another area that is becoming important is the sustainability of sport facilities. The advancement of LEED-certifications into the consciousness of customers has now become an expectation.

Ultimately, an integrated facility operations system that enhances the experiences for customers and participants and that incorporates the most experienced staff and partners will ultimately increase efficiency and reliability, help in managing costs, allow for the effective control of the venue, and optimize the operations management functions of a sport facility.

Source: Charlotte Jensen-Murphy. (2016, November). A day in the life of stadium management. Here are six ways to improve stadium facility operations – and the guest experience in the meantime. Retrieved May 28, 2019, from https://facilityexecutive.com/2016/11/a-day-in-the-life-of-stadium-management/

BIBLIOGRAPHY

Abdi, S. N. A., Awan, H. M., & Bhatti, M. I. (2008). Is quality management a prime requisite for globalization? Some facts from the sports industry. *Quality and Quantity*, *42*(6), 821–833. https://doi.org/10.1007/s11135-007-9135-x

Chen, H. H., Chen, K. K., Chang, T. T., & Hsu, C. C. (2010). An application of Six Sigma methodology to enhance leisure service quality. *Quality and Quantity*, *44*(6), 1151–1164. https://doi.org/10.1007/s11135-009-9271-6

Friday, S., & Cotts, D. G. (1994). *Quality facility management: A marketing and customer service approach*. New York: Wiley.

Hon Yin Lee, H., & Scott, D. (2009). Strategic and operational factors' influence on the management of building maintenance operation processes in sports and leisure facilities, Hong Kong. *Journal of Retail and Leisure Property*, *8*(1), 25–37. https://doi.org/10.1057/rlp.2008.29

International Organization for Standardization. (2018). *ISO 9000 family: Quality management*. Retrieved November 21, 2018, from www.iso.org/iso-9001-quality-management.html

Ip, K., She, K., & Adeyeye, K. (2018). Life-cycle impacts of shower water waste heat recovery: Case study of an installation at a university sport facility in the UK. *Environmental Science and Pollution Research*, *25*(20), 19247–19258. https://doi.org/10.1007/s11356-017-0409-0

Liu, W. (2014). The optimized design and material saving of sports architecture. *Journal of Chemical and Pharmaceutical Research, 6*(5), 1586–1591.

McAdam, R. (2000). Three leafed clover? TQM, organisational excellence and business improvement. *The TQM Magazine, 12*(5), 314–320. https://doi.org/10.1108/09544780010341897

Moxham, C., & Wiseman, F. (2009). Examining the development, delivery and measurement of service quality in the fitness industry: A case study. *Total Quality Management & Business Excellence, 20*(5), 467–482. https://doi.org/10.1080/14783360902863614

Roper, K. O., & Payant, R. P. (2014). *The facility management handbook* (4th ed.). New York: Amacom Books.

Ross, J. E. (2017). *Total quality management: Text, cases, and readings* (3rd ed.). New York: Routledge.

Speegle, M. (2016). *Process technology plant operations* (2nd ed.). Independence, KY: Cengage Learning.

Stenqvist, C., Nielsen, S. B., & Bengtsson, P. O. (2015). *Dialogue and collaboration for energy efficient facilities management: Municipal sector strategies and the role of external service providers*. Retrieved November 21, 2018, from http://orbit.dtu.dk/files/110807431/Dialogue_and_collaboration.pdf

Uecker-Mercado, H., & Walker, M. (2012). The value of environmental social responsibility to facility managers: Revealing the perceptions and motives for adopting ESR. *Journal of Business Ethics, 110*(3), 269–284. https://doi.org/10.1007/s10551-011-1153-x

SECTION III

IMPLEMENTING SPORT FACILITY OPERATIONS MANAGEMENT

CHAPTER 9

MULTICHANNEL MARKETING AND COMMUNICATIONS

CHAPTER OUTLINE

- Introduction to sport facility marketing management
  - The sport marketing mix and sport facilities
- Understanding the sport consumer in sport facilities
  - Market research and information systems
  - Consumer behavior
- Sport marketing infrastructure for sport facilities
  - Product and service management
  - Branding
  - Sales management
- Promotional communications for sport facilities
  - Advertising
  - Sponsorship
  - Enhancement of other promotional mix elements
- Sport facility marketing utilizing social, digital and mobile media
- Chapter review

CHAPTER OBJECTIVES

This chapter articulates the significant role of communications and sport market-ing in sport facility operations management. The goal is for the reader to develop knowledge and skill in the marketing process as it relates to understanding the sport consumer, logistics, and promotional activities in sport facilities. Studying and understanding the consumer in terms of marketing a sport facility, developing marketing strategies for the facility, clarifying its needs and goals, and implementing sport marketing plans to support the management and operations of a sport facility through market research and information systems, as well as consumer behavior, are integral to success. As part of these responsibilities, the sport facility manager must understand how to develop and implement a sport marketing plan through logistical functions, including product and service management, branding, and sales management. They must also be able to communicate this information through various promotional efforts including advertising, sponsorship, and public relations. Furthermore, the communication of information about sport facilities is especially crucial in consideration of the evolution of social, digital, and mobile media marketing to target and attract Millennials and Generation Z to sport facilities.

INTRODUCTION TO SPORT FACILITY MARKETING MANAGEMENT

One of the biggest misconceptions in sport facility management is that facility managers do not need to be involved with marketing – that their sole job is related to the operations and management of the actual facility. On the contrary, facility managers need to have a solid foundation in marketing and should be involved in all aspects of marketing relating to the sport facility. The knowledge of the facility manager with relation to operations and management of the facility actually can serve as a significant asset in the development of marketing plans. This will lead to helping with the understanding of the consumers who use the facility, efficient infrastructural and logistical administration of marketing efforts, and effective application of promotional activities though facility advertising, sponsorships, public and media relations, and atmospherics.

The purpose of this chapter is to provide an overview of how the association of sport marketing and sport facilities can interact to provide products and services that satisfy the needs, wants, and desires of the consumer. This knowledge also helps with the planning, organizing, directing, controlling, budgeting, leading, and evaluation of a facility whose primary products and services are related to sport, recreation, leisure, and entertainment. This will allow the sport facility manager to better understand how the application of marketing principles can advance the transfer of goods and services from the producer (the sport facility, the events in the facility, and the organizations utilizing the facility) to the consumer (spectators and participants), resulting in more customers for the sport facility.

The sport marketing mix and sport facilities

The sport facility manager must have a clear understanding of the sport marketing mix. The focal point of these marketing functions is on four specific areas known as the 4 Cs of marketing analysis: the consumer, the company itself, the competition, and the climate.

The *consumer* is an individual or organization that purchases or obtains goods and services for direct use or ownership. In the case of the sport facility, most often someone becomes a customer by purchasing a ticket to gain access to a facility for experiencing an event. Sport marketers reach sport consumers through a series of processes. First is through segmentation, which is the concept of dividing a large, diverse group with multiple attributes into smaller groups with distinctive characteristics. This is followed by targeting specific consumers to find the best way to get a product's image – in this case, a sport facility or the event it is hosting – into the minds of consumers, resulting in the purchase of a ticket to attend the event. This is accomplished by analyzing multiple aspects of the marketing mix that may include the product (the event in the facility), the price (the cost of attending), the place (the facility itself), or an analysis of the promotional and publicity efforts (for example, advertising, sponsorship, media relations). Through this analysis, the sport facility manager then must determine how to position the facility and event in such a way that it influences the perceptions of potential and current customers about the image of the facility and its products and services related to attending an event at the facility. Ultimately, the sport facility manager must deliver by providing high-quality facility operations and service to all stakeholders including event promoters, participants, and spectators.

With regard to the *company* and *competition*, the framework is centered on a situation (SWOT) analysis. The managerial function of a sport facility is concerned mostly with internal strengths and weaknesses of the organization, while the leadership of the sport facility tends to focus on the external opportunities and external threats posed by competition and the environment. The *climate* involves forecasting the factors that will have a direct effect on the internal and external functioning of the sport facility, including changes in societal values and beliefs, the economy, legal and political issues, the media, and changes in technology. Sport facility managers must be concerned with both the managerial and leadership functions inherent to sport marketing. Fortunately, because of their experience within the climate, their understanding of the diverse consumers who come to the facility for various events, their knowledge of how similar facilities operate, and their direct involvement with the internal functions of the sport facility, facility managers are a crucial part of the marketing management team for the sport facility.

However, the facility manager faces significant challenges because while the sport facility itself is a tangible building, the sport product is generally intangible, subjective, and variable. This makes the sport marketing efforts for a sport facility unique for numerous reasons but most importantly because the primary sport product and hence the market are traditionally demand based, whereas most generic products are marketed based on need. The sport product takes many forms including a consumer good, a consumer service, a commercial good, or a commercial service; hence, it has a wide and varied appeal. The sport facility manager has to have an equally wide and varied understanding of the multiple types and aspects of sport

191

products and services that may take place in their sport facility, as well as how best to deliver what is promised to the consumers.

The sport facility manager must also recognize that since sport product is often publicly consumed, the environment provided by the facility directly affects consumer satisfaction. As a result of the strong emotional connections elicited by the involvement with the sport product and the fact that since the sport product is an event form – a perishable commodity – the sport facility manager must do everything possible to ensure that, from the facility standpoint, the customer is satisfied. This is most often accomplished by working with all departments associated with the facility to ensure that the product extension within the sport facility is adequate – including such things as quality concession stands, functional and clean lavatories, simple ingress/egress, good flow within the facility (including directions within the facility), top-quality security, and overall cleanliness of the sport facility. Anything a sport facility manager can do to enhance the customer experience aids in marketing efforts.

UNDERSTANDING THE SPORT CONSUMER IN SPORT FACILITIES

The purpose of a sport facility is to provide a place for people to congregate and participate in sport- and leisure-related activities. As such, it is the responsibility of the sport facility manager to understand who their customers are – ranging from participants to spectators. Sport facility managers are increasingly investing time and resources into understanding their sport consumers in two ways. First is through the creation of a sport management information system, which consists of all department, activities, and people within a sport facility being responsible for gathering, organizing, analyzing, evaluating and distributing marketing information to ensure efficient and effective decision making regarding customer wants and needs. Second is understanding consumer behavior, which is the conduct that sport consumers display in seeking out, ordering, buying, using, and assessing products and services that the consumers expect will satisfy their needs and wants.

Market research and information systems

In order to understand consumers, sport facility managers must be able to incorporate a marketing information system into their marketing efforts efficiently and effectively. The purpose of a marketing information system is to collect the various data available in one place for use in making sport marketing decisions. It comprises an intricate structure of interacting with people, combined with infrastructure and techniques, in order to gather, sort, analyze, evaluate, and distribute relevant, well-timed, accurate information for use by sport facility managers so that they can develop, implement, and manage marketing plans. The marketing information system is made up of four elements: the marketing research system, the internal reports system, the marketing intelligence system, and the marketing decision support system.

The *marketing research system* is the process of designing, gathering, analyzing, and reporting information that is utilized to resolve a specified sport marketing issue or problem. The sport facility manager must engage in a process to determine where information about a need – ranging from the available target market to a need within the facility – is lacking. As a result of a problem being defined, the sport facility manager comes up with a list of potential solutions, articulated in terms of goals and objectives, and then engages in the research process. This process includes collecting primary and secondary data through various methods (surveys, focus groups, case study analysis, market tracking studies, industry standard reports, etc.); tabulating and evaluating the data collected; and utilizing the information to develop programs to meet the needs of the consumer or to modify policies and procedures as necessary.

The *internal reports system* serves as a framework for the marketing information system by enabling the sport facility director to examine the internal operations of the sport organization in order to enhance the marketing efforts of the facility and associated events. Utilizing the information collected from various departments through inputs from the order-to-payment cycle, the point-of-sale system, and data mining, the sport facility manager is better able to understand the sport organization they are working with and hence its relationship to prospective and current customers.

The *marketing intelligence system* is a crucial element of the marketing information system because it opens the door to understanding the external environment that affects the sport facility and the organizations it serves. By utilizing the primary and secondary intelligence collected through the various methods of scanning, then evaluating that data through the scanning dissemination process, the sport facility manager can gain a better understanding of the opportunities, threats, and trends that can affect the sport facility. In addition, this intelligence is utilized to enhance the internal reports of the sport facility and can serve as a framework for future sport marketing research.

The *marketing decision support system* (DSS) assists sport facility managers and other decision makers within both the sport facility and the organizations it serves by taking advantage of information that is available from the various sources and using that information to make strategic decisions, control decisions, operational decisions, and marketing decisions. This system looks at both the decision process and decision outcomes, with the goal of making changes in selected sport marketing that lead to higher profits, a stronger and more positive image for the sport facility, and an increase in sport consumer satisfaction. Therefore, the results from the decision support system are utilized to make strategic, control, operational, and marketing decisions that interact with all parts of the sport facility and the associated organizations.

Consumer behavior

While it is important to have knowledge about the marketing information system, this is only the functional part of understanding the sport consumer. The sport facility manager, to engage in marketing management effectively, must also comprehend and apply the principles of consumer behavior. *Consumer behavior* is the conduct that consumers display in seeking out, ordering, buying, using, and assessing products and services that consumers expect will satisfy their needs and wants.

The sport facility manager must understand the internal and external factors that affect sport consumers. The *internal factors* include the personality of the sport consumer, the learning process of sport consumers, the process of motivating sport consumers, the attitudes of the sport consumer, and the perceptions developed by those consumers about a sport product. *External factors*, resulting from environmental influences, include culture, subculture, international and global interaction, social setting, and social class. In addition, the sport facility manager must understand the marketing concept, which is a consumer-oriented philosophy suggesting that satisfaction of consumer needs provides the focus for product development and marketing strategy to enable the firm to meet its own organizational goals. In terms of sport facility management, the marketing concept focuses on the socialization, involvement, and commitment of spectators and participants through the sport product itself, the production of sport (through the experience of the 'event'), and the sale of sport (including product extensions).

The sport facility manager will also be an active member of the problem-solving and decision-making processes to ensure that the needs and wants of the consumer are being met. In problem solving, the sport facility manager will engage in brainstorming, formulating various solutions, analyzing all solutions to determine a course of action, implementing the course of action, and evaluating the success of the course of action chosen to ensure that optimal success is attained from a facility operations standpoint. The decision-making process works hand in hand with problem solving, focusing on the economic, passive, cognitive, and emotional needs of customers before they enter the facility, while they are in the facility, and after they have left. Ultimately, sport facility managers look at three key determinants of success as related to marketing management. First is whether the marketing program influenced sport consumers to come to the facility. Second is whether the advertisements and other collateral materials stimulate sport consumer purchases to come to the facility. Finally is determining whether the spread of information about the sport facility via word of mouth and social media was in an effective, controlled, and positive manner. The overriding goal is to market the facility utilizing the various processes in consumer behavior to influence the sport consumer into coming to the sport facility for an event. Once in the facility, the goal is to have the sport consumer believe that the sport facility is delivering a sport product and experience that meets and satisfies their needs, which in turn results in the sport consumer's purchasing another sport product in the future and hence using the sport facility.

SPORT MARKETING INFRASTRUCTURE FOR SPORT FACILITIES

Once sport facility managers understand the intricacies of the sport consumer, they then need to understand the major logistical functions in sport marketing that affect how they position their sport facility and deliver the sport product through it. The major logistical functions a sport facility manager must understand in terms of sport marketing are product and service management, branding, and sales management.

Product and service management

Sport *product and service management* usually starts as a function of the sport marketing planning process. This process involves the development of the sport organization's products and services marketing strategies, including the tactics and programs to be implemented during the life span of the plan. It starts by defining the competitive set, which is the process of determining the direct competitors to a sport organization in the specific product or service area. Then the sport organization engages in category attractiveness analysis, in which aggregate marketing factors, segment factors, and environmental factors are considered. This is followed up with a competitor and consumer analyses.

Sport facility managers have products and services that they have total control over (internal) and products and services they have limited control over (external). Internal products include the facility itself – the playing surface and related equipment, seating, scoreboard/message boards, bathrooms, concession areas, and the general infrastructure. Internal services include maintenance, housekeeping, security, customer service, and first aid. External products include all aspects of the event being conducted at the facility. External services are the added benefits provided by the event and other external entities to enhance the experience of the customer. Marketing of internal products and services is an important job that the facility manager must undertake. Just as with any other product or service, increasing awareness and image are crucial to attracting events to the facility, as well as customers to attend them. Hence, the sport facility manager must be acutely aware of the sport product and service life cycle, as well as how each stage is directly affected by the realities of competition, saturation, and change.

The internal development stage begins with the idea of a new product or service (in the case of a new facility) or a new twist on an existing product or service (in the case of a modified facility). *Introduction to market* is the time when the sport organization puts its plan into action and starts capturing market share by introducing products and services to the market. In this stage, the benefits of holding events in the facility to event coordinators and of building brand awareness and equity within the community are vital. The *growth stage* is when the facility that offers the best product and/or service (both in the types of events and in the experience within the facility) rises to the top and separates itself from the competition. Maturity refers to the time at which the sport facility has maximized profits and is seeking to maintain a stable place in the market through regular events and a standard schedule. The goal is to maintain a regular place in the market as long as possible. However, as with any product, there will come a time when the saturation point is reached. This is when the sport facility manager must come to the realization that it needs to reevaluate their place in the market because they are no longer increasing their market share. Often this means that events and people are not coming to the venue because it is viewed as deteriorating or moving toward obsolescence. The decline stage is the last stage before obsolescence, and either the sport facility will have introduced new services or a next generation of the product (such as a renovation or refurbishment) or it needs to exit the market (usually through demolition and replacement).

Marketing of external products and services works in a similar manner. Sport facility managers keep their eye out for new products or services that can be presented through the sport facility, such as a new event in the marketplace that is of interest to the public. At the same time, regular events such as local teams and annual events need to be on the radar of the sport facility manager and plans made to attract them to the facility. When the event is introduced to the market, the goal is to attract these new events to the facility – hence capturing market share. The growth stage is when the reputation of the facility grows, and the best events want to appear in the facility. As that calendar of events grows, there is a period of maturity, where the image and awareness of the facility are at its highest, and the job of the facility manager is to balance the schedule and not go beyond the capability of the facility. At this time of maturity, the sport facility manager also needs to realize that, as events grow in scope (and hence their needs expand) and more modern facilities open, events may move on to other venues. The goal, as with the internal plan, is to maintain a regular place in the market as long as possible through positioning and differentiation.

Branding

Regardless of the size or type of sport facility, its most valuable asset is the facility itself, closely followed by the brands with whom it is associated. This may include naming rights sponsors, teams and organizations calling the facility home, and in many cases, the community the facility is located in. A *brand* is a name, term, design, symbol, or feature that identifies one sport product or services as being different from another. *Branding* is the perception of a potential stakeholder or what a consumer thinks of upon hearing or seeing the name or image of the sport facility. Defining the sport facility as a brand is the foundation for all other marketing, image, and equity elements of the sport facility and distinguishes one sport facility from another. Ultimately, the purpose of branding in sport facility operations management is to communicate reputation, build awareness, and articulate the status of the sport facility within a given marketplace as compared to that of competition. This marketplace can range from the local community (for example, one fitness center versus another fitness center), a region (for example, competition for attracting events between Madison Square Garden and the Barclay's Center in New York City), a country (for example, Emirates Stadium in London versus Etihad Stadium in Manchester in England), or globally (for example, Melbourne Cricket Ground in Australia versus Allianz Arena in Germany).

Sport facility managers are responsible for working with other marketing staff to develop and communicate various brand elements to the public to differentiate and position their venue based on either their name, location, or unique design and services. Hence, it is important to create a brand structure or brand architecture focusing on communicating the value and benefits that the sport facility provides to stakeholders. A clear brand structure is the main drivers of the marketing strategy for a sport facility, as well as for the associated extensions, partnerships, and sponsorships.

To design a relevant brand architecture, the sport facility manager must work in partnership with the marketing staff to select the most appropriate elements for marketing the sport brand and develop strategies that create value for the sport facility. Potential brand elements may be as simple as the name of the facility but are often enhanced using other elements such as logos and symbols, slogans, nicknames, or even endorsements by celebrities or athletes. Brand elements should be memorable, descriptive, persuasive, positive, adaptable to a dynamic environment, and transferable to extensions and partners. Selecting the correct brand elements maximizes brand awareness by the public, creates positive perceptions by the community, and may improve the opportunity to attract brand partnerships that can further advance the brand of the sport facility. When applied consistently with a focus on maximizing value, the enhancement of the brand identity, awareness, and image of the sport facility is a vital tool influencing competitive advantage in the marketplace.

Sales management

Sales are the backbone of any sport organization, and this is equally true of sport facilities. While the facility manager may not necessarily have direct involvement in the sales process, they need to have an acute awareness of the entire process and be prepared to offer advice, consultation, and opinions about sales efforts related to facility inventories. In addition, the facility manager, through their staff, builds and nurture personal relationships with customers – since many of the facility staff become the face of the facility because of their direct contact with the guests.

Facility managers are involved with the sales process on numerous facility inventories, including leasing/rental of the facility for events; ticketing and box office management; premium access (suites, club seating, permanent seating licenses/debentures); product branding through pouring rights (they are known quantity in sport marketing – the rights a sport facility has with a beverage provider (beer company, soft drink company) to sell those products in the facility) and various promotional sales efforts including advertising (signage and promotions) and sponsorships (naming rights and endorsements). Facility managers are also often in charge of selling their facility to potential clients for a variety of events, including sports, concerts, corporate rentals, hospitality events, graduation, fund-raisers, and a number of other types of events. The facility manager is often involved in the negotiation of these rental contracts – covering everything from costs of the spaces to be used to various costs including setup/breakdown, security, housekeeping, electrical/technology, special equipment usage, permits, fire/police clearance, storage, and insurance.

Another major area facility managers must oversee is ticketing and box office management. From a ticketing standpoint, the facility manager needs to coordinate with teams and events to understand the various ticketing structures, inform ticket-taking staff of those structures, employing enough staff to serve the guests and ensure that ushers and security understand the level of access that tickets (and in many cases credentials) allow. As for the box office, many do not realize that the facility owns the box office – not teams or events. There are times when some of the box office operations are outsourced (for example, via team/event ticketing or outside vendors such as Ticketmaster), but all ticketing for events at some point must go through the box office. Usually, a box office employee reports to and works with the facility manager to determine ticketing based on space available, facility configuration for a specific event, and changes that may occur after the event has been set up. The box office is also responsible for creating a manifest, which is a listing of every seat available in a facility that is used to coordinate with teams, customers, promoters/booking agents, and outsourcing vendors to track pricing and availability of seating in the venue. This master list serves as the main source of information for every event. In addition to manifesting and ticketing, the facility manager is also responsible for coordinating relationships with the tenants of the facility, security of the box office (since a lot of money does go through the box office daily), and event day ingress/egress. They are also actively involved with overseeing on-sales for new events coming to the facility, both marketing of the on-sale and the management of the on-sale day.

Premium access is a financially lucrative part of running a sport facility, and facility managers need to pay special attention to ensure that users of these inventories are receiving value for the money they have paid. There are four main types of premium access seating: premium seating, club seating, luxury boxes/suites, and personal (or sometimes permanent) seat licenses (PSLs). Premium seating is the best of seats in the facility – front row at the basketball game, behind the plate or dugout at a baseball game or midfield at a soccer or rugby games. Club seating is specialized seating in the facility with special access and amenities that usually include food and beverage with the price of admission. Luxury boxes/suites are private rooms with seating for those with access to the box/suite, a lounge area, private bathroom, and food/beverage service either catered or available through wait staff. PSLs, which are also known as debentures, are where customers pay a one-time fee to gain ownership of a specific seat; they must pay a yearly season ticket fee to maintain the license.

The food and beverage industry is an integral part of the sport facility. While the operations may be kept either in-house or outsourced to another company, product branding through pouring rights is one area in which the facility manager must be closely involved. Because of exclusive agreements with beverage companies such as Coca-Cola and Pepsi or alcohol companies such as Anheuser Busch, Miller, or Coors, the facility manager is often the individual who is involved with these negotiations. Usually, their involvement involves leveraging the contract to include dedicated funds for facility upgrades and improvements, along with specific guidelines on how the branding of the facility by the vendor can be implemented.

TECHNOLOGY NOW! 1HUDDLE (UNITED STATES)

Within the realm of marketing for sport facilities, one of the most important departments is sales. The sales function for a sport facility may range from selling tickets to events through the box office to selling advertisement and sponsorship within the facility. As the new Millennial generation enters the workplace, the challenge of training them in the areas of sales and service is often a challenge. One of the reasons for this challenge is the way the new millennial employee prefers to learn new skills. According to Sam Caucci, CEO of 1Huddle (http://1huddle.co), '50% of Millennials will have logged over 10,000 hours on some type of gaming platform before the age of 21.' In addition, 'currently 91% of college graduates say they are unprepared entering the workforce, and 72% of companies do little or no training, resulting in 42% of college graduates being either unemployed or underemployed.'

This has resulted in sport industry professionals realizing that the new generation of employees have the skills necessary to succeed in the workforce but lack the experiences needed to develop those skills and habits further to aid in succeeding at their job. Since Millennials and Generation Z have grown up with the Internet and gaming platforms, it seems to make sense to use gaming mechanics that place employees in situations that enhance the likelihood of developing the necessary skills for the workforce

1HUDDLE Group has developed multiple platforms that can be used by sport facility operations managers to help prepare this new generation to succeed in sales and marketing, as well as in facility and event service management. The innovative simulation platform customized to a specific sport facility or organization using existing sales, service, and training processes, 'gamifying' them not only to meet the needs of this new generation of employees but also to provide an opportunity for repeated, 24/7 personalized training in real time in perpetuity, both in theoretical content and in real-world role-playing scenarios.

It is a functional tool that can be used in multiple environments because of its online capabilities. There are multiple styles of play from individualized training to team exercises, allowing the sport facility manager to create multiple training scenarios. The tools can also be used in a range of time formats from short refresher training to longer retreat or formal training sessions. Through the gaming platform, the training becomes fun, engaging, and competitive and provides opportunities to use real analytics to create rewards systems and incentive programs for employees. Ultimately, the goal of the tool is to create a culture of 'winning,' resulting in a higher level of success when applying these skills in real-world situations on the job.

Sport facility managers are also involved with numerous promotional sales efforts, including advertising and sponsorship sales. The final section of this chapter covers the promotional aspects of sport marketing and how the facility manager's involvement in promotional mix elements includes and goes beyond just the sale of advertising and sponsorship.

PROMOTIONAL COMMUNICATIONS FOR SPORT FACILITIES

Promotions are a very involved communications process that aids in providing information about the sport facility to consumers through the promotional mix. The elements of the sport promotional mix that sport facility managers work with include advertising, sponsorship, public relations, and atmospherics. To coordinate the interaction between the elements of the sport promotional mix, a strategy must be developed that focuses on building brand loyalty and product credibility, developing the image, and positioning the brand. The strategic process involves promotional integration, which is the actual creation and delivery of the promotional message. This involves defining how the message is to reach the consumer, ensuring that the promotional message will be received and understood and that the promotional message will lead to the purchase of a product or service – in the case of a sport facility, attending an event at the facility. The ultimate goal is to build brand awareness for the facility through a series of integrations (image, functional, coordinated, consumer-based, stakeholder-based, and relationship management) that will lead to the overall strategic promotional implementation. A number of generalizations can be made about promotions. Promotions temporarily increase sales substantially. Promotions in one product category affect sales of brands in complementary and competitive categories. Promotions also can result in increased traffic to the sport facility. Most of the generalizations are true; however, it is important to understand how to utilize these elements in order to ensure that the results are long-lasting and lead to maintaining current customers and attracting new customers to the sport facility.

Advertising

Advertising is the process of attracting public attention to a sport product or sport business through paid announcements in the print, broadcast, or electronic media. As a primary element of the sport promotions mix, the communication process is utilized most often in sport marketing for sport facilities. Through advertisements, advertising campaigns, and integrated brand promotion, advertising helps establish and maintain relationships with sport consumers by providing a conduit for listening and reacting to sport consumers through their attendance at an event hosted by the sport facility.

Advertising in sport facilities is an integral tool of marketing as related to brand development and management, segmentation, differentiation, and positioning. As a result, advertising efforts need to be congruent with the sport facility's brand strategy and the branding process. The brand strategy has a direct impact on the sport facility's value in terms of market capitalization and corporate value. The branding process provides the sport consumer with a clear understanding of the attributes and values of the sport facility. Sport facility advertising efforts will be unique to each facility and to the events and services being offered; however, the ultimate goal is to utilize the advertising efforts to enhance sport facility loyalty through brand association and to build a brand image through the association with the brands being advertised.

The sport facility manager is involved with the marketing, sales, and implementation of advertising in a sport facility. The goal of sport facility advertising is to maximize the visibility of the brand's image and to build brand association and loyalty with customers to the sport facility – while enhancing the image and awareness of the sport facility. Sport facility managers are involved with developing the partnerships since they are the ones who are ultimately involved with implementing and managing the advertisement efforts within the sport facility. The majority of this implementation usually involves signage in the facility. The most common types of signage include banners, infrastructure (embedded in the facility framework), field/court surfaces, and scoreboard/computerized. However, in recent years, sport facility managers have become very creative with the inventories available for advertising signage. These include step signage, wall wraps, turnstiles, garbage cans, bathrooms, and in-game equipment (such as silhouetted advertisements on nets above the glass in ice hockey arenas or field goal nets behind football uprights).

Sponsorship

Sport sponsorship involves acquiring the rights to be affiliated with a sport product or business in order to obtain benefits from that association. Sport sponsorships play a significant role in the sport promotional mix and take place at multiple levels of the sport business landscape. Especially in the United States, the most lucrative sponsorship agreements are naming rights with sport facilities. As such, sport facility managers are involved with the management of these sponsorships to ensure that these terms of the sponsorship are being upheld in terms of exclusivity, signage within the facility, implementation of promotional activities, and accuracy in the delivery of the corporate image and likeness.

Sport sponsorship agreements between corporations and sport facilities are documented within a sponsorship proposal. These packages are designed to articulate the benefits derived from the agreement for all parties involved. The reason for entering into a sport sponsorship agreement varies from organization to organization. Corporations have numerous goals resulting from sport sponsorship, including increasing public awareness, enhancing their company image, building business and trade relationships with other sponsoring organizations, changing or improving public perception of their company, increasing community involvement in the target area, and enhancing personnel relations by offering opportunities for employees to attend sponsored events, including attendance at hospitality areas. The goals of a sport facility related to sponsorship include taking in additional revenue from the agreement and increasing target market awareness, image, sales, and market share.

Sport facility sponsorships are naming rights agreements for stadiums, arenas, and other sport facilities. Since 2000, this is the fastest growing area of sport sponsorship, as many sport facilities around the world have sold their naming rights to sport corporations. These deals are usually long term and significant in value. In addition, the value of the sponsorship will vary with the size of the market, the level of competition playing, and the assortment of events scheduled by the facility. In Table 9.1 are some examples of major sport facility naming rights deals currently in place around the world. You will note that the deals in the United States are significantly longer in term and have a higher cost per year than in other parts of the world.

Table 9.1 Global sport facility naming rights deals

Location	Name of Facility	Location	Terms (in millions)
United States (in USD)	MetLife Stadium	New York	$425 for 25 years
	Citi Field	East Rutherford, NJ	$400 for 20 years
	Mercedes-Benz Stadium	Atlanta, GA	$324 for 27 years
	Reliant Stadium	Houston, TX	$310 for 31 years
	Chase Center	San Francisco, CA	$300 for 20 years
	Levi's Stadium	San Francisco, CA	$220 for 20 years
Canada (in CND)	Scotiabank Arena	Toronto, ON	$800 for 20 years
	Rogers Arena	Vancouver, BC	$70 for 10 years
	Bell Centre	Montreal, QC	$64 for 20 years
	BMO Field	Toronto, ON	$23.7 for 10 years
Europe (local currency)	Etihad Stadium	Manchester, England	£100 for 10 years
	Allianz Arena	Munich, Germany	£60 for 15 years
	Aviva Stadium	Dublin, Ireland	€50 for 10 years
Asia (local currency)	Nissan Stadium	Yokohama, Japan	¥470 for 5 years
	Mercedes-Benz Arena	Shanghai, China	CNY397 for 10 years
Africa (local currency)	Bidvest Stadium	South Africa	ZAR450 for 5 years
Australia (in AUD)	Marvel Stadium	Melbourne, VIC	AU$70 for 8 years
	Optus Stadium	Perth, WA	AU$50 for 10 years
	ANZ Stadium	Sydney, NSW	AU$31.5 for 7 years
	AAMI Park	Melbourne, VIC	AU$10 for 8 years
South America (local currency)	Allianz Parque	Sao Paulo, Brazil	BRL$300 for 20 years

Enhancement of other promotional mix elements

Sport facility managers also are involved in enhancing other aspects of the promo-tional mix – especially public relations and atmospherics. *Public relations* is the collection of activities, communications, and media coverage that convey what the sport organization is and what it has to offer, all in the effort to enhance their image and prestige. Through public relations, the sport facility director focuses on getting information out to the public through various methods to enhance the image and awareness of the facility and the events to be hosted. In order to get the best value, facility managers focus on the use of unpaid, nonpersonal promotion of the facil-ity through a third party (usually the media) that publishes print media or presents information through radio, television, or the Internet. The goal of any good publicity is that it is viewed as coming from an unbiased, neutral source. A sport facility manager understands that utilizing public relations is critical to success, as it is the management function that helps to evaluate public attitudes, articulate the policies and procedures of an organization that may be of public interest, and execute programs of action to acquire public understanding and approval.

The most important relationship is with the media. Media relations are the activities that involve working directly with individuals responsible for the production of mass media including news, features, public service announcements, and sponsored programming. Effective media relations maximize the coverage and placement of messages and information in the mass media without paying for it directly through advertising. Most media relations activities are designed to get free media coverage for programs and issues. As such, the sport facility manager engages in a number of efforts to give the media more access than the general customer does. This includes a press box/press row exclusively for the media; credentials for sideline/on field access/locker room, and behind-the-scenes access; areas for holding exclusive and group press conferences/interviews; and access to communications (phones/faxes/Internet technology) to file stories efficiently. Since the media will also be at the events in the facility for longer than the general public, the facility manager works with catering to ensure that food and beverage services are provided either in the press box or in a press-only dining area. The goal of providing a significant amount of access and service to the media is to get free media coverage that shows the sport facility in a positive light among the significant competition that is vying for a limited amount of airtime or print space.

Another aspect of promotions that is under the major control of the sport facility director is atmospherics. *Atmospherics* utilizes the design of visual communications in an environment to entice the sport consumer's perceptual and emotional responses to purchase the sport product or service. As a result of this operational function, the sport facility manager is able to control the environment based on the needs and wants of the consumer. Examples of sensory aesthetics include temperature, lighting, sound, color/appearance, and traffic flow.

SPORT FACILITY MARKETING UTILIZING SOCIAL, DIGITAL AND MOBILE MEDIA

While it is not possible to completely forecast the future of sport facility marketing, one area that has evolved significantly over the past decade is that of social, digital, and mobile media.

Communications in the past were mostly one-way, that is, asynchronous, where sport facility marketers struggled to identify and directly interact with customers unless they were physically in a facility. The evolution of these communications through social media, digital media, and mobile technologies have provided greater synchronous and asynchronous methods for directly getting and staying in touch with stakeholders. This allows sport facility managers to gather quality marketing information about the perceptions of the facility and the needs of the stakeholders, as well as to deliver value-added services to enhance the facility experience.

The initial evolution into this new generation of communication is social media, which is a dynamic, multiconnection communication technology that allows users to have instantaneous access to web-based tools to create content. The user-generated content through social media is disseminated through multiple Internet platforms including blogs, content aggregators, content communities, forums and bulletin boards, and social networks. At the time of publication, the social media sites Facebook, Instagram, Twitter, and YouTube are four of the top 20 most visited websites globally. These platforms all offer the viability of sharing activities in real time, can be stored long-term in perpetuity, and allow for contributions and results evaluation anywhere and anytime.

This co-creation of content can be used for a multitude of personal and business reasons. For sport facilities, social media is driven by a variety of stakeholders both internal and external to the organization and can directly influence the business continuity, brand, and image of a sport facility. Facility managers need to ensure that the information posted on all social media platforms is continuously updated, provides value-added information for the stakeholder, and seeks to enhance the relationship between stakeholders and the facility. This responsibility can range from posting changes to opening times for a facility for an event, to interactive diagrams and maps for easy ingress, egress, and movement in the facility, to games and contests promoting the facility and encouraging connections. Ultimately, sport facility managers seek to use social media to capitalize on opportunities across multiple platforms delivering the same message while maintaining the uniqueness and individuality of each platform. Sport facility managers must recognize the benefits of social media as a vital marketing communication tool that is well integrated across all marketing, operations, and service efforts.

In line with the growth of social media is the evolution of both digital media and mobile technologies. As with social media, the growth of digital and mobile communications has further changed the way sport is consumed and how sport facilities need to connect with stakeholders.

FACILITY FOCUS: MARKETING SINGAPORE AS A SPORTING DESTINATION: SINGAPORE SPORTS HUB, SINGAPORE

As a part of the Singapore government's Vision 2030 sports master plan, the Singapore Sports Hub opened in June 2014 and is an integrated land and water sports and lifestyle complex with not only world-class sporting facilities but also extensive retail and commercial space. It was built with a vision of delivering a sustainable, differentiated and competitive advantage for marketing Singapore as a sport destination location. It won the 2013 World Architecture Festival (WAF) award for best future project in the leisure-led development category and in 2017 entered the Guinness Book of World Records as having the largest true dome.

The Singapore Sports Hub includes the following facilities:

- A 55,000-seat, retractable-roof National Stadium
- A 13,000-seat indoor stadium
- A 6,000-seat aquatics center
- A 3,000-seat multipurpose arena
- A water sports center that includes programming for canoeing and kayaking
- The Kallang Wave Mall – a 41,000-square-meter retail and dining area
- A Sports Information and Resource Center with an exhibition center, library, and sport museum
- A water park for children
- Numerous open spaces for community, sport, and recreational activities

Entertainment events such as the 28th Southeast Asian Games, International Champions Cup, HSBC Singapore Rugby Sevens, international football friendlies, as well as internationally acclaimed artists, take place regularly at the Singapore Sports Hub.

In their first full year of operation (2015), they had over 3.5 million visitors, which included 1.4 million guests across 124 sport and entertainment events, nearly 550,000 users of recreational and leisure facilities and programs, and over 1.6 million attendees to festivals and carnivals.

They also offer their innovative Sports Hub Tix – a one-stop ticketing service designed with an enhanced user experience that is interactive, intuitive, and integrated. It allows users the ability to view the vantage point from that section before making an informed purchase, and it then prints their tickets at home or delivers them to their smartphone.

For more information, go to www.sportshub.com.sg

Sport facility managers also now need to manage additional levels of broadcasting and entertainment offerings to meet the needs of marketing professionals and wants of consumers and stakeholders. As new digital applications continue to evolve, the opportunity for sport facilities to enhance their advertising and promotional activities expands exponentially. The amount of broadcasting from a sport facility also increases significantly, further communicating the brand and image. Also, the evolution of Millennial and Generation Z sport activities will provide more opportunities for sport facilities to offer new and diverse events. At publication time, the advances in virtual reality personalization and the growth of augmented reality – especially through the growth of eSports – seems to be the first wave of this new growth.

Millennials and Generation Z are rapidly becoming the influencers of sport consumption. Millennials – also known as Generation Y or GenNext – are individuals who were born between 1985 and 2000. They are seen as being the first global generation, due to shared values across borders, who can view international events in real time through digital and social media. These digital pioneers prefer collaborations via digital connections but will engage in new opportunities based on interactions with opinion leaders. Generation Z, also known as the iGeneration, are individuals who were born after 2000. This generation has evolved into viewing themselves as global citizens who want more face-to-face collaborations and on-demand learning within a safe and secure environment.

The way sport facility managers connect, engage, and attract customers from different generations requires different methods. This is especially true with Millennials and Generation Z and has been a driver of the growth of social, digital, and mobile media technologies. There has been a shift from the media and sport organizations being the drivers of content to fans providing user-generated content (UGC), resulting in virtually unlimited opportunities to distribute and receive content to an increasingly segmented consumer markets across hundreds (if not thousands) of distribution channels. This has created a shift in the commercialization of sport from a mass audience focus toward the implementation of specialized one-to-one sport marketing efforts. Hence, sport facility managers must evolve from simply using mass marketing and traditional marketing methods through marketing mix elements to new innovative methods of reaching Millennials and Generation Z. This includes the evolution of sport facilities to deliver sport data analytics and the ability to build data transformation systems, develop the algorithms, and creatively combine various big data sets that will deliver higher-order information to supplement the in-facility experience.

For sport facility managers, the bottom line of 'bums on seats' has not changed, but the customers have. Engaging Millennials and Generation Z via UGC and data analytics using social media, digital media, and mobile technologies is crucial for future success. Sport facility managers must understand how to scale their efforts using new technologies based on the type of facility from the local community to large-scale stadia. The key is sport facility managers working side by side with sport marketing professionals to create content that users want in a timely manner across multiple platforms and devices with fast access, accurate content, and pleasing visual aesthetics.

eSPORTS AND THE NEW SPORT ARENA FOR MILLENNIALS AND GEN Z

The way sport marketers connect, engage, and attract customers from different generations requires different methods. This is especially true with Millennials and Generation Z. For example, there has been a shift from the media and sport organizations being the drivers of content; fans being able to provide user-generated content (UGC) has resulted in a virtually unlimited opportunity to distribute and receive content to increasingly segmented consumer markets across hundreds (if not thousands) of distribution channels. This has also created a shift in the type of sporting activities that are becoming part of the mainstream of global sport. Advances in virtual reality personalization and the growth of augmented reality are driving these changes, but it is the major advances of eSports in the sporting landscape that is leading the way of connecting to and engaging with future stakeholders.

The evolution of eSports in the mainstream of international sport business is validated by the international sport marketing strategies currently implemented by professional leagues, including the Australian Football League (AFL), the National Football League (NFL), and the National Basketball Association (NBA). From a sport facility management standpoint, this has ranged from the need to have the latest technologies and equipment in order to be considered as a host for these events to the development of stand-alone facilities for eSports. These eSports facilities range from stand-alone facilities (the first being the eSports Arena in Santa Ana, California) to eSports facilities being connected to existing traditional sport facilities (such as the new eSports high-performance center in Australia at the Sydney Cricket Ground) to facilities associated with other ventures (the eSports arena at the Luxor Hotel in Las Vegas).

How important will these new types of facilities be? According to Newzoo, a leading company that tracks marketing intelligence in the digital games industry, it was estimated that at press time of this book over 1.5 billion people worldwide were aware of eSports, 215 million were considered eSports enthusiasts, and revenue for global eSports was projected to hit $1 billion for the first time by the end of 2019 (ESPN, 2016).

Suggested discussion topics

1   One of the recent evolutions, as noted in the case study, is the creation of an eSports high-performance center at the Sydney Cricket Ground in Australia in 2018. Research the center, and explain the management and operational uniqueness of this type of facility as compared to a traditional sport facility.

Implementing operations management

2　What challenges and opportunities are inherent with replicating the development of a high-performance center such as the one at the Sydney Cricket Ground in Australia to other existing sport facilities globally?

3　How are leagues that own eSports franchises, such as the Australian Football League (AFL), the National Football League (NFL), and the National Basketball Association (NBA), creating or modifying facilities to host these new ventures?

CHAPTER REVIEW

Facility managers need to have a solid foundation in marketing and should be involved in all aspects of marketing that relate to the sport facility. The association of sport marketing and sport facilities interact to best provide products and services that satisfy the needs, wants, and desires of the consumer and aid in the planning, organizing, directing, controlling, budgeting, leading, and evaluation of a facility whose primary product and service is related to sport, recreation, leisure, and entertainment.

The focal point of these marketing functions is in four specific areas known as the 4 Cs of marketing analysis: the consumer, the company itself, the competition, and the climate. Sport marketers reach sport consumers through segmenting the population, targeting specific groups, positioning the sport facility to influence potential customers to attend an event at the facility, and then deliver on what is promised. With regard to the company and competition, the framework is centered on a situation (SWOT) analysis – internal strengths and weakness of the company and external opportunities and threats posed by competition and the environment. The climate involves forecasting the factors that will have a direct effect on the internal and external functioning of the sport facility.

The sport consumer can be broken down into numerous categories. After a simple breakdown – participants and spectators – in reality, there are multiple levels of spectators, including sport fanatics, club/team loyalists, social viewers, opportunistic viewers, star-struck spectators, and sport-indifferent consumers. In order to understand these various consumers, sport facility managers must be able to incorporate an effective marketing information system into their marketing efforts to compile the various data available in one place for use in making marketing decisions. In addition, the sport facility manager must also comprehend and apply the principles of consumer behavior, which is the conduct consumers display in seeking out, ordering, buying, using, and assessing products and services that the consumers expect will satisfy their needs and wants. The sport facility manager must also understand the major logistical functions in sport marketing that affect how they position their sport facility and deliver the sport product through the sport facility. The major logistical functions a sport facility manager must understand in terms of sport marketing are product and service management, branding, and sales management.

Understanding these foundational sport marketing concepts assists the sport facility manager with developing and applying various promotional efforts to market the sport facility. Promotions are a collection of communications processes that aid in providing information about the sport facility to consumers through advertising, sponsorship, public relations, media relations, and atmospherics. While many of the traditional promotional communication efforts were based on one-way communication with stakeholders, the evolution of social media, digital media, and mobile technologies have changed the way in which sport facility managers market their venue. This requires the development of content that users want in a timely manner across multiple platforms and devices with fast access, accurate content, and visually pleasing aesthetics. This is especially important if sport facility managers want to attract Millennials and Generation Z customers to their venues as users and customers.

IN THE FIELD . . .

Naming rights at Marvel Stadium, Melbourne, Australia

Located in the Docklands district in Melbourne, the stadium now called Marvel Stadium has had a long history of names. Built during 1997–2000 as a replacement stadium for Australian Rules Football (AFL) games, it has always had the general moniker of Docklands Stadium no matter the naming rights. However, from a naming rights perspective, it starts as Colonial Stadium as part of a ten-year naming rights agreement with Colonial State Bank. When Commonwealth Bank took over Colonial, rather than renaming the stadium, they sold the rights to telecommunications company Telstra, who then renamed the venue Telstra Dome. This lasted until 2009 when Etihad Airways took over the naming rights and renamed the venue Etihad Stadium. As of 2019, the name has changed again to Marvel Stadium due to a new partnership with Disney.

While the multiple name changes from Colonial to Telstra to Etihad were mainly business functions of a cash infusion for the stadium owners and brand awareness for the corporate partner, the latest name change came with many more operational, marketing, and strategic outcomes. To start is the ownership of the facility. The AFL was set to take hold of the stadium for $30 in 2025 as part of the original deal for the stadium to be built. A consortium of super and

Implementing operations management

investment funds that bought the venue from Seven West Media in 2006 had privately owned the stadium. The AFL wanted to take over ownership sooner because they believed they could bring back in-house marketing, ticketing, human resource, and event management functions that would save money in the long run, while the owners wanted to maximize their returns well in advance of having to give up the facility in 2025. So in November 2016, an agreement and purchase were finalized for the AFL to take over ownership and management of the stadium.

With the agreement with Etihad ending in 2019, this provided an opportunity for the AFL to negotiate a new naming rights deal to maximize revenue from the facility sponsorship. However, and more importantly, the AFL was looking for a partner to help maximize the experience for customers. You will see how it did so in the continuation of this facility focus in Chapter 11.

BIBLIOGRAPHY

Funk, D. C., & James, J. D. (2004a). Exploring origins of involvement: Understanding the relationship between consumer motives and involvement with professional sport teams. *Leisure Sciences*, *26*(1), 35–61. https://doi.org/10.1080/01490400490272440

Funk, D. C., & James, J. D. (2004b). The Fan Attitude Network (FAN) model: Exploring attitude formation and change among sport consumers. *Sport Management Review*, *7*(1), 1–26. https://doi.org/10.1016/s1441-3523(04)70043-1

Hassanien, A., & Dale, C. (2012). Drivers and barriers of new product development and innovation in event venues: A multiple case study. *Journal of Facilities Management*, *10*(1), 75–92. https://doi.org/10.1108/14725961211200414

Hock, C., Ringle, C. M., & Sarstedt, M. (2010). Management of multi-purpose stadiums: Importance and performance measurements of service interfaces. *International Journal of Services Technology and Management*, *14*(2/3), 188–207. https://doi.org/10.1504/ijstm.2010.034327

Murray, D., & Howat, G. (2002). The relationships among service quality, value, satisfaction, and future intentions of customers at an Australian sports and leisure centre. *Sport Management Review*, *5*(1), 25–43. https://doi.org/10.1016/s1441-3523(02)70060-0

Rovell, D. (2016). *427 million people will be watching esports by 2019, reports Newzoo*. Retrieved February 5, 2019, from www.espn.com/esports/story/_/id/15508214/427-million-people-watching-esports-2019-reports-newzoo

Schwarz, E. C., & Hunter, J. D. (2017). *Advanced theory and practice in sport marketing* (3rd ed.). London: Routledge.

Wang, J. (2013). Research on market development and management mode of stadiums of colleges and universities in Hunan Province. *Journal of Applied Sciences*, *13*(21), 4744–4748. https://doi.org/10.3923/jas.2013.4744.4748

Westerbeek, H. M., & Shilbury, D. (1999). Increasing the focus on 'place' in the marketing mix for facility dependent sport services. *Sport Management Review*, *2*(1), 1–23. https://doi.org/10.1016/S1441-3523(99)70087-2

Westerbeek, H. M., & Shilbury, D. (2003). A conceptual model for sport services marketing research: Integrating quality, value and satisfaction. *International Journal of Sports Marketing and Sponsorship*, *5*(1), 3–23. https://doi.org/10.1108/IJSMS-05-01-2003-B002

Yoshida, M., & James, J. D. (2010). Customer satisfaction with game and service experiences: Antecedents and consequences. *Journal of Sport Management*, *24*(3), 338–361. https://doi.org/10.1123/jsm.24.3.338

CHAPTER 10

REVENUE GENERATION AND DIVERSIFICATION

CHAPTER OUTLINE

- Introduction to revenue generation and diversification
- The importance of space and time
- Selling the core product
- Other forms of income generation
    - Visitor attractions
    - Conference venue/trade shows
    - Celebrations and adverse events
    - Other assets
- Future directions
- Chapter review

CHAPTER OBJECTIVES

Constructing sport facilities is an expensive business with costs now running at hundreds of millions and, in extreme cases, over a billion dollars. It is quite unlikely that any single investor would have the resources to make that kind of investment unilaterally; hence, it now requires numerous investors to share the financial risks with an expectation of a decent return on their investment. Thus for the very simple reason that the managers of a facility need to make sufficient money to be able to service their loans, pay their other expenses, and ultimately make a profit, it follows that revenue generation and diversification are vital issues to manage if a facility is to be commercially viable. In this chapter, we look at the challenges of generating and diversifying revenue in sport facilities and review examples of how the industry is taking advantage of the opportunities being offered by technological advances.

INTRODUCTION TO REVENUE GENERATION AND DIVERSIFICATION

Whether it is large multipurpose stadiums whose costs are now extending beyond one billion dollars USD or smaller-scale sport facilities such as gyms, swimming pools, and tennis courts; the financial resources needed to build and manage these types of venues while providing a return on investment to stakeholders and hopefully generating a profit can be quite daunting. The need for sport facility managers to generate revenue from diverse sources is vital to ensure financial viability. Beyond the basic commercial argument of being able to convince investors that your facility is sufficiently viable to justify their investment, there are wider arguments as to why sport facilities need to make money. First, much of the justification for public sector investment is the likely economic impact a development will have on its host community. The more events that take place in a facility, the greater the number of out-of-town visitors who come to the area, who in turn support local businesses with their spending. The net effect of this spending is an increased level of economic activity in the local area, which in turn leads to employment and increased activity all the way down the supply chain.

Second, facilities have the potential to create jobs. These occur during the construction phase for a limited period, and once a facility is operational, it will provide meaningful work for a variety of people with differing skill sets in all levels of the job market, including cleaners, retail assistants, electricians, plumbers, stewards, grounds staff, administrators, marketing and sales, sponsorship, matchday hosts, and senior management. To provide people with regular employment a facility must be run profitably in order to pay the staff their wages and salaries.

The greater the scale of sport facility, the greater the potential is for economic impact and employment opportunities. Most major sport facilities such as stadia tend to be dedicated to a primary purpose. For example, Old Trafford in Manchester, England, is the home to Manchester United Football Club. Also known as The Theatre of Dreams, Old Trafford has a seating capacity of 75,000. The club takes part in the English Premier League (EPL) in which 20 teams play one another home and away during the football season. Thus, each team will play 38 matches per season, of which 19 will be at home and 19 will be away. In addition, there may be additional home matches depending on the draws for knockout cup competitions such as the FA Cup and the League Cup. If the team is successful, it can qualify for the European Champions' League, which will also guarantee more home matches. Even in a perfect season, during which a club like, say, Manchester United was to win the FA Cup, the League Cup, and the Champions' League, the maximum number of home matches played would be around 35. Even in this extreme set of unlikely circumstances, the primary purpose of professional football would not fill the stadium for 10% of the days in a year. For this reason, the owners of sport facilities seek to generate revenues from other sources in order to service loans, pay shareholders, keep people in jobs, and make a profit.

In the case of Manchester United, the ground is used to host other events such as Rugby League matches (e.g., internationals and the Super League Grand Final), pop concerts (e.g., The Rolling Stones in June 2018), and Rugby Union internationals (it was a venue for the 2015 Rugby World Cup). Built into the stadium and its surroundings are a museum, retail outlets, meeting and conference facilities, car parks, and restaurants and bars. With daily stadium and museum tours hosting around 300,000 visitors per year, Old Trafford is a tourist attraction in its own right with a diversified offer that ensures the stadium is not wholly dependent on matchday income. However, there are many more challenges and opportunities related to generating and diversifying revenue in sport facilities. These include but are not limited to attracting sufficient events or 'product' to the facility, ensuring that these events are successful commercially, and delivering a high-quality experience for customers and sponsors.

THE IMPORTANCE OF SPACE AND TIME

If we consider what we are selling at a sport facility, we can summarize the offer as consisting of two things: space and time. Old Trafford stadium has a capacity of 75,000 seats that range from uncovered seats behind the goal to the last word in comfort and fine dining in the Centennial Club Suite. Between these extremes are various levels of comfort and price designed to meet the needs of numerous different market segments. Therefore, challenge number one is to sell as much space as possible at the best possible price to optimize income. A game of football (soccer) lasts for 90 minutes, and with half time and stoppage time, typically a game will last for nearly two hours. Consequently what we are also selling is time. It is widely held in the tourism and day visit worlds that longer dwell time generally equates to higher expenditure. For example, people who come to the stadium an hour before kickoff are more likely to purchase food and drink in the stadium than those who arrive at the last minute. Challenge number two, then, is to provide opportunities for people to increase their dwell time for the facility to benefit from their additional expenditure. Notable examples include pre-match entertainment to draw people in early or keeping bars and restaurants open after a match so that people have the choice to remain on site, perhaps to avoid the queues for public transport or for getting out of car parks. If we draw on the principles of basic economics and marketing, we can conclude that space and time are limited resources and are perishable in the sense that, once an event has started, any unsold space or time is lost forever. The overall challenge, then, for sport facility managers is to realize that they are in charge of finite resources and to organize their activities in such a way as to maximize income, bearing in mind the constraints of space and time. An indication of the scale of the revenues generated by matchdays can be seen in the published financial statements from Manchester United Football club over the five years 2014–2018 inclusive, as shown in Table 10.1.

Table 10.1 Manchester United matchday revenues and games, 2014–2018

Measure	2018	2017	2016	2015	2014
Matchday revenue	£109,776,000	£111,635,000	£106,587,000	£90,583,000	£108,103,000
Matches played	26	31	29	21	28
Revenue per match	£4.22 million	£3.60 million	£3.68 million	£4.31 million	£3.86 million
Annual revenue per seat	£1,464	£1,488	£1,421	£1,208	£1,441
Revenue per seat per match	£56	£48	£49	£58	£51

Source: www.sec.gov

In Table 10.1, the importance of space and time is shown in stark relief. Each unit of space at Old Trafford (one of the 75,000 seats) generated an average of £1,464 in the 2017/2018 season. Each unit of time (a match) generated £4.22 million, or the equivalent of £56 per seat. As a sport facility manager in this type of environment, you need to be willing to accept the challenge to generate the revenue required to achieve the company's commercial objectives. You can rest assured that your performance will be monitored and your career trajectory will depend on the extent to which you are capable of delivering!

SELLING THE CORE PRODUCT

The most important concept to grasp when thinking about selling the space and time within a sport facility is that of market segmentation. The people who attend sport events have different requirements as to what they wish to get out of their experience. At one end of the continuum might be the children who want to see their heroes as often as possible and at as a low cost as possible. At the other end might be sponsors who wish to entertain their clients in an exclusive hospitality box complete with a fine dining experience in order to maintain and influence business relationships. There are many different customer experience points between these two extremes, but the basic principle is that in the case of Old Trafford, although there are 75,000 seats to sell, not all seats are the same, and different market segments have different expectations of their experience. The challenge for venue managers is to identify and meet these varying needs profitably. They accomplish this by varying the prices for seats through the creation of a seating manifest.

Implementing operations management

SEATING MANIFESTS: HOW MUCH TO CHARGE FOR ENTRY?

One of the biggest challenges in selling the core product in a sport facility is determining the price for entry. This can vary based on a number of factors including the type of event, how much the market is willing to pay for a ticket, and the location of the seating in the sport facility. To manage this, box office managers in partnership with sport facility managers and event promoters develop a seating manifest, which is a listing of every individual seat within a sport facility based on section, row, and seat number. This manifest then allows for the pricing of every individual seat in the facility for a specific event.

Why is the seating manifest so important? First, it provides an accurate inventory of seating available for an event. Available seating can differ based on event setup including so-called seat kills (seating not available because of obstructions such as staging or cameras for broadcasting) or additional seating on the floor of the stadium or arena. It can also be affected by infrastructure issues such as seating not available during renovations or availability of space to build out more seating. Second is the ability to identify special seating in a sport facility ranging from corporate boxes to disability accessible seating. Third, it creates a visual map of all seating within a venue that can then be used to identify seats sold and still available and hence accurately project potential revenues from ticket sales. Finally, it becomes a central repository of information that can be used by all authorized sellers of tickets, including the box office itself, the team or event ticket sales representatives, and outsourced ticketing agencies such as Ticketmaster.

Speaking of Ticketmaster, their customer relationship management (CRM) platform Archtics is one of the world's leading in-house ticketing solutions used by sport facilities to enhance their box office, marketing, ticketing, and fan engagement capabilities. The platform allows for efficient seating manifest creation, management, and maintenance to configure pricing to maximize revenue and provide accurate information to stakeholders.

Suggested discussion questions

1   What factors would you need to consider when coming up with different seating pricing structures for an arena hosting a professional basketball team versus a concert at the same venue versus a WWE event?

217

2 What role does a seating manifest play in delivering:
  a Ticket resale?
  b Event cancellation?
  c Marketing of future events at the venue?

The application of the seating manifest provides a blueprint to address the most common form of market segmentation in sport facilities, which is by ticket type. This is shown for the 2018/2019 season at Old Trafford in Figure 10.1.

SEASON TICKET PRICES 2018/19

SEASON TICKETS 2018/19

AREA	SEASON TICKET INDIVIDUAL MATCH PRICE	ADULT (21-64) SEASON TICKET	*UNDER 16 SEASON TICKET	16-17 SEASON TICKET	18-20 SEASON TICKET	65+ SEASON TICKET
	£50	£950	—	£380	£712.50	£380
	£47	£893	—	£380	£669.75	£380
	£44	£836	£380*	£380	£627	£380
	£42	£798	£380*	£380	£598.50	£380
	£38	£722	—	£361	£541.50	£361
	£37	£703	£351.80*	£351.50	£527.25	£351.50
	£35	£665	£190	£332.50	£498.75	£332.50
	£34	£646	£190	£323	£484.50	£323
	£28	£532	—	£266	£399	£266

*Season Tickets for Under 16s continue to be half-price in all of the Second Tier, with the exception of Stretford End Tier 2.

NEW YOUTH PRICING STRUCTURE
Introduction of new 'youth' pricing structure for supporters aged 18-25 years in the pitchside seating blocks of the Stretford End lower tier.

SEASON TICKET PRICE = £285   INDIVIDUAL MATCH PRICE = £15

Figure 10.1 Season ticket prices and segments at Old Trafford 2018/2019

Source: https://www.manutd.com/en/tickets-and-hospitality/season-tickets

The cheapest seats are those immediately behind the goal at each end of the stadium (£28 per match), and these are followed by those seats that are the farthest away from the pitch in the third tier of the Sir Alex Ferguson Stand (£34). By contrast, the more expensive seats have a side-on view to the pitch and are elevated so that spectators are looking down onto the pitch from an optimal vantage point (£50). The view afforded by your seat is only one form of market segmentation, with others based on the preferences of spectators and the services available at the venue. Note how in Figure 10.1 age is used as a form of market segmentation whereby the same seats are sold to season ticket holders for £950 if you are an adult aged 21–64 (and assumed to be employed); £380 for those aged 16–17; £669.75 for those aged 18–20; and £380 for those aged 65+ (and assumed to be retired). For Manchester United, some of the other forms of market segmentation include season tickets or casuals, regulars versus premiums and corporate, and the type of match or event being staged.

There are 75,000 seats to sell at Old Trafford, and although the club is one of the most well supported in the world, the first consideration in market segmentation is the balance to be struck between selling them all to regular season ticket holders or to one-off or infrequent attendees known as casuals. In practice, Manchester United sells around 55,000 season tickets (73% of the stadium's capacity), and the remaining 20,000 tickets (27%) are retained for less frequent visitors. These include an allocation for visiting supporters for whom a trip to The Theatre of Dreams is one of the highlights of their season. Other groups include members of the club who like to attend matches occasionally but who cannot get or commit to season ticket ownership. Manchester United is so well supported that in order to access tickets not allocated to season ticket holders, you must have an official club membership, which costs £32 per year and gives members the right to be included in ballots for tickets when they are available. The season ticket holders provide a guaranteed income for the club, which offsets some of the financial risk attached to having so many seats to fill. The season ticket holders also play an important role in the 'production process' of a match. First, they are integral to creating the atmosphere in the stadium, which is often cited as one of the key motivations for watching live sport. Second, the atmosphere in a stadium can be a contributory factor to the so-called home advantage or home ground effect, whereby teams tend to perform better at home as compared to away. Third, spectators contribute to the wider spectacle of an event by making a stadium look full. In addition to the spectators in the venues, television viewers elsewhere are watching matches and events.

A full stadium looks good on television, whereas swathes of empty seats are not an attractive proposition and can devalue the product. This leads to an obvious question: 'If demand is so high, why not sell all of the tickets to season ticket holders?' The rationale for retaining some tickets for infrequent attendees is that these customers tend to spend more. For those who attend frequently, the novelty of arriving early, buying a program, visiting the merchandising stores, and buying food and drink wears off. Often these customers spend little beyond the face value of their tickets. By contrast, for infrequent attendees, securing match tickets is one of the social highlights of their year. They will arrive early, immerse themselves fully in the matchday experience, and probably spend considerably on ancillary products such as merchandise and food and drink. In short, these relatively infrequent customers are more profitable to the club than the season ticketholders on matchdays. We can make a connection between Table 10.1, where we find that in

2018 each seat generated £56 per matchday, and Figure 10.1, which shows that the cheapest tickets can be bought for £28 (half the average revenue per seat). It must hold true that if some people are generating less than the average revenue per seat, then some must be generating more. One group that generates more revenue for professional sports teams is that of occasional or casual visitors.

A second area of market segmentation is the balance between regulars versus premium and corporate customers. While the vast majority of spectators at sporting events are collections of regular individuals such as couples, families, and groups of friends, a relatively small but highly significant group is premium or corporate clients. These might be high-profile sponsors who hire an executive box to entertain clients and staff or groups of people looking to celebrate a milestone event. Regardless of their motivations, these corporate and premium customers demand a very different product from their stadium experience, compared with the regular spectators. To illustrate the point, consider the case of the Centennial Club Suites at Old Trafford. At a cost of £180,000 per year, corporate clients can enjoy the following list of benefits:

- Watch the game from your own private terrace with 16 luxury padded Directors' armchairs, or view the game from the comfort of your suite;
- Dedicated private entrance and lift to your suite;
- Access to your box three hours before kick-off and two hours post-match;
- All home Premier League, Domestic Cup, and European fixtures included;
- Option to brand and personalize your suite;
- Complimentary use of your suite for non-matchday meetings;
- 42-inch plasma, surround sound TV and Wi-Fi technology;
- VIP pitch side matchday tour;
- Five-course gourmet à la carte menu;
- Half-time and full-time refreshments;
- Full complimentary bar in your suite including signature wines and champagne;
- Gift of a framed signed shirt;
- Eight reserved car parking spaces included; and
- Matchday programs.

The Centennial Club is described in the sales brochure as 'truly one of the finest experiences in world sport.' In 2018, each of the 16 seats in a suite would have realized £11,250 across the 26 matches played, or £433 per match. Clearly, this cost is a radically different proposition to season ticket holders with seats behind the goal paying an average of £28 per match. Between these two extremes of an offer to spectators are numerous other levels of upgrade or downgrade depending on your starting point. At Old Trafford, for example, premium packages vary from around £275 to £600 per head per match. To put the value of premium and corporate customers into perspective, they typically represent around 10% of the capacity of Old Trafford and generate around 50% of the matchday income.

The type of matches or events taking place is another consideration when segmenting markets, as some matches or events are more attractive to customers as compared to others. A team in the NFL that has no chance of qualifying for the playoffs is a much more difficult sell than the Super Bowl. So too a team with whom there is an intense rivalry is an easier sell than one with which there is not. These sorts of factors have a bearing on the demand for tickets, and the astute sport facility manager will have the presence of mind to realize that maximizing revenue generation may involve having differential pricing for different types of event. In the case of Manchester United, there are intense rivalries with near neighbors Manchester City and old rivals Liverpool Football Club. The commercial manager of the club is aware of this and exploits it to the full. An entry-level hospitality package involves a match ticket in executive surroundings followed by a postmatch meal in the club's museum. For an opposition such as Fulham (a recently promoted side), the price for this package would be £275, whereas for a match against Liverpool the same package will sell for £450. Similarly, the hospitality suite called No. 7 at Old Trafford is available for £600 per person for the Fulham game and for £2,000 per person for the Liverpool game. In both cases, the difference between the two packages is simply the demand for them based on the perceived quality of the opposition.

It is important to understand that there is no one-size-fits-all approach to market segmentation other than to say that it exists and is used extensively in the sport and entertainment industries. In this chapter, we have looked briefly at three types of market segmentation in addition to age, but there could be many other different ways of analyzing your market. Understanding who your customers are and how to meet their needs with the infrastructure you have at your disposal is one of the great skills of venue management. While the core product for sport events is for the most part the price of admission, there are also opportunities to increase matchday revenues by secondary spend on products such as parking, food and drink, programs, and merchandise. Again, market segmentation techniques will be at play. We have seen how at one end of the continuum premium and corporate clients might like to enjoy gourmet dining and fine wines. At the other end of the continuum, regular customers might require handheld snack food such as a beer and a hotdog. The challenge for the venue manager is to anticipate the different types of demand across the customer base and to be able to deliver it. Just to make things more demanding, you have to realize that the window of opportunity to sell food and drink to customers is limited. There may be a rush before a match starts and particularly intense rushes during intervals, but while the core product is taking place, retail outlets in a stadium will be relatively quiet. During the intense periods, sport facility managers need to be able to answer numerous questions positively:

- Do we have enough staff on duty?
- Do we have enough stock available to sell?
- Can our equipment deal with the amount of heating or cooking we need to do?

- Can we serve quickly enough?
- Do we have enough means of taking payment?
- Is there enough change in the tills for customers paying by cash?
- Does our offer look clean and inviting?
- Are our staff good ambassadors for our brand?

In short, assuming you have a good core product to sell, the key to maximizing revenues depends on understanding your market via market segmentation techniques and then delivering an offer to these segments that meets or exceeds their expectations. While being able to manage the core product effectively is a good starting point for any sport facility manager, the job is much bigger than that, and facilities have to be put to even harder work to achieve their owners' commercial objectives. This notion of diversification is the subject of the next section.

OTHER FORMS OF INCOME GENERATION

It is important to realize that a sport facility such as a stadium is an asset and that assets need to be put to work in order to extract the maximum return from them. These assets are said to be 'properties' and to have 'property rights' attached to them. In practice, what this means is that those who own the property rights can sell them or rent them out in order to generate revenue. For example, in the United States, it is common practice for facility owners to sell the naming rights for a stadium. In return for a substantial investment in cash or in kind, investors have the opportunity to name a facility and to use this association to add value to their brand. Some high-profile examples from various professional team sports in the United States are shown in Table 10.2.

Table 10.2 Sample naming rights deals in the United States

Stadium	Team	League	Amount (millions)	From	To	$ per year (millions)
M&T Bank Stadium	Baltimore Ravens	NFL	USD$60	2017	2027	$6.0
Barclays Center	Brooklyn Nets	NBA	USD$200	2012	2032	$10.0
Chase Field	Arizona Diamondbacks	MLB	USD$66.4	1998	2028	$2.2
SunTrust Park	Atlanta Braves	MLB	USD$250	2016	2042	$10.0

It is interesting in Table 10.2 that the four companies that have purchased the naming rights of the various stadia are banks or financial services organizations. Finance is an area of business in which it is difficult to differentiate products, and so providers seek to create an emotional connection with customers, which they cannot achieve through traditional means such as advertising. Other naming rights sponsors tend to be drawn from business sectors like energy, telecommunications, and airlines, which are all products that can be difficult to differentiate. For the stadium owners, naming rights often contribute toward the building costs or help to offset day-to-day running expenses. If the stadium owner also happens to be the owner of the resident franchise, then the income from naming rights can be used to improve teams. Naming rights of facilities are particularly important in the world of sport sponsorship as they represent the most prestigious opportunity for businesses to connect with consumers. The number of stadia available to sponsors is relatively low, and the competition to sponsor them is high. While widely accepted in the United States, naming rights are less common and less lucrative in Europe where a minority of stadia are named after commercial sponsors. Notable examples include the Allianz Arena in Germany, which is home to Bayern Munich; the Etihad Stadium in Manchester, England, which is home to Manchester City; and the Turk Telekom Arena in Istanbul, Turkey, the home of Galatasaray. Again, note how these examples of stadium name sponsors are drawn from the financial services, airlines, and telecommunications sectors. Naming rights, although prestigious, are but one form of income generation beyond ticketing. In the same way that seats and corporate boxes are a form of selling space, so too other spaces in and around a sport facility can be sold. If you visit a sport stadium and look around, the chances are you will see sponsors' logos and brand images on some or all of the following: playing areas, perimeter boards at all levels, scoreboards, the outside walls of the facility, concourses, steps and risers, and seats.

When you are next at a sport facility or watching a game on television or mobile device, look around and see what is being sponsored and who is sponsoring it, and think about what the sponsors are hoping to achieve from their investment. Much of what we have discussed thus far relates to the core product of staging sport events in a stadium. However, stadia can be used flexibly and serve a variety of purposes other than being the home stadium of a sports team. A very common use of stadia, particularly during the close season, is to stage events either in other sports or, more broadly, from the world of entertainment. To illustrate the point, we can consider the cases of Wembley Stadium in London, England, which is the largest stadium in the UK with a capacity of 90,000. Wembley is the home of the England football (soccer) team and has hosted an average of six matches per year since it was reopened in 2007. This level of activity is clearly unsustainable in its own right, and the stadium is put to use throughout the year staging other events such as the FA Cup semifinals and finals, the FA Vase Trophy, playoff finals in the professional leagues below the English Premier League, the Rugby League Challenge Cup Final, Rugby League and Rugby union international matches, American football games (currently four per season), boxing matches, and pop concerts, in addition to being the home for Premier League team Tottenham Hotspur during the 2017/2018 and 2018/2019 seasons while its new stadium was being built.

This extensive level of activity at Wembley Stadium is relatively modest when we examine the case of what is considered the world's most profitable stadium, the STAPLES Center in Los Angeles, which is the home venue for four professional sports teams in basketball and ice hockey as well as being a concert and conference venue. The four sports teams provide the STAPLES Center with around 140 matchdays per year excluding playoff games, and much of the remaining time is put to use hosting concerts, WWE events, UFC events, Disney on Ice tours, political conventions, and award shows. That this venue has only around 19,000 seats and turns over some $350 million per year (nearly $1 million per day) shows what can be achieved when a state-of-the-art facility is put to effective use. While the STAPLES Center is perhaps an extreme example, other practices from around the world demonstrate how sport facilities can be used to generate income and diversify the business away from reliance on matchday revenues.

Visitor attractions

Stadia can exploit the emotional attachment fans place on sports teams and their facilities. Dublin in the Republic of Ireland has Europe's third largest stadium in Croke Park, the home of the Gaelic Athletic Association (GAA). The stadium is a focal point for Irish culture and a popular visitor attraction in its own right. Visitors are able to visit the GAA Museum, have a tour of the stadium, and walk the 17-story-high Croke Park Skyline, which is the highest open-air viewing point in low-rise Dublin. The GAA Museum welcomes around 150,000 visitors per year and is regarded as one of Dublin's top ten visitor attractions. Across the city of Dublin is the Aviva Stadium – the home of Irish football (soccer) and rugby union. Note how the stadium is named after the insurance company Aviva, who paid for a ten-year naming rights' deal from 2009 to 2019. In 2015, the Aviva Stadium played host to the annual conference of the European Association for Sport Management (EASM). With around 600 delegates attending the four-day event, the hospitality boxes overlooking the pitch were converted into small lecture theaters to hold the 400 or so presentations that took place during the conference. The catering facilities, which look after the needs of thousands of guests on matchdays, were easily capable of keeping meals and hot drinks flowing throughout the conference, which was a financial shot in the arm to the stadium during a period when no matches were being held. To develop the notion of visitor attraction, some venues integrate accommodation into their offer. Twickenham Stadium in London, the home of England Rugby, has integrated into its South Stand a 152-room, four-star hotel that has six hospitality suites that can be used as executive boxes on matchdays. Allied to a spa and health club and a performance venue/conference space, it is possible to appreciate how Twickenham Stadium can be used to generate revenue year-round and is not solely dependent on rugby matches for its revenue streams.

Conference venue/trade shows

For conferences and trade shows, the promoters of these events need space, catering facilities, toilets, parking facilities, and technical services. Sport stadia have these facilities and have expert staff who can adapt them to different uses. It is quite likely that a sport stadium will be the biggest catering outlet in its locality. This infrastructure can be used to service events such as conferences and shows. Stadia also have concourses, and these can be ideal for trade exhibitors to display their wares and for show visitors to be able to circulate freely. Venues that have a retractable roof such as the NRG Stadium in Houston, Texas, can turn the playing surface into large a convention center with all activity taking place on a flat surface that protects the stadium against the elements. On a smaller scale, public sport and leisure facilities are routinely used in the UK for computer fairs, dog shows, and formal dinners.

Celebrations and adverse events

The emotional attachment that fans have with their club and the stadium it plays in is a major source of differentiation and competitive advantage. Exploiting the potential of meeting spaces and hospitality areas, it is possible for fans to get married at certain sport stadia safe in the knowledge that all of the facilities are in place for a perfect day. There have also been examples of fans who have asked for their funeral wakes to be held at their favorite soccer club and for their ashes to be scattered on the pitch. Clubs have, however, realized that this is not good for the grass! Regardless of the occasion, whether it be a christening, birthday, bar or bat mitzvah, birthday, wedding, wedding anniversary, graduation, or funeral wake, sport facilities can be used to service the needs of customers by using their existing infrastructure and expertise. The facilities that sport stadia have can be put into stark relief when we consider how they can be used to deal with adverse events. It is routine practice in the UK, when there is flooding or severe snow, for publicly owned leisure facilities to be used as temporary shelters. There is space for people to sleep, catering facilities, showers, toilets, heating, and quite often secondary power supplies so that if the main electricity is lost, generators can be used. These sport facilities provide a focal point for communities when they are temporarily unable to use their homes. Although much criticized for its lack of preparedness, the then Louisiana Superdome was used as a shelter of last resort in August 2005 when Hurricane Katrina ravaged New Orleans.

Other assets

Other assets such as parking can become lucrative sources of revenue for sport facilities. If they are near places of work, they can be used for routine parking during business hours. The can also be used for specific events such as car boot sales, flea markets, or swap meets where private individuals come together to sell or trade goods. Chesterfield, a small town near Sheffield, England, has a car boot sale most Sundays that takes place on Chesterfield Football Club's car park. There is space for 150 pitches at £10 per pitch. Just by selling these pitches, the club can raise £1,500 in a few hours when the car park (an asset) would otherwise be idle, and it can make additional money from selling food and drink. Within the infrastructure of a stadium, there can often be space, notably underneath unused stands. Enterprising facility owners have put this space to use in the form of health and fitness clubs, shops, and office space that can be rented out. These sorts of activity help the assets of the stadium to work harder and to generate additional sources of revenue from the facility.

There is no blueprint to how a facility might be used to diversify its income streams, save to say that it is an important part of the sport facility manager's skill set. As a sport facility manager, you have to adapt your offer to take into account the physical capabilities of your facility, the expertise of your staff, and the likely demands that will be made of you by your host community. You cannot afford to stand still and have to constantly adapt your offer to take advantage of the latest technological innovations and market demands. Some of the more recent innovations being discussed around 2018 are discussed here.

TECHNOLOGY NOW! HALLAM ACTIVE (UNITED KINGDOM)

Providing sport services within a university environment poses particular managerial challenges that can be met by the effective use of technology. In the United Kingdom, a bachelor's degree lasts for three years of which each year is made up of a nine-month academic year and three months' summer vacation. Sheffield Hallam University has a student community of around 34,000, and many like to take part in a range of activities such as health and fitness, club sport, and elite sport. In the past, there used to be long queues at the start of the academic year as students attempted to enroll or reenroll to use the facilities. This was off-putting for students and placed considerable strain on the front office staff.

With the help of Gladstone MRM, a leading supplier of membership management software, innovative solutions have been devised that help to overcome problems and optimize revenue. The heart of the system is a database that can subsequently be used to deliver benefits to both gym members and staff. Students can now register to join the gym online, which eliminates queuing and enables front office staff to concentrate on value-adding activities. The software has the functionality to set up direct debits, which spreads the cost of membership over the year via monthly payments. Because of the nature of the academic year, it has been found that there is better retention of members if there is the option to freeze membership during the summer and then to reactivate it once the new academic year begins. What this means is that students do not have to make a decision at the start of each academic year as to whether or not to join the gym as continuity of membership is assumed.

Members can also derive further value from their membership using the online system. It is easy to book places on fitness classes using the online booking system, which can be accessed via computers all over the campus or indeed via smartphones. To keep members motivated and inclined to use the gym more frequently, smartcards enable users to monitor their progress over time and to receive feedback on their performance from specific pieces of equipment. For the staff, online bookings provide a clear sense of the level of demand for classes, which in turn helps to ensure that the correct number of classes is put on and that best use is made of instructor time (and costs).

Using technology in this way is important because it helps managers to realize that revenue generation and revenue protection best achieve financial success. The vast majority of costs in the gym are fixed and do not vary in proportion to activity. Therefore, the good manager will set about putting in place a strategy that will maximize revenue within the fixed cost base. This means enabling easy access to the membership via the online membership system, minimizing the pain of payment via the direct debit system, giving good value for money via the 'freeze membership' option, and increasing personal motivation and frequency of usage by progress monitoring. The system in place at Sheffield Hallam University provides personalized service for some 4,500 members, which would simply not be possible without the applied use of database technology.

FUTURE DIRECTIONS

Digital technology is providing the means by which to improve the customer experience in a facility and the potential for increased revenue generation or cost savings. Even before we reach a stadium nowadays, digital technology will have had an impact. There is no need for paper-based tickets anymore. We can buy tickets online and download a barcode to our phones that will be scanned at the entrance to provide us with access to a facility. There is no need for tickets to be sent out by post or to be collected from the box office, which saves on postage and labor costs. Tickets no longer have to be checked physically, which in turn can reduce the number of staff required on turnstiles, who in turn can be redeployed to more value-adding activities such as service and selling rather than access control.

Once inside the stadium, the old practice of buying a program will be diminished as teams will communicate with their fans via mobile applications (Apps). The use of Apps means that data such as team news can be as up to date as possible. Furthermore, at say events such as Golf Majors and Tennis Grand Slam tournaments, Apps enable people to keep up-to-date with scores elsewhere on the golf course or on other tennis courts. Greater interactivity with fans can be encouraged through social media with pictures taken by fans uploaded instantly to big screens around a stadium. This type of activity helps to improve the customer experience, which in turn improves the likelihood of repeat visits and the potential to charge higher prices for an enhanced experience. Underpinning these advances is the installation of advanced technology in stadia. These include sufficient wireless Internet capability to service the needs of tens of thousands of customers in a relatively confined space. Similarly, large high-definition scoreboards, screens, and perimeter advertising boards provide new areas on which to display branding messages (increase revenue) or customer interactions (better customer experience). With a stadium App downloaded to their phones, fans can enjoy an at-seat service. Rather than stand in a queue to get popcorn or Coke, fans are able to order and pay for catering to be delivered to their seats. This facility might not be available throughout a stadium, but it is a service enhancement that adds to the customer experience. Furthermore, market segmentation techniques can be used to charge premium prices over areas where an at-seat service is not available.

In addition to ticketless stadia, there is also a move toward cashless stadia via contactless bank cards, mobile phone payment systems such as Apple Pay, and preloaded purchase cards. Rather than customers worrying if they have brought enough cash with them, they can pay for catering and merchandise using their phones. This approach is flexible because customer spending is not limited to how much cash they have on them and enables them to make opportunistic purchases. For the sport facility manager, there is no longer any need to worry about whether there is enough change in the tills or whether cash is going missing because of fraud, and there is no need for the security costs involved in guarding and banking cash. Every time customers use an App, make a purchase, or visit the website, important information about actual fan behavior can be obtained and used to adapt the facility's offer accordingly. It is possible to identify the most profitable fans and to use this intelligence within a customer relationship management (CRM) package to understand customers more fully and to satisfy their needs profitably.

Where might it all end up? A glimpse into the near future suggests the convergence of the physical with the digital. For example, using up to 200 high-definition

Implementing operations management

cameras in a venue where the Super Bowl is being played will make it possible to recreate a hologram of the game in numerous other stadia across the world where people have come together for the shared experience of watching the event. The holographic representation of the game will be better than the quality of images that people can see in their homes and will be a sufficient draw to persuade them to leave the comfort of their homes. Too far-fetched – or not far-fetched enough? Time will tell.

FACILITY FOCUS: STADIUM DESIGN FOR DIVERSE REVENUE GENERATION: TOTTENHAM HOTSPUR STADIUM, LONDON, UNITED KINGDOM

Built at a cost of £750 million and with around 62,000 seats, Tottenham Hotspur Stadium opened in April 2019. The facility will be unlike any other in the UK. Not only is there a conventional soccer pitch, but 1.5 meters underneath the grass surface is an artificial grass pitch that will be used to stage two NFL games as well as about 16 music concerts per year. The grass pitch has been designed in three retractable trays that are stored underneath the South Stand. The basic turnaround time to change from a grass pitch to a synthetic pitch is estimated at around 25 minutes. For fans in the UK, there has been nothing quite like it. Novel features include a microbrewery that can make one million pints of beer per year and dispense 10,000 pints per minute during busy halftime breaks. Some of these beers will be served from what is thought to be the UK's longest bar. For food lovers, the in-house bakery will provide everything from artisan breads to pastries, which will be supplied to all of the food outlets across the stadium. For those who want to see things that are normally hidden from view, Tunnel Club members will be able to peer through a glass wall at the players in the tunnel before they run out onto the pitch. For premium customers, there are heated seats complete with USB chargers to top up the power in their phones. The stadium is designed with market segmentation in mind with an offer for those who just want to see a match to those who want an exclusive high-end experience and numerous price points in between. The current name of the venue, Tottenham Hotspur Stadium, is a temporary title as the club seeks to sell the naming rights. The figure sought is estimated to be £20 million annually for a 10- or 20-year deal.

Source: Retrieved March 23, 2019, from www.tottenhamhotspur.com/the-stadium

CHAPTER REVIEW

People embarking on a career in sport facility management might look at sport facilities generally and prestigious stadia specifically, as the glamorous end of the sport management business. There is some truth to this notion, but the reality is that it is no different from any other form of management. As a sport facility manager, you have at your disposal the fundamental economic resources of land, people, capital, and entrepreneurship. These have to be mixed in various ways by which to deliver a required economic outcome. At least in part, this outcome will be to generate a sufficient return to justify the investment in a facility, to pay the people (staff), and to provide a worthwhile return on the capital invested and the risk taken by the entrepreneurs behind a development.

When we apply these basic principles to managing a sport stadium, for example, we find that we can draw three useful principles from management theory that will help us in this regard. The first is that customers are not homogeneous, and therefore we need to segment our offer to identify the market segments, their needs, and how we can satisfy these needs profitably. To illustrate the point, let us revisit the case of Manchester United and a match against its fierce rivals Liverpool Football Club. At one end of the continuum are season ticket holders who attend every game and are content with a seat behind the goal looking down the full length of the pitch. On average, these supporters pay an average of £28 for each matchday ticket (see Figure 10.1). By contrast, at the other end of the continuum are customers who are prepared to pay £2,000 per head for access to the exclusive No. 7 at Old Trafford hospitality suite, where they can enjoy fine wines, gourmet catering, and the best views in the house. Numerous market segments between the extremes pay differing amounts of money for their experience and have different expectations of the service they receive.

The second useful principle is that sport stadia and facilities need to be put to work by diversifying their offer. We can appreciate this point by reminding ourselves of the notions of space and time. Sport facilities are but spaces, and the job of sport facility managers is to sell those spaces. If we revisit the case of the STAPLES Center, we see a facility that can sell its space for 140 days of the year just by way of the regular season games of the four franchises that use the venue as their home. At a micro scale, we can sell space to advertisers on our perimeter boards, scoreboards, concourses, steps, and seats. In terms of time, it is widely held that customers spend more the longer their dwell time. Therefore, beyond the duration of a game or an event, we need to provide an offer that encourages at least some people to come early and to leave late. We saw in the case of the premium hospitality that customers can access their executive boxes three hours before kickoff for drinks and lunch and can stay for two hours after the match for further refreshments and networking activity. Taking full advantage of this offer would make watching a two-hour match a seven-hour experience. Away from a stadium's primary purpose, it is important to diversify the income streams so that you are not overly reliant on matchday business. Whether this is an alternative event, such as a concert, conference, or trade show, or hiring out space and expertise for celebration events such as weddings, the basic point remains that it is important to make your assets work hard.

The third and final useful principle is the importance of innovating your offer in order to improve the customer experience, increase revenue-generating opportunities, and take advantage of cost reduction measures. The potential of digital technology enables us to save money by using digital tickets, to increase revenue by enabling at-seat service, and to reduce expenditure by becoming a cashless venue. Suppose that, when you go for a job interview, you can say to a prospective employer, 'I have ideas to improve the customer experience, to generate you more income, and to cut down on costs.' This is far more likely to make a favorable impression than saying, 'I'm a lifelong Dallas Cowboys fan, and I want to work where they play.' Finally, we need to commit to embracing innovation on a continuous basis. With eSports transferring to stadium settings and holograms being a distinct possibility, sport facility managers cannot afford to stand still.

IN THE FIELD . . .

With Iain Mckinney, head of sport services, Sheffield Hallam University, Sheffield, United Kingdom

Iain is the head of sport services and responsible for the strategic management of sport and physical activity opportunities at Sheffield Hallam University (SHU). The service includes a range of facilities such as gyms, an athletics track, and a multi-pitch facility. In addition to these facilities, his teams oversee sport and physical activity at both the performance and the participation levels, with an increasing focus on improving student health and well-being through physical activity. The team includes over 40 university staff, graduate interns, sports coaches, and students being supported to apply their learning within the service, all of which increases the wider team to over 100 people. Iain's key challenge is to generate sufficient income to meet the cost of providing the basic service while having sufficient funds available to cross-subsidize activities that will never make money but that are socially important, such as activities to support the mental well-being of students and staff.

Here are Iain's top tips for someone whose experience includes having been a professional athlete, an academic, and a senior leader:

- Take every opportunity to build your professional network.
- Keep up to speed with what is current in your industry or area of interest.

- You will always need to work with or lead people. Work hard to build trust and positive relationships, especially as a manager.
- Always focus on solutions rather than the size of the challenge or how difficult it might be to overcome.
- Do not fear change. It can be disruptive but often provides opportunity and variety that can keep you motivated in your work.

BIBLIOGRAPHY

Anonymous. (2016). Marketing and Gaelic football: How segmentation bases boost strategy. *Strategic Direction*, *32*(8), 15–17. https://doi-org.wallaby.vu.edu.au:4433/10.1108/SD-05-2016-0079

Cunningham, G., Fink, J., & Doherty, A. (2016). *Routledge handbook of theory in sport management*. Oxford: Routledge.

Gallagher, D., O'Connor, C., & Gilmore, A. (2016). An exploratory examination of the strategic direction of the Gaelic Athletic Association via the application of sports marketing segmentation bases. *Marketing Intelligence and Planning*, *34*(2), 203–222. https://doi.org/10.1108/MIP-09-2014-0188

Heatley, M. (2006). *European football stadiums*. London: Compendium.

KPMG. (2013). *A blueprint for successful stadium development*. Retrieved December 5, 2018, from https://assets.kpmg.com/content/dam/kpmg/pdf/2013/11/blueprint-successful-stadium-development.pdf

Manchester United. (2018). *Season ticket prices 2018–2019*. Retrieved November 6, 2018, from https://www.manutd.com/en/tickets-and-hospitality/season-tickets

McDonald, M. (2012). *Market segmentation and how to do it and how to profit from it*. West Sussex, UK: John Wiley & Sons.

Robinson, L., Chelladurai, P., Bodet, G., & Downward, P. (2012). *Routledge handbook of sport management*. Oxford: Routledge.

Schwarz, E. C., & Hunter, J. D. (2018). *Advanced theory and practice in sport marketing* (3rd ed.). Oxford: Routledge.

Schwarz, E. C., Westerbeek, H., Liu, D., Emery, P., & Turner, P. (2017). *Managing sport facilities and major events*. Oxford: Routledge.

Security and Exchange Commission. (2018). *United States Securities and Exchange Commission form 20-F for Manchester United plc for the year ended June 2018*. Retrieved November 6, 2018, from www.sec.gov/Archives/edgar/data/1549107/000104746913009876/a2217035z20-f.htm

Taylor, P. (Ed.). (2011). *Torkildsen's sport and leisure management* (6th ed.). Oxford: Routledge.

Trendberth, L., & Hassan, D. (2012). *Managing sport business: An introduction*. Abingdon: Routledge. [Notably chapters 8, 12, and 20].

Wimmer, A. (2008). *Stadiums: Market places of the future*. New York: Springer Wien.

CHAPTER 11

CUSTOMER EXPERIENCES – FROM EVENT PLANNING TO ACTIVATION

CHAPTER OUTLINE

- Sport facility event planning process
- Who are our customers?
- Activating the facility event marketing plan
- Event implementation and activation from the facility viewpoint
  - Level of involvement of facility personnel in managing events
- Event experiences at sport facilities from the customer viewpoint
- Evaluation of events by facility ownership and management
  - Key components of the SESA Assessment cycle
- Chapter review

CHAPTER OBJECTIVES

Without events, there would be no purpose for a sport facility. Events can range from free open recreation time to a full-scale hallmark event such as the Olympic Games or the FIFA World Cup. The purpose of this chapter is to explore the relationship between facility operations and management and event planning. This chapter is not intended to provide an in-depth analysis or explanation of event management; it is intended to articulate the role facility management plays in supporting event management. This first important factor is understanding the entire sport facility event planning process, as well as the various event relationships that a facility manager may engage with. This will lead to examining the sport facility's role in pre-event, during the event, and post-event operations including the activation of a facility event marketing plan, event implementation, level of involvement in managing events, preparation for the unexpected, and evaluation after the event has taken place. Throughout the chapter, the experience of customers – including spectators and participants – will be discussed as a vital component of the successful management and operation of a sport facility in terms of what customers want and how sport facility operation managers must manage the customer experience to meet their needs.

SPORT FACILITY EVENT PLANNING PROCESS

The sport facility event planning process involves the development of the event from conceptualization through activation to implementation and eventual evaluation by event managers. However, a part of the process that is often not described is that sport facility management and ownership go through a similar process in preparation for events coming to the sport facility. Hence the sport facility event planning process will mirror the sport event planning process but with some intricate differences. This first section of this chapter will discuss the planning process from setting objectives and developing conceptualizations to contract signing and moving forward toward implementation of the event in consideration of addressing the needs and wants of customers through the event experience at a facility.

The first step in the event planning process is setting objectives. All sport facility managers and owners need to make some decision as to what type of events they want their facility to host. Often, these decisions go back to the philosophy, mission, and vision (PMV) of the sport facility. For instance, if this were a community-based recreation facility, the types of events to be hosted would need to be focused on community building and the needs of that local municipality. In contrast, a large, commercial-focused stadium or arena is seeking to maximize revenues through high attendance rates at high-profile events. However, regardless of the size or type of facility, the interests of potential customers must be taken into account because without attendees, there is no reason for a facility to host an event. Additionally, there will always be questions at this stage about events that may be beneficial socially or financially to a sport facility but may be contrary to its mission. These may include events that may be politically motivated (ranging from a local politician speaking engagement to a political convention), culturally oriented (religious ceremonies), or socially driven (events such as an arts and crafts show) and may cause questions in the community. Furthermore, certain sporting events, depending on the jurisdiction, may not be considered appropriate – the most common sport this occurs with today is mixed martial arts (MMA).

When setting objectives for determining what events will be held in a sport facility, there will be a general list of accepted events and a process in place to consider other options that may be financially and socially viable. Some of the questions that should be answered to set these objectives include:

- What does the sport facility management ownership want to achieve by hosting the event?
- Who are your target audiences and participants?
- Is there an understanding of the history of the potential event?
- Does the event have a track record of success or failure?
- Does the sport facility have access to partnerships that can aid in the success of the event?
- Is there support from key stakeholders and partners for hosting the event in the sport facility?

After objectives are understood, the sport facility management needs to develop concepts of how it views these potential events in their facility. In conjunction with all pertinent personnel from the facility, the ownership and management will lay out what the general framework of these various events would look like. This includes the functions of ingress/egress, seating, timing, scale, facilities and equipment needed, marketing plans, as well as setup, during the event responsibilities, breakdown, and evaluation processes. As a part of this process, the sport facility manager will develop a series of strategies for the successful implementation of the event. These strategies should (1) be realistic, (2) result in having a positive influence on the sport facility, the event, and the community, (3) be able to be accomplished within the available infrastructure, and (4) be able to be realized within the available budget. In conjunction with effectively creating these strategies, three main questions need to be answered:

1   What is the importance of the event to the sport facility and the community?
2   What are the benefits of hosting the event to the sport facility and the community?
3   Who are the parties within the sport facility (and potentially the community) that should have input into creating the strategies?

Once these functions are analyzed, the sport facility ownership and management must determine whether it is feasible to host each type of event being analyzed. Feasibility is determined by first conducting a strategic analysis (SWOC) to see what strengths the sport facility brings to the table for this type of event, where the weaknesses are that can prevent success, and the opportunities and challenges that this event brings to the sport facility. In addition, an analysis of the competition will be conducted for two reasons. First, if this is a bid process for a larger event, there is a need to gain information that will aid in the success of securing the bid. Second, it is important to see whether those competitors have run similar events and attempt to acquire information that will help in managing that type of event.

When all of this research and analysis is completed, the information is evaluated and a determination needs to be made whether to host this type of event in the sport facility. If the evaluation is no, then either reconceptualization of the event needs to take place to determine whether, through modification, the event would be appropriate for the facility, or the event is deemed not appropriate – and future negotiation for those types of events will not be conducted. If it is determined that the event would be a good fit for the sport facility, it is time to seek out those events (just as events are seeking out facilities) and get the parties together to negotiate contracts.

Prior to negotiating contracts, the sport facility managers and owners will develop a pro forma budget to anticipate the general costs of hosting an event. This budget will become more detailed once contracts are negotiated and signed, but this advanced budget creates a general financial framework place for the specific type of events and a starting place for negotiations. If similar events have been held at the sport facility in the past, those final budgets can be used to support the developing budget for the new event. It is also important that the developers of the budget keep in mind political, economic, and infrastructural issues that may skew or change costs. In general, when creating a budget, the following questions should be considered:

- Is there information from previous event budgets that can help create the current event budget?
- Have all pertinent costs been included in the budget?
- Have all internal and external factors related to the sport facility been taken into account?
- Have errors and omissions been built into the budget for unforeseen expenses, unexpected costs, or miscalculation of budget numbers?
- Who from the sport facility is ultimately in charge of managing the budget and controlling cash flow?
- Who from the sport facility will be the second level of budget management in charge of auditing and monitoring the budget?

When the parties responsible for negotiating on behalf of the sport facility and the event get together, the end goals are to sign a contract agreeing to the use of the facility to host the event and to come up with a plan for the implementation of pre-event processes. Usually representing the sport facility is the facility manager and his or her designee (depending on the scope of the facility and/or the event), as they are usually the persons responsible for scheduling and booking the facility and have been actively involved with marketing the facility to event managers and promoters. From the event side, a promoter usually will negotiate on behalf of the event; however, again depending on the scope of the event, the actual event manager or owner may be involved. The biggest challenge in this process is the differing missions of the event and the facility. The event owner (ranging from teams to concert promoters to hallmark event managers) is concerned only about the event itself and maximizing profits through the event. On the other hand, the facility is mostly concerned about how the event is presented and produced because the appearance is a reflection on the sport facility in the community. These clashing philosophies often lead to some contentious discussions, and hence it is strongly recommended that all discussions and agreements be clearly documented in all contracts and agreements. This includes the implementation of pre-event planning, such as determining:

- Who is responsible for marketing what aspects of the event . . . and where?
- What event staff is going to be provided through the sport facility, and what staff will the event be providing?
- How long before the event can ingress for setup begin?
- How long before the event must setup be completed so that proper authorizations (as needed) can be given by the facility manager, police department, fire marshal, and others.
- What time will the doors open?
- Who is responsible for what from the time the doors open through the event and until the doors close?
- How long does the event have to break down and egress from the facility?
- How will any financial issues be settled at the end of the event?

This list is only an example of the numerous questions that should be answered during the pre-event planning process. This time of negotiating contracts and responsibilities not only serves to set parameters for the event's use of the facility but also provides an opportunity for the sport facility manager (and in some cases the ownership) to understand the relationships that are being forged. The most significant of these relationships is between the facility manager (and the appropriate staff) and the event manager (and designated staff) as just discussed. Another relationship will be with the media, with the scope of the event determining the level of involvement. The relationship with media for local, small events will be limited. For larger events, media involvement will grow. For instance, a local secondary school basketball tournament at a municipal facility will certainly have less media coverage than a professional football match at the Mercedes-Benz Stadium in Atlanta. Moreover, that media coverage will pale in comparison to the media coverage when the New National Stadium in Tokyo or the Stade de France in Paris hosts the Opening Ceremonies of the 2020 and 2024 Summer Olympics, respectively.

Another relationship is with potential sponsors. Depending on the scope of the event, this relationship could be minimal or on a grand scale. The biggest issue regarding this relationship is ensuring that facility sponsors do not clash with event sponsors. When this happens, significant problems can occur, as the following case study shows.

'DIS'AGREEMENTS BETWEEN FACILITY NAMING RIGHTS VERSUS HALLMARK EVENT SPONSORS

The Pepsi Center in Denver, Colorado, has been the scene of a multitude of conflicts between sport facility operations and management and external events throughout the life of the facility. The first two incidents are covered in this case study, with the third discussed later in the 'Facility Focus' for this chapter

Setting the scene

In 1999, the Colorado Avalanche of the National Hockey League (NHL) submitted a bid for the 2001 All-Star Weekend in the arena they played in at that time – McNichols Arena. During this same time in Denver, a new arena was being built to house the Denver Nuggets of the National Basketball Association (NBA) and the Colorado Avalanche (NHL). Naming rights were sold later that year (1999) to PepsiCo for $3.4 million per year for 20 years. The major dilemma came because Coca Cola is the official nonalcoholic drink sponsor of the NHL. So the NHL All-Star Game, with the NHL's sponsor Coca-Cola in tow, would be held at the Pepsi Center.

At the same time, the Denver Nuggets of the NBA kept a close eye on this situation. They were looking for ways to host the 2003 NBA All-Star Game at the Pepsi Center, but the NBA contract with Coca-Cola is even stronger than that of with the NHL. The contract between the NBA and the Sprite brand name is a 100-year global marketing alliance estimated to be worth well in excess of $1 billion.

How could the clashing naming rights of the facility and the sponsorship of the hallmark event be solved so that Denver could reap the rewards of hosting these two all-star events?

NHL All-Star Weekend: Coca-Cola wins this battle

During the 1980s and 1990s, in an effort to become the number 1 soft drink company in the United States, Coca Cola and Pepsi engaged in mutually targeted advertisements on all media fronts and marketing campaigns. Now in 2000 and 2001, the fight was on over whose name would be allowed to appear in conjunction with the NHL All-Star Weekend: Pepsi as the facility sponsor or Coca-Cola as the event sponsor. The main issues were (1) previous partnerships are considered in negotiations, but it is one item to consider among many, and (2) despite venue exclusivity, there are permitted exceptions for certain events, including those deemed as 'jewel events' such as all-star games. After months of negotiations and threatened litigation, it was determined that Coca-Cola would have precedent over Pepsi for this one-time event because the contract was signed for the All-Star event to be played in the old arena, and the move to the new arena and subsequent naming rights by Pepsi did not hold precedence over the Coca Cola event sponsorship. As a result:

- Coca-Cola forced the Colorado Avalanche and the NHL to erase the formal name of the arena (Pepsi Center) from all all-star tickets.
- The NHL required the broadcaster of the game (ABC) not to refer to the venue as the Pepsi Center. The only approved references for the arena were 'Home of the Colorado Avalanche'; 'Welcome back to Denver'; 'Coming to you from Denver'; and 'Back in Denver.' In addition, any blimp or other aerial shots had to be from the side of the facility so the title of the arena could not be seen.
- Since Pepsi, as the facility sponsor, had pouring rights, it was still served – but in generic, NHL cups.
- Coca-Cola, still not totally satisfied, withdrew some of its financial support for the event – and the Pepsi Center had to cut the NHL an undisclosed six-figure check to host the All-Star Game to make up for the deficit created by Coca-Cola's reduction in support.

NBA All-Star Weekend: Pepsi scores a victory

The Denver Nuggets had lobbied for years to host the event but feared it would not be for at least 100 years because they did not believe the NBA would want to alienate a top sponsor by bringing All-Star Weekend to an arena named after its competitor. Fortunately, the NBA decided in 2003 that the All-Star Game would come to Denver and be played in the Pepsi Center. Coca Cola was, of course, not happy about it because the reverse was happening: The Pepsi Center facility sponsorship came before the event contract with the NBA. However, Coca-Cola did put some pressure on the NBA and insisted that some mutual agreements with Pepsi had to occur. They included:

- All Pepsi signage in the arena could remain visible, but the floor where the game would be played could not say Pepsi Center
- Sprite (a Coca-Cola product) would be the prominent presenting sponsor of the Slam Dunk competition across all media and branded on scorer's tables, judge's tables and scorecards, and in the staging area for athletes.

- In the hospitality areas, all vending machines would be Coca-Cola products, however, if any product was brought out of hospitality into the arena, either the drinks needed to be poured in cups (for cans) or labels taken off plastic bottles. For patrons or media members who did not, an usher would approach them and ask them to comply.
- During media coverage by TNT (Turner Network Television), the Pepsi Center could be named only once verbally and once via an on-screen graphic during the broadcast on All-Star Saturday; the rest of the time, the event was referred to as being in Denver. For the All-Star Game on Sunday, TNT was asked to limit their use of the arena title; according to Front Row Marketing, the Pepsi Center received 12 seconds of on-screen graphics, 5 verbal mentions, and 40 seconds of visible in-arena signage (and no blimp or aerial coverage of the front of the arena – only the side).

Suggested discussion topics

1 TherehasalwaysbeenacontentiousrelationshipbetweenCocaColaandPepsi– but that is not the only industry segment where corporations have had issues with their sponsors. Review the issues with the original United States Olympic Basketball Dream Team in 1992, and explain the issues between Nike and Reebok that led to some athletes covering the Reebok logo with the American Flag during the medals ceremony.
2 Explain how the individual player partnership and endorsement deals of independent contractor athletes are handled when their sponsor is a direct competitor of an event sponsor? (An example is a professional golfer sponsored by Toyota or Mercedes wearing the company's logo on his or her shirt or hat while playing in the Honda Classic or the BMW Championship.)

WHO ARE OUR CUSTOMERS?

Also crucial to consider during this pre-event planning process are the customers – both spectators and participants – and the experiences that the event offers to meet their needs and wants. *Customers* are individuals or organizations that purchase or obtain goods and services for direct use or ownership. For those utilizing sport facilities, this ownership can range from the use of the facility for active participation to engaging in an experience as a spectator. Regardless of the type of customer, the sport facility manager must be able to define the needs and wants of a variety of customers within a single event.

So who are the customers for a sport facility? The largest customer population is the consumer market that purchases goods and services for personal or household consumption. As spectators, these customers purchase tickets to enter sport facilities to watch a variety of sport events and spend additional money on ancillary products and services including but not limited to food and beverage, merchandise, and parking. Consumers can also be participants – using facilities for a variety of reasons ranging from personal use such as a fitness center to producing events such as a player on a sports team or a band for a concert.

Another group of customers is the business market. These are organizations that purchase goods and services that benefit their own businesses in terms of either production or entertainment. The most significant business markets are event owners and promoters that hire out a facility to produce their event. Other business markets may include media companies that wish to broadcast an event, sponsors that seek an association with a facility or event for promoting their own organization and its products, and corporate box/suite holders who use the attendance at events as a business perk, entertainment opportunity, or meeting location.

Sport facility managers must use different strategies to attract and retain the various customer groups; however, in general, the sport facility is providing infrastructure to offer events as a service to these consumer markets in the form of experiences. Hence, the sport facility manager must find events that provide quality, value, and satisfaction to the sport consumer by providing the expected quality standard of operation that enhances the experience.

This requires the sport facility manager to be effective in the application of the service marketing principles of intangibility, perishability, inseparability, and variability. Experiences are *intangible* – only the memory of the experience can be taken home – and may be further articulated and remembered through capture technologies such as pictures or social media posts. The events that take place in most sport facilities are *perishable*, with a definitive end time at the completion of the event. The experience cannot be stored in inventory similar to a piece of merchandise or food from the concessions stand. There is also the facet of *inseparability*, where the production and consumption of events in a sport facility are produced and consumed simultaneously. This directly affects *variability* from a sport facility operations and management standpoint. The need to be consistent, from one event to the next, with a similar service quality expectation whether it is a sporting event, concert, conference, or cultural event. Hence, the challenge for sport facility managers is to find this consistency when the parties that directly influence the service experience – the primary customer, the service provider(s), and other customers – all have different needs and wants but expect to receive consistent levels of quality.

In order to gain a better understanding of our customers, sport facility managers must understand and be actively engaged in the implementation of the application of sport marketing plans. Marketing is a social and managerial process by which individuals and groups obtain what they need and want through creating and exchanging products and value with others. As noted previously, the needs and wants of customers span several different types, and their identification can be complex. However, creating and implementing an effective facility event marketing plan can be an important tool for sport facility managers to engage and deliver experiences that meet the needs and wants of customers.

ACTIVATING THE FACILITY EVENT MARKETING PLAN

Just as an event would engage in marketing, a sport facility also will engage in the marketing of the events they host. Some of these marketing efforts will be in partnership with events, while others will be independent of each other. Ultimately, it is important to remember that partnered marketing efforts will focus on the event's desire to maximize attendance and profits, and the independent facility marketing will focus on the presentation and production of the event desired by the community and on the appearance of the facility as a significantly positive reflection of that community.

The facility event marketing plan is a comprehensive framework for identifying and achieving the marketing goals and objectives of the sport facility through the event. A marketing plan is developed by the sport facility managers and personnel for each individual event and includes the following steps:

- Identify the purpose of the plan in terms of the event, including developing mission and vision statements; creating goals and objectives; and ensuring involvement and communication with all pertinent sport facility personnel.
- Analyze the event in terms of tangible goods, intangible support services, and the event itself.
- Conduct a situation (SWOT) analysis to forecast the market climate/environment in terms of the strengths, weaknesses, opportunities, and threats related to the event.
- Position the sport facility in terms of the event to your primary and secondary markets.
- Segment and target the market based on pertinent market research concepts related to the event – that is, demographics, psychographics, and geographics.
- Package the event so it becomes attractive to the consumer. This may include special packages with hospitality opportunities or advanced on-sale of tickets.
- Work with the event management and the box office to price the event appropriately.
- Promote the facility first and the event as an add-on through advertising, the media, community relations, word of mouth, promotional efforts, public relations, and sponsorship partnerships.
- Set up a plan for the effective distribution of tickets or other admissions efforts for the event. This includes coordination with the facility box office and working

with it to meet the needs of secondary and tertiary box offices such as teams, the events themselves, and online ticket agencies.

- Once marketing efforts have started and throughout the process of marketing the facility and the event, conduct evaluations and collect feedback to maximize marketing efforts.

There are two main issues to remember here. It is important to make sure that although some marketing efforts by sport facilities and sport events may be conducted independently of each other, both parties must be aware of what the other is doing to avoid conflicting information being publicized. Second, if conflicting information is being publicized, the two parties must get together and ensure that the problem is rectified immediately. Ultimately, both parties want a full facility for the event, and confusion among customers will only lead to problems. In most cases, the facility personnel will be the individuals to deal with the problem, as they are the local entity the customer will expect to get answers from, and the facility wants to ensure that their image is not tarnished in the mind of the community.

EVENT IMPLEMENTATION AND ACTIVATION FROM THE FACILITY VIEWPOINT

Event implementation planning from the sport facility viewpoint starts the day a contract is signed for an event. From that point, the sport facility manager determines the scope of the work necessary to have the event staged in the facility; itemizes and analyzes the tasks that need to be completed; establishes schedules and timelines; and assigns personnel with responsibilities to complete. The scope of the work to be completed will vary based on the size of the event, the contract stipulations, and the amount of work that can be conducted prior to the day of the event.

The busiest time for a sport facility is the 24-hour period that encompasses the ingress, set-up, implementation, activation, breakdown, and egress of the event. This usually includes the 12–16 hours or so before the doors open, the entire duration of the event, and usually the four hours after the doors close. During this time, the level of involvement of facility personnel with the event significantly increases. Special relationships also need to be addressed, including those with unions and outsourced vendors. In addition, throughout this process, there is a constant need to prepare for unexpected situations that may cause chaos during the event.

Level of involvement of facility personnel in managing events

Again, the level of involvement in the activation is strictly stipulated in the contract between the sport facility and the event. The sport facility manager will often have a checklist of responsibilities that need to be accomplished prior to opening the doors. These checklists usually encompass three areas. First are work break-down structures, which are itemized by task, personnel, and operational area. Second is an inventory of assignments sequenced in a priority listing to ensure which tasks are accomplished first and how long it should take to complete the tasks. The third is an event life cycle or schedule/timeline of events scripted to the minute. Among the biggest challenges for the sport facility manager is when two events are back-to-back . . . and even more so when multiple events are scheduled on a single day. This means that while one event is breaking down, another is trying to set up. Keeping this phase of event activation organized is crucial to success.

However, in many facilities, these processes of setup and breakdown are not totally controlled by the management of the sport facility. Many sport facility managers and event promoters have the additional challenge of coordinating operations within a unionized facility. As such, many of the functions that need to be accomplished as related to daily operations, event setup, activation and implementation, and breakdown are controlled by union guidelines. This may include the number of hours a person can work and required breaks, the minimum number of union employees for certain tasks, weight limitations on lifting and moving, specialists required for certain tasks (examples include forklift drivers, electricians, plumbing, construction, and sound/lighting), and overtime stipulations.

In addition, as most events come in from the outside, the management of the sport facility also has a responsibility to act as a liaison between the event and ancillary services. These ancillary services may be managed in-house by the sport facility or may be outsourced to vendors. One of the biggest challenges for a sport facility manager is maintaining the quality expected of the sport facility and dealing with the multitude of expectations of an event. Coordination of event needs has to be communicated to various constituencies, including concessionaires (especially food service and catering), parking, security, and house-keeping/custodial. In some cases, the sport facility will provide these services for a fee within the event contract. The bigger challenge is when the event has its own ancillary services (such as their own concessionaires and security personnel). The need to communicate and coordinate with the sport facility services to ensure that everyone is on the same page and understands the parameters of their responsibilities is vital to the success of both the event and the proper management of the sport facility.

As with any event within a sport facility, problems are bound to occur. The sport facility manager's reaction to these unexpected issues is crucial to event success and to keeping the reputation of the sport facility at its highest level. Some issues are beyond the control of the facility manager such as acts of God and power outages. This requires facility managers to always remember Murphy's Law: 'Anything that can go wrong will go wrong with little advanced notice.' Facility managers and personnel that can, on a moment's notice, dissect a problem and solve it without

Implementing operations management

customers knowing anything happened are high-quality sport facility personnel. Hence, sport facility managers need to remember the six Ps of facility and event management: 'Prior proper planning prevents poor performance,' which is also stated as 'If you fail to plan, then you plan to fail.'

If you engage in quality and complete planning as far in advance as possible, the likelihood of a problem or poor performance is reduced exponentially. However, as you will see in the 'Facility Focus' at the end of the chapter, poor decisions fully within the grasp of the facility manager or owner can result in unnecessary dilemmas.

EVENT EXPERIENCES AT SPORT FACILITIES FROM THE CUSTOMER VIEWPOINT

The goal of any sport facility manager is to create memorable customer experiences that place the facility is a positive light and encourage customers to return for future events. These memorable experiences need to take into account those features most expected from customers, including safety, the value of the experience, entertainment, quality service, and hedonism. To fulfill these needs, customers seek out and pay premium prices to engage in these experiences with the hope of being present during extraordinary moments.

To create these memorable customer experiences, the sport facility manager and the staff seek to provide an environment through events that builds the experience beforehand, allows the customers to watch the experience unfold and to feel as though they are a part of it, and retain the experience so it is valued beyond the event and shared with others. Hence, it is important that the facility play its role in providing a holistic experience through multiple interactive moments. From the facility's standpoint, this could include a multitude of areas including but not limited to the cleanliness of restrooms and the facility itself, ease of ingress and egress, diversity and ease of food service, and overall feelings of safety due to quality security protocols. This requires sport facility managers to understand how spectators' experiences translate into positive emotion encounters. Hence, creative offerings and opportunities should be developed that stimulate the senses and valued-added moments of the live experience. This is, however, a challenge as spectators want to control their own individual experience space and expect authentic spontaneous surprises, while sport facility managers are highly accountable and must provide safe experiences for all stakeholders. It is also important for sport facility managers to understand that the first and last impressions of an event are critical to the memorable nature of the spectator experience, so ensuring that getting the pre- and post-event experiences correct is just as important and in some cases more important than the event experience itself.

IN THE FIELD . . .

Customer experiences at Marvel Stadium, Melbourne, Australia

The naming rights history of Marvel Stadium in Melbourne, Australia, was discussed back in Chapter 9. Beyond the financial benefits of the agreement, the Australian Football league (AFL) was looking for a partner to help maximize the experience for customers in a facility that had been notorious for a less-than-exciting spectator experience.

In the rebranding of the facility, the goal was to enhance the experience for customers. According to Michael Green the CEO of Melbourne Stadiums Limited:

> Marvel is a powerhouse in the entertainment industry and one of the most recognized brand names in the world. It is a brand dedicated to audience experiences, which firmly aligns with our vision to create incredible experiences for fans. This partnership will allow us to take the stadium atmosphere to the next level and create memorable experiences for a vast array of audiences and we look forward to delivering a truly game-changing experience.

To start, a Marvel retail store and various experience activations at the stadium are bringing the Marvel characters to life. Furthermore, a guest arriving at the stadium for events is greeted with street art, interactive displays, and technological installations. It is obvious that fan engagement and immersive activities for kids are a major focus to enhance the overall experience for customers without taking away from the core event on the field.

The Millennials demographics (1985–2000) brought back a new age of reading comic books and following superheroes (think about television's Big Bang Theory or the influx of Marvel movies from *Ironman* to *Deadpool* and the return of historical classics such as the Hulk and Captain America). This generation has discretionary income and a close connection to superheroes. Then there is Generation Z (born since 2000), who not only are the most significant influencers of spending in households, they want activities that include technological interactions and in many cases are the children of Millennials. Hence, the crossover opportunities through customer experiences that connect both are vital to quality event activation and spectatorship. It seems the partnership between Marvel and the AFL is seeking to do that while not taking away from the on-field and in-stadium experience craved by the AFL's most passionate fans.

Therefore, sport facility managers need to provide a level of service quality that creates customer satisfaction and positive impressions leading to customer retention. This requires an understanding of relationship marketing and experience marketing. *Relationship marketing* is concerned with building, maintaining, and enhancing long-term customer relationships for the benefit of both the customer and the sport facility, while *experience marketing* seeks to offer more value to entice customers to want to come back because of their positive experience at the sport facility.

A useful tool for sport facility managers interested in maximizing the quality of their services and hence customer satisfaction is the sport-specific adaptation of the *servuction model*. This model depicts the different elements that constitute the facility and event service experience and how the service experience is created. The sport facility manager is most concerned with the 'visible' parts of the model, namely facility, design, and physical evidence; the contact people, including staff and service providers; and the interaction with customers. The relationship between quality, satisfaction, and retention in association with these components has the potential to positively – as well as to negatively – influence a customer's service experience. Facility design in terms of the infrastructure and inanimate environment during the facility experience may include atmospherics such as music, lighting, and odors. It also includes physical evidence such as the scoreboards and technology available for customer use. For example, an air-conditioned suite with digital television, access to real-time statistical analytics and Wi-Fi, quality furnishings, and premium food and beverage is an example of how the facility design and physical evidence can positively influence the experience of the corporate customer. In terms of contact people, there are both direct and indirect interactions. *Direct interactions* include security screenings as a condition of entry to the building and selling beverages from a food service concession stand. *Indirect interactions* are remote in nature, such as spectators watching warm-ups, the game itself, or game break entertainment. For interactions with customers, sport facility managers and staff want to ensure a positive experience through fan interactions, the atmosphere created by a full house, and communications that are free from antisocial behaviors. Hence, the implementation and adherence to policies and procedures for fan behavior that hold all parties accountable can also positively influence the spectator's experience.

Another model that has been utilized by sport facilities is the Sportscape model. The framework for this model was derived from Bitner's Servicescape model, with the primary dimension of service focusing on the surrounding conditions, the functionality and layout of the infrastructure, and the signs and symbols associated with the experiences. The physical environment created through a sport facility and, by connection, the associated events taking place in a sport facility have a direct effect on the perceptions spectators have about the experience. This directly influences their decision-making process whether to stay longer at an event or return to the facility for future events. Sport facility managers need to consider the Sportscape in terms of facility ingress and egress, aesthetics, seating comfort, accessibility, space allocation, signage, and the latest technologies as factors that potentially influence spectators to stay at an event and repeat their patronage in the future.

Ultimately, customers of sport facilities desire easy access, quality aesthetics, good seating, the latest technology, cleanliness, and an overall positive event experience. Sport facility managers strive to meet the needs and wants of customers across all of these areas to improve the perceptions of those customers about the quality of the sport facility. If this perception is high, positive customer satisfaction is likely, resulting in positive word of mouth through social media communications about the sport facility. This, in turn, can lead to more customers attending events at the facility, as well as other events seeking to come to the facility. However, it is important to be able to evaluate all of these experiences to make an informed decision on the operation and management of the sport facility and to choose appropriate events to host.

EVALUATION OF EVENTS BY FACILITY OWNERSHIP AND MANAGEMENT

Once you have supported an event and the event has left the building, it is time to sit back and reflect on the successes and failures of the event. This is usually accomplished through an outcomes assessment process. When the facility event management plan was put together, goals and objectives should have been created. Those goals and objectives need to be measurable in order to effectively measure them. These measurements include the event as a whole, specific task analyses, and performance evaluations of both the facility personnel and of the outside event. These evaluations will result in one of four decisions:

1   Decide to host the event at the sport facility again in the future with no modifications (which does not happen 99.9% of the time).
2   Host the event at the sport facility again with enhancements or modifications.
3   Host the event again but with significant changes.
4   No longer host the event in the future.

The National Center for Spectator Sports Safety and Security (NCS[4]), at The University of Southern Mississippi, offers a security planning process designed to promote a standardized methodology for security planning at sporting venues and events throughout the United States. This planning process, known as Sport Event Security Aware (SESA), defines a minimum threshold for security policies, procedures, and operational plans. SESA was designed and developed by NCS[4] personnel (Dr. Walter Cooper, Dr. Stacey A. Hall, Dr. Lou Marciani, Jim McGee, and Frederick Gardy), funded by grants from Mississippi Homeland Security and the United

248

States Department of Homeland Security (DHS), and it receives continuous support from sport safety and security subject matter experts, DHS, and NCS[4] National Advisory Board. SESA assessments are available to all professional, collegiate, high school, and event organizations that own or operate sport facilities. The assessment is designed to be a repeated cycle implemented by venue or event managers to enhance preparedness, prevention, response, and recovery efforts.

Key components of the SESA Assessment Cycle

See Figure 11.1. The first component is a risk assessment. During this process, a list of recommended self- assessments are provided for use by the individual sport facility to conduct a self-assessment of risks to the venue or event. The goal is to identify gaps in existing security and response plans, identify areas in which targeted investment in security enhancements would reduce risk, and revise plans for a long-term security strategy.

The second component is training. Appropriate training can come from a collection of currently available local, state, and federal catalogs – recommended training courses typically include leadership, supervisory, and line staff training.

The third is exercise planning and performance. Venues or event organizations implementing the SESA process participate in planned and directed discussions as well as tabletop exercise. Personnel from organizations that own/operate venues or events supporting those venues during events are expected to participate in this

Figure 11.1 SESA Assessment Cycle

exercise. Exercise scenarios are determined for the venue or event based on the results of risk assessments and venue feedback at prior events with an emphasis on the evaluation of plans, procedures, and operational utility.

The final component is recommendations. After assessing plans, procedures, training, exercise outcomes, and event operations, a written report of the assessment is provided to the sport facility. The assessment will provide a determination of whether the individual venue or event implements best practices in the industry for the safety and security of venues or events. It also recommends measures for improving general security, counterterrorism security, and emergency preparedness.

TECHNOLOGY NOW! CERM PI (AUSTRALIA)

In Australia and New Zealand, the University of South Australia operates the CERM Performance Indicators Project. Designed for public aquatic centers and leisure centers, it now extends to a range of sport and leisure services, including golf courses, caravan and tourist parks, campgrounds, skate parks, and outdoor centers. CERM PIs provides benchmarks for 26 performance indicators, including services (e.g., program opportunities per week), marketing (e.g., promotion cost as a proportion of total cost), organization (e.g., cleaning and maintenance cost per visit), and finance (e.g., surplus/subsidy per visit).

In 2018, CERM PI commenced an online platform that focused on collecting data from customer service quality and operational management surveys. In providing a simple and customized experience for clients, the platform will provide not only benchmarking data against other facilities but, more importantly, individualized reports measuring customer satisfaction and loyalty. It also provides information about improvements to the experience that need to be considered for both retaining existing customers and attracting new ones.

The information to evaluate customer experiences is provided by information gathered through the CERM PI Customer Service Quality Survey. This survey collects information about customer experiences at facilities and perceptions of service quality across a multitude of categories including cleanliness of the facility, staff responsiveness to issues, and whether customers feel they are receiving value for money. The data collected can be used by facility managers to improve operations by making modifications to processes and procedures to maximize efficiency and customer satisfaction.

Source: University of South Australia. (2019). CERM PI. Retrieved May 30, 2019, from http://unisabusinessschool.edu.au/cerm-pi/

The evaluation of events by facility ownership and management is further buoyed by the information provided through the significant advances in performance analytics, which is discussed in depth in Chapter 14. These benchmarking and performance analytics provide significant information for sport facility managers to more effectively measure performance and achieve positive results. However, before considering performance analytics, two additional operations and management areas must be addressed: legal issues and risk assessment (Chapter 12) and security planning and management (Chapter 13).

CHAPTER REVIEW

No matter the size or type, facilities need events – and events need facilities. Sport facilities engage in their own independent sport event planning process as a part of its operations and management. The sport event planning process from the standpoint of the sport facility involves the development of the event from conceptualization through activation to implementation and eventual evaluation as related to the infrastructure and support services offered. This planning process involves setting objectives; developing a conceptualization of how the event will be implemented; creating realistic strategies that can be accomplished within the infrastructure at a cost that is affordable and that brings a positive image to all constituencies; and finalizing both a feasibility study and a strategic (SWOC) analysis. This also includes determining who the customers are for such an event.

Once accomplished and a decision is made to move forward with an event, the sport facility manager and ownership will enter into negotiations to host the event. This may be accomplished through a series of bid processes or through direct contact with an event promoter. As a part of negotiating contracts, a pro forma budget is created in advance to anticipate the general costs of hosting an event. Once all terms are agreed upon, contracts are signed and pre-event preparation begins immediately.

A major responsibility of the sport facility manager at this point is ensuring that the event is presented and produced in a professional manner, as the appearance is a reflection on the sport facility in the community, and that the facility is not damaged. This is a challenge at times because event promoters are often concerned only about the event itself and maximizing profits. In addition, as a result of the event, the sport facility manager must often also forge additional relationships with the media and sponsors to ensure there is no conflict.

Some of the responsibilities of the sport facility manager at this point include activating the facility's event marketing plan, implementing and activating the event plan, determining the level of involvement of facility personnel, coordinating tasks with unions and facility services, and preparing for any unexpected problems.

The goal of any sport facility manager is to create memorable customer experiences that place the facility in a positive light and encourage customers to return for future events. To create these memorable customer experiences, the sport facility manager and the staff of the facility seek to utilize events to provide an environment that builds the experience beforehand, allows the customers to watch the experience unfold and feel as though they are a part of it, and retain the experience so that it is valued beyond the event and shared with others. Therefore, the sport facility needs to understand the concepts of relationship marketing and experience marketing to deliver a level of service quality that drives customer satisfaction and positive impressions that lead to customer retention. The sport servuction model and the Sportscape model can also be used as a foundation for maximizing service quality, customer satisfaction, and the overall experience.

Ultimately, customers of sport facilities desire easy access, quality aesthetics, good seating, the latest technology, cleanliness, and an overall positive event experience. To ensure that sport facility managers are delivering these outcomes, an evaluation process must take place to determine whether to have the event at the sport facility again in the future or not. Through a performance evaluation process such as the SESA Assessment Cycle, the areas of risk assessment, training, exercise planning and performance, and recommendation can be assessed to determine the successful attainment of those outcomes.

FACILITY FOCUS: FACILITY AND EVENT SPONSORSHIP CONFLICTS: PEPSI CENTER, DENVER, COLORADO, UNITED STATES

Earlier in the chapter, we discussed two scenarios related to facility and event sponsorship conflicts at the Pepsi Center. Another situation in 2008 and 2009 resulting from the double booking of the arena played out creating more dramas for this sport facility.

In August 2008, Stan Kroenke and Kroenke Sport Enterprises, owners of the Pepsi Center, signed a contract with World Wrestling Entertainment (WWE) to hold their Monday Night Raw wrestling show that is televised worldwide on Memorial Day, May 25, 2009.

The WWE contract was signed well in advance of the 2008–2009 NBA season. Despite that, a verbal agreement with the Denver Nuggets of the NBA (also owned by Kroenke) to host game 4 of the Western Conference Finals ended up being scheduled on the same date if the team made it that far in the playoffs. When the team made it to the conference finals and despite having a legal and binding contract, the WWE was bumped from the facility for the Denver Nuggets – less than one week before the WWE event. The owner defended his move by stating that the Nuggets game would take precedence.

The results of this issue included the WWE having to refund tickets to over 11,000 fans and having to move the event to the Staples Center in Los Angeles. It also resulted in a lot of bad press from WWE Chairman Vince McMahon about the ineptness of Kroenke Sports and, by association, the Pepsi Center. The WWE also went out of its way to communicate that the blame for what they called The Denver Debacle was on the owners of the Pepsi Center, creating significant bad press for the facility.

BIBLIOGRAPHY

Bitner, M. J. (1992). Servicescapes: The impact of physical surroundings on customers and employees. *Journal of Marketing, 56*, 57–71. https://doi.org/10.1177/002224299205600205

Covell, D., & Walker, S. (2013). *Managing sport organizations: Responsibility for performance* (3rd ed.). London: Routledge.

Greenwell, T. C., Fink, J. S., & Pastore, D. L. (2002). Assessing the influence of the physical sports facility on customer satisfaction within the context of the service experience. *Sport Management Review, 5*(2), 129–148. https://doi.org/10.1016/s1441-3523(02)70064-8

Hock, C., Ringle, C. M., & Sarstedt, M. (2010). Management of multi-purpose stadiums: Importance and performance measurement of service interfaces. *International Journal of Services Technology and Management, 14*(2–3), 188–207. https://doi.org/10.1504/ijstm.2010.034327

Lindgreen, A., Vanhamme, J., & Beverland, M. B. (2009). *Memorable customer experiences: A research anthology.* Farnham: Gower.

Masterman, G. (2014). *Strategic sports event management* (3rd ed.). London: Routledge.

Schwarz, E. C., & Hunter, J. D. (2017). *Advanced theory and practice in sport marketing* (3rd ed.). London: Routledge.

Schwarz, E. C., Westerbeek, H., Liu, D., Emery, P., & Turner, P. (2017). *Managing sport facilities and major events* (2nd ed.). Oxford: Routledge.

Shilbury, D., Westerbeek, H., Quick, S., Funk, D. C., & Karg, A. (2014). *Strategic sport marketing* (4th ed.). Sydney: Allen and Unwin.

Van der Wagen, L., & White, L. (2018). *Event management: For tourism, cultural, business and sporting events.* Melbourne: Cengage Learning.

CHAPTER 12

LEGAL ISSUES AND RISK ASSESSMENT

CHAPTER OUTLINE

- Effects of the legal environment on sport facility operations
- Legal principles and standards related to sport facility management
  - Negligence law and unintentional torts
  - Criminal law and intentional torts
  - Contract law
- Risk management
- Risk assessment
- Sport venue risk assessment model
  - Step 1.0: Identification of the sport event security action team (SESAT)
  - Step 2.0: Characterization of assets
  - Step 3.0: Threat assessment
  - Step 4.0: Vulnerability assessment
  - Step 5.0: Consequence evaluation
  - Step 6.0: Risk assessment
  - Step 7.0: Consequence reduction proposals
- Risk Probability, consequence severity, and financial loss
- Risk control and response strategies
  - Risk avoidance
  - Risk reduction
  - Risk transfer
  - Risk retention
- Chapter review

EFFECTS OF THE LEGAL ENVIRONMENT ON SPORT FACILITY OPERATIONS

The law permeates all aspects of sport facility operations management such as ownership structures and governance, finances, design and construction, security planning, and human resource management. While we cannot articulate all the laws and legal concerns that may affect a sport facility manager or owner (especially with the global differences in laws based on individual countries), we can communicate the effect of the law on the operation and management of a sport facility, along with the major legal and risk management principles that are prevalent globally.

Laws are a body of rules that govern individual or collective actions and conduct as defined by an authorized governing body that have binding legal force. Laws provide accountability and justice for citizens and, in the case of this text, for the users and related constituencies of a sport facility. However, the challenge is that laws are constantly evolving through modifications and change and that legal evolution has a direct effect on the daily conduct of the management and operation of a sport facility.

The governments of the world and their designees create a great majority of laws. These laws may be created at the highest level (usually federal or parliamentary), at regional levels (states and provinces), or at the local level by municipalities. In addition, some laws are administrative in nature and are set by governing bodies such as the International Olympic Committee and the various sport leagues and tournaments around the world. In an attempt to generalize the categories of law, we present the following four categories:

- *Constitutional law*: Laws embedded in the constitution or charter of a country or region
- *Statutory law*: Laws created and affirmed by sanctioned legislative bodies
- *Common law*: Laws created based on past legal decisions (precedence)
- *Administrative law*: Rules and regulations created, implemented, and enforced by a specifically authorized agency

While it would be impossible for a sport facility manager or owner to know every law that has a direct effect on the management and operation of the facility, they do have a duty of care to their users and associated constituents to act legally. As such, sport facility managers and owners must have a basic understanding of the legal principles and standards that directly affect them.

LEGAL PRINCIPLES AND STANDARDS RELATED TO SPORT FACILITY MANAGEMENT

Managers and owners should have a basic understanding of the legal principles and standards that are inherent to proper sport facility management and operations. Tort laws are the most significant set of laws that sport facilities encounter. Unintentional torts fall under the category of negligence, and intentional torts fall under the realm of criminal law. Managers and owners also deal with legal ramifications of their management and operations of a sport facility as related contract laws. In addition, two of the most prevalent legislative issues to impact sport facilities globally in the 21st century relate to intellectual properties and ambush marketing.

Negligence law and unintentional torts

An *unintentional tort*, more commonly known as negligence, is a failure to act in a manner equal to how a reasonable person would act under the same circumstances. As related to sport facilities, for there to be negligence, four elements must be proven: duty, the act itself, proximate cause, and damages. First is whether the designees of the facility had a duty of care or a duty to act. This duty can arise from an inherent relationship between the personnel or owners of the sport facility and a user or from duties that are required because of legal standing (employment laws, supervisory obligations, and administration of first aid are three examples). Second, the act usually relates to foreseeing risks and preventing harm. Ultimately, all actions should meet a standard of care that limits the inherent risks of activities in the sport facility and prevents negligence behavior by those engaged in activities within the sport facility. The third is proximate cause, which means, for a charge of negligence to be valid, the action of negligence causes a loss or injury. The fourth element is damages, or that there was an actual injury, loss, or emotional harm.

Any party associated with a sport facility can be liable for negligence, ranging from individual employees to administrative staff to ownership. There are numerous ways to protect against negligence – the most widely used in sport facilities are *waivers*, by which users contractually release the facility and their agents from liability. There is also the assumption of risk statutes that can protect sport facilities against negligence claims for injuries suffered from acts that are inherent and known to be part of an activity. Other ways to limit negligence liability is by using independent contractors for events – in essence transferring the risk of negligence to the contractor and purchasing insurance to protect the entire operation in case a negligent act takes place.

Criminal law and intentional torts

An *intentional tort* is a civil wrong based on an intentional act. These types of torts fall under criminal law, and the purpose of these laws is to protect the general health, safety, and welfare of the public. As a result of the inherent activities in sports, there are times, both on the field/court and off, that disagreements and actions may go beyond the realm of what is acceptable in society and cross over to a criminal act. In addition, because of potential interactions between staff and uncooperative patrons, there must be an understanding of crossing the line from what is a duty of care or action and a criminal act.

The major intentional torts that may take place in sport facilities are:

- *Assault*: When one individual tries to physically harm another in a way that makes the second person under attack feel immediately threatened. There does not need to be actual physical contact; threats, gestures, and other actions that would raise the suspicions of a reasonable person can constitute an assault.
- *Battery*: The unlawful and unwanted physical contact by one person to a second person with the intention to harm
- *Defamation*: Written (libel) or verbal (slander) communication of nonfactual information with the intent to create a negative image
- *Invasion of privacy*: Interference with the right to be left alone, ranging from the handling of membership data to having a personal locker with a lock on it

Contract law

Contracts are a major part of facility management. Other than employment contracts, the largest and most significant contracts are those with events that utilize the sport facility and sponsorship contracts. No matter the type, any contract has five elements: (1) the offer, (2) the acceptance, (3) consideration, (4) legality, and (5) capacity. The *offer* and *acceptance* are when one party tenders the contract, and a second party agrees to the terms. *Consideration* involves the exchange of value between the two parties. Hence there must be a benefit of some type to both parties: In an event contract, it is usually a fee to the sport facility for the event to acquire a venue. *Legality* is simply that the contract must not be against the law, and *capacity* is that both parties entering into the agreement have the authority to do so. All contracts have additional language covering a multitude of issues. Some of the most common are terms and cancellation clauses with remedies, confidentiality statements, and damages should a breach of contract occur.

Event contracts are usually more detailed because a number of specialized elements need to be included. First, the event itself is only a small part of the contract; the pre-event setup and post-event breakdown must also be detailed. In addition, any specialized lease agreements for facilities, equipment, and rentals must be spelled out and are often added as an addendum. There must also be an articulation of other ancillary benefits and options, including marketing and sponsorship efforts, concessions and merchandising offerings, and personnel inclusions (examples are setup/breakdown staff, security, ushers, contractors, and site managers).

A *facility sponsorship contract* could be for naming rights on the entire complex or on a specific part of the facility (a court, field, or room). Depending on the size of the facility and the location, these agreements can net up to USD$40 million per year over 50 years (for example, the current deal between Citi and the New York Mets). In England, the Football Association (FA) will offer advertising rights to Wembley Stadium (i.e., Wembley Stadium 'sponsored by' or 'in association with'), which they anticipate will bring in an additional £5 million per year. In addition to advertising and promotions specifications, the contracts may also include statements of exclusivity (which prevent other sponsors in the same industry to enter into an agreement with the facility) or nonexclusivity, options to renew, rights of first refusal for renewal, and any intellectual property rights concerns.

RISK MANAGEMENT

A *risk* is the possibility of loss from a hazard such as personal injury, property damage, or economic loss. Risk cannot be eliminated from the environment, but with careful planning, it can be managed. Risk is best understood as the product of the consequence (severity) of an event and the probability (frequency) of the event occurring, also represented as:

Risk = Probability × Consequence severity

Risk increases as the consequences and probability of occurrence increases (see Figure 12.1). When risk probability is low and consequence severity is low, the risk level is depicted in Figure 12.1 as RP1, CS1. As the level of risk probability and level of consequence severity increase, the risk level increases to RP2, CS2. The three main types of risk are mission (function) risks, asset risks, and security risks. Mission risks prevent an organization from accomplishing its mission. Asset risks may harm an organization's physical assets, and security risks have the potential to harm actual data and people.

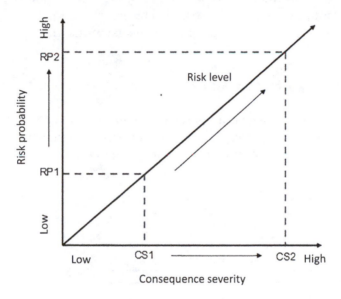

Figure 12.1 Risk probability and consequence severity

Quality risk management practices are imperative to reduce legal exposure, prevent financial and human loss, protect facility assets, ensure business continuity, and minimize damage to the sport organization's reputation. Primarily, facility owners or operators must act prudently. They have a duty of care to provide a reasonably safe environment for patrons. In the event of an incident, organizational plans and policies will be reviewed to assess the standard of care provided. Sport managers tend to understand the need and value of risk management but fail to do the necessary planning, thereby exposing their programs to risk and eventual financial loss. Sport managers tend to react to events and circumstances rather than taking a proactive approach and implementing effective plans and policies to prevent catastrophic losses. Sport facility managers must develop an effective risk management program to reduce risks and mitigate the consequences of incidents.

RISK ASSESSMENT

The Department of Homeland Security in the United States identified major sport stadiums and arenas as key assets. *Key assets* are individual targets whose destruction could create local disaster or damage to the nation's morale or confidence. Sport facility managers face a significant challenge in determining potential threats and must prepare for a wide range of possible incidents. In order to identify potential threats, sport facility managers should conduct a risk assessment of their facility. *Risk assessment* is the process of evaluating security-related risks from threats to an organization, its assets, or personnel. The assessment process gathers critical information to aid the facility manager in the decision-making process.

SPORT VENUE RISK ASSESSMENT MODEL

The National Center for Spectator Sports Safety and Security (NCS[4]) has developed a sport venue risk assessment model based on the United States Department of Homeland Security risk assessment principles (see Figure 12.2).

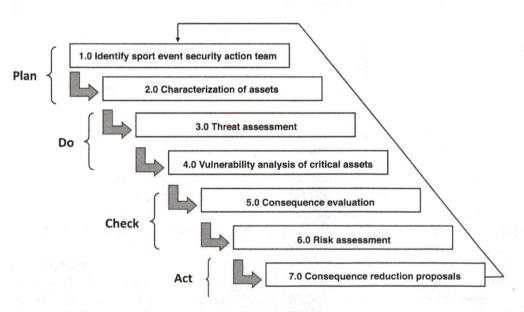

Figure 12.2 Sport Event Security Assessment Model (SESAM)

Step 1.0: Identification of the sport event security action team (SESAT)

Step 1.0 involves identifying the sport event security action team (SESAT), or working group. These individuals are key players in facility security planning and operations related to sport events. The team is responsible for providing information about the sport facility and the surrounding area. SESAT members may include the sport facility manager, local police chief, local emergency management director, emergency medical services, fire/HAZMAT, public health, and public relations. A combination of representatives from all agencies ensures multidisciplinary cooperation and the ability to gather knowledge and information from different perspectives.

Step 2.0: Characterization of assets

Step 2.0 allows managers to characterize assets. An *asset* is a person, place, or thing and can be assigned a monetary value. Assets to be assessed include both facility assets and surrounding area (community) assets. Assets to be protected may include people (i.e., athletes), physical assets (i.e., a stadium), information (i.e., electronic data), and processes (i.e., supply chains and procedures). Table 12.1 provides examples of assets under each category:

Table 12.1 Sport venue assets

Human assets	Physical assets	Information and processes
Athletes	Facility buildings	Electronic data
Spectators	Stadiums/arenas and contents	Nonelectronic data
Staff	Command post	Supply chains
Contractors	Police department	
Visitors	Fire department	
Community residents	Hospitals	
	Public works	

Step 3.0: Threat assessment

Step 3.0 identifies potential threats. A *threat* is a product of intention and capability of an adversary to take action that would be detrimental to an asset. The most relevant threats to the sport industry that need to be addressed include terrorism, hooliganism, crowd disorder, vandalism, personal assault, theft, fraud, logistical failure, and inclement weather. Facility managers must decide what their main threats are at an early stage and determine how vulnerable the organization is to an incident.

Terrorism is one of the most commonly cited risks associated with the security of sport venues. Sporting events are at high risk due to the common elements of large crowds, national/international participants, national/international audience, and the known date, time, and location of events.

Numerous sport facility threats need to be assessed, including terrorism, hooliganism, crowd disorder, vandalism, personal assault, theft, fraud, logistical failure, and inclement weather.

Terrorism

The Federal Bureau of Investigation (FBI) in the United States defines terrorism as the unlawful use of force or violence against persons or property to intimidate or coerce a government, the civilian population or any segment thereof, in furtherance of political or social objectives. A sport stadium or arena is considered a high-value terrorist target because of the potentially high casualty rate. There are two primary categories of terrorism: domestic terrorism and international terrorism. *Domestic terrorism* is the unlawful use or threatened use of force or violence by a group or individual based and operating entirely within the home country. *International terrorism* is the unlawful use of force or violence against persons or property committed by a group or individual who has some connection to a foreign power or whose activities transcend national boundaries.

Hooliganism

Hooliganism involves disorderly fan behavior and criminal activity that occur before and after events. Incidents may be organized (preplanned) or spontaneous. *Spontaneous hooliganism* is a low-level disorder in or around stadiums and is not as violent. *Organized hooliganism* is the more serious form of hooliganism where violence is the norm and people are injured or killed. The primary purpose is to fight rival supporters and/or police officials and to cause disruption at the event and destroy property. Hooliganism has been known as the English Disease because of its origination in Britain, but it is prevalent elsewhere in Europe.

Crowd disorder

Crowd disorder may involve demonstrations or protests inside and outside the venue or spectator intrusions onto the playing field. Fan celebrations are sometimes overexuberant, resulting in 'rushing the field.' Crowd congestion has been the cause of many horrific incidents in the sporting world. This problem has primarily been the result of the number of fans exceeding venue capacity. Other reasons may include excessive alcohol consumption, inadequate access control, or inadequate design of facility structure.

Vandalism

Webster's dictionary defines *vandalism* as the willful or malicious destruction or defacement of public or private property. Individuals or groups may cause damage to the stadium or arena building or equipment installed at the venue. Acts of vandalism can range from graffiti to arson, normally occur during non-event days when security is lenient.

Personal assault

Sport facility managers must plan for all types of assault, including player and fan violence. Assault cases on and off the playing field have become a major problem in recent years, especially at youth sports events. In many previous cases, parents have assaulted one another or an officiating referee.

Theft

Sport organizations and associations need to plan for financial loss caused by the illegal disappearance of money or inventory. Management, employees, and visitors are all capable of theft and/or embezzlement. Many organizations experience 'shrinkage' of inventory that may be attributed to an outsider or staff member. This reinforces the need for employee background checks or similar policies to prevent hiring dishonest staff.

Fraud

Ticket scalping and fraudulent tickets are a problem in the sport industry. Entities selling tickets are sometimes selling above face value, which is illegal in some parts of the world. Furthermore, fraudulent tickets infiltrating the ticket market has caused serious problems in the past, especially the sale of these tickets through online Internet sites. An example of this problem transpired at the 2007 Liverpool–Milan UEFA Champions League Final in Athens, Greece. Many fans with valid tickets were locked out of the Athens Olympic stadium for the final match because fans with counterfeit tickets purchased on the black market had successfully gained entry to the venue.

Logistical failure

Sport facility event operations may be disrupted due to logistical failure (i.e., loss of power and/or resources). Plans need to be developed to address unplanned incidents and to ensure continuity of operations through backup systems or event relocation agreements. Mutual aid agreements with a neighboring facility may provide relief in case the unexpected happens and the facility is unable to host an event.

Natural disasters or inclement weather can cause chaos to sporting organizations and their events. In fall 2005, Hurricane Katrina caused massive devastation to the South Gulf region of the United States including the New Orleans area. Many professional and collegiate sport programs in the affected areas suffered major destruction and financial loss. Some programs were eliminated or relocated to other parts of the country. The New Orleans Saints Football team relocated to Baton Rouge, Louisiana, for the 2005 season and returned to its home venue in September 2006. It cost an estimated $180 million to renovate the Superdome facility. The sudden onset of storms, tornadoes, or lightning can pose real problems for facility operators, resulting in mass evacuations of stadiums and arenas.

Table 12.2 provides examples of sport event incidents from around the world. Besides the major threats to sport facilities previously discussed, the facility manager must also identify specific risks associated with the venue and its activities. These may include employee accidents, breach of contract, negligence, product defects, discrimination, environmental hazards (i.e., slippery surfaces), infrastructure hazards (i.e., design defects), programmatic hazards (i.e., supervision and training), emergency care hazards (i.e., appropriate treatment), and transportation hazards (i.e., properly maintained vehicles).

Table 12.2 Global sport event incidents

1972: At the Munich Olympic Games, a group known as Black September took several Israeli athletes hostage.

1985: At the European Cup soccer match between English and Italian teams at Heysel Stadium, Brussels, Belgium, 41 persons died when a crowd barrier collapsed under the weight of people trying to escape from the rioting between rival fans.

1988: A violent Nepalese hailstorm resulted in 93 fatalities and over 100 casualties during a soccer match at the national stadium in Nepal. Hundreds of spectators attempted to exit the open stands when the storm broke, but the gates were locked, and many fans were trampled to death.

1989: In San Francisco, an earthquake occurred during game 3 of the Major League Baseball (MLB) World Series between the San Francisco Giants and Oakland As at Candlestick Park. The stadium remained intact, and no fans received serious injuries.

1989: The Sheffield, England, stadium disaster killed 95. Crushing took place in a standing area of the stadium. Fans entering the stadium through a vomitory were unaware that the pushing was crushing people at the fence line of the terrace, and officials were slow to detect the crush and relieve the pressure.

1993: In what is known as the Monica Seles Stabbing, during the second set of a quarterfinal match in Hamburg, Seles was stabbed between the shoulder blades with a 25-centimeter knife by a fan. Seles was unable to return to playing tennis for 28 months because of the psychological harm.

1993: Some 12,000 fans rush the field in Madison, Wisconsin, United States, at a college football game between Michigan and Wisconsin at Camp Randall Stadium. Fans were hurt when chain-link and rail fences collapsed under a wave of jubilant Wisconsin fans pushing toward the field after the game.

1996: At the Atlanta Olympic Games, two people died and 110 were injured from a pipe bomb blast at Centennial Olympic Park during an open-air concert.

1996: One hundred died in a crowd crush at a tunnel leading to soccer stadium seating in Guatemala City at a World Cup qualifying match. Too many tickets had been sold.

2000: Thirteen people were trampled to death in a riot at a 2002 FIFA World Cup qualifying match in Zimbabwe between South Africa and Zimbabwe.

2002: An FBI alert warned that Al-Qaeda's *Manual of Afghan Jihad* proposed U.S. football stadiums as a possible terrorist target. People with links to terrorist groups were downloading stadium images.

2002: A father and son attacked Major League Baseball (MLB) Kansas City Royals first base coach Tom Gamboa at Comiskey Park.

2004: Mayhem broke out at a National Basketball Association (NBA) Indiana–Pacers game when fans and players exchanged punches in the stands.

2004: A street reveler was killed at a Boston Red Sox celebration when she was hit in the eye by a projectile filled with pepper spray.

2005: The UEFA Champions League quarterfinal match between AC Milan and Inter Milan was abandoned after Inter fans threw missiles and flares onto the pitch. One of the flares hit the AC Milan goalkeeper.

2005: Hurricane Katrina caused the displacement of many professional and collegiate sports programs in New Orleans and the Gulf Coast region of the United States.

2005: An Oklahoma University student killed himself by prematurely detonating a bomb strapped to his body outside an 84,000-seat stadium.

2006: The National Football League (NFL) received a radiological dirty bomb threat that indicated several stadiums were subject to attack.

2007: A police officer was killed in Sicily, Italy, when fans rioted at a Series A soccer match between Catania and Palermo, leading to the suspension of all league matches and a safety assessment on all stadiums.

2007: In the UEFA Champions League lockout, many fans with valid tickets were locked out of the Athens Olympic stadium for the final match between Milan and Liverpool. It is alleged that fans with counterfeit tickets purchased on the black market had successfully gained entry to the venue.

2008: At the Summer Olympics in China, Cuban Taekwondo champion Angel Matos kicked a Swedish referee in the head, pushed a judge, and spat on the floor after being disqualified in the Bronze Medal match due to his Kye-shi time-out having elapsed.

2009: Philadelphia Phillies fan, David Sale (22), was beaten to death outside the Philadelphia Citizens Bank Park after an argument over a spilled beer.

2009: A 60-year-old female spectator at the Tour De France cycling event was killed after being hit by a police motorcycle accompanying the cyclists.

2010: Near the end of an international cricket match between Australia and Pakistan, a drunken Australian fan ran onto the field and tackled Pakistan's Khalid Latif before being detained by security.

2011: Texas Rangers baseball fan, Shannon Stone (39), died after falling from the stands at Arlington Stadium while trying to catch a ball tossed toward him by Rangers outfielder Josh Hamilton.

(Continued)

Table 12.2 (Continued)

2011: Bryan Stow was nearly beaten to death in a parking lot after the 2011 opener in Los Angeles between the Dodgers and Giants. He suffered brain damage and is permanently disabled, requiring constant physical therapy.

2012: A soccer match ended in riots and civil unrest in Port Said, Egypt, after Port Said's Al-Masry beat Cairo's Al Ahly 3–1. This incident resulted in 73 deaths.

2013: During the 117th Boston Marathon on April 15, 2013, two pressure cooker bombs exploded near the finish line, killing three people and injuring an estimated 264 others.

2014: During a UEFA Euro 2016 qualifying match between Serbia and Albania in Belgrade, Serbia, a small remote-controlled drone with Albania's flag suspended from it hovered over the stadium. An Albania player removed the flag, which led to a large brawl involving players, staff, and spectators from both teams. The game was suspended at 0–0 in the 41st minute

2015: An attempted suicide bombing was foiled at a France–Germany international friendly soccer match in Paris. At least one of the attackers outside the Stade de France stadium had a ticket to the match and tried to gain entry. A security guard who discovered the vest in a routine check 15 minutes after kickoff thwarted the attempted entrance into the stadium. The bomber then backed away and detonated the vest that was loaded with explosives and bolts. Police reported that one civilian was killed in these attacks.

2016: A phishing scheme exposed the NBA's Milwaukee Bucks Team tax records. Fraudsters impersonated the team president in an e-mail requesting the players and staff's W-2 records for the previous year that revealed social security numbers, dates of birth, compensation packages, and other financial statements.

2017: An unauthorized drone crashed into the upper deck seating at a MLB game at Petco Park between the San Diego Padres and Arizona Diamondbacks. The MLB has prohibited drone use at all of their parks.

2018: A group of around 50 intruders forced their way into Sporting Lisbon's training center during a practice session to assault players and staff and cause damage to the changing room. This was shortly after Sporting Lisbon missed out on a Champions League place to their bitter rivals Benfica.

Step 4.0: Vulnerability assessment

Step 4.0 assesses current vulnerabilities. *Vulnerability* is defined as an exploitable security weakness or deficiency at a facility. Vulnerabilities expose the facility to a threat and eventual loss. A vulnerability assessment identifies weaknesses in physical structures, personnel systems, and processes that may be exploited and is a key component of the risk assessment process. Common vulnerabilities at major sport venues include the lack of emergency preparedness, perimeter control, physical protection systems, access control, credentialing, training, and communication capabilities.

Step 5.0: Consequence evaluation

Step 5.0 evaluates the potential consequences of an incident. This includes analyzing the potential number of people requiring hospitalization, potential loss of life and infrastructure, economic impact, and level of social trauma. There will be consequences to all types of incidents, for example, a slip-and-fall accident may result in one personal injury and a single lawsuit. Alternatively, a major crowd-crushing incident could cause hundreds of casualties, huge financial loss, and a social stigma for the sport team, league, or governing body. Consequence is also referred to as the 'criticality' impact of loss that differs at each facility. The greater the potential for loss or damage to human and physical assets, the higher the impact of the loss. Consequence evaluation can be classified as essential (catastrophic loss), critical (serious loss), important (moderate loss), or not important (minor loss). Consequence classifications are discussed later in the chapter.

FACILITY FOCUS: MANAGING SECURITY FOR 100K GUESTS: DARRELL K ROYAL (DKR)–TEXAS MEMORIAL STADIUM, AUSTIN, TEXAS, UNITED STATES

Texas Memorial Stadium is the home to the University of Texas (UT) at Austin Longhorn NCAA Division I football program. Longhorn football games regularly sell out, hosting more than 100,000 fans. Considered a high-profile target because of its capacity, UT Austin personnel also address severe weather challenges, the fact that the stadium is part of an urban campus in a metropolitan city, and thousands of fans tailgating around the stadium, who are considered soft targets.

According to Mr. Johnson, assistant VP for campus safety, 'the potential for adverse outcomes is high, so we look at threats, vulnerabilities, and consequences associated with these incidents and occurrences. We identify, analyze, and assess what the risk is and how we either accept, avoid, transfer, or try to control it based on an acceptable level of risk and an acceptable cost.' To ensure a fan's security experience is unobtrusive as possible, communication and training are key, including:

1 Providing guidance to fans during emergency situations;
2 Providing information to peers, supervisors, and subordinates who are working events;
3 Demonstrating a familiarization with the stadium to all people working on game day; and
4 Understanding what needs to be done in the event of an emergency – shelter in place or go into lockdown.

UT Austin also does cross-messaging at other sport events, and security news can be included with ticketing packets, e-mails, the website, and disseminated throughout the University's Longhorn Foundation. UT Austin implemented a clear-bag policy in 2017, taking its lead from the NFL. A fan text messaging service is utilized to send alerts to staff if they notice a problem. Staffing for game days includes around 3,500 people, and 26 different agencies are represented in the emergency operations center (EOC). During the week of the game, the university holds general operations meetings and briefs with police and security partners about VIP attendance and contingency plans. There is also a police briefing three hours before the game to discuss any emerging threats. Training is a continuous cycle with supervisors undergoing extensive training and practicing shelter and evacuation plans annually.

Source: *Security Magazine.* (2018, July). How the University of Texas at Austin secures 100,000-fan football games. Retrieved May 30, 2019, from www. securitymagazine.com/articles/89211-how-the-university-of-texas-at-austin-secures-100000-fan-football-games

Step 6.0: Risk assessment

Step 6.0 involves determining the overall risk level for the facility. After analyzing the threat, vulnerability, and consequence levels of each potential incident, a total risk level for the facility is determined. The level of risk may be categorized as high, moderate, or low. The facility manager must decide whether the determined risk level is acceptable or not and make the necessary adjustments to safety and security policies and procedures.

Step 7.0: Consequence reduction proposals

Step 7.0 is the final stage in the process that offers the opportunity to provide consequence reduction proposals (countermeasure improvements), which are provided to management to enhance decision-making abilities. Possible security measures to reduce risk may include physical security, good personnel practices, and information security. Facility managers should conduct regular reviews of security measures and exercise plans to ensure that they remain accurate and workable. Furthermore, all staff should understand the importance of security and assume responsibility to raise concerns and report observations. Other consequence reduction options include policy review, evacuation routes, traffic rerouting, vendor/usher/volunteer training, stadium lockdown, lighting upgrades, parking restrictions, and emergency lights and signs.

The sport venue risk assessment model is a cyclical model. Assessments must be continuously completed on facilities to ensure that adequate plans and security measures are in place and updated over a period of time. A sport facility's threat and vulnerability level may change depending upon circumstances in the country or local community. Evaluations of potential threats and existing vulnerabilities are used to determine what dangers to prepare for, how to address them, and how to prioritize preparedness efforts. Determining which threats are the most dangerous allows managers to decide where they should invest their time and effort in preparedness methods.

PANORAMA STADIUM THREAT ASSESSMENT

Panorama Stadium is a multipurpose outdoor facility, hosting soccer, rugby, and other athletic events. The facility management team has decided to conduct a threat assessment in order to identify potential risks and gaps in their security operational system.

The Panorama Stadium facility management team appointed a sport event security action team (SESAT), representing police, firefighters, emergency medical services, public relations, and public health officials. A pre-planning meeting occurred to inform agencies of the situation and their role in the assessment process. Facility and surrounding assets were characterized, and potential facility threats were discussed.

Stadium location and features

- Built in 1994
- 69,000 club seats, plus 1,000 box seats
- Located in a major metropolitan city
- Access to major public transportation systems
- Residential and business areas surrounding the facility
- 16 main entrances with turnstiles
- Parking immediately adjacent to the facility
- Press box with CCTV capabilities
- Command post in the press box area
- Concession deliveries scheduled once a week
- Event security outsourced to a local security provider
- Local police, fire, and emergency medical services available on the event day

Assets

- Stadium infrastructure
- Human assets (i.e., spectators, athletes, officials)
- Equipment storage area
- Residential and business assets
- Public transportation infrastructure
- Local response agencies

Threats

- Active political activists in a city area
- Biological agent release in the facility
- Active shooter incident

269

- Suicide bomber
- Fan/player violence
- Tornado warning
- Vehicle borne improvised explosive device (VBIED)

The sport event security action team discussed the following issues:

1 The facility was built in 1994 with little focus on security features.
2 The multipurpose facility hosts soccer, rugby, and other athletic events.
3 Fan demographics are different according to the sport.
4 Previous incidents of fan violence have occurred.
5 Spectators entering the facility are screened.
6 Alcohol is consumed.
7 Evacuation procedures (full, partial, or shelter-in-place) have not been established.
8 There is concern over training requirements for security staff and volunteers.
9 Facility break-ins have occurred in the past year, resulting in the theft of property.
10 Restricted areas of the facility are unsecured during event time.
11 There is inadequate facility lighting at entry gates and in parking areas.
12 Credentialing of athletes, officials, and security is inadequate.
13 Control and monitoring of concession deliveries are not controlled and monitored.
14 Facility equipment and maintenance storage are unsecured and stored chemicals may be used for terrorist purposes.
15 If an incident were to occur, the possible hospital surge of casualties would overwhelm current emergency medical resources in the city.

After further discussion, the team decided to implement the following countermeasure improvements:

1 Conduct a structural assessment of the facility and reevaluate/redesign security features within the facility.
2 Evaluate threats and risks for each event as they may differ.
3 Utilize security technologies, that is, the text messaging system, to identify troublemakers.
4 Develop emergency response and evacuation plans.
5 Practice evacuation drills to test operations.
6 Require all staff to complete security training, that is, terrorism awareness training

7 Ensure proper and consistent screening procedures.

8 Schedule concession deliveries when security officials are present.

9 Ensure that all restricted areas (for example, pressroom, storage space) are secured at all times.

10 Establish mutual aid agreements with response agencies and ensure alternative playing sites for continuity of operations.

Discussion questions

1 Discuss the risk assessment process. Are there any other potential threats or vulnerabilities to the Panorama Stadium? What additional countermeasure improvements would you recommend?

2 Identify potential threats and vulnerabilities at a local sport venue.

3 Research the 2015 Stade de France bombing incident. Discuss the event operations and response strategies.

RISK PROBABILITY, CONSEQUENCE SEVERITY, AND FINANCIAL LOSS

Risk probability refers to how frequent a risk may occur, which is dependent on the current vulnerability levels. If existing countermeasures are effectively protecting the facility from all threats, the vulnerability will be low, and in essence, the risk probability will be low. However, the reverse is also true. If current facility vulnerabilities are not protected, the facility is exposed to a high potential for loss. Sport organizations can classify the probability (frequency) of risks into four categories: extremely high, high, medium, and low.

The consequence severity of a threat and eventual loss must also be evaluated. The manager must consider both the severity and financial impact on the sport program. Each threat must be evaluated individually, along with the impact it will have on the facility or organization to perform its mission. Consequence severity (impact of loss) can be classified into four categories: essential, critical, important, and not important. Consequently, the resulting financial loss is equated as catastrophic, serious, moderate, or minor:

- *Essential*: A successful threat would cause complete loss of facility operations, resulting in a *catastrophic* loss.
- *Critical*: A successful threat would cause severe impairment to facility operations, resulting in a *serious* loss.

271

- *Important*: A successful threat would cause a noticeable impact on facility operations, resulting in a *moderate* loss.
- *Not important*: A successful threat would not cause a noticeable impact on facility operations, resulting in a *minor* loss.

A catastrophic loss is one that requires major tax or fee increases or, in private industry, may result in bankruptcy. A critical loss would require major service cutbacks, facility closings, and/or program cancellations. Moderate loss indicates temporary service reductions or minor fee increases. Minor losses can be absorbed by the organization with current operating revenues and no program reductions. In order to aid sport facility managers in risk management decisions, consequence and probability data is presented in a risk logic matrix in Figure 12.3.

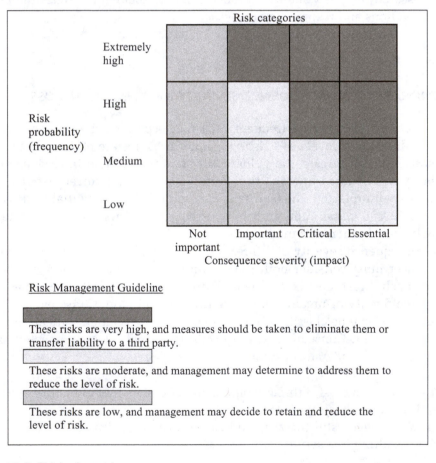

Figure 12.3 Risk logic matrix

Implementing operations management

TECHNOLOGY NOW! SPORT SECURITY AND TECHNOLOGY (GENERIC/GLOBAL)

Sport security professionals are using a wide variety of technology – social media, simulation software, phone apps, security cameras, digital two-way radios, license plate recognition software, and unmanned aircraft systems, commonly known as drones – to mitigate risks to fans, players, and personnel at sporting events.

Social media: Monitoring Facebook and Twitter posts can yield information on potential security threats. Monitoring social media before, during, and after an event can help identify any plans or ideas for illegal activity.

Simulation software: The National Center for Spectator Sports Safety and Security (NCS[4]), in conjunction with INCONTROL, developed simulation software called SportEvac to help with emergency response training and planning. This software allows venues to exercise scenarios specific to their sites, such as ingress and egress under normal circumstances, or evacuation during an emergency incident.

Phone apps and text messaging: Today's sport venues have phone apps for facility maps, seat upgrades, food service, and security assistance. Some venues have an anonymous text messaging system to report problems and request security assistance. The information is monitored in the command center and relayed to security staff on the ground in order to resolve a problem efficiently before it escalates.

Security cameras: Camera capabilities and their associated systems have been one of the most innovative improvements in recent years. For example, cameras that have analytics enable you to discern certain behaviors. Computerized searching has also made it possible to find things almost instantaneously in hours of recording.

Digital two-way radios: According to *RCR Wireless News*, digital two-way radios are cost-effective, have excellent sound audio and high level of security, and offer the ability to look up necessary information instantly. They also have the ability to contact certain groups of people, such as those near an incident. The radio has a GPS locator so that users can identify the closest persons to the scene and dispatch them immediately to handle the problem.

License plate recognition software: Casinos were the first to use license plate recognition. Facilities such as racetracks also use this technology as quite a number of people are banned for various integrity reasons.

Evaluating risk and potential loss assists the facility manager's decision-making process to reduce, reassign, transfer, or accept identified risks. The asset manager (facility manager) or owner usually determines an acceptable level of risk.

Risk avoidance

Severe risks that have the potential for a high degree of loss and that may occur frequently should be avoided. These risks need to be identified prior to an incident and avoided completely. Risks that are categorized in the black zone in Figure 12.3 should be avoided, or significant safety and security upgrades should be implemented to reduce risk to the greatest degree possible. For example, if a sport activity or event has a history of potentially fatal accidents or crowd management problems, the facility manager may wish to eliminate the activity or cancel the event.

Risk reduction

Facility managers can reduce risk through staff training, preventative maintenance, and development of a risk management plan. Risks that are categorized in the light gray zone in Figure 12.3 may be reduced. For example, if a facility manager has experienced acts of hooliganism at the facility, it would be prudent to identify the culprits and ban them from future events to prevent future incidents. Alternatively, the manager may wish to implement buffer zones between rival fans to prevent confrontational issues. Sport facility managers can also reduce the likelihood of threats by improving physical protection systems such as implementing access controls, closed-circuit television (CCTV) security cameras, venue lighting, personnel background checks, credentialing measures, interoperable communication networks, and developing emergency response and evacuation plans. Further safety and security measures to reduce threats and risks are presented in Chapter 13.

Risk transfer

Average frequency and moderate-severity risks can be transferred to someone who is willing to assume the risk. Risks categorized in the light gray zone in Figure 12.3 may be transferred to a third party. Commonly used transfer methods are insurance, independent contractors, liability waivers, and indemnification clauses. The two main types of insurance available to the facility manager are personal injury liability insurance and property insurance.

Personal injury liability coverage is protective insurance in case a spectator, participant, or employee is physically injured by something a facility manager did or did not do. For example, a spectator is injured by a stray baseball that traveled through an undiscovered hole in the protective barrier around the field. This incident may result in a lawsuit in order for the victim to recover damages for direct injuries and for pain and suffering. *Property insurance* is important when considering protecting the facility and its contents from damage or destruction. There are two types of property insurance: named perils and all-risk. *Named perils insurance* will cover only what is stated in the policy. Most commonly named perils are natural occurrences such as fire, hail, explosion, lightning, malicious mischief, tornadoes, vandalism, and smoke.

Other methods of risk transfer include waivers, independent contractors, indemnification clauses, and leasing or rental agreements. A *waiver* transfers risk from the facility management team or owner to the person signing the document. Several principles are to be followed for a waiver to be valid. An adult must voluntarily sign the waiver. The waiver must be explicit and in clear language, stating that the waiver is for the negligence of the provider and acknowledgment of inherent risks of an activity. The participant must be aware that they are signing a waiver; however, the waiver cannot release the facility management team from intentional, willful and wanton acts, or gross negligence.

Some sport programs may wish to use *independent contractors* to conduct an activity or provide a service. Independent contractors can be individuals or organizations. Employees such as event staff and security officials can be utilized to transfer risk. These individuals are responsible for the liability of their services and for their own insurance coverage. The sport program may contract with private organizations to provide a program or service. For example, an organization may wish to contract with firms for concessions, facility maintenance, or security. It is important to note that when selecting an independent contractor, facility management must take reasonable care to select a competent person or organization that possesses the necessary credentials.

Sometimes facility management will *lease or rent* the facility for other events such as concerts. In this case, facility management should include an *indemnification clause* (sometimes referred to as hold harmless agreements) to allow the facility to be compensated by entities leasing or renting the facility if damage occurs during the event.

Risk retention

Facility managers may decide to retain the risk and assume responsibility. Risks categorized in the dark gray zone in Figure 12.2 may be retained. Facilities choosing to retain the risks become financially responsible for any injuries or financial risks associated with an incident. Risk financing strategies for retention may include current expensing, unfunded reserves, funded reserves, and borrowing. In a *current expensing* (or pay-as-you-go) system, the organization pays for losses as they arise out of their budget. An *unfunded reserve* is an accounting technique by noting the likelihood of future loss payments that remind management of future expenses for financial losses. A *funded reserve* is money set aside in the organization's budget to pay for future losses. *Borrowing* is an option for the organization when it does not have sufficient resources to pay for losses. The organization can borrow from internal or external sources, although it is often difficult to borrow from external sources to pay for a loss. Table 12.3 illustrates examples of facility risks, the probability of occurrence, consequence severity, risk control response, and possible financing options.

Table 12.3 Risk control and response matrix

	Threat/risk identification	Risk probability	Consequence severity	Risk control	Financing option
1	Vandalism	Medium	Not important (minor loss)	Reduce	Retention (current expensing)
2	Terrorist attack	Low	Essential (catastrophic loss)	Avoid/ transfer	Transfer (insurance)
3	Theft/ embezzlement	Medium	Critical/ important (serious/ moderate loss)	Reduce	Retention (current expensing)
4	Spectator or participant injury	Medium	Either (dependent upon extent)	Reduce/ transfer	Transfer (insurance, waiver)

Implementing operations management

CHAPTER REVIEW

The law has a significant relationship to almost all aspects of sport facility operations management. Laws are a body of rules that govern individual or collective actions and conduct as defined by an authorized governing body and having binding legal force. The four major areas of law that sport facility managers and owners deal with are constitutional law, statutory law, common law, and administrative law. While it would be impossible for sport facility managers or owners to know every law that has a direct effect on their management and operation of the sport facility, they do have a duty of care to their users and associated constituents to act legally.

Sport facility managers and owners must have a basic understanding of the legal principles and standards that directly affect them. Negligence law involves unintentional and intentional torts. Contract law is a major part of facility management, especially as related to employment contracts, event contracts, and sponsorship contracts.

A risk is the possibility of loss from a threat. Risk increases as the consequences and probability of occurrence increases. Risk management is important to facility managers in order to meet legal obligations, prevent financial loss, and ensure business continuity. An all-hazards approach must be employed when assessing potential threats and risks (including human-made and natural events, that is, terrorism, crowd management, natural disasters, theft, and fraud). Risk assessment involves the following key steps: identify SESAT, characterize assets, assess threats, assess vulnerabilities, evaluate consequences, analyze risk levels, and provide countermeasure improvements. Countermeasures are used to reduce the probability and consequent severity of a threat/risk. The facility manager can control risk through several strategies. They can avoid, transfer, reduce, or retain identified risks.

IN THE FIELD . . .

With David Born, senior director of security, STAPLES Center, Los Angeles, California, United States

David Born, senior director of security for the STAPLES Center in Los Angeles oversees the safety and security of one of the busiest venues in the United States with more than 250 events every year. Mr. Born has more than 25 years of experience in the sport venue industry and enjoys the diversity his job brings while managing sport events from concerts to family shows. He also enjoys working with his security team of professionals. During his tenure in the sport industry, Born has seen changes in the types of incidents he must prepare for. Initially concerned about incidents between fans, he must plan for the safety of all guests, team members, players, and performers from venue entry to departure at the event conclusion. Keeping up with current events and risks is essential, as well as with security technology updates and establishing and maintaining critical relationships with safety stakeholders such as law enforcement partners, Department of Homeland Security, and the FBI. In addition, Born believes those at the top of an organization must support security efforts. One of his challenges is inconsistent operations due to a diverse and large number of team members working an event. He understands the importance of maintaining policies and procedures and to invest in training programs. Born works closely with different associations and committees to maintain a prominent position among peers.

Source: S. Ludwig. (2016, November). David Born: Entertaining security trendsetting. *Security Magazine*. Retrieved May 30, 2019, from www.securitymagazine.com/articles/87532-david-born-entertaining-security-trendsetting

BIBLIOGRAPHY

Ammon, R., Southall, R., & Nagel, M. (2016). *Sport facility management: Organizing events and mitigating risks* (3rd ed.). Morgantown, WV: Fitness Information Technology.

Connors, E. (2007). *Planning and managing security for major sports events: Guidelines for law enforcement*. Alexandria, VA: Institute for Law and Justice.

Fried, G. (2015). *Managing sports facilities* (3rd ed.). Champaign, IL: Human Kinetics.

Hall, S., Marciani, L., Cooper, W. E., & Rolen, R. (2007). Introducing a risk assessment model for sport venues. *The Sport Journal, 10*(2), 1–6.

National Counterterrorism Security Office. (2006). *Counter terrorism protective security advice for stadia and arenas*. Retrieved February 2, 2015, from https://assets.publishing.service.gov.uk/government/uploads/system/uploads/attachment_data/file/375168/Stadia_and_Arenas_Reviewed.pdf

Nemeth, C. P. (2017). *Homeland security* (3rd ed.). Boca Raton, FL: CRC Press.

Stevens, A. (2007). *Sports security and safety: Evolving strategies for a changing world*. London: Sport Business Group.

Wolohan, J. T. (2017). *Law for recreation and sport managers* (7th ed.). Dubuque, IA: Kendall/Hunt Publishing Company.

CHAPTER 13

SECURITY PLANNING FOR FACILITY MANAGEMENT

CHAPTER OUTLINE

- Security management
  - Lessons learned from the United Kingdom
- Protective measures
  - Venue design and safety
  - Physical protection systems
  - Perimeter control
  - Access control and credentialing
  - Communications
  - Security personnel
  - Training and exercise
  - Crowd management
  - Emergency management
  - Business continuity
- Chapter review

CHAPTER OBJECTIVES

This chapter will address global security issues involved in protecting sport facilities from threats and risks identified in Chapter 12. Security best practices, systems, and planning options are provided to equip sport facility managers with an all-hazards approach to facility security planning. Security management and planning involve the development of plans, policies, and protective measures. Protective

SECURITY MANAGEMENT

Security management systems are employed to reduce risk and exposure to facility vulnerabilities. A facility manager is expected to act in a reasonably prudent manner regarding the safety and security of the facility. This includes keeping the facility in safe repair, inspecting the facility to discover hazards, removing hazards or warning of their presence, protecting patrons from foreseeable dangers, and conducting facility operations with reasonable care for the safety of all. Sport facility managers reduce liability exposure by successfully managing risks and foreseeable actions that lead to injuries. Several legal issues related to event security management include inadequate security, negligent employment practices, and handling disturbances, ejections, and arrests.

Security management requires the coordination and collaboration of many individuals, government agencies, and private contractors. Figure 13.1 illustrates the

Figure 13.1 Sport event security stakeholders

multiple stakeholders involved in providing a safe and secure sporting environment. Sport organizations should designate a security director to oversee security operations and coordinate security efforts with stakeholders. The security director forms a leadership (planning) team with representatives from the stakeholder groups, known as a sport event security action team (SESAT). Facility managers, owners, or operators are normally responsible for the safety and security management of events. However, they may rely upon other agencies, locally and regionally, in the case of a major incident. Regardless of the type and criticality of an incident, the sport organization should have established a working relationship with external agencies. Multiagency collaboration ensures effective planning, response, and recovery efforts.

Planning is a critical component of the overall security management system. In order to effectively plan, the sport manager must first identify facility risks, threats, and vulnerabilities. Addressing specific threats ensures that appropriate planning measures are implemented, such as relevant policies, procedures, and security measures. To reduce risk, the sport facility should develop a list of essential venue safety and security policies, such as alcohol policy, fan conduct policy, search policy. A facility emergency response plan should be developed with annexes for game day operations, evacuation procedures, incident response, and business continuity and recovery. A game day operations plan provides the general administrative, operational and security strategies for the game day. A game day operations plan may include the following items:

- Ticketing policies
- Ticket samples
- Seating policies
- Radio communications
- TV broadcast information
- Stadium staff directory
- Gate designations
- Parking information
- Parking maps
- Parking pass samples
- Traffic flow information
- Credential samples
- Tailgating policies
- Severe weather plans
- General information policies:
    - For example, admission, prohibited behavior/items, alcohol, camera, first aid, disability accommodations, guest services, lost and found

To successfully implement security plans, facility managers, event staff, security personnel, and emergency response personnel require adequate training in their respective roles and responsibilities. Crowd control methods, spectator safety, and terrorism awareness training are essential for security staff to detect suspicious behavior or criminal activity. Training should be conducted on a continuous basis and refresher courses utilized to emphasize individual tasks. Beyond basic training, security stakeholders should conduct some type of exercise to test security plans for effectiveness and to identify resource gaps.

Post 9/11, professional sport organizations in the United States enhanced security efforts. The National Football League (NFL), National Basketball Association (NBA), and National Hockey League (NHL) developed a best practices guide of recommended protective security measures to assist league members. Security management was also upgraded at the collegiate level. The National Collegiate Athletic Association (NCAA) issued a Security-Planning Options guide for American college athletic programs. The NCAA is a voluntary organization that governs American college and university athletic programs. The NCAA national office staff consulted with stadium managers and law enforcement representatives from across the United States to compile a list of options to assist NCAA members with security planning. Planning options included items related to deliveries, facility personnel, coordination with public safety agencies, lockdown, metal detectors, parking and perimeter, prohibited items, and publicity. A 38-item Game Day Security Operations Checklist of pre-event, game time and post-event considerations are presented in Table 13.1.

Table 13.1 Game day security operations checklist

Pre-event considerations
- Write a formal risk management plan.
- Implement a pre-event training program for all event staff.
- Be aware of nearby dangerous/explosive sites.
- Be aware of the quantities of antidotes within the region.
- Coordinate your plans with the local and state police.
- Conduct background checks on all employees including students and seasonal employees.
- Verify that first responders have a small stockpile of drugs and medications for rapid response use should a biological weapon be released.
- Utilize 24-hour live security teams in concert with a sophisticated surveillance system.
- Lock down the venue prior to the event.
- Prohibit all concessions deliveries 90 minutes prior to the event.
- Utilize bomb-sniffing dogs.
- Test air quality prior to the event.
- Issue holographic personal identification cards for all media.
- Purchase and install clear refuse bags and receptacles.
- Escort all cleaning crews.

Game time considerations
- Secure no-fly zones over the venue.
- Patrol air space above the venue, parking lots, and adjacent access roads.
- Secure the services of a mobile emergency room to be on site.
- Utilize portable biological detection equipment.

- Use undercover surveillance teams/individuals.
- Utilize one crowd observer for every 250 spectators.
- Utilize radio-equipped security personnel in parking lots and key access points.
- Have key personnel wear inexpensive HAZMAT smart strips that detect the presence of nerve agents, cyanide, and other chemicals.
- Invoke periodic broadcasts detailing security practices and restricted areas within the facility.
- Implement electronic scanning of all tickets, and match these records with detailed records of all your season ticket holders.
- Frisk/wand every spectator.
- Ban all carry-ins and backpacks.
- Prohibit reentry by spectators.

Post-event and general considerations
- Implement a formal post-event debriefing of all personnel.
- Vary your security practices so as not to create a pattern in your system.

Adapted from M. J. Pantera, R. Accorsi, C. Winter, R. Gobeille, S. Griveas, D. Queen, J. Insalaco, & B. Domanoski. (2003). Best practices for game day security at athletic & sport venues. *The Sport Journal*, 6(4). Retrieved January 10, 2019, from https://thesportjournal.org/article/best-practices-for-game-day-security-at-athletic-sport/

Lessons learned from the United Kingdom

Britain is a pioneer in the implementation of security standards through government regulation. Hooliganism in British football (soccer) has been well documented for many years, and legislative and administrative changes introduced by the English Football Association (FA) and the British government have helped control the problem.

The Hillsborough disaster was the worst stadium disaster in English football history, resulting in the deaths of 96 people. On April 15, 1989, the FA Cup semifinal match between Liverpool FC and Nottingham Forest at the Hillsborough football stadium was called off six minutes into the game due to a human stampede in the Leppings Lane end of the stadium holding Liverpool fans.

Since the 1989 Hillsborough disaster and the 1990 Taylor Report on football stadium safety, new legislation and safety and security measures have been imposed on football teams. The Football Disorder Act (1989), Football Spectators Act (1989), Football Offenses Act (1991), Football Act (1999), Football Disorder Act (2000), and Football Disorder Bill (2001) were enacted by the government. These pieces of legislation prohibited hooliganism, categorized the different offenses that a person would be charged with, covered both domestic and international terrorist threats to sport stadiums, and assured that individuals who were banned would be prevented from attending matches inside and outside of Britain. Additionally, the Football Intelligence Unit was created to collect and disseminate information and intelligence about domestic and international issues that occur at or near sport stadiums. Football Intelligence officers are assigned to each football team to gather intelligence and identify potential troublemakers or banned offenders from entering the stadium.

Most significant, under new safety legislation, each football club is required to hold a stadium Safety Certificate. The government produced and published a set of safety requirements in the *Guide to Safety at Sports Grounds* for every club playing in the top four divisions in England. The local government authority (municipality) is responsible for issuing the safety certificate and ensuring that the stadium complies with the requirements issued in the safety guide. In addition, each football club is assigned a safety officer to assist facility management with safety strategies on matchday. Safety officers are responsible for the recruitment and training of all stewards. The safety officers formed the Football Safety Officer's Association to share best practices (www.fsoa.org.uk). Specific safety and security measures utilized in the English football system are:

- Football clubs ban any person who is arrested or ejected from a stadium.
- Football clubs operate travel clubs for away matches and issues tickets only to supporters who are members.
- Each club in the top two divisions (Premier League and the Championship) are required to restrict the admission of spectators to seated accommodation only.
- National legislation introduced by government outlaws: (1) the possession of alcohol on trains and/or coaches when traveling to a match, (2) entering a stadium drunk or in possession of alcohol, (3) throwing objects toward the pitch or spectators, (4) entering the pitch, (5) indecent or racist chanting, and (6) ticket touting.
- Any person convicted of a football-related offense receives a banning order preventing the offender from attending matches at home or abroad for three years. Failure to obey this ban is a criminal offense.

PROTECTIVE MEASURES

Facility managers must have adequate security measures in place to protect spectators, athletes, officials, and staff. Protective security measures reduce facility vulnerabilities and enhance preparedness among supporting agencies to respond and resolve potential incidents. Protective measures are designed to meet one or more of the following objectives:

- *Devalue*: Lower the value of a facility to terrorists, criminal activity, or crowd management issues, thereby making the facility less attractive as a target for illegal or unruly behavior.
- *Detect*: Spot the presence of suspicious people, unruly fan behavior, and/or dangerous materials and provide responders with the information needed to execute an effective response.

- *Deter*: Make the facility difficult to attack or less vulnerable to fan/player violence and criminal activity.
- *Defend*: Respond to an attack, protect the facility, and mitigate any effects of an incident.

Some protective measures are designed to be implemented permanently to serve as routine protection for a facility and are sometimes referred to as baseline security measures. Other measures may be enforced as security threats arise. To establish a facility's baseline security measures, the facility manager must assess facility threats and vulnerabilities (as discussed in Chapter 12). Specific facility threats, vulnerabilities, and organizational policies provide a foundation for the development of baseline protective security measures. Sport organizations should consider protective security measures in the following key areas:

- Venue design and safety
- Physical protection systems
- Perimeter control
- Access control and credentialing
- Communications
- Security personnel
- Training and exercise
- Crowd management
- Emergency management
- Business continuity

Venue design and safety

Venue design and safety features are predetermined to an extent by occupational safety and health administration regulations, environmental regulations, fire codes, seismic safety codes, life safety codes, transportation regulations, and zoning regulations. However, security trends in the 21st century are guiding the work of sport architects and engineers developing the next generation of facilities. Designers are now working in collaboration with security professionals and first responders during the design process.

Designers can control stadium accessibility by restricting the size of grounds surrounding the stadium to provide limited space for loitering, less space for event staff to patrol, and reduced vehicle access to the stadium. Securing the facility perimeter can be established by installing vertical posts or bollards around the stadium to create a physical separation. Parking garages should not be attached to a facility and should be separated with as much distance as possible so terrorists cannot park a vehicle loaded with explosives. Design standards set forth by the Association of Chief of Police Officers (ACPO) set parameters for construction and design of grounds to reduce crowd management issues and the likelihood of attacks. The planning scheme includes a high-level CCTV system, a fully equipped control room, and its own on-site mini jail (or custody suite).

Most stadiums built today include a modern command center (also known as a command post) with communication capabilities for security forces to monitor events inside and outside of the stadium. The command center controls the security functions of the sport event. The center is normally staffed with the security director, facility management (operations and security), fire, police, emergency medical services, private security, and media representatives. Copies of security plans, phone directories, and backup technology systems are normally located in the command center in case of an incident. The center has reliable communications and the capability to access the facility public announcement system, fire alarm system, voice activation system, turnstile system, and door access control system.

Physical protection systems

Physical security is imperative in preventing a multitude of threats and vulnerabilities. An annual structural inspection of the facility will determine current structural damage or future problems. Alarm and card access entry points can restrict parts of the building to unauthorized persons. Restricted areas can be used to protect food sources, communication centers, and public media outlets. Facility managers can protect restricted areas by requiring a magnetic-striped key for entrance to ensure access to authorized individuals. The stadium and press box should be equipped with an integrated security management System (ISMS) consisting of CCTV. Cameras may be utilized to monitor the sport facility, including the perimeter, concourses, playing field, and concession areas. Facility managers should monitor (1) stadium entrances and exits, (2) spectators and employees for suspicious behavior, and (3) individuals standing in prohibited areas, taking pictures of the stadium without consent, drawing maps, or appearing in large groups outside the stadium during the event.

Sufficient lighting at gate areas is needed for adequate searching of bags and persons. Ventilation systems should be secured and capable of blocking hazardous agents such as anthrax. Air quality monitors can detect changes in air quality and identify biohazards and radioactive materials. Additionally, a mobile command center may be utilized. In England, a mobile command center known as the Hoolivan is located at high-profile football matches. The vehicle is equipped with CCTV for surveillance operations and maintains radio contact with officers inside and outside the stadium.

Perimeter control

Establishing perimeter control measures helps prevent illegal entry onto premises or into the sport facility. A secure outer perimeter of at least 100 feet should be established around the facility. This normally encompasses the facility property boundary, including parking areas. Roads and streets adjacent to the facility should be blocked off when feasible. Security forces may utilize barricades, such as jersey barriers, concrete planters, or bollards. Clear ingress and egress routes are established for emergency medical services, fire, and police in case of emergencies. An inner perimeter should be established around the stadium with limited and controlled pedestrian access points 12 hours prior to the event. The stadium should be locked down 24 hours prior to an event and allow only controlled access during this period. During events, security personnel is assigned to guard vulnerable systems. All buildings located within 100 feet of the stadium should be inspected prior to the event and secured by a lock or security guard. Vehicles should be requested to park more than 100 feet away from the stadium. If a vehicle needs to be parked close to the stadium, permission must be granted ahead of time from stadium officials.

Access control and credentialing

Access control and credentialing measures are enforced to prevent unwanted persons or vehicles from entering the facility premises or restricted areas of the facility building. Access control considerations include prohibiting coolers, bags, large backpacks, containers, weapons, and outside food or beverages, except as required for medical or family needs. Some stadiums implement a no-reentry policy, except for medical emergencies. Event staff can divide spectators into two groups for stadium entry: one with bags and other items and those with no items. The NFL and most college sports leagues have adopted a clear-bag policy to ensure that screening of personal items is as efficient as possible. This allows for better traffic flow into the stadium. The use of portable metal detectors and standard pat-down procedures at stadium entry gates have been employed at many major sport stadiums.

Technology-based security solutions include electronic scanning of tickets or contact cards capable of capturing season ticket holder information. Several UK football teams (e.g., Manchester City, Wigan Athletic, Fulham, and Rangers FC) use a smart card system for fans. Instead of paper-based tickets, fans are issued a plastic card containing a microchip stored with ticket and gate access information. Fans scan their card at turnstile locations at their designated gate entrances. This method of entry provides reliable information to the facility manager as spectator data is collected and analyzed in real time. For security purposes, it minimizes queues and reveals exactly who is sitting where. The smart card technology is also used for marketing and customer relation purposes. These cards provide consumer profiles and insight into consumer buying habits; this, in turn, enables the football club to target specific audiences for matches. The smart card can be charged with electronic credit, allowing fans to buy match tickets, refreshments, and merchandise.

Additional technology-based security tools, such as FaceTrac and Biometric systems, are used to identify fans, run database searches, and send images to security personnel on the grounds. The NFL has used facial recognition technology for every

Super Bowl since 2001. This technology locates faces, constructs facial print templates, and matches facial images with those previously stored in a database allowing law enforcement to identify suspicious facial photos. Biometric systems are suitable for use in protecting facilities with a high-risk rating (i.e., government) or high-risk areas within a sport facility, such as a command center. During the 2018 FIFA World Cup in Russia, biometric facial data was scanned through police databases to identify known hooligans and suspected troublemakers. Defense drones have been used in recent years, for example, at the 2018 winter games in South Korea, these drones were capable of snatching possible bomb-carrying enemy drones out of the air. These drones have been used for major events in the United States including Super Bowls.

TECHNOLOGY NOW! UNMANNED AIRCRAFT SYSTEMS (GENERIC/GLOBAL)

The use of unmanned aircraft systems (UAS), commonly known as drones, has increased significantly in the last few years. According to the Federal Aviation Administration, the number of registered commercial drones will increase from 80,000 units in 2017 to 420,000 units by 2021 with a global market worth $127 billion by 2020 (up from $2 billion in 2018).

Benefits of drone use

- *Risk assessments*: Drones provide a different point of view when conducting an analysis of gaps and vulnerabilities and can subsequently change the dynamic of how managers position security countermeasures.
- *Perimeter control*: Drones can monitor perimeters in the nighttime as well as daytime with a thermal imagining camera.
- *Inspections*: Security teams can inspect and monitor roofs and other high places with ease from the ground.
- *Safety*: A drone can usually get to a spectator incident or other issue much faster than a security officer and is also able to assess the risk so that management will know the best way to respond. Drones also have the capability to analyze images, and audio and video sensors can differentiate between gunfire and explosions.
- Emergency relief: Drones can be used to find people inside collapsed buildings.
- Cost savings: The use of drones could potentially alleviate the cost of security officers, cameras, or physical barriers.

Source: S. Ludwig. (2018, March). Drones: A security tool, threat and challenge. *Security Magazine*. Retrieved May 31, 2019, from www.securitymagazine. com/articles/88803-drones-a-security-tool-threat-and-challenge

Credentialing considerations include conducting background checks on all vendors, employees, contractors, and volunteers. Credential systems can be simplified by indicating zone access and color code by game function. Management should issue a photo credential to all regular game day employees, staff, media, vendors, and subcontractors and require those designated to pick up their credentials to do so in person, using a government-issued photo ID. Management should schedule limited daily or weekly delivery times for vendors and ensure that food dispensing and handling procedures are secure to prevent contamination. Credentials need to be worn at all times and clearly displayed. Credentials will include name, photograph, personal identification number, and areas of authorized access. Additionally, a record of persons issued credentials should be maintained for control purposes.

Communications

The sport organization should have an interoperable communication system in place with access to the stadium's command center. According to the United States Department of Homeland Security, an efficient interoperable communication system may require handheld portable multichannel radios, cell phones, pagers, or a combination thereof. All responding agencies must be able to communicate with one another on the same network to coordinate security management, response, and recovery efforts. Security personnel on the ground must have the capability to report problems to authorities at the center and receive relevant intelligence on disruptive behavior or suspicious activity. The NFL implemented a new text-messaging system that allows fans to report drunk or disorderly fans without confronting them. Fans send a quick text message to the stadium's command center for security to respond. Teams are able to compile databases of complaints and details about how they were resolved. They can also track areas in a stadium where complaints are frequent.

FACILITY FOCUS: SECURITY IN THE OUTFIELD: CITI FIELD BALLPARK, NEW YORK CITY, UNITED STATES

The game day command center at Citi Field is staffed with representatives from emergency medical services, the fire department (FDNY), police department (NYPD), parking company, concessions company, ballpark operations, and security supervisor. These stakeholders meet at 3:30 p.m. each game day to review the plan of the day, including promotions and VIP attendance. Technology and personnel work hand in hand to secure fans and players. Facial recognition technology is used through cameras at the main entrance to check faces against a blacklist. If a camera detects a 'Do Not Admit' – someone who has been banned from future Citi Field events (i.e., for fighting, larceny, or assault), the officer at the entrance is instructed by the operations center to approach the person and check their ID. If it matches, the matter is handed over to the NYPD as a trespassing violation.

The command center monitors social media, checking tweets and posts from within a geo-fence around the field. This helps with awareness of potential field invasions or runners, fan complaints of rowdy or intoxicated fans, or a maintenance issue. The command center also monitors the field's 187 surveillance cameras and 115 doors and card readers, and its platform is integrated with Live Earth, which forms an interactive map of Citi Field and surrounding areas, including traffic information. The platform also includes weather alerts and can show delays on public transportation systems. For example, if a subway line is delayed before a game, Citi Field security team can change its staffing plan at entrances to be prepared for a late rush of fans. The Citi Field security team also practices for emergencies through tabletop and full-scale exercises collaborating with all stakeholders.

Source: *Security Magazine*. (2018, August). Security in the outfield: At Citi Field in New York City, technology and personnel team up for threat detection. Retrieved May 31, 2019, from www.securitymagazine.com/articles/89369-security-over-center-field

In addition to possessing adequate communication equipment and systems, the sport organization should have a risk communication system in place that is operational and ready to be activated. Successful risk communication reduces the length, strength, and frequencies of controversies resulting from an incident. Sport organizations should develop contingencies for a post-incident press conference with key representatives including emergency services. Risk communication needs to take into consideration the target audience, including cultural background, shared interests, concerns and fears, and social attitudes.

Security personnel

The sport organization should appoint an experienced employee as the security director to deal with daily security matters and emergency incidents. A successful security staff plan has properly screened, trained, and educated staff. An employee background screening program for all facility personnel and contracted staff should be established. All personnel and contracted staff working events should be trained in appropriate standard operating procedures (SOPs) for emergency response, security awareness (i.e., suspicious persons and packages), and notification protocols.

Recommended training for security personnel includes first aid, CPR, crowd management, drug awareness, emergency response, and defensive techniques. The sport organization may utilize outsourced personnel in the form of contractors, vendors, or security force.

There should be adequate supervision and oversight of facility employees. The number of security personnel needed to staff an event or facility may vary according to the type of event, stadium capacity, or relevant intelligence. The National Fire Protection Association (NFPA) industry standards for fire prevention and safety apply to crowd management principles. There should be one trained crowd management professional for every 250 spectators in any facility with a capacity of over 250 people. It is important that security personnel are visible during the event. Visible security forces may deter illegal activity or unruly fan behavior; additionally, personnel are easily accessible to spectators in case of an emergency. Major sport events such as the Olympics and FIFA World Cup require a very large workforce. An estimated 60,000 South Korean personnel, including 50,000 soldiers were deployed throughout the Olympic venues for the 2018 Pyeongchang Winter Games. This was almost twice as many as those employed at the 2016 games in Brazil.

Training and exercise

Staff training is a key component in protecting critical infrastructures such as sport stadia and arenas. The three main levels of staff training are multiagency team training, supervisory training, and event staff training. *Multiagency team training* is conducted with the sport event security action team (SESAT) (leadership/planning team). *Supervisory training* is conducted with main supervisors in charge of event staff and security personnel. *Event staff training* is conducted for all other venue staff (full-time, part-time, or volunteer). These may include parking attendants, contracted security personnel, gate security, ticket takers, ushers, concessionaires, vendors, and maintenance. Training should be conducted at routine times, for example, preseason, during the season, and postseason. Written responsibilities and duties for each position, including how each position's job function is linked to the overall facility safety and security program, should be made available.

Sport organizations should conduct exercises to test plans and promote awareness of staff roles and responsibilities during an incident scenario. Seven types of exercises are defined by the United States Department of Homeland Security Exercise and Evaluation Program (HSEEP) and are considered either discussion based or operations based. *Discussion-based exercises* familiarize participants with current plans and policies or may be used to develop new plans and policies. Types of discussion-based exercises include seminars, workshops, tabletop exercises, or game simulations. *Operations-based exercises* validate plans and policies, clarify roles, and identify resource gaps in security operations. Types of operations-based exercises include drills, functional exercises, and full-scale exercises.

Crowd management

Crowds need to be managed for several reasons. Large gatherings of people increase the odds of something happening and make changes in action slower and more complex. Furthermore, communications tend to be slower and more complicated than normal. Most importantly, in the event of an incident at a mass gathering, the possible number of injuries increases. People have been injured or killed at sport venues around the world from crowd crushes, fires, bombs, heat exhaustion, structural collapses, over-crowding, and rioting. Critical components of a crowd management plan include:

- *Trained staff in crowd control methods*: Staff training has been emphasized in several areas of this chapter. It is evident that human capital is critical to the effective coordination and response efforts of all security and safety-related pro-grams. Employees should have an understanding of the facility, including the location of emergency medical services to assist fans.
- *Established policies and procedures for possible incidents*: Specific policies and procedures are needed to address incidents such as disruptive and unruly fans or public drunkenness and disorder. Parking and traffic control is critical in the management of crowds entering or exiting the facility. Poor traffic and parking control can result in stalled crowd ingress, delay of the event's start, or aggressive behavior by fans because of frustration.
- *Effective communication systems*: An effective communication network inte-grated with the stadium command center allows for efficient reporting of inci-dents and response and recovery efforts.
- *Appropriate signage*: Adequate signage is the final component of the crowd management plan. There should be prominent signage providing guidance on responding to and reporting suspicious behavior.

A crowd management plan should include an alcohol policy. Protective measures concerning alcohol include staff training in alcohol management, identification checks to prevent underage drinking, limiting the number of alcohol drinks sold to one individual, and ending alcohol sales at a certain point during the event. For example, the NFL requires stadiums to stop selling beer at the end of the third quarter.

The NFL has gone even a step further to prevent unruly fan behavior by imple-menting a fan code of conduct to promote a positive fan environment and address behavior that detracts from the fan experience. Introduced in 2008, the NFL Fan Code of Conduct is committed to 'creating a safe, comfortable, and enjoyable expe-rience for all fans in the stadium and the parking lot.' The policy, implemented by the league and all 32 teams, covers the following:

- Behavior that is unruly, disruptive, or illegal in nature
- Intoxication or other signs of alcohol impairment that results in irresponsible behavior

- Foul or abusive language or obscene gestures
- Interference with the progress of the game (including throwing objects onto the field)
- Failing to follow instructions of stadium personnel
- Verbal or physical harassment of opposing team fans

The policy provides the authority to stadium staff to intervene to support an experience free from those behaviors. The policy also provides a mechanism to eject patrons without refund, the potential of being arrested, and possible loss of entry to future games and events at the stadium. Additionally, the NFL has collaborated with the AJ Novak Group to create an online educational fan conduct class before a banned patron is allowed to attend a future event. The four-hour class covered a multitude of topics, including:

- Stadium Code of Conduct;
- Alcohol abuse and public intoxication;
- What disruptive fan behavior is;
- Preventing interference with the progress of the game such as by throwing objects onto the field;
- Skills in improving empathy toward other fans;
- Skills for becoming less impulsive and improving judgment;
- Skills for better managing stress and learning new ways of staying in control during the game day experience;
- Preventative communication skills (foul or abusive language or obscene gestures);
- Verbal or physical harassment of opposing team fans; and
- Smoking policies.

Controlling fan violence must be a priority for sport organizations. To manage crowd behavior and effectively design fan violence prevention efforts, one must understand the basic principles that underlie individual decision making. It can be argued that humans are a product of their environment and make decisions based on what is happening around them, as well as a personal cost-benefit analysis. According to the situational crime prevention (SCP) model developed by crime scientist Ronald V. Clarke, people choose a course of action by using physical and social cues in their environment by answering the following questions:

1   How much effort is needed, and is this the easiest course of action?
2   What are the risks involved, and will I be detected or harmed?
3   What are the rewards, and are the benefits worth the risk?
4   Do I feel provoked, and will this satisfy an immediate/pressing need?
5   Can I excuse my behavior, and will I be able to justify it to others?

293

This model insinuates that people are more likely to engage in behavior that requires little effort or risk while offering high rewards and that will likely act when they feel provoked and can rationalize their actions. According to Dr. Tamara Madensen, director of the Crowd Management Research Council at the University of Nevada–Las Vegas, crowds provoke violence due to unwanted physical contact between strangers, increased wait times increase frustration and stress, movement is more difficult, and mass panic emergencies can lead to crowd crushes. Furthermore, large crowds also make engaging in violence easier, less risky, more rewarding, and excusable. That being said, Dr. Madensen believes that it is possible to manipulate environmental cues in sport facilities to make violence a less attractive option. Sport facility managers may do so by using the SCP model, which presents 25 different prevention techniques – five techniques for each perceptual dimension – as shown in Figure 13.2.

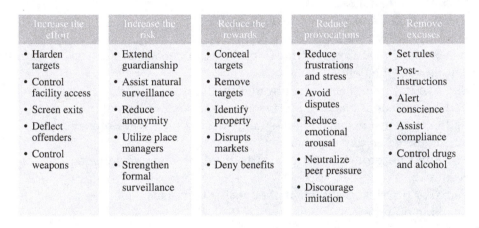

Increase the effort	Increase the risk	Reduce the rewards	Reduce provocations	Remove excuses
• Harden targets	• Extend guardianship	• Conceal targets	• Reduce frustrations and stress	• Set rules
• Control facility access	• Assist natural surveillance	• Remove targets	• Avoid disputes	• Post-instructions
• Screen exits	• Reduce anonymity	• Identify property	• Reduce emotional arousal	• Alert conscience
• Deflect offenders	• Utilize place managers	• Disrupts markets	• Neutralize peer pressure	• Assist compliance
• Control weapons	• Strengthen formal surveillance	• Deny benefits	• Discourage imitation	• Control drugs and alcohol

Figure 13.2 Situational crime prevention (SCP) model

Emergency management

The four primary components to all-hazards emergency management are mitigation, preparedness, response, and recovery. *Mitigation* activities try to prevent emergencies or lessen the damage of unavoidable disasters. *Preparedness* activities such as training and exercise drills enhance the ability of agencies to respond quickly in the aftermath of an incident. *Response* activities focus on damage assessment or assisting the affected population. *Recovery* actions, such as providing economic aid, ensure the successful recovery of the affected location. Figure 13.3 depicts the interrelated components and offers potential considerations in each area.

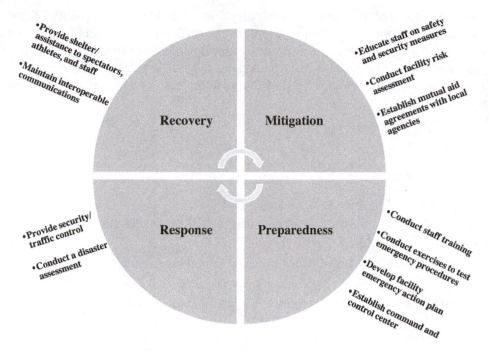

Figure 13.3 Principles and components of sport event emergency management

Source: Adapted from S. Hall, L. Marciani, & W. E. Cooper, W.E (2008). Emergency management and planning at major sports events. *Journal of Emergency Management, 6*(1), 43–47.

Business continuity

Business continuity involves developing measures and safeguards allowing an organization to continue to operate under adverse conditions. The development of a business continuity program includes the formation of a sound contingency plan. A contingency plan includes the steps taken before, during, and after an incident. Contingency plans include the facility's emergency management policy, personnel responsibilities, emergency scenarios that could occur, and where response operations will be managed. The plan highlights how core elements of the emergency management system will be organized such as communications, community outreach, recovery and restoration of systems, operations, administration, and logistics. Supporting documentation to the plan may include building and site maps, floor plans, escape routes, emergency equipment inventories, emergency procedures, and personnel call lists. Additionally, contracts should be in place for immediate restoration and secondary locations identified to hold event bookings in case of an incident. To put this in perspective, the London 2012 Olympic Games Organizing Committee had a contingency budget of £2.7 billion to address these issues.

The ultimate goal is to return the facility and its stakeholder's quality of life to the same level it was before the incident. In the online supplements for this book, you will find a sample Business Continuity and Disaster Preparedness Plan that can be adapted for use by sport facility managers. In addition, sport facility managers may use the continuity capability checklist in Table 13.2 as a resource tool for planning purposes.

Table 13.2 Continuity capability checklist

Continuity capabilities	*Yes*	*No*
Essential functions have been identified and prioritized.		
A plan is available to manage essential functions throughout an emergency.		
Employees are aware of the authority of leadership.		
Delegations of authority are established to ensure a rapid response.		
Delegations of authority are predetermined to make policy decisions.		
A vulnerability assessment has been conducted on the location of the continuity facility.		
Access to a continuity facility can be achieved within 12 hours.		
Communications can be maintained in the event of a catastrophic disaster.		
Communications can be maintained with leadership personnel while transitioning to continuity facilities.		
Plans that facilitate the immediate transfer of essential functions to other agencies are available in case of a catastrophe.		
Devolution plans are established that address emergencies rendering key personnel unavailable to perform essential functions.		
Plans for transitioning back to the original operating facility are in place.		
Procedures for phasing down alternate facility operations and returning operations, personnel, records, and equipment to the primary facility are in place.		
Vital records are kept to ensure confidentiality of records during a disruption of normal operations.		
Vital records are protected either by use of duplicate hardcopy or electronic files.		
Procedures are in place that addresses the needs of personnel during a continuity event (i.e., pay, communication, hiring).		
An action plan is in place for hiring new personnel due to the unavailability of personnel during an emergency.		
A written document has been developed for conducting training and exercise programs regarding the continuity plan.		
Exercises are conducted regularly using the components of the continuity plan.		
The likelihood of potential threats or hazards has been identified and assessed.		

Strategies have been created to minimize the likelihood of high-risk scenarios.

Budgetary procedures that allow for the availability of resources before, during, and after a continuity event are in place.

Procedures to acquire resources necessary for continuity operations are available on an emergency basis.

Procedures are in place that reviews the best course of action based on the organization's readiness posture.

The organization is prepared to implement executive decisions based on a review of emergencies.

2013 BOSTON MARATHON BOMBING

During the 117th Boston Marathon April 15, 2013, two pressure cooker bombs exploded near the finish line, killing three people and injuring an estimated 264 others. The bombs exploded about 13 seconds and 210 yards (190 meters) apart with more than 5,700 runners yet to finish the race. At least 14 people required amputations, with some suffering traumatic amputations as a direct result of the blasts. As the attack occurred at the finishing line, Emergency Medical Technicians (EMTs) and triage stations were available to respond quickly to the immediate aftermath of the explosions. Casualties were treated in 27 local hospitals.

Officials had swept the area for bombs twice before the explosions; with the second sweep occurring one hour before the bombs detonated. The blasts blew out windows on nearby buildings but did not cause any structural damage. The marathon was halted abruptly. Police, following emergency plans, diverted the remaining runners away from the finish line and evacuated nearby buildings. Many people dropped backpacks and other bags as they fled, requiring each to be treated as a potential bomb. Police closed down a 15-block area around the blast site. As a precaution, the Federal Aviation Administration restricted airspace over Boston and issued a temporary ground stop for Boston's Logan International Airport.

The Massachusetts Emergency Management Agency suggested that people trying to contact those in the vicinity use text messaging instead of voice calls because of crowded cell phone lines. The American Red Cross helped concerned family and friends receive information about runners and casualties. The Boston Police Department also set up a helpline for people concerned about relatives or acquaintances to contact and a line for people to provide information. Google Person Finder activated their disaster service under Boston Marathon Explosions to log known information about missing persons as a publicly viewable file.

The Federal Bureau of Investigation led the investigation, assisted by the Bureau of Alcohol, Tobacco, Firearms, and Explosives, the Central Intelligence Agency, the National Counterterrorism Center, and the Drug Enforcement Administration. United States government officials stated that no intelligence reports had indicated such a bombing would take place. House Intelligence Committee Representative Peter King stated that he received two top-secret briefings on the current threat levels in the United States the previous week to the event, and there was no evidence of an imminent attack.

Police identified two suspects after the immediate investigation and review of video surveillance, photographs, and social media materials. Russian-born brothers, Dzhokhar and Tamerlan Tsarnaev (26 and 19 years old, respectively), who subsequently had become U.S. citizens, had planned and implemented the bombing attacks. After an extensive manhunt, on April 19, one brother was captured and the other died in an exchange of fire between the suspects and police forces.

Key factors

First responders: Qualified emergency medical teams (EMTs) and associated resources in close proximity to the bombings ensured that injuries were treated quickly and effectively. The success of the immediate response efforts was also a function of where the bombings took place. If the bombs had detonated at less notable points on the marathon route, the death toll may have been higher due to the lack of EMTs, first responders, and hospital facilities nearby. The start and finish lines are the two most secure and prepared locations on a marathon route.

Surveillance: Law enforcement officials were able to process huge amounts of video, photography, and social media offered by the public in response to a request for their help in the identification of potential suspects. The role of the community in providing data, videos, and photographs of the bombing scenes and suspects were crucial in the evidence collection process.

Crowd management: Security officials along the marathon route were primarily facing the athletes because in the past, the primary concern was security breaches that would interrupt the runners. Police would observe the crowd for disruptive activities that could impact athletes on the course; they were not looking for individuals with an intention to injure spectators.

Lessons learned

Critical role of first responders: When dealing with an open-access event, locations where spectators and athletes are the most vulnerable and where officials are most prepared for dealing with a crisis, must be identified. Enhancing the security of an event may include an increased EMT presence and actively recruiting volunteers who have backgrounds in emergency response.

Evolving role of surveillance: Officials are able to observe assets, athletes, and the crowd during an event and are able to return to the time of a security breach and collect evidence. Video technology can be an important asset in emergency response, recovery, and crisis management throughout a post-event investigation. Following the Boston Marathon bombings, there may be a greater need and demand for additional surveillance at open-access sporting events.

Crowd management personnel training: Open-access sporting event officials may decide to distribute their focus and attention equally among the athletes, the event, and the crowd/spectators.

Community education programs: Empowering communities and providing them the tools, education, and awareness knowledge to identify suspicious behaviors and anomalies are critical in a constantly evolving threat environment. Cooperation between the community and law enforcement is fundamental in identifying and preventing potential terrorist threats.

Source: K. E. Todt. (2013). Lessons in response and resilience from the Boston Marathon bombing. *International Center for Sport Security Journal*, *1*(2). Retrieved May 31, 2019, from https://libertygroupventures.com/lessons-in-response-and-resilience-from-the-boston-marathon-bombing/

Discussion questions

1 What were the key strengths of the response effort, and what areas needed improvement?
2 What suggestions would you recommend for securing open-access events?
3 What additional training would you suggest for crowd management personnel?
4 Do you think surveillance efforts should be increased at all open-access events? Why?

CHAPTER REVIEW

Security management systems are employed to reduce risk and exposure to facility vulnerabilities. Facility managers are responsible for keeping the facility in safe repair, discovering potential hazards and protecting patrons from foreseeable dangers. Security management requires the coordination and collaboration of many stakeholders, including individuals, government agencies, and private contractors. The facility manager should develop a facility emergency response plan with annexes for game day operations, evacuation procedures, and incident response to various emergency scenarios.

Industry best practices, planning options, and guidelines are available to the facility manager for assistance in security planning. Britain has successfully implemented national legislation and standard stadium requirements and protocols to combat hooliganism. Protective security measures are designed to devalue, detect, deter, and defend the facility from attack or illegal activity. Baseline protective security measures should be implemented on a permanent basis as routine inspection for a facility. Protective security measures should be considered in the following key areas: venue site design, safety, sustainability, physical protection systems, perimeter control, access control, communications, security personnel, training and exercise, crowd management, emergency management, and business continuity and recovery.

IN THE FIELD . . .

With various sport security leaders from the United States and Puerto Rico

Security Magazine assembled a panel of experts in sport security with various security and venue backgrounds, including:

- James DeMeo, president and CEO of Unified Sports & Entertainment Security Consulting LLC in New York;
- Toby McSwain, director of security at Sea Pines Resort in Hilton Head, South Carolina;
- Richard Fenton, vice president at Ilitch Holdings in Detroit, Michigan, which provides security to the Detroit Red Wings and Detroit Tigers; and
- Hector Rivera, executive advisor for security, safety and compliance, Puerto Rico Professional Baseball League.

Security Magazine: What are the biggest and fastest growing challenges inside and outside of sport venues?

James DeMeo: There are numerous challenges within the space: workplace violence, IEDs, active shooter, terrorism, the extremely unpredictable lone wolf. Even intoxicated patrons, or extreme weather. We have to look at safeguarding confined spaces and view security from multiple angles. It's definitely about looking at the space from a holistic point of view. Ownership groups are understanding the importance of having the security group sit a little closer to the head of the table. You don't want to be that one ownership group that cut corners on security. You don't want to be that organization that's used as an example for all the wrong reasons. The one thing that keeps you up at night is a security breach.

Toby McSwain: From a professional golf standpoint, the biggest challenge is the open venue. When you start looking at professional golf tournaments, some have controlled access points. The RBC Heritage is one of several tournaments where there is limited controlled access points. The golf course stretches out for over three miles, with homes on both sides of the fairway, and spectators are coming from 100 different directions – as opposed to an arena where everybody goes through a checkpoint with a magnetometer. We work very closely together with the PGA TOUR in preparing our security plan. They have security personnel on the course all week focusing on the safety of the players and caddies. My responsibility focuses on the spectators, sponsors, and volunteers.

Hector Rivera: There are six teams in our league every winter, and then we have the Caribbean series, where other nations come in. In Puerto Rico, the stadium is owned by the municipality, which is responsible for security. We help them when it comes to temporary staff and also coordination with local law enforcement. We have not only the police department but other first responders and even space for federal agents. The league itself does not employ anyone. We have a benchmark standard of what each club should do. Then, we're more of a watchdog. Inside the stadium, we have no major issues. One of the challenges we have is with the credentialing [for admittance to the stadium]. I hope by next winter we're going to have something in place. Now everyone has something different, and we don't know who's who.

Richard Fenton: Security challenges facing the sports and entertainment industry, similar to other locations that host large mass gatherings, continually evolve as the result of terrorist acts internationally and domestically. We work collaboratively with a myriad of intelligence agencies, professional sports leagues security departments, and federal, state, county, and local public safety agencies to address these evolving tactics and challenges.

Source: Excerpt from E. Finkel. (2017, July). Growing terrorism threats lead sports security leaders to change tactics. *Security Magazine*. Retrieved May 31, 2019, from www.securitymagazine.com/articles/88104-growing-terrorism-threats-lead-sports-security-leaders-to-change-tactics

BIBLIOGRAPHY

Allen, K., & Gutman, M. (2018, February 8). *Intense security measures ahead of Olympics in South Korea*. Retrieved January 2, 2019, from https://abcnews.go.com/beta-story-container/International/intense-security-measures-place-ahead-olympics-south-korea/story?id=52925816

Department of Homeland Security. (2008). *Protective measures for U.S. sports leagues*. Washington, DC: Author.

Department of Homeland Security. (2013). *Homeland Security Exercise and Evaluation Program (HSEEP)*. Washington, DC: Author. Retrieved February 2, 2019, from www.fema.gov/media-library-data/20130726-1914-25045-8890/hseep_apr13_.pdf

Hall, S., Marciani, L., & Cooper, W. E. (2008). Emergency management and planning at major sports events. *Journal of Emergency Management, 6*(1), 43–47.

International Association of Assembly Managers. (2002). *Safety and security task force best practices planning guide: Arenas, stadiums, and amphitheaters*. Retrieved February 1, 2019, from www.iwi-associates.co.uk/library/2011/iaam_sstf_planningguide.pdf

Madensen, T. (2014, October). *Understanding crowds key to controlling fan violence*. Retrieved October 23, 2014, from www.athleticbusiness.com/event-security/understanding-crowd-dynamics-key-to-controlling-fan-violence.html

National Center for Spectator Sports Safety and Security. (2017). *Intercollegiate athletics safety and security best practices guide*. Hattiesburg, MS: Author. Retrieved February 2, 2019, from www.ncaa.org/sites/default/files/2017DIIISpo_NCS4IntercollegiateBestPractices_20171220.pdf

National Counterterrorism Security Office. (2006). *Counter terrorism protective security advice for stadia and arenas*. Retrieved February 2, 2015, from https://assets.publishing.service.gov.uk/government/uploads/system/uploads/attachment_data/file/375168/Stadia_and_Arenas_Reviewed.pdf

Social Issues Research Centre. (n.d.). *Football violence and hooliganism in Europe*. Retrieved February 1, 2019, from www.sirc.org/publik/football_violence.html

Sports Grounds Safety Authority. (2018). *Guide to safety at sports grounds* (6th ed.). London: Stationary Office.

SECTION IV

EFFECTIVENESS OF MANAGEMENT AND OPERATIONS

CHAPTER 14

PERFORMANCE ANALYTICS FOR SPORT FACILITIES

CHAPTER OUTLINE

- ▦ Introduction to performance management and benchmarking
- ▦ Performance management frameworks
  - ▦ The European Foundation for Quality Management Excellence Model (EFQM)
  - ▦ Toward an Excellent Service (TAES)
- ▦ Performance management principles
  - ▦ Objectives
  - ▦ Performance
  - ▦ Performance indicators
  - ▦ Targets
  - ▦ Balanced scorecard
- ▦ Benchmarking
- ▦ Conclusions about performance management and benchmarking
- ▦ Chapter review

CHAPTER OBJECTIVES

This capstone chapter will ensure that the book concludes on a high note by bringing together various concepts that out of necessity have been treated separately earlier in the book such as strategic management; financial management; the four e's of economy, efficiency, effectiveness, and equity; customer satisfaction; and service quality. It will draw on internationally recognized best practice, notably the thinking behind Sport England's National Benchmarking Service. The basic point is 'that which gets measured gets managed.' Therefore, managers need to be clear about what their priorities are and the measures they need to monitor in order to demonstrate personal, team, facility, and corporate effectiveness.

The word 'analytics' is used to describe the broad area of data analysis in the field of management. In the case of sport facility management, analytics are used for two distinct but complementary purposes. First, managers might conduct research into historical data to look for trends. For example, there might be a relationship between temperature and the type of drinks sold at a match. On cold days, hot drinks will be popular, whereas on hot days cold drinks are more likely to be in demand. By looking for patterns in the previous data, it might be possible to anticipate a situation and make sure that the concessions are suitably prepared with the right products to deal with the expected weather conditions. Second, having made, for example, the decision on a cold day to stock up on hot drinks in favor of cold drinks, we can use analytics to assess the impact or effectiveness of whether it was actually a good decision. The ultimate purpose of using analytics is to help managers to improve their operations by acquiring useful information that can be used to deliver positive outcomes. These outcomes might include increased revenue, reduced costs, or indeed a combination of the two. The overall objective of the chapter is to demonstrate how the use of analytics can provide sport facility managers with the information they require for planning, decision-making, and control purposes.

INTRODUCTION TO PERFORMANCE MANAGEMENT AND BENCHMARKING

Performance management and benchmarking are important techniques for facility managers, for three key reasons. First, they help facility managers to achieve better results by enabling them to understand and influence the drivers of performance. This is achieved by both *data benchmarking*, comparing statistical performance with others, and by *process benchmarking*, comparing the key decisions made to achieve good performance. Second, benchmarks provide much more authoritative reporting of performance than an organization's performance reported in isolation. Third, when benchmarking/performance management techniques become established as part of organizational culture, they provide the basis for a clear focus on the business essentials as well as on the direction for continuous improvement.

It might be tempting to suggest that good managers are intuitive, with natural skills for dealing with people and making decisions, using charisma and entrepreneurial flair. This romantic vision of management probably fits a few inspirational leaders but is inappropriate for the large majority of good managers. All the principles of good management suggest that, as well as personal skills, it is important to have, among other things, evidence to guide decisions. At the heart of this chapter, therefore, is the concept of good performance evidence. It is this evidence that will:

- Demonstrate whether strategies and objectives are being realized;
- Identify key financial changes and guide financial decision making;
- Demonstrate how customers are feeling about products or services and guide marketing decisions; and
- Identify the quality of service provision and guide human resource decisions.

Furthermore, it is not advisable to examine the evidence for one's own organization in isolation. External comparisons are also important in order to judge how the organization is doing in relation to other providers of similar products or services, whether or not they are competitors, and in relation to previous periods. For example, a 20,000-seat arena might sell food and drink at an average of $5 per head. Is this good, bad, or indifferent? One way in which we might interpret the quality of performance is by comparing it against what others are doing or by what has gone before. If a comparable rival arena is selling food and drink at $10 per head, we might think that $5 dollars per head is relatively poor performance and use this information as a basis to drive improvement. By contrast, if in the previous six months we had been selling at $4 per head, we might be congratulating ourselves for the significant improvement.

Utilizing appropriate evidence about organizational performance in order to improve decision making and comparing this evidence with similar providers and past achievements are the essentials of performance management and benchmarking. This chapter first provides examples of performance management frameworks, the organizational processes that stimulate the right evidence, and the right use of it. Second, concepts of performance are examined, demonstrating that it is a multifaceted phenomenon. Third, appropriate performance indicators are discussed (i.e., the pieces of data that are selected to represent organizational performance). Finally, benchmarking is considered, with the help of a case study of a benchmarking service used for sport facilities in the UK.

The term 'performance management' is often used interchangeably with 'quality management' because they cover very similar principles.

- *Performance management* is defined by IDeA, the Improvement and Development Agency for local government in the UK, as 'taking action in response to actual performances to make outcomes for users and the public better than they would otherwise be' (IDeA, 2009). It is a process of improving organizational performance by informing management decisions with appropriate planning, objectives, targets, performance measurement, and review.
- *Quality management* is defined by The Chartered Institute of Quality as 'an organization-wide approach to understanding precisely what customers need and

consistently delivering accurate solutions within budget, on time and with the minimum loss to society' (Chartered Institute of Quality, 2009). Broader in concept than performance management, quality management also includes measuring and analyzing performance using a process designed to achieve continual improvement in products, services, and the methods that deliver them to the customer.

PERFORMANCE MANAGEMENT FRAMEWORKS

A number of frameworks have been devised to facilitate performance management. We examine two in this chapter, the first a general model for any organization (EFQM) and the second a framework specifically designed for public sector cultural services in the UK (TAES).

The European Foundation for Quality Management Excellence Model (EFQM)

EFQM was established on the premise that to be successful, an organization needs to establish an appropriate management system. The EFQM Excellence Model is a practical tool to help organizations do this. It does so by measuring where they are on the path to excellence, helping managers to understand the weaknesses in performance and then stimulating solutions through actions. It is similar to the Baldrige Excellence Framework that is common in the United States and has been used by around 2 million businesses since 1988.

The EFQM Excellence Model is a management framework that can be used to provide continuous improvement to any organization in any area of activity. It works by self-assessment by an organization's managers rather than by external assessment. An organization is assessed by its managers against the relevant criteria that constitute quality performance, and a score is allocated.

By matching the organization against the model's criteria, strengths and weaknesses can be identified. Within this nonprescriptive approach, some fundamental concepts underpin the model:

- *Results orientation*: Satisfying the needs of all stakeholders is the orientation.
- *Customer focus*: The essence of service quality is to identify the needs of customers and to satisfy these needs.
- *Leadership and constancy of purpose*: Without effective leadership in seeking continuous improvement, it is unlikely to be achieved.
- *Management by processes and facts*: Systematic management is based on reliable evidence.
- *People development and involvement*: The potential of staff is realized through a culture of trust and empowerment.

- *Continuous learning, innovation, and improvement*: Sharing and an organizational culture that embraces change and development are required.
- *Partnership development*: Mutually beneficial relationships are based on trust.
- *Corporate social responsibility*: An ethical approach to service delivery demonstrates responsibility to the wider community.

The EFQM Business Excellence Model is based on nine criteria and is reproduced in Figure 14.1. Five of these criteria are Enablers, covering what an organization does. Four are Results covering what an organization achieves. Feedback from Results help to improve the Enablers.

The EFQM is the most widely used organizational framework in Europe and has become the basis for many national and regional Quality Awards.

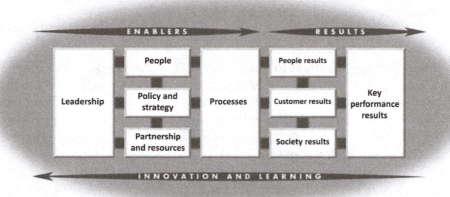

Figure 14.1 Business Excellence Model: EFQM

Toward an Excellent Service (TAES)

In the UK, TAES is a national framework for performance management in cultural services.

TAES is a self-assessment and improvement planning toolkit, which is designed to complement and embrace other quality frameworks and awards such as EFQM. It is described by IDeA as a 'journey' rather than as a scheme because it is a continuous process of improvement. Continuous improvement is necessary because of the continuous changes in both community needs and customer expectations. Continuous improvement requires an organization to:

- Clearly establish what it is trying to achieve (i.e., objectives);
- Establish what causes success;

- Identify current performance;
- Take actions to improve on a continuous basis; and
- Go back to step one and carry on (IDeA, 2006).

TAES identifies eight key 'themes' that influence the quality of cultural services, with 'equality' and 'service access' integrated into every theme:

1 Leadership;
2 Policy and strategy;
3 Community engagement;
4 Partnership working;
5 Use of resources;
6 People management;
7 Standards of service; and
8 Performance measurement and learning.

(IDeA, 2006).

The similarity of these criteria to those of the EFQM Excellence Model is deliberate: It is designed to complement EFQM. Within each of the themes are criteria that define key aspects of high-quality service. A number of 'descriptors' for the criteria allow performance in them to be measured. The system is evidence based – evidence schedules identify the sorts of evidence required to demonstrate that a particular criterion has or has not been met – 'the evidence schedules are vital to the integrity of the framework' (IDeA, 2006, p. 12). From the evidence emerging from self-assessment, an organization can identify its position in relation to four levels of performance: poor, fair, good, or excellent. A lack of evidence automatically leads to a rating of poor under the TAES self-assessment and reinforces the point made throughout this book that sensible decision making is best done on the basis of high-quality supporting information.

IDeA focuses on the improvement plan as the most important part of the TAES process – 'it is the very reason for carrying out the self-assessment in the first place' (IDeA, 2006, p. 12). Key attributes of an improvement plan are:

- Improvements are prioritized, focusing first on those that will make the biggest impact;
- The plan must be such that specific tasks are identified that are realistic, resourced, with clear accountability and deadlines set for delivery; and
- The improvements are themselves measurable, and you can monitor whether the actions planned are having the desired effect (IDeA, 2006, p. 12).

PERFORMANCE MANAGEMENT PRINCIPLES

A well-designed performance management system must be based on:

- A systematic analysis of the relationships between the objectives of the organization;
- The performance indicators employed in representing these objectives;
- The management targets set for the performance of the organization; and
- The actions taken to realize these targets.

To some sport managers, the differences between these concepts have been vague. However, more recently, a range of performance management systems have been devised to help managers achieve continuous improvement. However, why measure performance? As noted in Figure 14.2, it is likely that without the right evidence it is not easy to see where you are, let alone what is right or wrong with an organization.

1. What gets measured gets done.

2. If you do not measure results,
you cannot tell success from failure.

3. If you cannot see success, you cannot reward it.

4. If you cannot reward success,
you are probably rewarding failure.

5. If you cannot see success, you cannot learn from it.

6. If you cannot recognize failure, you cannot correct it.

7. If you can demonstrate results, you can win public support.

Figure 14.2 Why measure performance?

Source: Audit Commission. (2000a). *Aiming to improve: The principles of performance measurement.* London: Audit Commission.

Objectives

An essential first stage in performance management is setting appropriate organizational objectives. *Objectives* are a desired future position and should have certain desirable attributes as outlined by Taylor (1996).

- Objectives should be specified so that, at the end of an appropriate period, it is clear whether they have been achieved or not. This means that objectives need to be quantifiable. Each objective requires appropriate performance indicators, by which measurement of performance is possible. Remember when we looked at financial management (Chapter 7), we said that the budget was an organization's objectives expressed in financial terms.
- Objectives are concerned with ends not means. For example, it is not an objective to 'set low prices for disadvantaged groups in the community'; the objective here is 'to increase visits to the service by people from disadvantaged groups,' and this objective can be served by a number of means, with pricing being one of the primary objectives.
- The prioritization of objectives is important. Sometimes objectives may conflict; for example, 'increase revenue' might conflict with 'increase usage of a sport facility by the lowest socio-economic groups in the community.' Where trade-offs between conflicting objectives are apparent, priorities need to be identified. Failure to specify such priorities means that targets and management actions become compromised.

The attributes of appropriate objectives can be summarized in the mnemonic MASTER:

M = measurable
A = actionable
S = specific
T = time-specified
E = ends not means
R = ranked

It has often been the case, particularly in the public sector, that organizational objectives are expressed vaguely or generally so that it is difficult if not impossible to identify whether they have been achieved. Such inaccurately specified objectives include 'achieving sport for all,' 'serving the community's needs,' and 'providing a high-quality sporting experience.' These are 'aims' rather than objectives; they are broadly based and nonmeasurable. They require more specific, measurable objectives to be monitored through performance indicators, which in turn are used for management decision making.

Objectives for public sector sport organizations are likely to be more complicated than those of private, commercial firms because social, nonprofit objectives such as usage by disadvantaged groups are of importance to public sector organizations, as well as financial and customer satisfaction objectives. Social objectives extend to the impacts of public services, such as improved health and citizenship and reduced crime and vandalism. Impacts are typically less easily expressed in a measurable form than operational objectives.

Performance

Performance for a sport organization can mean any number of things, depending on what objectives are specified. It is possible, however, to generalize about the nature of performance and do so in the context of any type of organization. Before discussing specific performance indicators, it is important to identify the different aspects of performance that sport facility managers will be interested in.

The most common type of performance found in the commercial sector is financial performance. This is often simplified to mean profits, but, in fact, financial performance means much more than this. It can include income, growth, profit margins, level of debt, liquidity, and risk.

Related to financial performance is the concept of *economy*. This is concerned solely with the input side of the production process and with costs. It is not concerned with outputs. Economy is achieved if inputs are acquired at a minimum cost. Overemphasis on economy is not wise unless it is seen as the main reason for weak performance. In the public sector, it has often been the case that performance has been 'measured' by expenditure on inputs, i.e., increased spending is taken to mean an increase in service output. This is no measure of performance at all, as it says nothing about the actual outputs of the service, which could be highly wasteful of resources despite the rising expenditure.

Efficiency is concerned with achieving objectives and targets at minimum cost. Therefore, efficiency considers the best possible relationships between inputs and outputs. It is sometimes given the terms 'cost effectiveness' or 'cost efficiency' and is also what is meant by the terms 'productivity' and 'value for money.'

Effectiveness is concerned solely with the achievement of output targets. Hence, it does not consider the costs of achieving the output targets. A basic measure of effectiveness is throughput volume, such as the number of visits in a given time period, an example being the number of bathers at a swimming pool. However, this is a rather basic indicator because it contains no indication of the types of visitors that have been attracted or of the extent to which the service has met the needs of the visitors.

Effectiveness is an important performance aspect in public sector leisure services since they are concerned with social objectives that are largely nonfinancial in nature. These objectives include education, notably with services such as swimming and other activity classes. They also include increasing visits by particular, disadvantaged target groups such as people from minority ethnic groups.

In the public sector, organizations are also interested in the effectiveness of services in terms of achieving impacts on society. Therefore, while throughput is concerned with the volume of visitors, and outputs are concerned with direct effects such as the type of visitors or the revenue they provide, impacts are concerned with broader effects on society, such as improvements in health, citizenship, or quality of life.

In addition to economy, efficiency, and effectiveness, sometimes another *e* is added to the list of important performance dimensions, particularly in public sector organizations. This is equity, which is concerned with fairness in the treatment of all customers. This has a variety of interpretations, such as prioritizing visits by the most disadvantaged members of society or ensuring equality of opportunity to use a facility.

Another performance dimension that is increasingly common is customer satisfaction. This can be measured directly by such methods as questionnaire surveys, comment slips, complaints, and increasingly through technology-enabled means such as smartphones and instant feedback devices. Have you ever left the changing rooms of a sport facility and noticed on your way out a panel or tablet inviting you to press a button or touch a screen to indicate your level of satisfaction with, say, facility cleanliness? This type of feedback information provides managers with real-time analytics with which to make decisions. For example, it would be possible to program the devices so that if there were two consecutive 'dissatisfied' ratings, a duty manager is immediately alerted to visit the location and to take action.

Performance indicators

Ideally, indicators of performance should have certain qualities to make them suitable for management purposes. A set of performance indicators should:

- Reflect all the objectives of the leisure service accurately;
- Cover different dimensions of performance, such as effectiveness and efficiency;
- Be capable of being measured for separate parts of the service, since it is likely that different objectives and different targets are applicable to different parts of the service, even within the same facility;
- Be administratively manageable and easily understood; and
- Be consistent over time and between service elements and different organizations, which is particularly important for benchmarking exercises.

In the UK public sector, the Audit Commission has provided two forms of advice in relation to performance measurement. Although designed for the public sector, much of this general advice is transferable to other sectors. First, it is necessary to consider the general characteristics of indicators that can help to ensure that proposed indicators will be useful and effective. Second, it is important that the data collected is reliable. Good quality data is an essential ingredient for reliable performance information.

The Audit Commission identified 13 criteria for assessing the robustness of a performance indicator (see Table 14.1). Devising a performance indicator that fulfills all of the criteria in this table is challenging. Inevitably, a performance indicator will score less well against some criteria. Indicators that are published for the benefit of the local community should primarily be relevant and easy to understand.

Table 14.1 Criteria for good performance indicators

Criteria	Explanation
Relevant	Indicators should be relevant to the organization's strategic goals and objectives.
Clear definition	The performance indicators should have a clear and intelligible definition in order to ensure consistent collection and fair comparison.
Easy to understand and use	Performance indicators should be described in terms that the user of the information will understand.
Comparable	Indicators should be consistently comparable between organizations and be comparable on a consistent basis over time.
Verifiable	The indicator also needs to be collected and calculated in a way that enables the information and data to be verified. Therefore, it should be based on robust and verifiable data collection systems.
Cost-effective	There is a need to balance the cost of collecting information with its usefulness. Indicators should be based on information already available and linked to existing data collection activities.
Unambiguous	A change in an indicator should be capable of unambiguous interpretation so that it is clear whether an increase in an indicator value represents an improvement or deterioration in service.
Attributable	Service managers should be able to influence the performance measured by the indicator.
Responsive	Indicators should be responsive to change. An indicator where changes in performance are likely to be too small to register will be of limited use.
Avoid perverse incentives	Indicators should not be easily manipulated because this might encourage counterproductive activity.
Allow innovation	Indicators that focus on the outcome and user satisfaction are more likely to encourage innovation than indicators based on existing processes.
Statistically valid	Indicators should be statistically valid.
Timely	Data for the performance indicator should be available within a reasonable timescale.

Source: Audit Commission. (2000b). *On target: The practice of performance indicators*. London: Audit Commission.

The Audit Commission defined six key characteristics that can be used to assess the quality of data used to construct performance indicator scores (see Table 14.2). Most of these criteria directly echo those stipulated for performance indicators in Table 14.1. The one additional consideration in Table 14.2 is completeness – an important reminder that validity and reliability are as much dependent on what is missing as on what is collected.

Having stated these requirements, however, it is necessary to stress that any set of indicators is unlikely to fulfill all of these properties. This is simply because these qualities are difficult to achieve – all indicators have their good points and their bad points. However, using the basic principles outlined in Tables 14.1 and 14.2 provides the basis for a robust framework around which to construct a set of context-specific performance measures.

Table 14.2 Criteria for suitable performance indicators' data

Dimension	Description
Accuracy	Data should be sufficiently accurate for its intended purposes, representing clearly and in detail the interaction provided at the point of activity. Data should be captured once only, although it may have multiple uses. Accuracy is most likely to be secured if data is captured as close to the point of activity as possible. The need for accuracy must be balanced with the importance of the uses for the data and the costs and effort of collection. For example, it may be appropriate to accept some degree of inaccuracy where timeliness is important. Where compromises have to be made on accuracy, the resulting limitations of the data should be clear to its users.
Validity	Data should be recorded and used in compliance with relevant requirements, including the correct application of any rules or definitions. This will ensure consistency between periods and with similar organizations. Where proxy data is used to compensate for an absence of actual data, organizations must consider how well this data is able to satisfy the intended purpose.
Reliability	Data should reflect stable and consistent data collection processes across collection points and over time. Managers and stakeholders should be confident that progress toward performance targets reflects real changes rather than variations in data collection approaches or methods.
Timeliness	Data should be captured as quickly as possible after the event or activity and must be available for the intended use within a reasonable time. Data must be available quickly and frequently enough to support information needs and to influence the appropriate level of decision making.

Table 14.2 (Continued)

Dimension	Description
Relevance	Data captured should be relevant to the purposes for which it is used. This entails periodic review of requirements to reflect changing needs.
	It may be necessary to capture data at the point of the activity that is relevant only for other purposes rather than for the current intervention. Quality assurance processes are needed to ensure the quality of such data.
Completeness	Data requirements should be clearly specified based on the information needs of the organization and data collection processes matched to these requirements. Monitoring missing, incomplete, or invalid records can provide an indication of data quality and can point to problems in the recording of certain data items.

Source: Audit Commission. (2007). *Improving information to support decision making: Standards for better quality data.* London: Audit Commission.

Private, commercial sector

For a private, commercial organization, performance is, in the main, specified in financial terms, although there are other important considerations. Business accounting measures are often expressed as ratios and are designed principally for planning (strategic appraisal) and control purposes (operational appraisal). The ratios are concerned not just with profit but also with gross profit, growth, and productivity. An indicative sample of such ratios is given in Table 14.3.

Table 14.3 Performance ratios for commercial organizations

Profitability 1 Overall profit margin: $$\frac{\text{Net Profit}}{\text{Total Income}}$$	No rules of thumb. It varies widely among industries and firms but a very clear indicator as to whether the selling price is higher than the cost.
2 Sales margin: $$\frac{\text{Sales}}{\text{Cost of goods sold}}$$	The sales margin or gross profit margin shows the contribution toward fixed costs as a result of selling.
Growth 1 Income growth %: $$\frac{\text{Income this year} - \text{Income last year}}{\text{Income last year}} \times 100$$	All businesses need to grow just to stand still because over time their costs increase. Furthermore, in order to invest in a better customer experience, we need money for investment.
2 Profit growth %: $$\frac{\text{Profit this year} - \text{Profit last year}}{\text{Profit last year}} \times 100$$	It is one thing to grow income, but what is more important is how much of that income is left over as profit. Therefore, profits and profit growth are good insights into an organization's financial performance.

(Continued)

317

Table 14.3 (Continued)

Productivity	Productivity measures provide us with an indication as to how well our resources are working. The first example, sales per employee, gives us an insight into how much income each employee generates on average.
1 Sales per employee: $$\frac{\text{Sales}}{\text{Number of employees}}$$	
2 Staff cost effectiveness: $$\frac{\text{Sales}}{\text{Staff costs}}$$	The second example develops the first by looking at how much income we are generating from each dollar of staff costs. As ever, we are looking for sales to be more than costs.
3 Secondary sales per head: $$\frac{\text{Sales of food and drink}}{\text{Number of admissions}}$$	An alternative way of looking at things is how much income are we extracting for each customer on secondary sales? Sales per head is one of the all-time classic measures of productivity and one that you will learn to judge yourself and your staff by if you work in sport facility management.

A major advantage of ratios is that they put performance into a consistent perspective. For instance, it is one thing to declare $100,000 profit, but this figure takes on more meaning if it is put in the context of income as our overall profit margin percentage does (see Table 14.3). Ratios commonly involve two monetary sums, such as the ratio of a firm's profit to its income, so they enable financial comparisons to be made over time, without having to worry about adjusting for inflation. They also hide potentially sensitive or confidential information by expressing data as a ratio rather than disclosing the absolute value, for example, sales expressed as a function of staff costs reveals neither the actual sales nor the actual staff costs.

Ratios, however, have to be interpreted very carefully. Many are more appropriate for comparing a single firm's performance over time than comparing different firms, particularly if the firms are from a different industry or sector. You would not ordinarily seek to compare the financial performance of a sport stadium with that of a swimming pool in any meaningful way. Some ratios involve estimates that can be calculated in various ways, so comparing like with like can be problematic – for example valuing inventories and intangible assets.

Private firms are also interested in other aspects of performance apart from financial ratios. Market share is a particularly important objective that is normally measurable, even at the local or regional level as it provides an indication of the demand for a product. It is vital for any organization, from whatever sector, to be informed about changes in demand for the service it is providing. If competition is low and market share is high, this is the basis for perhaps raising prices. By contrast, if the competition is increasing and there is a threat to market share, then techniques such as promotion and improved customer service become more important.

Market research, either formal (e.g., commissioning a study) or informal (e.g., being aware of what is happening in your locality), is a typical means of generating this evidence.

Most large private leisure organizations have marketing departments with market research functions. As well as continual monitoring demand for their goods and services by this means, they regularly employ outside market research agencies or consultancies to conduct specialist market research. This point reinforces the importance for organizations to be outward looking in addition to inward looking. It might be great news to find out that your business has grown by 10% compared with its performance last year, but if the sector as a whole has grown by 20%, then you have actually lost ground to your rivals who in turn have reduced your market share.

Public sector

Public sector sport providers have had to become accustomed to performance measurement in the UK, with the advent of fundamental reviews of the way in which public services are provided. Local authorities no longer have a divine right to be providers of services, and their role has shifted toward being enablers, particularly when more cost-effective alternatives exist. The management of sport facilities and leisure centers is increasingly being undertaken by private sector organizations and trusts that can provide better services at a lower cost than the local authorities themselves can.

In order to ensure that organizations that provide an outsourcing solution to managing sport facilities for local authorities are actually providing a worthwhile service to the community, performance indicators are used to ensure compliance with the conditions of the contract. One suite of indicators is Sport England's National Benchmarking Service (NBS) for sport and leisure centers, which compiles data for 47 performance indicators across four dimensions of performance. These four dimensions (access, utilization, financial efficiency, and customer service) are outlined in Table 14.4.

The list of indicators in Table 14.4, used for the National Benchmarking Service, illustrates the compromise that is often necessary between what indicators are desirable and what indicators can be measured reliably and at a reasonable cost. The NBS does not attempt to measure wider long-term impacts of sports provision, such as improvements in health, improved quality of life, reduced crime and vandalism, or education benefits; these are considered too difficult to measure regularly in the specific context of sports provision. However, the NBS does provide indicators relevant to another impact objective – social inclusion – via the access indicators. The NBS also does not measure nonusers' attitudes and barriers – this would require expensive research in local communities – or the views, behavior, etc. of young people under 14 years old, who are not considered suitable for the questionnaire survey employed.

(a) Access: Usage by specific groups or market segments

Key

% visits 14–25 years ÷ % catchment population 14–25 years
% visits from NS-SEC classes 6&7 ÷ % catchment population in NS-SEC classes 6 & 7[1]
% visits 65 + years ÷ % catchment population 65+ years
% visits from black, Asian, & other ethnic groups ÷ % catchment population in the same groups
% visits disabled, <65 years ÷ % catchment population disabled, <65 years

Other

% visits 26–64 years ÷ % catchment population in the same group
% of visits that were first visits
% visits with a discount card
% visits with discount cards for 'disadvantage'[2]
% visits female
% visits disabled, 65 years+ ÷ % catchment population disabled, 65+ years
% visits unemployed

Notes:

1 NS-SEC classes 6 & 7 are the two lowest socioeconomic classes in the official classification used in the UK. People from these groups account for around 25% of the population and are some of the most deprived and 'hard to reach' members of society. A subsidy is often justified on the grounds of providing sport and leisure opportunities for people from these disadvantaged groups.
2 Disadvantage eligibility for discount cards includes over-50s, students, unemployed, disabled, single parents, government support, government-funded trainees, widows, exercise referrals, and elite performers.

(b) Utilization

Key

annual visits per square meter (of usable space)

Other

annual visits per square meter (of total indoor space)
% of visits casual, instead of organized
weekly number of people visiting the center as % of the catchment population

(c) Financial efficiency

Key

subsidy per visit

Other

% cost recovery
subsidy per resident
subsidy per square meter
total operating cost per visit
total operating cost per square meter
maintenance and repair costs per square meter
energy costs per square meter
total income per visit
total income per square meter
direct income per visit
secondary income per visit

(d) Service attributes for customer service

Accessibility

Activity available at convenient times
Ease of booking
Activity charge/fee
Range of activities available

Quality of facilities/services

Quality of flooring in the sports hall
Quality of lighting in the sports hall
Quality of equipment
Water quality in the swimming pool
Water temperature of the swimming pool
Number of people in the pool
Quality of car parking on site
Quality of food and drink

Cleanliness

Cleanliness of changing areas
Cleanliness of activity spaces

Staff

Helpfulness of reception staff
Helpfulness of other staff
Standard of coaching/instruction

Value for money

Value for money of the activities
Value for money of food/drink

Overall

Overall satisfaction with the visit
Net Promoter Score (NPS)

It is really up to each organization to choose a manageable array of indicators to reflect its objectives and performance priorities. For a public sector provider, this may include throughput indicators for particular groups of clients, such as women, the elderly, lower socioeconomic groups, and the disabled, since this would monitor the effectiveness of the organization in reaching important target groups. It may also include very conventional indicators of financial performance such as those relevant to a private supplier, as shown in Table 14.3, particularly for parts of the service that have no particular 'social service' function, such as the bar, cafe, vending machines, and other merchandise sales. For these aspects of a business, measures like gross profit and sales per head are vitally important indicators of operational efficiency that are easy to convey the importance of to your staff.

How often should performance indicators' evidence be produced? It is very common for performance indicators to be calculated annually. However, there are good reasons for wanting operational performance indicators to be available on a far more regular basis. Decisions about promotion, programming, and staffing arrangements may be modified at any time, so a regular flow of up-to-date information assists such decisions. Technology such as bar code readers at the point of sale enables managers to know at any point in time how much income should be in the till and how much merchandise should be left in stock. This type of knowledge is useful because it can be used to motivate people to sell and encourages staff to look after the stock under their control. It is by doing these basics correctly that profits can be realized and used to run a business sustainably.

Targets

Targets are precise statements of what is to be achieved by when and by whom. They are an obvious implication of measuring performance indicators that reflect management objectives. A target provides a concrete and unambiguous reference point against which to ask, 'Is this objective being achieved?' A target typically takes the form of a numerical target, such as, 'We need to achieve 1,000 admissions per week.' Targets also can be applied to nonfinancial data. For example, given the objective of increasing usage by the disabled and using as an indicator the ratio of percentage of visits by the disabled to the percentage of local population who are disabled, a target figure of one would mean trying to increase usage by the disabled to a level that is representative of their numbers in the local population. This is a good example of the way in which a target can provide a degree of specificity to an objective.

Evidence of previous performance or evidence of the performance of similar organizations elsewhere provides a quantitative basis for setting targets. Such evidence enables the target setter to reach the difficult balance between ambition and realism. Targets need to be challenging, but they also need to be achievable. If they are too easily reached, or if they are impossible to reach, they quickly fall into disrepute. Targets can and do change in the course of time. They need to remain under continuing scrutiny for their relevance to the operating circumstances of the organization.

Balanced scorecard

One of the best-known models for performance measurement is the Balanced Scorecard, a system devised by Kaplan and Norton (1992). A motivation for the Balanced Scorecard was to add strategic nonfinancial performance measures to the traditional financial measures in order to give a more 'balanced' view.

The structure of the Balanced Scorecard is represented in Figure 14.3. The figure demonstrates not just the development of performance measurement beyond the financial but also a consistent process of specifying objectives, devising measures

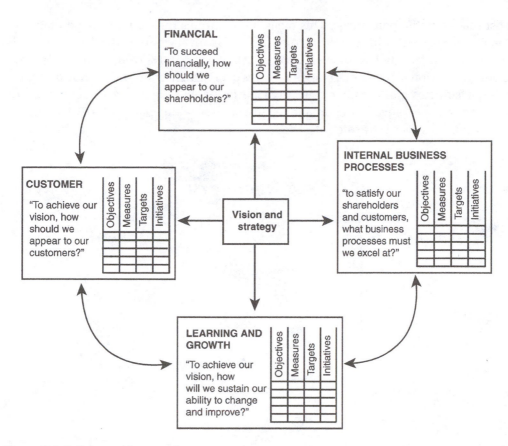

Figure 14.3 Balanced Scorecard structure

for these, setting targets, and devising initiatives to achieve the targets. The last of these processes turn the Balanced Scorecard into a performance management system, not just a performance measurement tool.

BENCHMARKING

So far, we have been discussing evidence that is appropriate for an organization to collect in order for its managers to know how the organization is performing and whether changes are occurring because of their decisions. However, it is also likely that the organization will want comparisons to be made with other similar organizations. Benchmarking is a process that facilitates this.

Data benchmarking involves comparison with numerical standards (e.g., averages) calculated for performance indicators in a particular service. In the UK public leisure centers, one of the most important measures of performance is what is known as the cost recovery rate percentage. This measure quantifies the extent to which facilities recover their costs with earned income. A cost recovery rate of 100%, for example, means that a facility breaks even because it recovers 100% of its costs. Using data from the National Benchmarking Service, we can illustrate industry norms against which facilities can compare their own performance. Figure 14.4 shows the cost recovery rates achieved by sport and leisure centers taking part in the 2018 National Benchmarking Service exercise.

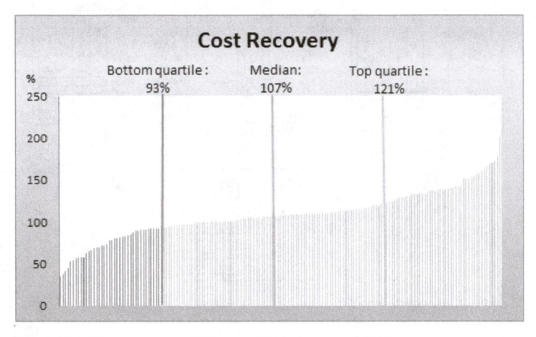

Figure 14.4 Cost recovery rates in UK sport and leisure centers in 2018

Source: Sport Industry Research Centre, National Benchmarking Service Annual Report 2018.

In 2018, the median benchmark for cost recovery was 107%; in other words, it is average practice for public sport and leisure centers to be run profitably with a surplus of 7% on expenditure. However, it also quite clear that there are wide variations in cost recovery with the bottom quartile around 93% and centers in the top quartile achieving 121% and higher. Armed with this data about industry norms, it becomes possible for managers to set realistic targets about what is achievable and what a realistic target for improvement might be. It is possible to break the data in Figure 14.4 into more granular levels, for example, swimming pools only, so that comparisons and target setting are done on a like-for-like basis as much as possible. It is one thing to benchmark data, and this is useful for answering a question such as, 'How much?' However, if appropriate action is to be taken, it is also important to know about 'how?' and 'why?' Answers to these types of question are the role of process benchmarking.

Effectiveness of management and operations

Process benchmarking involves the comparison of different procedures adopted in different organizations. Used in conjunction with performance data, process benchmarking facilitates an understanding of the procedures that improve performance. Imagine, for example, that on the user satisfaction survey of the NBS, one facility scores 2 out of 5 for its cleanliness of the changing areas and a similar center is the top scorer with 4.5 out of 5. As a matter of routine, to help drive up standards and to help managers strive for continuous improvement, the identities of the top 25% of facilities for each benchmark are made public. By doing this, centers that perform less well are able to contact the top performers to find out how they perform so well and whether any learning is transferable. Thus for a facility struggling with its cleanliness scores, the manager might contact the manager of a facility that has a strong score. For the cleanliness attribute, key features of the top performers tend to be:

- All staff take collective ownership for facility cleanliness;
- Changing areas are inspected every hour;
- Those who inspect a changing area sign off on a sheet that is on public display;
- Complaints are listened to and acted upon immediately;
- Mystery customers are used to conducting occasional checks on facilities;
- Instant feedback devices are used to gauge customer satisfaction in real time; and
- Bonuses are awarded for cleanliness performance as well as for conventional performance such as selling memberships.

External benchmarks for performance are important because they enable a judgment to be made on the relative performance of an organization, which in turn gives it competitive impetus. They also enable other bodies to assess the relative performance of each organization. This feature of benchmarks is particularly important in the public sector where the central government is very interested in monitoring the relative performance of individual local government services, if only because it directly funds around half the costs of these local services in the UK.

In the UK, Sport England's National Benchmarking Service for sport and leisure centers (NBS) provides data on management and finance with customer satisfaction as an optional extra. The NBS is featured in the following case study.

SPORT ENGLAND'S NATIONAL BENCHMARKING SERVICE (NBS)

The NBS measures performance standards for indoor sport and leisure centers with one or both of the following core facilities: a sport hall of four badminton courts or more and/or a swimming pool at least 20 meters in length. This helps to ensure that the service is focused on similar types of facilities. The performance indicators measured in this service are identified in Table 14.4.

They are designed to cover as many dimensions of performance as practical for a reasonable cost. However, as noted earlier, they do not cover many of the broader impacts of sport in the community, such as improvements in health and education.

To generate the data, the NBS requires clients to conduct a survey of customers and to submit a form with specified management and financial information. In addition, population data for the local catchment area is derived from the National Census. Data from clients is checked carefully – there can be considerable discrepancies and inaccuracies in quite basic pieces of management information, such as throughput counts and cost estimates. Similarly, the administration of the user survey has to ensure valid and reliable results. An NBS guidance document is designed to provide advice that seeks to ensure as much consistency in data as possible between clients.

The NBS results for access, finance, and utilization performance are compared with benchmarks for four families that have been empirically tested and proven to have structural effects on performance:

- *Type of center*: Wet, dry (with or without outdoor facilities), and mixed (with or without outdoor facilities)
- *The socioeconomics of a center's location*: High deprivation, medium deprivation, low deprivation – measured by the percentage of the catchment population in the bottom two socioeconomic classes
- *Size of the center*: Large, medium, and small – measured by floor space in predetermined bands
- *Management type at the center*: In-house local authority, local trust, or external commercial partner

Three benchmarks are employed. The 25%, 50%, and 75% benchmarks are the quarter, half, and three-quarters points in the distribution of scores for a performance indicator if all the centers' scores were organized from the lowest score at the bottom end of the distribution to the highest score at the top end.

Another important feature of the NBS output is the information on facility users from the user survey. Frequency distributions of responses to all the user survey questions include visit characteristics (e.g., activities engaged in, the frequency of visit) and the profile of visitors (e.g., travel distance and time, travel mode, home postal codes).

NBS clients have emphasized a number of benefits from the service:

- Awareness of the state of the service, often confirming preconceived ideas but objectively

- Challenges to preconceived ideas held by managers and politicians, causing a reassessment of priorities and delivery methods
- Real data to help set targets for objectives
- Experience of research data to develop an awareness of further information needs and helping to develop an evidence-based management culture
- Benchmarking data to enable the selection of process benchmarking partners with whom to discuss how to generate better performance for specific performance indicators

In addition, NBS clients have demonstrated a number of commendable responses to the processes of performance management:

- Generating the right information
- Interpreting the results meaningfully
- Utilizing the results in performance planning – that is, immediate action plans and longer-term contract specification and strategy development

As a 'killer fact,' it has been shown that the difference in financial performance between centers in the top quartile and the bottom quartile can be as much as £300,000 per year. This is a considerable wake-up call to the poor performing centers in the UK and has stimulated considerable interest in process benchmarking, that is, asking the questions of peers, 'What are you doing better than us, and how can we learn from you?'

Suggested discussion topics

1 Take one of the NBS indicators from each of the categories of access, utilization, and financial identified in Table 14.4, and consider its merits against the Audit Commission criteria in Table 14.1
2 As a sport facility manager, why would you want to compare the performance of your facility with benchmarks for other facilities?

The scope of benchmarking is almost unlimited and can be applied to almost any facet of facility management. In human resource management, one of the most disruptive issues managers encounter can be the turnover of staff. If you are the manager of a stadium, and you need 300 stewards on duty for every match or concert, you do not want to be spending all of your time recruiting staff who will be with you for one event and then gone forever. Thus if staff retention is important to you, then you measure it. The employee turnover ratio can be derived by calculating the proportion of employees who leave an organization over a set period (usually a year), expressed as a percentage of total staff numbers. If you have good staff, you want to retain them, and if we have a good working environment, then staff are more likely to stay. Under these conditions, a staff turnover ratio of 10% is much more preferable than one of 50%, particularly when large numbers of staff are involved.

Benchmarking is not the sole confine of managers. They can be used for operational purposes to help motivate staff and to focus their attention on what is important. So, for example, if you manage a stadium and have a target to sell an average of $10 per head on food and drink, this needs to be communicated to staff, and their individual performance needs to be monitored against the target. Those who achieve this target should be rewarded accordingly, and those who do not should be trained so that they meet the required standard or alternatively be replaced.

In day-to-day operations such as marketing, we can also use benchmarking. For certain events, the marketing department might take out an advertisement with a special offer such as a coupon giving free admission to one child for every full-paying adult. How would we know if this promotion had been successful? One method might be to have a target for how many are returned. Often vouchers used in mass media have a redemption rate of around 1%. If this were in a newspaper with a circulation of 200,000, it would mean 2,000 admissions. This would then need to be considered alongside other factors such as the original cost of the advertisement and whether the people using the vouchers were over and above the business-as-usual people or simply those who were planning to attend anyway and who received an unnecessary discount.

The point that unites these three examples is that they are all courses of action that are important to managers, who in turn require feedback as to whether the decisions they have made have been effective. The saying 'What gets measured gets done' could not be more appropriate.

FACILITY FOCUS: EFFICIENCY ANALYSIS OF AN ANONYMOUS
FACILITY USING THE NATIONAL BENCHMARKING SERVICE:
UNITED KINGDOM

The following table presents an extract of the efficiency data from an anonymized center that used the National Benchmarking Service in 2019. The scores for all facilities that take part (c. 250 per year) are aligned in ascending order and divided into quartiles. Each center's score on a particular indicator is allocated to the relevant quartile in order to paint a picture of overall efficiency performance, which is subsequently interpreted for a lay audience.

Efficiency indicators	Bottom quartile	25%	2nd quartile	50%	3rd quartile	75%	Top quartile
% cost recovery	3rd	3rd	3rd	3rd	3rd	3rd	3rd
total operating cost per visit	3rd	3rd	3rd	3rd	3rd	3rd	3rd
maintenance and repair costs per m²	50%	50%	50%	50%	50%	50%	50%
energy costs per m²	3rd	3rd	3rd	3rd	3rd	3rd	3rd
energy efficiency rating	2nd	2nd	2nd	2nd	2nd	2nd	2nd
staff costs as % of total income	2nd	2nd	2nd	2nd	2nd	2nd	2nd
central costs as % of total expenditure	2nd	2nd	2nd	2nd	2nd	2nd	2nd
income per m²	25%	25%	25%	25%	25%	25%	25%
direct income per visit	50%	50%	50%	50%	50%	50%	50%
secondary income per visit	2nd	2nd	2nd	2nd	2nd	2nd	2nd
annual visits per m² (usable space)	25%	25%	25%	25%	25%	25%	25%

How would we diagnose the performance shown?

1   High-level efficiency performance is above average relative to the National Benchmarks, with five of the indicators achieving performance at or above the median (50%) score. The all-important cost recovery indicator performs better than the industry average.
2   Two indicators perform at the 25th percentile level, which is regarded as weak performance relative to the industry averages, namely income per square meter (i.e., low income), and the low level of throughput (as measured by annual visits per square meter).
3   To improve performance, the most logical approach is to consider strategies that increase throughput and, in turn, income. We make this recommendation because operating costs are under control and income per visit (a measure of pricing) is average. The issue to address, then, is that the center has below-average customer throughput. This finding suggests that the basic asset of space is not being used as efficiently as it is in comparable facilities across England.

The important thing about NBS data is that is objective and provides the basis for a sensible conversation about the nature of corrective action to be taken if deemed necessary.

Source: Anonymized and simplified extract from an actual NBS efficiency report produced for a client by the Sport Industry Research Centre at Sheffield Hallam University.

CONCLUSIONS ABOUT PERFORMANCE MANAGEMENT AND BENCHMARKING

Performance management and benchmarking are essential tools in the quest for continuous improvement. At the heart of these systems is appropriate evidence of performance. However, acquiring appropriate evidence is not an easy matter. Performance indicators have to be selected that fully represent an organization's objectives. One of the problems encountered with the NBS is that feasible performance measurement falls short of desired performance measurement in public sector sport facilities. Much of the modern emphasis in justifying taxpayers' subsidies to such facilities rests on social impacts, particularly in improving users' health. However, measuring improvements in health and attributing them specifically to making use of sport facilities is a difficult task, one beyond the cost of a reasonable performance measurement system.

Another threat to the promise of performance management is the difficulty of assembling accurate and consistent measurement data. Financial data may be subject to accounting regulations, but even so, there is considerable variation in the way in which some standard ratios are calculated, and 'creative accounting' can be used to disguise problems if the wrong organizational culture has set in. Another increasingly essential component of management evidence is market research of customers, but there are enough precedents at the national and local levels to warn that market research can all too easily be conducted in an inappropriate manner, which can bias samples, or that lead respondents into answering questions in certain ways.

Nevertheless, if these constraints can be overcome, the promised land of performance management beckons, where the right evidence enables weaknesses to be identified, plans to be made, actions to be taken, and outcomes to be improved. The third millennium has seen an accelerated take-up of performance management and measurement systems. Benchmarking is increasingly seen as being the norm for facility managers. This development can only help to secure continuously improving performance in sport facilities and management practice.

TECHNOLOGY NOW! – A NEW AND IMPROVED NATIONAL BENCHMARKING SERVICE (UNITED KINGDOM)

The National Benchmarking Service (NBS) has existed as a resource for sport and leisure facilities in England since 2000. During this time, it has evolved from being a manual data entry and analysis system to one that is fully automated. In the latest generation of the NBS, data is entered and processed using a web-based platform that provides three key service improvements for users:

1   *Improved data presentation*: Data will be used only to inform current practice if it is easily understood such that managers have confidence in

it. The new NBS makes use of the latest data visualization technology to produce dashboards, dials, and other graphics that are much more user-friendly than the output that can be produced in spreadsheets.

2 *Bespoke analysis*: Subscribers to the NBS are now able to conduct their own secondary analysis of the data. Each client has its own password-protected log-in that provides access to the anonymized NBS data. If a particular indicator is a cause for concern, it is possible for managers to drill down deeper into the data to gain further insight into the problem as a first step toward identifying practical solutions.

3 *A benchmarking community*: The NBS online tool enables managers to interact with one another to share good practice. While it is useful to know how your center performs on a particular indicator, it is even more useful to take action to improve facility management and service delivery. Subscribers to the NBS can now communicate directly with a top-performing manager, which in turn facilitates the more important technique of process benchmarking.

The rationale for the NBS is to help drive up standards and performance in public sport and leisure facilities. The NBS online platform improves the efficiency of data entry and processing, enabling managers to focus on striving to achieve continuous improvement in service delivery and efficient use of resources.

Source: National Benchmarking Service. (2019). Retrieved March 23, 2019, from https://questnbs.org/nbs/options-and-guidance

CHAPTER REVIEW

This chapter started by looking at what the field of analytics is about and agreeing that it can be used to look for patterns in historical data as well as providing information as to whether decision making has been effective. We looked at the similarity between two concepts: performance management and quality management. Two examples of performance management frameworks are described – EFQM and TAES. EFQM is one of the oldest generic systems, and it is possible to see similarities between this and many other systems that have been subsequently developed. TAES is a system devised specifically for cultural services in the UK public sector.

Objectives are a cornerstone of good performance management, and they need to be specified much more specifically than organizational aims. Criteria for good objectives are given. The meaning of 'performance' is discussed, and while it is driven in an organization by its objectives, there are many different facets to performance. The major elements relevant to sport facility management are detailed.

Performance indicators have to be devised to represent the performance that is relevant to objectives. Indicators are the way in which performance is measured, and the chapter discusses the criteria for good performance indicators and the requirements for good data from which to calculate performance indicator values. Differences between the nature of performance indicators in the commercial sector and public sectors are demonstrated. As well as measuring performance indicators, it is important for organizational improvement to set targets for them. These targets will be determined by the objectives of the facility.

The Balanced Scorecard is an example of a performance measurement system, designed for the commercial sector to reflect more than simply financial performance. The Balanced Scorecard reinforces the essential principles of performance management: objectives, targets, measurement, action, and review. In addition, the concept of benchmarking is explained as a process of comparing performance either with other facilities or with previous performance. From the UK, the case of the National Benchmarking Services for sport and leisure facilities is featured as an extended case study.

IN THE FIELD . . .

With Mike Hill, joint director of Leisure-net Solutions Limited, Norfolk, United Kingdom

Mike is a joint director of Leisure-net Solutions, a company he founded after a successful career in sport facility management in which he gained experience working in both the private and the public sectors covering health and fitness, ice rinks, pools, and food and beverage. Mike set up Leisure-net Solutions in 1999, having seen the need for the industry to improve its knowledge base and understanding of the needs of its customers. Leisure-net Solutions is now seen as the go-to organization for customer insight into the sport and leisure industry in the United Kingdom. They are also leaders in the areas of business intelligence and consultation to the cultural services, active leisure and health, and fitness industries.

In providing advice to people entering the sport industry, Mike stated:

My advice would be to not specialize too early in your career, but when you do, make sure you are one of the best. I think it is really useful to have a good wide grounding in the sector that you wish to build your career in, there really is not anything like the experience of 'having done it myself,' when you are advising people on how to improve their business or drive forward customer service improvements.

Secondly, find a unique selling point (USP) for your services and concentrate on something that emphasizes that difference. For me, it was putting myself through a Net Promoter Score Partner course. At the time in the leisure sector, very few people knew about or were using the Net Promoter Score to benchmark their customer experience.

Finally, try to embed yourself in the sector you want to work in. If you want to work in the area of data analytics and benchmarking, try to work hand in hand with organizations in the industry that will have a stake in using the outputs.

BIBLIOGRAPHY

Audit Commission. (2000a). *Aiming to improve: The principles of performance measurement*. London: Audit Commission.

Audit Commission. (2000b). *On target: The practice of performance indicators*. London: Audit Commission.

Audit Commission. (2007). *Improving information to support decision making: Standards for better quality data*. London: Audit Commission.

Balanced Scorecard Institute. (2017). *What is the balanced scorecard?* Retrieved March 4, 2019, from www.balancedscorecard.org/BSCResources/AbouttheBalancedScorecard/tabid/55/Default.aspx

EFQM. (2013). *The EFQM excellence model*. Retrieved March 4, 2019, from www.efqm.org/index.php/efqm-model-2013

IDeA. (2006). *Towards an excellent service: A performance management framework for cultural services*. London: IDeA.

Kaplan, R. S., & Norton, D. P. (2005). The Balanced Scorecard: Measures that drive performance. *Harvard Business Review, 83*(7), 172–180.

Ramchandani, G., Shibli, S., & Kung, S. P. (2018). The performance of local authority sports facilities in England during a period of recession and austerity. *International Journal of Sport Policy and Politics, 10*(1), 95–111.

Sport Industry Research Centre. (2018). *The National Benchmarking Service annual report for 2018*. Sheffield: Sport Industry Research Centre/Sheffield Hallam University.

CHAPTER 15

IMPACTS AND LEGACIES THROUGH SUSTAINABILITY

CHAPTER OUTLINE

- Impacts of sport facilities
  - Economic impact
  - Social impact
  - Environmental impact
- Legacies of sport facilities
- Chapter review

CHAPTER OBJECTIVES

This closing chapter looks at the role sport facilities play in creating impacts and legacies for society through sustainable operations and management. Impacts look at the short-term influence a sport facility has on society, usually measured during the initial operations of the facility (first ten years). The term 'legacy' has been used with increasing frequency in describing the long-term social impact sport facilities have on society. The concepts of impacts and legacies are often linked to the concept of sustainable sport and leisure development and are becoming a vital component in measuring the effectiveness of sport facility management operations. This chapter examines the impacts and legacies of sport facility operations management leading to sustainable sport and leisure infrastructures.

IMPACTS OF SPORT FACILITIES

As we conclude this book on sport facility operations management, the authors have taken you through the pre-management and pre-operational issues, the application of management and operations principles, the implementation of sport facility operations management, and the evaluation of the effectiveness of management and operations. The efficient management and operations of sport facilities should then lead to short-term impacts and long-term legacies that create sustainable sport and leisure infrastructures. So let us start by looking at the triple bottom line.

An *impact* is a short-term impulse that creates an ongoing benefit to the users. For a sport facility, this involves how the users of that venue consume sport product or services that have a direct effect on maximizing a sustainable impact on relevant stakeholders. The way in which sport facilities are operated and managed over the short term plays a crucial role in driving what is known as the *triple bottom line* of impacts – economic impact, social impact, and environmental impact.

Economic impact

Economic impact is defined as the net economic change in a host community that is directly attributable to a facility or an event. Economic impact focuses on the effect a sport facility will have on a variety of factors ranging from local consumer spending and unemployment to visitor spending and business growth. For example, the construction and maintenance of sport facilities and the events they host represent substantial financial investments that have led to increasing significant economic impacts on the wider communities where they are located. Sport facilities and the events they host are expected to provide the community with economic benefit by inducing spending in the local area and profiting local businesses. As a result, economic impact is an important measure of facility performance.

Economic impact can be evaluated based on its components – direct, indirect, and induced impacts. *Direct economic impact* is the change in economic activity during the first round of spending by visitors directly stimulated by a facility, such as buying tickets to an event, customers needing to stay at hotels or going out to restaurants before and after the facility visit, or spending attributed to participants, organizers, and sponsors. *Indirect impact* is the economic activity generated in other businesses because of the facility. This would be what other additional business and jobs are created beyond the sport facility that supports direct economic activities. In marketing terms, it is how the supply chain is affected by the sport facility or major event. Therefore, this category could include the need for additional police presence at events or the need for the opening of new parking structures. *Induced impacts* are the expenditures by employees and businesses from earnings related to the sport facility. When this additional money is spent in the economy, there are businesses with additional revenue – and employees with extra income either from overtime or from taking on temporary positions. This additional economic power via spending of those earnings is the induced impact of the sport facility. The economic impact of sport facilities is measured through an economic impact study. This is a commissioned analysis that attempts to model the future economic impacts of a sport facility or to measure its actual economic impact.

Social impact

Social impact is a behavioral concept focused on how a sport facility can positively or negatively influence the behaviors and interests of stakeholders directly related to the quality of life for the community. These behaviors and interests are measured, evaluated, and managed through a social impact assessment. The focus of this assessment is on the advancement of social development, with the changes in the quality of life of residents of a destination based on the impact judged to be most important. Some of the most positive social impacts a sport facility may have on a community include further infrastructure development and image enhancement of the community, Negative social impacts may include increased traffic, security concerns, and possible social conflict at the events held in the facility.

Social impact is important to community members, who wish to ensure that facilities meet the attitudes, behaviors, and motivations of relevant stakeholders by accentuating the positive impacts and limiting the negative. This requires facility managers and owners to have alternative pathways for projects, infrastructure development, and event activations to maximize the positive social impacts. This could range from building a new facility in a different part of the community, limiting the size and scope of a facility, or setting parameters on the timing and types of events to be held at the facility. Ultimately, positive social impact is a mutually beneficial partnership that needs to be developed and nurtured between the sport facility and the community.

Environmental impact

Environmental impact focuses on how a sport facility directly affects the ecological footprint of a community. This can range from the carbon footprint in terms of emissions from facility operations to consumption related to waste generation and the efficiency of sustainability practices such as recycling, renewal, regeneration, and transformation.

The concept of recycling and reducing the amount of waste leads directly to the concepts of environmental management. Environmental management is the process of managing the interaction between the human environment and the physical

Effectiveness of management and operations

environment/habitats. Globally, ISO 14000 (International Organization for Standardization) guidelines provide requirements for environmental management systems and specify their relevance for organizations wishing to operate in an environmentally sustainable manner. In its latest update in 2015, the purpose of the standard is to reduce the environmental footprint of a business and to decrease the pollution and waste a business produces. In sport facility management, this has become more important as a marketing function than as an operations function. Sport facilities that take the initiative to be more socially responsible are publicly recognized for their efforts. While a direct correlation may not be visible in any accounting documents, the cost of environmental awareness is at least partially justified in the positive effect it has on the image of the facility, which is a large component of public relations.

Two of the most relevant environmental management concepts crucial to sport facility operations management are greening and sustainability. *Greening* is the process of transforming a space into a more environmentally friendly area. *Sustainability* is the process of being renewable for an indefinite period without damaging the environment. In energy management (Chapter 8), we discussed some of the ways to be more environmentally friendly (for example, energy saving bulbs) and management (for example, recycling). However, one of the biggest issues is the disturbance and reduction of plant life, trees, grasses, and other natural environments due to the construction of sport stadiums and arenas (and associated ancillary areas), artificial surface fields, and sport environments in the natural environment (ski resorts, golf courses, etc.).

LEGACIES OF SPORT FACILITIES

So how do impacts evolve into legacies? Whereas an impact focuses on the short term, *legacies* are longitudinal impacts that aim to create an ongoing benefit to the users over the long- term. So the longer a sport facility has an impact on a community and its stakeholders, eventually (usually after about 10–15 years), the impacts shift to legacies. The concept of legacy in terms of sport facilities was first looked at during the planning process for the 1996 Summer Olympic Games in Atlanta, Georgia. The organizing committee stated they wanted to 'leave a legacy,' tangibly and intangibly, through the Olympics that would have a lasting impact long after the Games left the city. At the time, they felt some of those legacies could be planned ahead of time, such as with the donation of the aquatics center to Georgia Tech for use as a recreation complex. They also acknowledged some would grow organically, while others – such as the tennis center at Stone Mountain – would become a negative legacy. However, in the end, most legacies focus on three areas: infrastructure legacies, heritage legacies, and sport participation legacies.

Infrastructure legacy focuses on how sporting venues that are constructed or renovated provide a benefit to society well beyond the initial purpose of their development. Many of these types of legacies are the result of major, hallmark, and mega events being hosted by a community with sport facilities being the obvious centerpieces. Many times this effect is more evident when new venues are built in a community where infrastructure had been lacking, but it can be equally important in world-leading sport communities. For example, when Melbourne, Australia, hosted the 2006 Commonwealth Games, the sport facility legacy included the rebuilding of half of the Melbourne Cricket Ground (MCG), and new pitch surfaces and an environmentally-sustainable watering system was added to the State Netball Hockey Centre.

Heritage legacies in sport facilities are where history and culture are captured for people to remember for years to come. People travel the world to visit former Olympic Stadiums to acknowledge the history of the Games, but probably the most significant evolving area of heritage legacies in sport facilities is that of museums. In Pyeongchang, South Korea, most of the main Olympic Stadium from the 2018 Winter Olympics has been taken down with only the Olympic cauldron remaining. In its place, they are planning to build an Olympic museum to attract tourists and to retain the history of the venue. Another area of heritage legacies is when a sport facility is renovated into another use but the historical significance is remembered and revered. A perfect example of this is the old Montreal Forum in Canada, which had been known as the most storied building in hockey history. When the Montreal Canadians moved to a new arena in 1996, the Forum was gutted and converted into an entertainment center with movie theatres, restaurants, and retail shops. To acknowledge the heritage of the venue, center ice was recreated in the middle of the complex, including a section of the stands and a statue of one of the most famous players, Maurice Richard. They also have taken original seats from the Forum and repurposed them as benches throughout the complex.

Another very important legacy of sport facilities is to increase participation in sporting activities. Having facilities used by the community long after a sporting event has left or for years after a venue is built or renovated is possibly the most important legacy. In many communities where this has been unsuccessful, it is often because of 'white elephant' stadiums being built – that is, a facility is built in a community where there is not enough use of a sport facility or the community cannot afford the upkeep of the infrastructure. This is currently an evolving area of research and examination.

CHAPTER REVIEW

Impacts evaluate the short-term influence a sport facility has, as a direct effect, on the future development of societal benefits. These are usually measured during the initial operation of the facility (first ten years) across economic, social, and environmental dimensions. In contrast, legacies focus on the long-term impact that sport facilities have on society across infrastructural, historical, and sport developmental dimensions. The concepts of impacts and legacies are often linked to the concept of sustainable sport and leisure development and operations. Ultimately, impact and legacy are directly influenced by the manner in which sport facility managers lead, manage, and operate the sport facility. Understanding the concepts inherent to quality facility management and operations management is vital to success. This book has systematically taken the reader through pre-management and pre-operational issues, the application of management and operations principles, the implementation of sport facility operations management, and the methods for measuring the effectiveness of those efforts. While the knowledge provided throughout this book provides a framework for understanding, combining this information with real-world experience working in sport facilities is vital to fully comprehend the scope of responsibilities inherent to sport facility operations management.

BIBLIOGRAPHY

Crompton, J. L. (1999). Economic impact analysis of sports facilities and events: Eleven sources of misapplication. *Journal of Sport Management*, *9*(1), 14–35.

Gratton, C., & Preuss, H. (2008). Maximizing Olympic impacts by building up legacies. *The International Journal of the History of Sport*, *25*(14), 1922–1938.

Holt, R., Ruta, D., & Panter, J. (2015). *Routledge handbook on sport and legacy*. Oxford: Routledge.

International Organization for Standardization. (2018). *ISO 14000 family: Environmental management*. Retrieved November 21, 2018, from www.iso.org/iso-14001-environmental-management.html

Preuss, H. (2015). A framework for identifying the legacies of a mega sport event. *Leisure Studies*, *34*(6), 643–664.

INDEX

Note: Numbers in **bold** indicate a table and numbers in *italics* indicate a figure.

ABM Industries, New York City, United States 183
accounting rate of return (ARR) 66–68, **67**, **76**, **77**, 78, **79**
Accra Sports Stadium disaster 4
Allen, Paul 15
Anschutz Entertainment Group 29
ANZ Stadium, Sydney, Australia **203**; *see also* stadiums by name
Arena Network 124
arenas 22, 50, 52, 170, 338; checkpoints 301; commercial 234; environmental and sustainability issues 337; evacuations of 264; food sales (concessions) 307; ice 165, 202; as key assets 260, **261**; parking for 172; seating arrangements and pricing 217; staff training for 291; as terrorist target 262; vandalism 263
arenas by name: Allianz Arena, Munich, Germany 197, **202**, 223; Antel Arena, Montevideo, Uruguay 23; Buenos Aires Arena, Argentina 23; Cadillac Arena, Beijing, China 23; Dubai Arena, Dubai, UAE 23; Ericsson Globe Arena, Stockholm 23; eSport Arena, Luxor Hotel, Las Vegas, United States 208; eSport Arena, Santa Ana, California, United States 208; flyDSA Arena 158; Key Arena, Seattle, Washington, United States 53; König Pilsener Arena, Germany 22; Margaret Court Arena, Melbourne, Australia 40; McNichols Arena, Denver, Colorado, United States 238; Mercedes-Benz Arena, Shanghai, China 23, 29–30, **202**; Pepsi Center, Denver, Colorado, United States 239–240, 252; T-Mobile Arena, Las Vegas 23; Turk Telekom, Istanbul, Turkey 223, O2 Arena in London 23; Odyssey Arena, Northern Ireland 22; Perth Arena, Perth, Australia 23; Phillips Arena, Atlanta, Georgia, United States 175; Qudos Bank Arena, Sydney, Australia 23; Rod Laver Arena, Melbourne, Australia 40–41; Rogers Arena, Canada **202**; Scotiabank Arena, Toronto, Canada **202**; Singapore Sports Hub arena 206; Suncorp Stadium, Brisbane, Australia 23
Armand Cesari Stadium, Bastia, Island of Corsica, France 4
assets: characterization of 254, 261, **261**, 277; facility 180; fixed 59, 61, 80; disposal of 56; human and physical 267; key 260, 261; management of 14; other 226; personal 15; private entity **50**; property as 222; public ownership of 19; 'sweating your assets' 139
assets, sport venues *see* sport venues assets
astrodomes: Houston 96
Astroturf 96
AT&T Stadium (Dallas) 52; *see also* stadiums by name
Athens Olympic Stadium, Athens, Greece 263; *see also* stadiums by name
Audit Commission, UK 31

Australia 54; ANZ Stadium, Sydney **203**; Marvel Stadium, Melbourne 210, 246; National Tennis Center, Melbourne 40; Optus Stadium, Perth 104

AutoCAD (United States) 93

AwareManager (United States) 174

benchmarking 8, 86, **90**, 102, 177, 179, 182; data 306; performance management 323–331, *324*; process 306; *see also* National Benchmarking Service

Born, David 277–278

Boston Marathon bombing 5, 266, 297

Boston Red Sox, Boston, Massachusetts, United States 19, 265

Brailey, Steve 158

Business Continuity and Disaster Preparedness Plan 296

business structures, three main categories 32

calculated risk 59, 79

capital employed percentage, returns on 66–67

capital investment appraisal (CAP) xvii, 6, 9, 59–82; gym example **63**, **76**; modern methods 69–75; purpose of 61–62; raw data 62– 64, **63**; summary of three competing projects **79**; traditional methods 64–69

Capital Investment Appraisal (CIA) skills 60

capital works and environmental impact (United Kingdom) 79

case studies: Boston Marathon bombing 297; eSports and the new sport arena 208; facility naming rights versus hallmark event sponsors 238; Global volunteerism 118; Highmark Stadium and the Pittsburgh Riverhounds 137; natural grass or synthetic turf 96; Panorama Stadium 181, 269; private management of public facilities 22; seating manifests 217; Sport England's National Benchmarking Service (NBS) 325; sport facility financing investment 52; United States' most expensive sport stadia 60

centers/centres by name: Barclay's Center, New York City 53, **222**; Change Our Game Sports Leadership Center, Victoria, Australia 54; Chase Center, San Francisco, California **203**; Moda Center, Portland, Oregon 15; National Counterterrorism Center 298; National Tennis Center, Melbourne, Australia 40; Pepsi Center, Denver, Colorado 238–240,

252–253; Staples Center 224, 230, 277, 253, 277–278; Virginia Mason Athletic Center; World Cup Expo Cultural Center, Shanghai, 29

CERM Performance Indicators Project, Australia 250

Chargers *see* Los Angeles Chargers

charities 26, 54, 120

Chartered Institute of Management Accountants (CIMA) 39

Chartered Institute of Quality 307–308

Chesterfield Football Club, England 226

China: Cadillac Arena, Beijing 23; Mercedes-Benz Arena, Shanghai 23, 29, **203**; Summer Olympics 2008 **265**

Citi Field Ballpark, New York City, United States *203*, 289–290

Citizens Bank Park, Philadelphia, Pennsylvania, United States 265

Coca-Cola 199; NBA contract 238–240; NHL sponsorship 238–239

Colorado: Pepsi Center, Denver 238, 252

Colorado Avalanche hockey team, United States 238–239

C-corporation 17

compounding and discounting 69, *70*; international rate of return (IRR) 72, **72**, **73**, 74; net present value (NPV) 71–73, **71**, **72**

concessions *see* sports facilities services

consequence reduction proposals 254–271

consequential evaluation 267

continuity capability checklist **296**

contracts and contract law 17, 26, **254**, 255, 258; approvals 22; event contracts 244, 258; facility sponsorship contracts 258

corporation 17; types of 18–20

corporates boxes, customized 169

costing matrix to show contribution **140**, **141**

criminal activities 262; detecting 282; reporting 171

criminal/background checks 123, 134

criminal law 254, 255, 256; and intentional torts 257

criteria for good performance indicators **315**

criteria for suitable performance indicators' data **316**

cross-cultural values 115, **115**; *see also* diversity

current expensing 276

customer experiences xvii, 8, 233–253; defining the customer 240–242; events from customer viewpoint 245–248; *see also* SESA

customer relationships management (CRM) 21
customer satisfaction 179, 182, 192–194, 247–252, 305; objectives 313; related to organizational performance 313; *see also* customer experiences; benchmarking
customer service 169, 173–174, 177–178, 182, 184; attributes **321**; desk 161, 174; product and service management 195; *see also* CERM PI
customers: and clients 121; defining 240–242

Dallas, Texas: AT&T Stadium 52
Dallas Cowboys football team, Dallas, Texas, United States 5, 231
Darrell K Royal (DKR)–Texas Memorial Stadium, Austin, Texas, United States 267–268
Deficit Reduction Act of 1984 (US) 51
Democratic Rules of Order 18
Denver Debacle 252–253
Denver: Mile High Stadium 175; Pepsi Center 238–240, 252–253
Denver Broncos, NHL team, Denver, Colorado, United States 175
Denver Nuggets basketball team, Denver, Colorado, United States 238, 252–252
diversity, cultural 23, 109, 114–116, 134
diversification (revenue) xvii, 7, 9, 213–221, 224, 230–231
Dover Motorsports Inc. (Dover, Delaware, United States) 33–34

economic impact studies 42
emergency action plan/preparedness 168, 250, 266–268, 273
emergency management 279, *280*, 294–295
emergency medical services 180, 261, 264, 269–270, *280*
eventIMPACTS (United Kingdom) 43–44
eSports 207, 231; new sport arena for Millennials and Gen Z 208–209
European Foundation for Quality Management Excellence Model (EFQM) 305, 308–309, *309*, 310, 331
event sponsorship *see* sponsorship
exercises: discussion-based 291; operation based 291

facility and event sponsorship conflicts 252
facility event: customer's experience of 245–248; evaluation by ownership and management 248–251; marketing plan 242–243

facility focus: Citi Field Ballpark, New York City, United States 289; Darrell K Royal (DKR)–Texas Memorial Stadium, Austin, Texas, United States 267; efficiency analysis of an anonymous facility using the National Benchmarking Service: United Kingdom 328; Hallamshire Tennis and Squash Club, Sheffield, United Kingdom 75; Hathersage Swimming Pool, United Kingdom 153; Melbourne Park Redevelopment, Melbourne, Australia 40; Mercedes-Benz Stadium, Atlanta, Georgia, United States 117; Mercedes-Benz Arena, Shanghai, China 29; Pepsi Center, Denver, Colorado, United States 238–240, 252–253; Ras Abu Aboud Stadium, Doha, Qatar 99; Santiago Bernabéu Stadium, Madrid, Spain 169; Singapore Sports Hub, Singapore 205; Tottenham Hotspur Stadium, London, United Kingdom 229
facility personnel: managing events 243–244
FAME *see* Financial Analysis Made Easy
Féderation Internationale de Football Association 4, 96, 137 *see also* FIFA World Cup
feasibility 57; study 83, 87, *88*, 89–90, **89–90**, 91, 103
Federal Bureau of Investigations (FBI), United States 262, **265**, 278, 298
fees 44, **46**, 62, 99, 163, 174; acquisition 258; additional service 244; business initiation 17; catastrophic loss 272; consultancy 98; governmental 17; hire 153; lease **50**; legal 18, 99; parking **49**, 152; PSLs 199
Female Friendly Facilities Fund, Australia 54
FIFA World Cup 233; South Africa 2010 5; Qatar 2022 5, 99, 104; Zimbabwe 2002 265
Financial Analysis Made Easy (FAME) 20–21
financial management *see* sport facility financial management
financing, sources of 44–57
financing concepts 37
financing sport facilities 36–58; business issues 37–38; costs of ownerships 38–41; economic impact analysis 41–44, *42*; future trends 52–55; history of 50–52
Football Act (1999) 283
Football Disorder Act (1989) 283
Football Disorder Act (2000) 283
Football Disorder Bill (2001) 283
Football Intelligence officers 283

Football Offenses Act (1991) 283
Football Spectators Act (1989) 283
forgery 4

Gaelic Athletic Association (GAA) 224
game day 267; operations plan 281–283;
    security operations checklist **282**
Gameday Merchandising 124
Gates, William (Bill) 15
global: audiences **47–48**; brand awareness
    29; citizens 207; investments 56; legal
    differences 255; recession 41; standards
    179
global governance structures for sports
    facilities 21
global models of organizational
    effectiveness **30–31**
global organizational behavior 109, 114–116
global security issues 279; companies 171
Global Spectrum 22–23
global sport event incidents **264–266**
global sport facility: naming rights **203**;
    management 102, 124–125; *see also* sport
    facility management
global sports marketing 1, 7, 55, 238;
    consumer behavior 194; *see also* facility
    event marketing plan
global volunteerism 118–121
global/generic sports security and
    technology 273
global/generic unmanned aircraft systems
    288
Greenwich Leisure Limited 26
Guide to Safety at Sports Grounds 253

Hall, Stacey v
Hallam Active (United Kingdom) 226–227
Hallamshire Tennis and Squash Club,
    Sheffield, United Kingdom 75
Hathersage Swimming Pool, United
    Kingdom 153
hazardous materials (HAZMAT) 168–169,
    261, *280*, 283
Heysel Stadium disaster 3
Highmark Stadium and the Pittsburgh
    Riverhounds 137–138
Hill, Mike 332
Hillsborough Stadium, United Kingdom 4,
    283
hiring, training, and retention 117; *see also*
    human resource management
Houston, Texas: Houston Astrodome 96;
    NRG Stadium 22, 225; Reliant Stadium
    203

Houston, Kristin 134
human resource management
Hurst, Ronnie 104

IDeA *see* Improvement and Development
    Agency
impacts and legacies 334, 337–339;
    economic 335–336; environmental
    336–337; social 336
Improvement and Development Agency
    307–308
In the Field: Born, STAPLES Center 277;
    Brailey, Sheffield International Venues
    Ltd (SIV) 158; customer experiences at
    Marvel Stadium 246; Hill, Leisure-net
    Solutions Limited 332; Hurst, Optus
    Stadium 104; Houston, Tampa Bay
    Buccaneers 134; Jensen-Murphy, ABM
    Industries 183; naming rights at Marvel
    Stadium 210; Mckinney, Sheffield Hallam
    University 226–227; Pathik, The Sports
    Facilities Advisory 57; Tatoian, Dover
    Motorsports Inc. 33; Whitaker, We Do
    Tennis Ltd 82; various sport security
    leaders 300
increasing income via facility hire 153
indemnification clauses 275, 276
independent contractors 275
injury, spectator or participant **276**; personal
    180, 183, 258, 267; proximate cause 257;
    risk 97
insurance: named perils 275; personal
    injury liability 275; property 275;
    protective 275
internal rate of return (IRR) 6, 72–81, **72**, *73*,
    74, 76, 79
investing for competitive advantage 75
investing for the future 40–41
Istanbul, Turkey: Turk Telekom Arena 223

Jensen-Murphy, Charlotte 183

Kansas City, Kansas, United States 52
Kansas City Royals baseball team **265**
Katmandu National Stadium, Nepal:
    tragedy 3
King, Peter 298
Kroenke, Stan 252
Kroenke Sports Enterprises 252–253

Las Vegas 52; Luxor Hotel 208; Oakland
    Raiders' relocation to 52; T-Mobile Arena
    23; University of Las Vegas 60; University
    of Nevada 294

Las Vegas Stadium 60
laws *see* contract law; criminal law; lawsuits; legal environment; negligence law
lawsuits 114, 133, 267, 275
legal environment: effects on sport facility operations 251, 255–256
legal issues xxvii, 19, 254–278; *see also* ownership structures
leisure development and activities 3, 8, 9, 29, 53; marketing management 190, 192, 206; private sector 319; public sector 313, 319, **320**, 323–324; 'trusts' 24, 26, 27, 158
Leisure-net Solutions Limited, Norfolk, United Kingdom 332
Levi's Stadium, San Francisco, United States 52, **203**
life cycle costing **39**
Liverpool, England 3, 4
Liverpool Football Club 19, 221, 230, 263
London, England 143; Budweiser Gardens 23; Emirates Stadium 197; Greenwich Leisure Limited 26; Hotspur Stadium 229; Olympic Park **42**; 2012 Olympic Games 41; Tottenham Hotspur Stadium 229–230; Twickenham Stadium 224; Wembley Stadium 56, 223
London Development Agency 37
Los Angeles, California, United States 52, **266**; Los Angeles Stadium 60; Staples Center 23, 224
Los Angeles Chargers 52, 60
Los Angeles Rams 52, 60
lotteries 54; and gaming tax **45**
Louisiana Superdome *see* superdomes by name

Major League Soccer (MLS) 137, 138, 175
management: performance 307; quality 307–308
marathons 118; *see also* Boston Marathon bombing
marketing plan, facility event *see* facility event marketing plan
managing security for 100k guests 267
Manchester (England) **203**; Etihad Stadium
Manchester City 221
Manchester United Football Club 19, 152, 197, 214–216; matchday revenues and games, 2014–2018 **216**; *see also* Old Trafford
material safety data sheets (MSDS) 168
Marvel Stadium, Melbourne, Australia 210; customer experiences 246

Mateo Flores National Stadium, Guatemala City 4
Mckinney, Iain 231–232
McNichols Arena, Denver, Colorado, United States 238
Melbourne Park Redevelopment, Melbourne, Australia 40
Mercedes-Benz Arena, Shanghai, China 23, 29
Mercedes-Benz Stadium, Atlanta, United States 52, 60, 117–118, **203**, 237
Met Life Stadium, New York City 52, 60
mixed martial arts (MMA) 234
MMA *see* mixed martial arts
Monica Seles Stabbing **26**
multichannel marketing and communications 189–190; *see also* sport facility marketing management
Munich Olympic Games 3, 264; *see also* Olympics

National Basketball Association (NBA) 15, 29, 209, 238; Atlanta Hawks 175; Brooklyn Nets **222**; Denver Nuggets 238–239, 252; eSports 208; Indiana Pacers **265**; Milwaukee Bucks **266**; Seattle Supersonics 53
National Benchmarking Service (NBS) (United Kingdom) 300, 319, 325–330
National Center for Spectator Sports Safety and Security (NCS⁴) *260*
National Counterterrorism Center, United States 298; *see also* Boston Marathon Bombing
National Football League (NFL), United States 15, **42**, 61, 208–209, 221, 229, 282; Baltimore Ravens **222**; bomb threats **265**; Denver Broncos 175; Los Angeles Chargers 52, 60; Los Angeles Rams 52; New England Patriots 175; Oakland Raiders 60; partnership with United Way 114; partnership with SAFE management 171; Seattle Seahawks 15
National Hockey League (NHL), United States 282; All-Star Weekend 238–239; New York Islanders 53; Pittsburgh Penguins 52
National Lottery, England 37, 79–80
natural grass or synthetic turf 96–97
negligence law 256–257
net present value (NPV) 71–76, **71**, **74**
New England Patriots, NHL team, Boston, Massachusetts, United States 175
New England Revolution MLS team, Boston, Massachusetts, United States 175

New National Stadium, Tokyo, Japan 237
New Orleans, Louisiana, United States 225,
    265; Mercedes-Benz Superdome 22
New Orleans Saints Football team 264
New York City: ABM Industries 183–184;
    Barclays Center 23, 197; MetLife Stadium
    52, 60, 203; Yankee Stadium 23
New York Giants 5, 60
New York Islanders 53
New York Jets 60
New York Yankees 60
NHL *see* National Hockey League
NRG stadium, Houston, Texas, United
    States, 22, 225

1HUDDLE, United States 199–200
Oakland Raiders football team 52, 60
Old Trafford Stadium 19, 214–219, *218*
Olympic Park, London **42**
Olympics 20, 93, 233; Atlanta 1996 265,
    337; London 2012 41, 295; Munich games
    3, 264; Summer 2020 Japan 121, 237;
    Summer 2024 237; Summer 2028 Los
    Angeles 60; Winter 2018 Pyeongchang,
    South Korea 291, 338
operations management 161–164, **164**
operations management, sports facility
    164–170; alterations 169; inventory 170;
    maintenance and cleaning 165–166; plant
    and field 164–165; safety 167–169; waste
    and recycling 166; utilities 166–167; *see*
    sports facility service
Optus Stadium, Perth, Australia 104;
    see also stadiums by name
organizational effectiveness, models of
    30–31, **30–31**
organizational leadership and human
    resource management 109–110; appraisal
    systems 129–130; leadership 111;
    contingency theories of 111–113; cultural
    diversity 114–116, **115**; customers and
    clients 121; employment process 122–123;
    individual behaviors in the workforce
    121–122; job analysis 123–124; job
    recruiting 124–127; managing human
    resources 115–121; manuals, creation of
    132–133; orientation and training 127;
    organizational culture and change 114–116;
    performance management 129; professional
    staff 116–118; promotions and successions
    130; termination 131; transformational and
    charismatic leadership 113–114; reward
    systems 130; volunteers 118–121
ownership structures 13–35

Panorama Stadium [hypothetical case] 181;
    threat assessment 269–271
parking 39, 98, 117, 145, 161, 170,
    172; conference and trade show 225;
    coordination 244; corporate clients 220;
    facility service 182, 226; fees **49**, 152;
    garages 47; lighting 270; management 183,
    281, **282**, **283**; private 48; restrictions 268;
    revenues 45, 221, 241; tragedies **266**
Pathik, Dev 57
partnership 15–16; limited partnerships
    16–17
Partnerships, Period of *see* Period of
    Partnerships
partnerships, public-private 49–50, **50**
payback method 64–66, **65**; discounted **74**
PepsiCo. 199, 238–240
Pepsi Center, Denver, Colorado, United
    States 238–240, 252–253; *see also* centers
    by name
performance analytics for sports facilities;
    see also benchmarking
performance management 307–308;
    balanced scorecard 322–323, *323*;
    benchmarking 323–331, *324*; objectives
    312–313; performance 313–314;
    performance indicators 314–315, **315**,
    316–317, **317–318**, **320–321**; public sector
    sports providers 319–21; principles 311,
    311; targets 322
performance management frameworks
    308; European Foundation for Quality
    Excellence 308–309, *309*; Toward an
    Excellent Service 309–310
performance measurement principles *311*
performance ratios for commercial
    organizations **317**
Period of: Antiquity 50; Change 51;
    Discontinuance 51; Growth 51;
    Partnerships 51; Revitalization 51
permanent/personal seat licenses (PSLs) 45,
    48, 198, 199
philosophy, mission, and vision (PMV) 89, 234
Pittsburgh Riverhounds 137–138
Porter, Dan vi
Portland, Oregon, United States: Moda
    Center 15; Portland Trailblazers 15
public-private partnership models 14, 36,
    44, 49–50, **50**, 56
public sector: facilities 38; financing 47, 51,
    56; money 37
public subsidies 22, 37, **47**, 51, 52–53
pre-management and pre-operative issues
    xvii, 9, 11–105; corporations 17–21;

organizational effectiveness, models of 30–31; ownership and governance structures 21–29; *see also* capital investment appraisal; financing sport facilities; project management
private management of public facilities 22
program analysis 89
project management 83–85; architect selection 91–92; construction 99; contractor selection 100; cost estimate 98–99; drawings 100; facility design 94–97, *95*; feasibility studies 89–90, **89–90**; groundbreaking 101; life cycle 85–87; master plan development 92–93; preliminary planning 87–88, *88*; planning committee 90–91; program analysis 89; site selection 98; timetables 98; training and management 102
project management, application of principles 107; *see also* organizational leadership and human resource management
Project Management Institute (PMI) 85
PSLs *see* permanent/personal seat licenses

Qatar 5, 99
quality bonds 44
quality management 85–86, 307; *see also* total quality management

Rams football team *see* Los Angeles Rams; National Football League
Ras Abu Aboud Stadium, Doha, Qatar 99
recycled stadium construction 99
reserve: funded 276; unfunded 276
revenue generation and diversification 213–232; celebrations and adverse events 225; conference/trade shows 225; future directions 227–229; importance of time and space 215–216, **216**; selling core product 216–221, *218*; other assets 225; other forms of income generation 222–224, **222**; visitor attractions 224–225
revenue, private sources **48**
risk assessment, sport venue 251, 260–271, **264–266**, 276; assets, characterization of 261, **261**; consequence evaluation 266–267; consequence reduction 268; crowd disorder 262; fraud 263; hooliganism 262; identification 261; inclement weather 264; logistical failure 263; personal assault 262; terrorism 262; threat assessment 261–262; vandalism 263; vulnerabilities 266; *see* Panorama Stadium

risk avoidance 274
risk control and response 273–276, **276**; avoidance 274; reduction 274–275; retention 276; theft 263; transfer 275–276
risk logic matrix *272*
risk management 258–260, *272*
risk probability *259*, 271–272, *272*
risk reduction 274–275
risk retention 276
risk transfer 275–276
Robert's Rules of Order 18

San Diego Padres 52
Santiago Bernabéu Stadium, Madrid, Spain 169
seating **48**, **49**, 169, 195, 235, 248; capacity 171; and customer satisfaction 252; general admission 172; maintenance 183; manifests 216, 217–218, *218*; Old Trafford 214, *218*; premium 51, 198–199; removable 99; specialized 52
security in the outfield 289
security management 280–284, **282**; access control and credentialing 287–280; business continuity 295–299, **296–297**; communication 289–290; crowd management 292–294, *294*; emergency management 294–295; perimeter control 286; physical design 286–287; principles and components *295*; protective measures 284–285; security personnel 290–291; training 291; venue design 285–286; *see also* Boston Marathon bombing
security planning and management 251
security stakeholders, sport event *280*
service marketing principles: intangibility, perishability, inseparability, and variability 241
SESA *see* Sport Event Security Awareness
Schwarz, Eric C. v
Sheffield Hallam University, Sheffield, United Kingdom 226–227
Sheffield International Venues Ltd (SIV), Sheffield, United Kingdom 158
Shibli, Simon v
Singapore 23, **115**; Singapore Sports Hub, Singapore 205–206
situation analysis (SWOT) 235
situational crime prevention (SCP) model 293–294, *294*
SIVTickets.com, United Kingdom 143
soccer (European football) 97, 104, 139, 215, 225; Irish 224; Major League Soccer (MLS) 137, 138, 175; Panorama Stadium

hypothetical 181; premium seating
198; Tottenham Hotspur Stadium 229;
tragedies 3, 4, 5; *see also* FIFA
sole proprietorship 14–15
space and time, importance of 215–216;
market segmentation 216; other forms of
income generation 222–223; selling the
core product 216–222
sponsors and sponsorship 7, **31**, 34, 43, 189,
214, 215; brand structure 197; corporate
52, 53; Mercedes-Benz Arena 29; naming
right 45, **48**, 196, 198; organizing 110;
promotional 190, 191, 199, 210; thanking
101; university/student **164**
Sport England's National Benchmarking
Service (NBS) 325
Sport Event Security Awareness (SESA)
248–251, *249*
sports event security action team (SESAT)
254, 261, 269, 277, 281, 291
sports events incidents, global **264–266**
sport event security management *see*
security management
sports facilities: delivering positive
economic benefits **42**; as key assets 260
sports facilities, general business structures
see general business structures for sports
facilities
sports facilities, impacts and legacies *see*
impact and legacies
sports facilities, performance analytics *see*
performance analytics
Sports Facilities Advisory, The 57
Sports Facilities Management, The 57
sport facility event planning process
234–253; evaluation by ownership
and management 248–251; customers
240–242; customer viewpoint 245–248;
facility event marketing plan, activation
of 242–243; facility viewpoint 243–245
sport facility financial management
137–139; budgeting 150–151, *151*;
cost behavior 139–140; costing matrix
140–144, **140**, **141**, *143*; costing, practical
applications of 144–149, **145**, **146**, **148**;
financial planning 150–157
sport facility financing, history of 50–52;
see also financing sports facilities
sport facility marketing management
190–211; advertisement 201–202;
branding 196–197; infrastructure
195–196; other promotional mix elements
203–204; promotional communications
200–201; sales management 197–199;

social, digital media 204–210;
sponsorship 202–203, **203**
sport facility marketing mix 190–192;
climate 191; company 191; competition
191; consumer 191, 192–193
sport facility service 170; concessions **49**,
51, 52, 117, 157, 161, 173, 192; customer
service 173–174; event management 174;
ISO 9000 standards 179–180; operations
manual, creation of 180–181; parking 172;
principle of continuous improvement
176; risk management 180; security 171;
Six Sigma 180; ticketing 171–172; total
quality management (TQM) 176–178;
see also customer service
sport facility ownership and governance
structures 21; nonprofit/voluntary
24; public 21–22; private 24; private
management of public facilities 22–23;
trusts 24–29, **25**
sport security and technology (generic/
global) 273
sport venues assets 261, **261**
sport venue risk assessment *see* risk
assessment, sport venue
stadium design for diverse revenue
generation 229
St. Louis, Missouri, United States 52
Stade de France, Paris, France 237
stadium 19, 29, 33, 62, 80, 300, 318;
access control 287; accessibility
285–286; ancillary revenues **49**;
benchmarking 328; communications
289; costs (example of) 139–144, **140**,
146, 147; commercial 234; crowd
management 292–293; customer
balance 220; and digital technology
227–228; diversification of income
streams 231; environmental impact
337; eSports 231; evacuations of 264;
as key asset 260, 261, **261**; lockdown
268; managing 230; multipurpose
214; naming and naming rights 53,
202, 222–223, **222**; NHL franchise **42**;
Olympic 338; parking 172; perimeter
control 287; privately financed 50;
seating 217, 219; security 290; sports
39, 68, 70; terrorism 262; ticket offices
172; tours 8; vandalism 263; virtual 52;
'white elephant' 338
stadium disasters 3–5, 265, 266, 283
stadium Safety Certificate 283
stadiums by name: Accra Sports Stadium
4; ANZ Stadium, Sydney, Australia

203; Armand Cesari Stadium, Bastia, France 4; AT&T Stadium, Dallas, Texas, United States 52; Aviva Stadium, Dublin, Ireland **203**, 224; Bernabéu Stadium, Spain, 169–170; Bidvest Stadium, South Africa **203**; DKR-Texas Memorial Stadium, Austin, Texas, United States 267–268; Gillette Stadium, Boston, United States 175; Emirates Stadium, London, England 197; Etihad Stadium, Manchester, England 197, **203**, 223; Highmark Stadium, Pittsburgh, United States 137–138; Hillsborough Stadium, Sheffield, England 4, 283; Las Vegas Stadium 60; Levi's Stadium, San Francisco, United States 52, **203**; Marvel Stadium, Australia **203**, 210–211, 246; Mateo Flores National Stadium 4; M&T Bank Stadium, Baltimore, Maryland, United States 175, **222**; Mercedes-Benz Stadium, Georgia, Atlanta 52, 60, 117–118, **203**, 237; MetLife Stadium, New York, United States 50, 60, **203**; Mile High Stadium, Denver, Colorado, United States 175; New National Stadium, Tokyo, Japan 237; NIB Stadium, Perth, Australia 104; Nissan Stadium, Japan **203**; NRG Stadium, Houston 22, 225; Old Trafford, England 19, 214–219, *218*; Optus Stadium, Perth, Australia **203**; Panorama Stadium [hypothetical case study] 181, 269–271; Ras Abu Aboud Stadium, Doha, Qatar 99; Reliant Stadium, Houston, Texas, United States **203**; Singapore Sports Hub National Stadium and Indoor Stadium 23, 206; Suncorp Stadium, Brisbane, Australia 23; Tottenham Hotspur Stadium, London, England 229–230; Twickenham Stadium, London, England 224, 225; University of Phoenix Stadium, Arizona, 23; U.S. Bank Stadium, Minneapolis, United States 52; Wembley Stadium, England 37, 55, 223, 224, 258; Wroclaw Stadium, Poland 22; Yankee Stadium, New York City, United States 37, 60
STAPLES Center, Los Angeles, California, United States 224, 277
Super Bowl, United States 118, 171, 221, 229, 287
superdomes by name: Mercedes-Benz Superdome, New Orleans, Louisiana, United States 22, 225, 264

swimming pool 39–40, 61, 78, 147, 318; annual running costs 148–149, **148**, 152; diversification 214; effectiveness 313; hazards 168; lifeguards 157; quality **321**; *see also* Hathersage Swimming Pool

Tampa Bay Buccaneers, Tampa, Florida, United States 134
Tatoian, Mike 33–34
tax-increment financing (TIF) **46**
taxes 39, **42**, **47**, 53; advantages 25; corporation 26; deductions 18; exempt 20; franchise 17; general property 56; hard and soft 44, **45**, 51, 56; liability 14, 16, 17; prepay 18; revenues 44; trusts 27; *see also* financing
Taylor Report 4, 283
TeamWork Online (United States) 124
Technology now!: AutoCAD (United States) 93; AwareManager (United States) 174; Capital works and environmental impact (United Kingdom) 79; CERM PI (Australia) 250; eventIMPACTS (United Kingdom) 43; Financial Analysis Made Easy (FAME) (United Kingdom) 20; Hallam Active (United Kingdom) 226; National Benchmarking Service (United Kingdom) 300; SIVTickets. com (United Kingdom) 143; sport security and technology (generic/global) 273; 1HUDDLE (United States) 199; TeamWork Online (United States) 124; unmanned aircraft systems (generic/global) 288
terrorism 175, 250, 255, 261–262, **276**, 277; training 270
Texas Memorial Stadium, Austin, Texas, United States 267
theft/embezzlement 261–262, 263, 270, **276**, 277; see also forgery
Tottenham Hotspur Stadium, London, United Kingdom 229
Toward an Excellent Service (TAES) 308, 309–310
total quality management (TQM) 161, 162, 176–178, 179
transnational venue management 29
trusts, three elements of 24, *25*
Turk Telekom Arena, Istanbul, Turkey, 223; *see also* arenas by name
Turner Network Television (TNT) 240
Twickenham Stadium, London, England 225

United Soccer League (USL) 97
United States: Department of Homeland Security 260; most expensive sport stadia 60; *see also* Boston; Dallas; Denver; Las Vegas; Los Angeles; New Orleans; New York City; Pittsburgh; Portland; San Francisco; Seattle; St. Louis
unmanned aircraft systems (generic/global) 288
University of Nevada-Las Vegas 60, 294
University of Phoenix Stadium 23
University of Texas at Austin 267–268
university sports complex 85, 163, **164**, 226
U. S. Bank Stadium (Minneapolis) 52

Valley Parde football stadium fire 3
vandalism 3, 261–263, 275, **276**
Virginia Mason Athletic Center 15

waivers 121, 257, 275, **276**
We Do Tennis Ltd, Welton, United Kingdom 82
what-if scenario **145**
Whitaker, Matt 82
World Cup *see* FIFA World Cup
World Wrestling Entertainment (WWE) **48**, 217, 224, 252–253

Yankee Stadium, New York City, United States 60; *see also* stadiums by name

CPSIA information can be obtained
at www.ICGtesting.com
Printed in the USA
LVHW061017091121
702849LV00018B/112

9 780367 133641